African Society of Evangelical Theology Series

We often hear these days that the center of Christianity is moving toward the Global South and Africa is a key player in that movement. This makes the study of African Christianity and African realities important – even more so when it is being done by Africans themselves and in their own context. The Africa Society of Evangelical Theology (ASET) was created to encourage research and sustained theological reflection on key issues facing Africa by and for African Christians and those working within African contexts. The volumes in this series constitute the best papers presented at the annual conferences of ASET and together they seek to fill this important gap in the literature of Christianity.

TITLES IN THIS SERIES

Christianity and Suffering: African Perspectives
2017 | 9781783683604

African Contextual Realities
2018 | 9781783684731

Governance and Christian Higher Education in the African Context
2019 | 9781783685455

God and Creation
2019 | 9781783687565

I0129353

Over the centuries, the African continent has not only been the cradle of human history, but also of human civilization. By and large, Africa has enjoyed many sustained, productive centuries of scholarship. The twenty-first century is yet another century in which African theologians are reclaiming the intellectual legacies that the continent has been known for.

Forgiveness, Peacemaking, and Reconciliation is one of the great pearls that African theologians have produced. It is a testament to what African collaborative partnership in scholarship can give to the global community. It is not only scholarly and academic work, but it also illustrates how African theologians are once again demonstrating their ability to engage in careful theological reflection on their social setting through vigorous empirical studies. It showcases an extensive grasp of a broad spectrum of issues – social, cultural, political, religious, and economic – which have perennial consequences. Indeed, this is the kind of book that can enormously contribute to the creation of "a new spirit of Africa" – *The Africa We Want* and God wants. Wole Soyinka, the Nigerian playwright, poet and essayist, and 1986 Nobel Price winner in literature, once said, "Books and all forms of writing terrorise those who do not want the truth to be exposed." Except for this category of people, every other literate African must have this book on their "to-read" list.

Rev. Sunday Bobai Agang, PhD
Professor of Christian Ethics, Theology and Public Policy,
Provost, ECWA Theological Seminary, Jos (JETS)
Director, African Research Consultancy Center, West African Region

Drs. Ngaruiya and Reed attempt an audacious project of compiling conference papers on the wide-ranging subject of the realities of forgiveness, peacemaking, and reconciliation in Africa. These very well researched and thoroughly engaging chapters range from biblical patristic to interpersonal and societal arenas. The human-divine angle as well as interdenominational and interfaith dimensions of these key subjects are also addressed. As the center of gravity of Christianity moves to the Global South, or Majority World, and especially to Africa, the offerings in this book will be a very welcome addition to the panoramic overview of the faith of African believers. The challenge of Jesus to us all to pursue forgiveness, peacemaking, and reconciliation at all levels is not yet exhausted, but neither is the supplementary literature encouraging us to do so. This book offers various theoretical frameworks from different angles to pursue these worthy aims. Highly recommended for church leaders and their precious members as well as students and the general public. May Jesus Christ be praised.

Rev. Casely B. Essamuah, ThD
Secretary, Global Christian Forum

ASET Series

Forgiveness, Peacemaking, and Reconciliation

Langham

GLOBAL LIBRARY

Forgiveness, Peacemaking, and Reconciliation

General Editors

**David K. Ngaruiya
and
Rodney L. Reed**

Langham
GLOBAL LIBRARY

© 2020 Africa Society of Evangelical Theology (ASET)

Published 2020 by Langham Global Library
An imprint of Langham Publishing
www.langhampublishing.org

Langham Publishing and its imprints are a ministry of Langham Partnership

Langham Partnership
PO Box 296, Carlisle, Cumbria, CA3 9WZ, UK
www.langham.org

ISBNs:
978-1-83973-053-5 Print
978-1-83973-099-3 ePub
978-1-83973-100-6 Mobi
978-1-83973-101-3 PDF

David K. Ngariuya and Rodney L. Reed hereby assert their moral right to be identified as the Author of the General Editor's part in the Work in accordance with sections 77 and 78 of the Copyright, Designs and Patents Act 1988. The Contributors have asserted their right to be identified as the Author of their portion of the Work under the same Act.

British Library Cataloguing-in-Publication Data
A catalogue record for this book is available from the British Library.

ISBN: 978-1-83973-053-5

Cover & Book Design: projectluz.com

CONTENTS

Preface

This volume explores the tripartite theme of forgiveness, peacemaking, and reconciliation, which together constitute the true "climate" for human flourishing. Without this quintessential tripartite gift to humanity nations, communities, and individuals falter and crumble. With forgiveness the deepest wounds are healed, with peacemaking human dignity is restored, and with reconciliation the current tumultuous world is restored toward political and more importantly spiritual stability.

What makes this collection of essays distinctive is their African flavor. They have all been written by scholars from, serving in, or having served in African countries. In the language of Agbonkhianmeghe E. Orobator, these contributions to the discussion of forgiveness, peacemaking, and reconciliation have all been "brewed in an African pot"! And across much of Africa there is a desperate need for informed theological and practical reflection on these themes. Even now in many quarters of the African continent, conflicts rage that call out for the grace of forgiveness, peacemaking, and reconciliation. This volume is offered up to speak into those situations as well as to inform the outside world about how Africans contextualize these themes.

First, the volume explores different facets of forgiveness having laid a biblical foundation as to the infiniteness of true forgiveness. It also explores the theological thinking of the early church fathers, many of whom were African, on unconditional forgiveness. Further, it also deals with how E-therapy can be of use as an intervention in post-traumatic stress disorder.

Second, this volume explores peacemaking. It commences by examining the overarching theme of the book based on a sociological examination of Genesis 31. The issue of albinism in Tanzania is also addressed. The perennial question of Christian–Muslim relations is also addressed from a historical lens of Spanish medieval *convivencia* (coexistence) of Christians, Jews, and Muslims. In addition this section explores a Wesleyan "Catholic Spirit" on matters of peace.

Lastly, the volume explores reconciliation from multiple perspectives. Situational irony is examined from the Hebrew concept of *shatal*, followed by an invitation to ethnic reconciliation from selected Johannine, Lukan, and Pauline texts. This last part also examines public theology derived through interreligious dialogue, and concludes with a framework for caring for and counseling victims of violence.

David K. Ngaruiya, PhD

Acknowledgments

The chapters that follow represent the best of the papers presented at the ninth annual conference of the Africa Society of Evangelical Theology (ASET) which took place at Pan Africa Christian University in Nairobi, Kenya, on 22–23 March 2019. Over the years we have witnessed the growth in number, diversity, and quality of the papers presented at these conferences. Truly ASET is meeting a need!

The Editorial Committee of ASET wishes to thank all of the contributors to this, our fifth volume with Langham Publishing. The contributors have labored over these chapters, "giving birth" to some beautiful "babies"! They have patiently allowed us to "pester" them with revision after revision. We wish to thank those who reviewed both the proposals for presentation prior to the ASET conference as well as the many papers that were submitted for publication. Their critique and review was essential to the success of this enterprise. Special thanks to eminent New Testament scholar Craig Keener, who was our keynote speaker and whose paper, originally published in *Evangelical Quarterly*, is represented as one of the chapters in this book.

Appreciation also goes to Pan Africa Christian University and their staff members who so graciously hosted this conference. They provided all that was needed and more for ASET to effectively hold its conference and annual meeting. We cannot overlook our publisher, Langham Publishing, without whom this series of books could not have happened. To Vivian Doub and her team at Langham, we give many thanks. To my editorial partner, David Ngaruiya, thank you so much for helping to shoulder the load. "Two are better than one, because they have a good return for their labor" (Eccl 4:9).

Rodney L. Reed, PhD

Part 1

Forgiveness

1

A Response to the Biblical Question "How Many Times Shall I Forgive My Brother?" (Matt 18:21–22)

Its Implications for Kenyan Communities

Micah Onserio Moenga

Pastor and Part-Time Lecturer

Africa International University (AIU) and Pan Africa Christian University (PACU)

Nairobi, Kenya

Abstract

One of the questions that is increasingly of major concern among political and religious leaders is "How can we build strong community bonds?" Shockingly, Kamaara notes, "While Christian values are expected to foster national cohesion and identity, more often than not Christianity has provided a convenient rallying point around which ethnic conflicts are mobilized."[1] It is true that national cohesion in Kenya remains a challenge five decades after independence. This is due to a number of factors, such as political, economic, and sociocultural challenges. These factors have hampered efforts toward building one nation as envisioned by the founding fathers. Hence the need to investigate Peter's question to Jesus: "Lord, how often shall my brother sin

---

1. Eunice Kamaara, "Towards Christian National Identity in Africa: A Historical Perspective to the Challenge of Ethnicity to the Church in Kenya," *Studies in World Christianity* 16, no. 2 (Jul. 2010): 126.

against me, and I forgive him?"[2] This question needs investigating in order to address the problem of the disintegration of Kenyan community.

The subject of forgiveness has gained interest among scholars in recent years. Schaeffer-Duffy, for instance, writes, "Forgiveness began to attract the attention of researchers in academia. Prior to 1985, the total number of forgiveness studies completed was five. Today there are approximately 55, and research continues, according to A Campaign for Forgiveness Research, a nonprofit organization directed by Worthington."[3] The year 1985 was just over three decades ago, and studies on forgiveness have surely burgeoned since then. The world today is in dire need of forgiveness. This is because forgiveness, peace, and reconciliation constitute the very essence of community existence and cohesion. Yet while forgiveness, peacemaking, and reconciliation are fundamental for the well-being of any society, they still remain a challenge for many societies.

This chapter therefore assesses Kenya's history since independence to ascertain some of the challenges to national cohesion. As a response to the identified challenges, the chapter examines biblical passages related to the subject of forgiveness within a biblical exegetical framework. Hence, the study is historical, exegetical, and theological, and is aimed at providing applicable solutions to the challenge of cohesion in the Kenyan context and Africa at large.

Key words: brotherhood, building bridges, ethnicity, forgiveness, national cohesion, robust community, tribalism.

Introduction

It is evident that the Kenyan community is yet to heal from the political, economic, and social upheavals since independence. Such upheavals are experienced especially during electioneering periods, which seem to open up old wounds to the extent of almost tearing the nation apart. The worst such period was the 2007–8 postelection violence which saw many lives lost and many people internally displaced. Subsequent elections have not been without their skirmishes either. In Kenya, after every election, the nation comes to a defining moment when everything seems to come to a standstill.

---

2. Matt 18:21 NKJV. The basic text followed in this chapter is the New King James Version of the Bible.

3. Claire Schaeffer-Duffy, "Building a Future of Hope," *National Catholic Reporter* 38, no. 25 (26 Apr. 2002): 24.

It is against this backdrop that this study seeks to highlight some of the problems believed to be the root causes of the challenge of unity and nation-building for a robust Kenyan community. A brief analysis of Kenya's history since independence will suffice to show that there is a problem regarding cohesion. The chapter responds to this by addressing the subject of forgiveness from a biblical point of view, as a key modality for fostering a robust united Kenyan community. Despite the abundant writings that have sought to address the question of reconciliation, there is little to demonstrate their impact. The question then is: What are we not doing right in addressing the problem?

In the practice of medicine, it is customary for diagnosis to precede prescription. Unfortunately, when it comes to finding a remedy for societal ills, the reverse seems to be true. Many approaches employed to address the challenges to cohesion in Kenya have offered a prescription prior to conducting a diagnostic procedure. This leaves the nation with the same problems recurring from time to time. It is my conviction that if we can get to the root causes of some of these problems, and with proper mechanisms and goodwill from the people in place, these problems will be greatly minimized. It has been argued that a solution that recognizes the need for structural change and the manner in which group differences are managed stands a good chance of success.[4] The question to ask, then, is: Where do we go from here in order to find a workable approach?

This chapter argues that forgiveness is an inevitable route toward peace and reconciliation. The study demonstrates this within an exegetical framework; that is to say, biblical exegesis is our primary method of addressing the questions raised. Therefore, our task involves analyzing relevant biblical passages in order to provide a workable solution to address the challenges of national cohesion in the country.

This chapter comprises four sections. The first section investigates some of the root problems of national cohesion in Kenya. The second section is an exegetical investigation of Peter's question to Jesus, "Lord, *how often shall my brother sin against me, and I forgive him?*" (Matt 18:21 NKJV, emphasis mine). The passage is investigated so as to provide possible solutions to Kenya's need to attain a robust, united community for a stable political, economic, and social environment. Other relevant passages are also investigated. Section 3 focuses on some practical ways to foster community cohesion in Kenya. Section 4 gives the research's findings, a summary, and a conclusion.

---

4. Aquiline Tarimo and Paulin Manwelo, *African Peacemaking and Governance*, Studies on Social Change in Africa (Nairobi: Acton, 2008), 11.

Challenges to Community Cohesion in Kenya

This section concerns itself with the investigation of some of the challenges to community cohesion in Kenya. It presents some of the problems believed to be the root causes of disunity. As stated earlier, it is an uphill task to begin treatment before discovering the cause of a particular illness. This chapter therefore proceeds on the basis that in order to deal with an ailment effectively, a diagnostic procedure must precede prescription. A number of factors have contributed to the derailing of the achievement of Kenya's vision to build one strong community as envisioned by the founding fathers. Three main factors are the political, economic, and sociocultural challenges. Research conducted between 1945 and 1994 among 163 ethnic groups revealed that most conflicts are due to political and socioeconomic factors.[5] Each of these factors is discussed briefly below.

Political Challenges

One major challenge for the achievement of national unity in Kenya is the political situation. A brief background to the genesis of politically motivated factors in Kenya will help in understanding this.

Generally speaking, in precolonial Kenya most communities lived harmoniously with each other. Kenya lived as one big community. There was unity and harmony among neighboring communities as they interacted with each other through trade and intermarriage.

However, things changed with the advent of the colonial powers. This period witnessed a rapid disintegration of communities along tribal lines. For instance, Ojuka and Ochieng assert, "In many instances, the colonial authorities helped to create the things called 'tribes,' in the sense of political and economic communities."[6] This implies that the term 'tribe' was alien to Africans. It was not until the arrival of the colonial powers that the term came into play, and in the long run it became a cancer that destroyed community cohesion. It is notable that the British colonial government helped draw up ethnic and administrative boundaries along tribal lines, and these have remained to this day. Kanyinga and Okello regretfully note, "This is the one colonial legacy that

5. Noël Bonneuil and Nadia Auriat, "Fifty Years of Ethnic Conflict and Cohesion: 1945–94," *Journal of Peace Research* 37, no. 5 (2000): 563–581.

6. Aloo Ojuka and William Ochieng, eds., *Politics and Leadership in Africa* (Kampala: East African Literature Bureau, 1975), 254.

has baited the country to the extent it is repugnant to development."[7] Indeed, tribalism is "repugnant" not only to development, but also to cohesion, as we shall see later.

Before we proceed further, it is fundamental to understand the term "tribalism" as well as its counterpart, "ethnicity." The term "tribalism" has been described variously by scholars. Ojuka and Ochieng state that, according to J. S. LaFontaine, "tribalism entails, among other things, a clinging to traditional life, as opposed to rapid change. Tribalism has also been used to designate (and often to deplore) nepotism in modern African states where the ties of common ethnic origins may be given precedence over other, more Western, allegiance."[8] This study is inclined toward the second aspect of the meaning of the term and shows how it has worked against the consolidation of the nation of Kenya.

For instance, John Reader states, "Tribalism is the most pernicious of the traditions which the colonial period bequeathed to Africa."[9] The introduction of tribalism by the colonialists had far-reaching implications. Its consequences affected not only the young nation but also the church. Faulkner notes, "It is true to say that the church had taken 'tribal' identities to heart."[10] The end result, as noted by Faulkner, was that "the dreams of a local church had been unwittingly reduced to a tribal church."[11] In similar vein, Maigadi argues, "Although the world is becoming a global village, at the same time it is also becoming fragmented ethnically, and the church does not seem to be exempted."[12] This clearly shows that tribalism is an enemy both of unity and of development. A solution must be found for dealing with it. Otherwise, the effort toward fostering a robust community will remain in limbo.

The next term to consider is "ethnicity." The *Cambridge English Dictionary* defines ethnicity as "a particular race of people, or the fact of being from a particular race of people." While in this regard "ethnicity" is a neutral word, it has often been used negatively. Crossman, for instance, states that "ethnicity

---

7. Kanyinga and Okello quoted in John O. Oucho, "Undercurrents of Post-Election Violence in Kenya: Issues in the Long-Term Agenda," in *Tensions and Reversals in Democratic Transitions: The Kenya 2007 General Elections* (Nairobi: Society for International Development: Institute for Development Studies, University of Nairobi, 2010), 496.

8. Ojuka and Ochieng, *Politics and Leadership*, 255–256.

9. Cited in Mark Faulkner, "Evangelizing Gone Awry: The Church in Kenya Has Fostered the Tribalism It Now Deplores," *National Catholic Reporter*, 22 February 2008, accessed 5 December 2018, http://natcath.org/NCR_Online/archives2/2008a/022208/022208p.htm.

10. Faulkner, "Evangelizing Gone Awry."

11. Faulkner.

12. Barje Sulmane Maigadi, *Divisive Ethnicity in the Church in Africa* (Kaduna, Nigeria: Baraka Press, 2006), 3.

is often a major source of social cohesion as well as social conflict."[13] While in itself there is nothing wrong with the term, it has been turned into a tool for mutual destruction. In modern African societies, for example, ethnicity is a source more of conflict than of social cohesion. Similarly, Kamaara views ethnicity as "the single major threat to national identity in Africa."[14] She further raises concerns about the role of the church in fostering national unity and identity in contemporary Africa. Kamaara's concern needs to catch the attention of every Kenyan, because when the church remains silent in the face of the problem of ethnicity, it invites trouble.

Strictly speaking, tribalism is a baby of the colonial powers who, after birthing it, abandoned it, leaving it to grow in the African soil. One can argue that the colonial administration, in its approach of divide and rule, divided the country along tribal lines and thus introduced a new "gene" of tribalism to a once-communal society. This has birthed in our country the problem of negative ethnicity. While it is true that tribal conflicts existed before the colonial era, the colonial period played a large role in solidifying and deepening the interethnic cleavages.[15] Christian missionaries followed the colonialist ideology of tribalism by encouraging the emergence of tribal-based denominations.[16]

Despite the negative effects of tribalism, successful regimes have sadly only helped perpetuate it, rather than eradicating it. For instance, Ojuka and Ochieng argue that "African politicians and elites whom they recruited into the civil and military services"[17] helped to perpetuate tribalism. This trend has continued in modern Kenya. This, in turn, has widened tribal animosities among Kenyan communities. Ojuka and Ochieng rightly assert, "Tribalism represents real divisions of the Kenyan people, and ways must be found to combat it."[18] Politics is now being used as a tool for gratifying selfish political ambition rather than making the lives of Kenyans better. With such a situation, there is a general feeling that some communities are being discriminated against, thus leading to community polarization. Some communities no longer feel they have any share in the political arena. These communities play a spectator role, with no

---

13. Ashley Crossman, "Ethnicity Definition in Sociology," ThoughtCo, accessed 29 January 2019, https://www.thoughtco.com/ethnicity-definition-3026311.

14. Kamaara, "Towards Christian National Identity."

15. Ojuka and Ochieng, *Politics and Leadership in Africa*, 258.

16. Ojuka and Ochieng, 258.

17. Ojuka and Ochieng, 276.

18. Ojuka and Ochieng, 268.

space left for their participation. In such a situation, building bridges toward a robust Kenyan community is an uphill task.

Political profiling is another major enemy hindering the progress toward a robust Kenyan community. This has divided the Kenyan nation into two camps famously termed in Swahili *wenye nchi* and *wana nchi*. In other words, certain communities are perceived to be the "owners" of the nation, while others are considered as merely belonging to the nation by statistics alone. Some communities feel completely cut off and not able to share equally in Kenya's resources.

This has created bitter hatred among communities, especially those that feel oppressed or disenfranchised by the dominant communities. Consequently, this kind of hatred that has been caused by political oppressors has been categorized among the "unforgivable sins" by the victims of oppression. This is because there is a lack of political goodwill and because political emancipation is far from being realized. In such circumstances it becomes almost impossible to imagine how to fix the breaches so as to build a strong Kenyan community.

Professor Wangari Maathai, in her book *The Challenge for Africa*, attempted to diagnose the challenge to national unity in African states. She says, "The modern African state is a superficial creation: a loose collection of ethnic communities or micro-nations, brought together in a single entity, or macro-nation, by the colonial powers."[19] Similarly, Nyasani describes Kenya as "a *sui generis*," meaning "nations in a nation."[20] This creation in itself poses numerous challenges to fostering national unity, as Maathai points out:

> Most Africans didn't understand or relate to the nation-state created for them by colonial powers; they understood, related to, and remained attached to the physical and psychological boundaries of their micro-nations. Consequently, even today, for many African peoples, a threat to their micro-nation or those they consider their leaders within their micro-nation carries more weight than a threat to the nation-state. At the same time, each community hopes to have access to the resources of the nation-state should someone from their micro-nation assume political power (particularly the post of president or prime minister). In

---

19. Wangari Maathai, *The Challenge for Africa*, 1st ed. (New York: Pantheon, 2009), 184.

20. Joseph M. Nyasani, "The Meaning and Implication of Ethnicity," in *Ethnicity, Conflict and the Future of African States*, edited by Aquiline Tarimo and Paulin Manwelo (Nairobi: Paulines Publications Africa, 2009), 17.

this way, the community will have, as is said in Kenya, it's "time to eat."[21]

What Professor Maathai helps us to understand is that many African states are still far from being fully integrated. The colonial powers who created the shambolic nation states cared nothing about the likely consequences that would follow as long as they got what they wanted (Africa's resources). Even though the African communities were perceived as being community conscious, sadly the seeds that the colonial masters sowed seem to have overtaken the African agenda. This is why even at independence, when the Kenyan government sought to retrace Kenya's roots, the effort came to an end, being an exercise in futility. The light that had begun shining at independence soon became darkness. The founding fathers of our nation did their best to restore the rapid erosion of community consciousness. Some of the efforts that were put in place were the development of the philosophy of peace, love, and unity.

In addition, the founding father Mzee Jomo Kenyatta promised to fight against poverty, ignorance, and diseases (the main challenges to progress) in order to achieve Kenya's dream of unity and prosperity. All this gave hope to the young nation. Unfortunately, as we will see, this was a brief "honeymoon" moment, as Meredith describes it.[22] Meredith further asserts, "The march of African nationalism seemed invincible. Africa, so it was thought, once freed from colonial rule, was destined for an era of unprecedented progress. African leaders even spoke of building new societies that might offer the world at large an inspiration."[23] Yet all these aspirations remained only wishes that never became a reality.

A number of factors suggest that Kenya started on the right footing. For instance, Kenya's national motto, *Harambee*, itself speaks volumes. *Harambee* is a Kiswahili word which literally means "pulling together." What a sign of unity! This clearly shows that the young nation sought to remain united as one community in the early years of independence. As a result of such great commitment to national unity and integration, Kenya became a united community fostering togetherness on every front. Development activities were done in the spirit of unity. For instance, schools, hospitals, and churches were built through communal initiatives. The community from which one came from did not matter.

---

21. Maathai, *Challenge for Africa*, 184.

22. Martin Meredith, *The State of Africa: A History of Fifty Years of Independence* (London: Free Press, 2006), 141.

23. Meredith, *State of Africa*, 141.

Additionally, various national symbols were used to signify Kenya's commitment to unity; for instance, the national anthem. The Kenyan national anthem is actually a prayer for the nation. It recognizes God as the creator of the universe. The anthem also acknowledges that blessings for the nation come from God, the creator of the universe. The national anthem is clearly a prayer for unity, peace, and liberty – key components for fostering national unity for a robust Kenyan community. Generally, unity is the main theme of the national anthem. Thus, at independence Kenya's aspirations began on good foundations.

Sadly, though, as stated above, all these aspirations for the young nation were short-lived. It did not take long before the nation started experiencing political and socioeconomic instability that was advanced through negative ethnicity.

Economic Challenges

After the postelection violence of 2007–8, which left the country more divided than ever, the National Cohesion and Integration Commission (NCIC) in conjunction with the National Cohesion and Constitutional Affairs (NCCA) was constituted and tasked with discovering the likely causes of Kenyan community disintegration. Among its findings in the *National Cohesion and Integration Training Manual*, published by the Ministry of Justice, the NCCA, and the NCIC, the Commission revealed that economic factors have worked to hamper national cohesion on many fronts. The manual cites a number of challenges facing the nation. These include inequality of access to national resources such as finance, land, technology, and communications. This is considered to be one of the major impediments to national unity and cohesion.

The manual identifies various components that result in the economic disadvantages of some groups. Topping the list is finance. This has been exacerbated by the problem of corruption, which has become one of the major vices posing a challenge to eradicate. Sadly, the problem of corruption has been politicized in Kenya, complicating efforts toward its eradication. For instance, Tarimo and Manwelo argue that "Practices of corruption promote political disorder in the most extreme form. They amount to state capture so that individuals can control the state by manipulating the machinery of government to serve private interests."[24] Corruption both at the individual and at the institutional level has become the "elephant in the room" in Kenya, and this has adversely affected efforts toward nation-building. Kibwana, Wanjala, and Owiti-Oketch argue that "while corruption affects all facets of society, it

---

24. Tarimo and Manwelo, *African Peacemaking and Governance*, 29.

is in the economic arena where both the causes and effects of corruption are most pronounced and manifested."[25] In a nutshell, corruption is an enemy of economic development, and in the long run it affects national cohesion in a negative way because it creates a disparity between the rich and the poor.

It has become almost impossible to hold victims of corruption to account since the suspects retreat into their communities to seek refuge from their wrongs. This has made communities point the finger at each other, increasing the disunity. Consequently, the nation is left under the control of a select few who control economic power at the expense of the masses. The economic bigwigs enjoy the nation's resources without regard for the state of their fellow countrymen. This has created animosity between the "haves" and the "have nots." For instance, Ogachi asserts, "One impact that the economic reforms have had in Africa has been the emergence of a 'social underclass' totally excluded from national society and economy."[26]

Another component that is mentioned in the manual is land. Land remains one of the thorniest issues hindering the country's efforts toward national cohesion. For instance, land was identified as one of the major factors in the postelection violence of 2007–8. Maathai, referring to the aftermath of the 2007–8 postelection violence, noted, "Communities fought each other over land and political power." Land was one of the most problematic issues among what came to be known as the "Agenda Four item" of the Kenya National Dialogue and Reconciliation mediation team (KNDR), which was formed of members from the government and the opposition. The team identified land as an issue that needed to be addressed urgently. Unfortunately, it has remained unresolved ever since a peace deal was brokered to end the impasse following the postelection violence of 2007–8. This is an indicator that as a country we are still far from attaining a united Kenya.

The fight for limited resources is another source of conflict in Kenya. Ogachi asserts, "Economic scarcity . . . seems to be the center of conflicts, within the context of gains and losses being counted by different communities. This situation is mediated through a series of political manipulations."[27] The unequal distribution of national wealth has become a major concern among Kenyan communities. Hence, for communities to have one of their own run

---

25. Kivutha Kibwana, Smokin Wanjala, and Owiti-Okech, eds., *The Anatomy of Corruption in Kenya: Legal, Political and Socio-Economic Perspectives* (Nairobi: Claripress, 1996), 107.

26. Oanda Ogachi, "Economic Reform, Political Liberalization and Economic Ethnic Conflict in Kenya," *Africa Development / Afrique et Développement* 24, no. 1/2 (1999): 83–107.

27. Ogachi, "Economic Reform."

for the presidency is seen as the only solution. This has further divided the Kenyan nation along tribal lines at the expense of national unity.

Sociocultural Challenges

In addressing sociocultural factors we again refer to the *National Cohesion and Integration Training Manual.* We have already discussed the issue of ethnicity, so for the purposes of this research we will here discuss two of the other factors addressed in the manual: the deterioration of morals and values, and cultural insensitivity.

It is evident that in modern society morals and values are deteriorating at an alarming rate, and this is a trend that poses a challenge to national cohesion. It is against this backdrop that crime is on the rise. Today, the entire globe is grappling with the issue of terrorism. Donald W. Wuerl observes, "The context of our efforts to bring about unity includes some realities we all face: a culture that is losing respect for human life and dignity, family and sacrifice for others. Violence and terror in our world destroy lives, [and] target people based on race, religion, sexual orientation or other differences."[28] This is the same in Kenya, where terrorism has become a major challenge toward achieving national cohesion and development. Many of our youths have become radicalized to join militia groups, and this has greatly accelerated the disintegration of moral values in the nation. Since the majority of the Kenyan population are youths with no employment, they are easily lured by terrorist compromisers and financiers who promise them a lucrative lifestyle at the expense of human dignity, thus compromising their morals and values. We are, however, in great danger when we lose a sense of human dignity.

Social injustices also pose a challenge to national unity. Social injustices did not end with colonial imperialism but have been carried over by neocolonialism, being perpetuated by Africans against Africans. This is witnessed on many fronts, including in the oppression of the poor and the discrimination of marginal communities when it comes to the distribution of national resources. A retired bishop of the Presbyterian Church of East Africa, Rev Dr Timothy Njoya, said in a television interview: "Kenya has become a fellowship of the rich for the rich."[29] This is the bitter truth of the situation in our country. In

---

28. Donald W. Wuerl, "Christian Unity in an Age of Social Division," *Priest* 73, no. 1 (Jan. 2017): 10–21.

29. Timothy M. Njoya, "On Live Citizen TV Inclusive Interview," 2019, News broadcast by Jeff Koinange.

such a situation, then, one wonders what will become of the large part of the population who are languishing in poverty. Social injustice did not end with colonial imperialism but has been carried over by neocolonialism, being perpetuated by Africans against Africans. This is witnessed on many fronts, including in the oppression of the poor and the discrimination of marginal communities when it comes to the distribution of national resources.

Cultural insensitivity is another factor that has led to community disintegration in Kenya. It should be realized that cultures can never be the same, and that no culture is superior to another. Sadly, our social and cultural differences have been wrongly construed, causing disintegration and erosion of the spirit of brotherhood. Social–cultural differences have been used negatively in Kenya and this has opened the door to conflict among many communities in Kenya. We are indeed different and diverse in many ways as a people, but this should not be used as a license for hatred. As Jones notes, "Throughout history, differences have been used to deny that one or another group of people are human like 'us.'"[30] As a result, some communities, based on their cultures, have been considered unworthy even to offer leadership of any sort. This is particularly seen when it comes to the office of the president. It is against this backdrop that divisive politics thrives. As a result, people select leaders on a tribal basis rather than because of their qualifications.

A Detailed Analysis of Matthew 18:20–35

Having looked at the different factors that have contributed to the disintegration of Kenyan community, we now turn to the biblical text to seek a remedy. We have selected Matthew 18:20–35 as the primary text for our consideration for the subject of forgiveness, peace, and reconciliation. It is important to note the literary structure of this text within its wider context in order to interpret it correctly. Matthew 18:20–35 is preceded by 18:15–18, a pericope on church discipline. It is therefore important to briefly highlight this pericope since it is connected to our text.

Settling of Disputes (Matt 18:15–20)

In Matthew 18:15–20, Jesus presents what could be described as a step-by-step procedure for settling disputes within a church context. Verse 15 begins with

---

30. L. G. Jones, "Unity and Diversity in Christ," *Christian Century* 109, no. 18 (20 May 1992): 540.

a subordinate conjunction Ἐὰν, a clear indication that this is a conditional construction. In this case, the condition in view is a situation in which a brother or sister happens to have sinned against another. The majority of the manuscripts have ἁμαρτήσῃ εἰς σὲ[31] ("sins against you"). This reading is most likely to be correct as it assumes that the conflict involves two believers within a church setting. In this case, Matthew proceeds to suggest that the offended party should go to his or her brother or sister and point out the fault. There is a similar sentiment in Leviticus 19:17. In this case, it was expected that the offended party was to show the offender the fault instead of feeling hatred for the offender in his or her heart. This is to happen just between the two believers, the offended party and the offender, as is indicated by the objective genitive μόνου (alone, "two of you"). In other words, this should happen in seclusion, not involving any other people yet. The main goal[32] for taking such a step is to win the offender back, probably to the church community. Schweizer argues, "The expression 'win back' shows that what matters is the sinner, not a 'pure community.'"[33] The offender is won back if he or she listens. Matthew uses the word ἀκούσῃ[34] (may listen) to depict the action expected of the offender.

The second step in the process of mending a broken relationship is occasioned by the possibility that the offender may fail to listen (μὴ ἀκούσῃ). In such a circumstance, the offended party is advised to take along one or two others to serve as witnesses of the matter at hand. This suggestion is in keeping with Jewish jurisprudence whereby witnesses (the minimum number of which was either two or three) were required for the confirmation of a matter.[35] Schweizer argues, "The presence of one or two of the brethren is meant to protect the sinner; the admonisher may well be wrong, or someone else may find the right words when he cannot."[36]

The next step is again occasioned by the possibility that the offender may also fail to hear the witnesses (παρακούσῃ αὐτῶν). At this point, the offended party is advised to present the matter to the ἐκκλησία, the assembly. However, if the brother or sister also fails to listen to the assembly, he or she is to be

---

31. The following MSS have ἁμαρτήσῃ εἰς σὲ such as D, K, L, X, Δ Θ Π.

32. The goal of this action is depicted vividly by the resultative aorist ἐκέρδησας.

33. Eduard Schweizer, *The Good News according to Matthew* (Atlanta: John Knox Press, 1975), 370.

34. The verb ἀκούω means to heed or listen to.

35. See Deut 17:6; 19:15; 2 Cor 13:1; 1 Tim 5:19; Heb 10:28; 1 John 5:8.

36. Schweizer, *Good News*, 371.

treated like a Gentile and a tax collector. Thus Matthew's Jesus presented his disciples with a procedure for settling disputes in the church context.

Forgiving Repeatedly (Matt 18:21–22)

This section presents a higher degree of strengthening relationships. Peter, who has been keenly following Jesus's teaching on settling disputes, raises a fundamental question on the relationship among brothers and sisters: "How often shall my brother sin against me, and I forgive him?"[37] Jesus had earlier taught about the necessity for forgiveness among his disciples (6:12, 14–15). Peter was thinking about the practicality of the whole issue. In this case, he suggested a tentative number – up to seven times? The basis for Peter's idea of forgiving an offender seven times is not certain. Blomberg, however, suggests, "Peter's words allude to the sevenfold avenging of Cain; Jesus's reply contrasts starkly with the seventy-sevenfold avenging of Lamech (Gen 4:24)."[38] Indeed, Jesus's reply made Peter's "seven times" more complex in a practical sense. Interestingly, Peter's suggestion to forgive up to seven times sounds good enough as it goes beyond the rabbinic maximum of forgiving three times (e.g. *b.* Yoma 86b, 87a).[39]

Peter was considering the practicality of the whole issue, but Jesus was thinking of how to maintain healthy relationships. This needs repeated forgiveness – seventy times seven! Hagner rightly argues that "'seventy times seven' points not to a limit of literally seventy-seven or even 490 times but indicates forgiving an unlimited number of times (cf. Luke 17:4: 'seven times in a day')."[40] Jesus's statement reveals that forgiveness should be a continuous exercise. It has to be rendered whenever an occasion to do so arises. Even though Peter had learned that forgiveness should take the place of vengeance, he was still asking about limits.[41] Peter had departed only quantitatively, not qualitatively, from the Jewish principle that a person may be forgiven once, twice, or three times, but not four times (albeit with reference to God's forgiveness).[42]

---

37. See Matt 18:21.

38. Craig L. Blomberg, *Matthew*, New American Commentary 22 (Nashville: Broadman, 1992), 281.

39. Blomberg, *Matthew*, 281.

40. Donald A. Hagner, *Matthew 14–28*, Word Biblical Commentary 33b (Dallas: Word, 1995), 537.

41. Schweizer, *Good News*, 377.

42. Schweizer, 377.

There is a difference between the two gospel records of Jesus's words. For instance, Luke mentions the issue of repentance as the ground for forgiveness: καὶ ἐὰν μετανοήσῃ ἄφες αὐτῷ (but if there is repentance then you must forgive him). There is a textual variation between Matthew's gospel and Luke's. For instance, according to Matthew's gospel record, the offended party must forgive the offender "up to seventy times seven" (18:22 NKJV), while Luke has added, "in a day" (Luke 17:3–4). If we take Luke's gospel to be closer to the original source, it becomes obvious that it is impractical for a person to sin seventy times in a day. This then implies that there should be no excuse for failing to forgive one's brother or sister. Indeed, he or she would not have sinned seventy times in a day!

Forgiveness Illustrated (Matt 18:23–35)

The parable that follows serves as an illustration of what Jesus has been teaching about, that is, forgiveness. Luz has identified the structure of the parable which has three main scenes. The first scene takes place between the king and his servant (vv. 24–27), the second between the servant and his fellow servant (vv. 28–30), and the third, once again, between the king and the servant (vv. 31–34).[43] This is clearly indicated by Διὰ τοῦτο ("on account of this," or "for this reason"). In these three parables, God is presented as the king[44] who desired to settle accounts with his servants. This is emphasized by the repeated use of ὁ κύριος (cf. vv. 25, 26, 31, 32, 34). The parable goes on to tell us that one of the servants who owed the king a sum of ten thousand talents was "brought in." Schweizer suggests, "That the servant was 'brought in' might mean that he is already lying in prison, having been unmasked as a swindler."[45] Some scholars view the parable as an exaggeration, especially given the mention of such a huge sum owed by the servant to the king.[46] Hagner argues, "The use of μυρίοι, 'myriad,' or 'ten thousand talents' which itself could mean 'beyond number,' is a deliberate hyperbole pointing to a debt that was so high it was

---

43. Ulrich Luz and Helmut Koester, *Matthew: A Commentary*, Hermeneia: A Critical and Historical Commentary on the Bible (Minneapolis: Augsburg, 2001), 468.

44. Blomberg, *Matthew*, explains that the "parable mirrors the most common form of rabbinic parable – a story involving a king with servants or sons. The king almost stands for God; the servants, for God's people. Often obedient and disobedient servants provide a contrast between righteous and wicked behaviour. Settling accounts is a natural metaphor for judgment."

45. Schweizer, *Good News*, 377. Also see T. W. Manson, *Sayings of Jesus* (London: SCM Press, 1949), 213.

46. See Schweizer, 377.

practically incalculable."[47] My understanding of this is simply that the debt owed by the servant was so great that he could not settle it. Indeed, as Hagner indicates, "parables by nature often employ hyperbole for effect, and there is no reason to require that every point corresponds to historical reality."[48] This is supported by the next phrase, in which the servant was ordered to be sold together with his wife, children, and possessions in order to settle the debt. Schweizer has pointed out that this action was not in keeping with Jewish law. However, foreign kings did act in this manner (2 Kgs 4:1 [children, but not the man's wife]; cf. Isa 50:1; Amos 2:6; 8:6; Neh 5:1–13).[49]

On realizing that this would be too much, the servant "prostrated himself" (προσεκύνει). The servant begged his master to be patient with him, promising that he would pay back everything (πάντα)! Was it true that the servant was going to pay back everything he owed the king? Not at all; it was merely a petition of desperation. The master, "moved with compassion" (σπλαγχνισθείς),[50] decided to release the servant and forgave him his debt. Two actions by the servant's master are critical for the current study. First, the king released the servant, perhaps from prison. Second, the king forgave the servant his debt. The verb ἀφίημι, as Hagner argues, literally means "to let go." It is the verb used regularly to refer to "forgiveness" pertaining to sin (cf. 6:12 [where the word for sins, ὀφειλήματα, is literally "debts"], 14–15; 9:2, 5–6; 12:31–32).[51] In other words, the king simply treated the debt as though it had never existed. The king's action is unparalleled, as Schweizer notes: "He grants not just postponement but total remission of the debt."[52] The phrase ὁ κύριος τοῦ δούλου ἐκείνου, "the lord of that servant," occurs again in 24:50 in the context of eschatological judgment.[53]

The next verses, 28–35, repeat the scene, but the reaction of the servant is different from that of his master. The demonstrative pronoun ἐκείνου ("of that") of verse 27 parallels ἐκεῖνος in verse 28, showing that the same servant is being referred to. It would have been expected that the forgiven servant would treat his fellow servant with the same compassion he had received, but

---

47. Hagner, *Matthew 14–28*, 538.

48. Hagner, 538.

49. Schweizer, *Good News*, 378.

50. Hagner observes that all the occurrences of the word "compassion" in Matthew refer to Jesus: 9:36; 14:14; 15:32; 20:34.

51. Hagner, *Matthew 14–28*, 539.

52. Schweizer, *Good News*, 378.

53. Hagner, *Matthew 14–28*, 539.

the reverse was the case. He instead began to pressurize his fellow servant, demanding that he pay a relatively small debt of a "hundred denarii" (ἑκατὸν δηνάρια), forgetting that he himself had received a reprieve of paying "ten thousand talents." The debt the servant was demanding his fellow servant pay was a far smaller amount than the amount he himself had owed his master. Again, the hyperbolic nature of parables should be taken into account here: the disparity between the huge amount forgiven of the first servant and the small amount owed by the other servant is the point of focus. The implication is that if the large debt was canceled, the small debt should definitely have been canceled as well. Surprisingly enough, the forgiven servant even resorted to physical violence in his demand to be paid: ἔπνιγεν, he began to choke him. What a forgetful servant he was! He had just been forgiven a huge debt, and now here he was, choking his fellow servant because of the debt he owed him. In a parallel text, 24:49, the wicked servant began beating his fellow servant as well. This showed how wicked the first servant was, and that he had never learned the lesson of reciprocation (of mercy). Jesus had earlier declared in his teachings of the Sermon on the Mount, "Blessed are the merciful, for they will receive mercy."[54] The obstinate servant had never learned Jesus's teaching.

The fellow servant pleaded (παρεκάλει) for mercy just as the forgiven servant had done, but his pleas landed on deaf ears. Matthew uses παρεκάλει here instead of προσεκύνει which he had used in the previous scene. Hagner argues, "'Pleaded' is more appropriate in reference to a fellow servant than the προσεκύνει, 'prostrated,' of v 26, used in reference to the master)."[55]

In the fellow servant's plea here in verse 29, the word πάντα is omitted. The reason for this is probably to depict the ingenuity of the first servant's claim to settle the debt fully. He wanted to justify himself as being willing to pay back his debt. This reminds us of another parable Jesus told, of the Pharisee and tax collector in Luke 18:9–14. The Pharisee who sought to justify himself is juxtaposed with the tax collector who humbly sought God's mercy. This probably explains the reason for the omission of πάντα for the second servant. The first servant followed through with his threats and threw the servant into prison (εἰς φυλακὴν)[56] until he could pay the debt. This demonstrates the degree of cruelty with which the first servant handled his fellow servant. How quickly he forgot the kindness shown him by his master!

---

54. See Matt 5:7 NRSV.

55. Hagner, *Matthew 14–28*, 539.

56. εἰς φυλακὴν is an accusative of termination with the focus on the place, in this case, prison.

This action made his fellow servants indignant, so they went and reported everything to their master. The master immediately summoned the servant and reprimanded him sharply: Δοῦλε πονηρέ ([you] evil servant!). The verb πονηρεύομαι literally means to "act wickedly" or to "play the rogue." Indeed, the servant had acted wickedly toward his fellow servant. The master calls him a wicked servant because he, the master, had forgiven him his debt in full, yet the servant was not willing to forgive his fellow servant. The master said he had had no mercy upon his fellow servant: οὐκ ἔδει καὶ σὲ ἐλεῆσαι τὸν σύνδουλόν σου, ὡς κἀγὼ σὲ ἠλέησα (was it not necessary for you to have mercy on your fellow servant, as I had mercy on you?). Matthew often emphasizes the need to show mercy to one another. Mercy is a virtue expected of those who belong to the kingdom of God (Matt 5:7). Jesus puts mercy above sacrifice (Matt 9:13). According to Matthew's Jesus, mercy is among the weightier matters of the law (23:23).

The virtue of mercy is a serious matter in the kingdom of God. Since the servant lacked this fundamental virtue he attracted his master's displeasure. Hence he was handed over to be tortured until he paid the entire debt. The parable concludes with a summary statement that God will likewise deal with those who do not forgive their brothers or sisters from their hearts. Matthew, in a characteristic way, uses the term "heart" in discussing issues of life. In the Sermon on the Mount, for instance, Jesus demonstrates that every action emanates from the human heart (5:28). That is probably the reason why he states, "Blessed are the pure in heart, for they will see God" (Matt 5:8 NRSV). The servant in question did not portray purity of heart and so was expelled from the presence of his master. Matthew believes that the heart is the center of our emotions, and for this reason it governs our actions. In other words, whatever we do as Christians is a reflection of our hearts.

The last verse clearly serves as an interpretation of the parable. Talbert has made some fine concluding remarks on this parable: first, the parable's language functions together with 18:21–22 to enable disciples to see that being a forgiving servant is rooted in the nature of God. Second, the parable reveals that forgiving others is rooted in God's forgiveness, and thus we should pass it on! Third, the parable aims to shock the disciples into realizing the seriousness of failing to show mercy to other disciples.[57]

---

57. Charles H. Talbert, *Matthew*, Paideia Commentaries on the New Testament (Grand Rapids, MI: Baker Academic, 2010), 224.

Some Ways to Enhance Community Cohesion

The following statement by Bacote is insightful: "Forgiveness is a vital practice because it is an absolute necessity if there is to be genuine healing and transformation regarding race and ethnicity."[58] This means that forgiveness is a vehicle through which societies can experience true healing and reconciliation. The inner desire to forgive those who have wronged us should be cultivated. In similar vein, Robinson argues, "Forgiveness is not so much an act as an attitude."[59] This statement is important for our consideration of the Kenyan context which, as has been demonstrated earlier in this chapter, is facing community disintegration caused by political, economic, and sociocultural factors. In this section, I suggest a number of ways to help us build a strong bond of unity. On the basis of our exegesis of Matthew 18:20–35 forgiveness is primary for the realization of peace and reconciliation. I therefore begin this section by discussing the importance of forgiveness irrespective of the wrongs done to us.

Developing an Attitude of Forgiveness

Many a time, when people discuss the subject of forgiveness, they focus on the right actions that should be undertaken. While that is not wrong, it should be realized that right actions begin with right attitudes. Since forgiveness is a matter of right attitudes, it is therefore a matter of the human heart. Ntamushobora reiterates that problems related to conflicts like that of the Rwandan genocide lie in the "human heart."[60] Forgiveness, therefore, is, as Robinson stated, not so much an action as an attitude. It is by having an attitude of forgiving those who offend us that we can take the next action of actually telling them that we have forgiven them. The attitude that forgives should be informed by the fact that none of us is perfect. While today it might be my neighbor who is in the wrong, tomorrow I might be the perpetrator of the offense. It is against this backdrop then that as humans we need to take forgiveness seriously. We should not hold grudges against each other, whether at an individual or community level. Instead, we need to develop an attitude of forgiveness toward one another.

---

58. Vincent Bacote, "Church as a Lifestyle: Distinctive or Typical?," in *This Side of Heaven: Race, Ethnicity, and Christian Faith*, edited by Alvaro L. Nieves and Robert J. Priest (Oxford: Oxford University Press, 2007), 208.

59. Theodore H. Robinson, *The Gospel of Matthew*, Moffat New Testament Commentary (London: Hodder & Stoughton, 1947), 156.

60. Faustin Ntamushobora, *Transformation through the Different Other: A Rendezvous of Giving and Receiving* (Eugene, OR: Wipf & Stock, 2013), 1.

Robinson has said that the greatest creditor in the universe is God; all wrongs affect him, and all sin is sin against him. And he forgives the whole, freely and without stint or reservation.[61] We should therefore realize that when we wrong someone, it is God whom we ultimately wrong. Lack of forgiveness complicates our lives and makes cohesion an uphill task. For instance, when we choose not to forgive others, it means that God will withhold his forgiveness from us as well.[62] Forgiveness, in this case, should be reciprocal; it should not be a blame game. We should make it a choice to forgive. Nelson Mandela once said, "We may never forget, we must forgive."[63]

It is high time communities agreed to realize the need for forgiveness. Of course, this must start from the top, with the leadership, and work down to the common citizen. I applaud the efforts both the President, Uhuru Kenyatta, and the then Leader of the Opposition, Raila Odinga, took in agreeing to come together and unite the country. The famous handshake which was witnessed on 9 March 2018 was a helpful gesture that forgiveness is possible even for perceived great enemies. As Tutu observes: "There is hope that a new situation could come about when enemies might become friends again when a dehumanized perpetrator might be helped to recover his lost humanity. This is not a wild irresponsible dream. It has happened and it is happening and there is hope that nightmares will end, hope that seemingly intractable problems will find solutions and that God has some tremendous fellow workers, some outstanding partners out there."[64]

Tutu's statement shows that all is not lost when it comes to building bridges, even in the worst of scenarios involving potential enemies. That God can use certain people to foster unity is a possibility, not a fantasy. For his part, Mandela said, "To make peace with an enemy, one must work with that enemy."[65] It is entirely possible to have a situation in which the government works with the opposition. For instance, the famous "handshake" came after the disputed Kenyan presidential election in August 2017. The Supreme Court of Kenya nullified Kenyatta's victory, citing flaws in the process, and ordered a rerun. This was the first time in Kenya's history that the election of an incumbent president was nullified. Subsequently, the Leader of the Opposition boycotted

61. Robinson, *Gospel of Matthew*, 156.

62. See Matt 6:14.

63. Cited by Brian Frost, *Struggling to Forgive: Nelson Mandela and South Africa's Search for Reconciliation* (London: Harper Collins, 1998), 2.

64. Desmond Tutu, *No Future without Forgiveness*, 1st ed. (New York: Doubleday, 1999), 158.

65. Cited by Frost, *Struggling to Forgive*, 2.

the elections, which he said would not be free and fair. This led to protests and violence that left at least ninety-two people dead. Yet as soon as the two leaders chose to forgive and come together, peace returned to the country.

It is not possible to talk about peace and reconciliation without forgiveness. Forgiveness creates an avenue toward peace and reconciliation. As we have seen from our textual analysis of Matthew, forgiveness is expected to the extent that there is a need. The leaders have a major role to play when it comes to political, economic, and social-cultural upheavals in the country. Leaders at both political and religious levels should find a way to work together to foster unity for the good of every citizen. Indeed, leaders at all levels should follow the example of the president and the opposition leader to begin building bridges for a robust Kenyan community. One of the areas they should work hard to sanitize is the political environment. Divisive politics must be avoided by all means and instead they should concentrate on building one strong nation as was envisioned by our forefathers. Verkuyl and Smedes rightly observe, "The Bible, as profoundly as it does simply, as divinely as it does humanly, reveals that the human family is in principle one."[66] This, of course, means that forgiveness is not an option but a "must" in order to build one strong nation.

The second step in forgiveness is taking the action of forgiveness itself. This action of forgiveness should move beyond words. Sometimes, it will involve retribution for the wrong committed. Forgiveness does not mean trampling justice underfoot. Matthew himself alludes to the idea of justice as a proper indication of repentance.[67] For instance, when it comes to cases of corruption, the offender should not only ask for forgiveness but also be willing to return the stolen public funds or property. This kind of action will reveal a truly repentant heart, and its implications are far-reaching. This, however, must be done voluntarily, out of the willingness of a repentant heart. In our text, what angered the master was the action the first servant took against his fellow servant. The first servant took for granted the forgiveness he had received from his master and harassed his fellow servant, thus revealing his unrepentant heart. Forgiveness is not and cannot be one-sided. It is not enough for it to be offered by the injured party; it remains incomplete until it has been accepted by the wrongdoer.[68] We are not here advocating for retributive justice, but restorative justice which demands the need to forgive besides returning stolen

---

66. Johannes Verkuyl and B. Lewis Smedes, *Break Down the Walls: A Christian Cry for Racial Justice* (Grand Rapids, MI: Eerdmans, 1973), 22.

67. See Matt 3:8.

68. Robinson, *Gospel of Matthew*, 157.

goods or funds. When public funds or property is stolen, a large number of people are hurt. So being asked to return the stolen funds or goods means restoring relationships, which is of far greater importance in order for a nation to experience peace. It is afterward that the need for forgiveness will have more weight.

Taking Part in the Process of Forgiveness

Forgiveness, peace, and reconciliation are not matters to be relegated to political leaders. In fact, the church has a mandate from God to spearhead the process.[69] The church is both to pray for peace and also to work toward attaining the same.[70] This does not mean that the state is to play a spectator role; rather, the state and the church should seek to work hand in hand in order to make the process a success.

Desmond Tutu, assessing the situation in Rwanda after the genocide of 1994 which claimed almost half a million lives, saw the need for forgiveness. He commented, "The cycle of reprisal and counter-reprisal that had characterized their national history [Rwanda] had to be broken and . . . the only way to do this was to go beyond retributive justice to restorative justice, to move on to forgiveness, because without it there was no future."[71] The task of initiating forgiveness, reconciliation, and peace should not be relegated to state machinery, but should be a corporate initiative between the church and the state. In other words, everyone must be involved. The reason for this is simple: all of us are in one way or another affected by the existence of peace or lack of it. The importance of forgiveness, peace, and reconciliation must be emphasized in order to realize a robust community.

As a country, we need to endeavor to build bridges of unity. This should be viewed as a task not just for the leadership but for every well-meaning Kenyan. This can be achieved through dialogue with one another. No one should exonerate himself or herself from being a channel of forgiveness. As our exegesis shows, we must explore all possible options available to achieve forgiveness. Many people give up too quickly and thereby jeopardize the process of reconciliation. This widens the differences and makes forgiveness even more difficult to attain. The parable that Jesus gave helps us see the need to make it our priority to forgive others just as God has forgiven us. One of

---

69. See Matt 5:9; Ps 34:14.

70. See Pss 34:14; 122:6.

71. Tutu, *No Future without Forgiveness*, 260.

the challenges that we encounter is that many people do not realize just how much God has forgiven them. Understanding how much God has forgiven us, even when we do not deserve it, should drive us toward forgiving others unreservedly. There are no perfect people; we only need to accommodate one another, being driven by the spirit of brotherhood. A brother might be wrong, but he remains a brother. A community might be wrong, but we all belong to the same country.

One of the questions that arises when it comes to forgiveness is whether one can actually forget the wrongs committed against oneself. The issue is not forgetting as compared to forgiving. This is because "to be a human being is to be a creature of history."[72] Our history, however, should be utilized in a cautionary manner so that it is not used against building a future of peace and harmony. Frost notes, "In this way, the truth about the past is acknowledged, but forgiveness frees people from the past for a new and hopefully different future."[73] For instance, as Kenyans, we should boldly face up to our past, however painful it may seem, but choose to turn every wrong around for a bright future. Forgiveness, though, is not as easy as said. Augsburger calls it "the hardest thing in the universe."[74] That means it requires a lot of sacrifice. Consider, for instance, how much the master of the first servant had to forgo in order to forgive his servant. We are told that the servant owed his master ten thousand bags of gold (Matt 18:24)! This was a huge sum to cancel as though it had never existed. Yet, shockingly enough, the master canceled the huge debt and let the servant go free. This requires real sacrifice. The sacrifice, however, is worth it, since relationships are more important than material things. In the case of our country, it should be realized that the nation is bigger than an individual.

It is high time that, as a nation, we realized that relationships are more important than the material things we value. We should be willing to sacrifice whatever it takes for the sake of peace and unity, for the sake of relationships. If we lose things, we can recover them through hard work, but if we lose relationships, it will take genuine forgiveness to restore them. This is the path that we as Kenyans must be willing to walk in order to restore our lost vision of peace, love, and unity. If we truly forgive one another and treat each other as equals before God, community disintegration will become a thing of the past.

---

72. Frost, *Struggling to Forgive*, 28.

73. Frost, 28.

74. David Augsburger, *The Freedom of Forgiveness: Seventy Times Seven* (Chicago: Moody, 1973), 19.

Often we fail to forgive because we fail to treat each other as equals. This seems to have been the case for the first servant in the passage we have analyzed. Indeed, the first servant could not have treated his fellow servant in the way he did if he had realized that the two were equal before God. This is one of the challenges that we face in Kenya when it comes to working toward cohesion. As we saw earlier, some communities or individuals think of themselves as superior to others. They think that it is their right to be treated fairly while they themselves are busy mistreating those around them. This obviously hampers the process of attaining peace and reconciliation for a cohesive society.

Forgiveness can only be possible for people who are conscious of having been forgiven themselves. Bash argues that "forgiven people become forgivers. If we are unforgiving, it will be because we ourselves have never properly received the gift of forgiveness."[75] I would add to Bash's statement that some people fail to forgive because they are not even aware that they have already been forgiven. Sometimes this becomes another impediment to cohesion: many people do not either realize or recognize that they have been forgiven as a result of the sacrifice of Jesus Christ on the cross.

Recognizing That Forgiveness Is a Process

Forgiveness is a continuous process; it is something that we must be willing to keep on doing as the need arises. We should not be tired of forgiving others. Bash points out that forgivingness is to be "lavish and generous."[76] Indeed, this is what Jesus meant when he told Peter "seventy times seven." As Schaeffer-Duffy asserts, "forgiveness is the necessary mortar for building a lasting peace."[77] We frequently see situations when even court trials fail to deliver justice to the victims. It is against this backdrop that forgiveness becomes the only means of true peace and reconciliation. As Schaeffer-Duffy observes, "Many victims feel better knowing where the bodies of their loved ones are than knowing someone is going to jail."[78] This shows that forgiveness is the surest remedy to societal ills.

---

75. Anthony Bash, *Just Forgiveness: Exploring the Bible, Weighing the Issues* (London: SPCK, 2011), 74.

76. Bash, *Just Forgiveness*, 79.

77. Schaeffer-Duffy, "Building a Future of Hope," 24.

78. Schaeffer-Duffy.

Conclusion

Through this study, we have seen that there are a number of factors that militate against the attainment of cohesion for a robust community in Kenya: political, economic, and social-cultural. These factors are deeply rooted in our history and therefore require a careful study of their causes. This follows from the proposition, borrowed from the medical field, that diagnosis precedes prescription. Once the root cause of an illness has been successfully identified, one can proceed to its treatment.

In the case of Kenya, the problems of cohesion are rooted in the country's history and go back to the colonial period. Unfortunately, previous regimes have only helped to perpetuate rather than eradicate them. This has made it difficult for the nation's realization of its dreams of peace, love, and unity for a prosperous Kenya; hence the need to find an amicable approach to solving these challenges in order to develop a robust, united Kenyan community. The surest approach is to choose forgiveness in place of revenge. Forgiveness is an attitude and is a task for everybody. It is important to note that forgiveness, as a process, takes time. One cannot simply wake up one morning and forgive one's enemies; it takes time to restore peace and reconciliation where hatred has previously reigned supreme. This therefore calls for concerted effort, sacrifice, and patience to see the fruit of forgiveness, which is peace and reconciliation.

Bibliography

Augsburger, David. *The Freedom of Forgiveness: Seventy Times Seven*. Chicago: Moody, 1973.

Bacote, Vincent. "Church as a Lifestyle: Distinctive or Typical?" In *This Side of Heaven: Race, Ethnicity, and Christian Faith*, edited by Alvaro L. Nieves and Robert J. Priest, 195–210. Oxford: Oxford University Press, 2007.

Bash, Anthony. *Just Forgiveness: Exploring the Bible, Weighing the Issues*. London: SPCK, 2011.

Blomberg, Craig L. *Matthew*. New American Commentary 22. Nashville: Broadman, 1992.

Bonneuil, Noël, and Nadia Auriat. "Fifty Years of Ethnic Conflict and Cohesion: 1945–94." *Journal of Peace Research* 37, no. 5 (2000): 563–581.

Crossman, Ashley. "Ethnicity Definition in Sociology." ThoughtCo. Accessed 29 January 2019. https://www.thoughtco.com/ethnicity-definition-3026311.

Faulkner, Mark. "Evangelizing Gone Awry: The Church in Kenya Has Fostered the Tribalism It Now Deplores." *National Catholic Reporter*, 22 February 2008. Accessed 5 December 2018. http://natcath.org/NCR_Online/archives2/2008a/022208/022208p.htm.

Frost, Brian. *Struggling to Forgive: Nelson Mandela and South Africa's Search for Reconciliation*. London: HarperCollins, 1998.

Hagner, Donald A. *Matthew 14–28*. Word Biblical Commentary 33b. Dallas: Word, 1995.

Jones, L. G. "Unity and Diversity in Christ." *Christian Century* 109, no. 18 (20 May 1992): 540.

Kamaara, Eunice. "Towards Christian National Identity in Africa: A Historical Perspective to the Challenge of Ethnicity to the Church in Kenya." *Studies in World Christianity* 16, no. 2 (Jul. 2010): 126–144. https://doi.org/10.3366/swc.2010.0002.

Kanyinga, Karuti, and Duncan Okello, eds. *Tensions and Reversals in Democratic Transitions: The Kenya 2007 General Elections*. Nairobi: Society for International Development: Institute for Development Studies, University of Nairobi, 2010.

Kibwana, Kivutha, Smokin Wanjala, and Owiti-Okech, eds. *The Anatomy of Corruption in Kenya: Legal, Political and Socio-Economic Perspectives*. Nairobi: Claripress, 1996.

Luz, Ulrich, and Helmut Koester. *Matthew: A Commentary*. Hermeneia: A Critical and Historical Commentary on the Bible. Minneapolis: Augsburg, 2001.

Maathai, Wangari. *The Challenge for Africa*. 1st ed. New York: Pantheon, 2009.

Maigadi, Barje Sulmane. *Divisive Ethnicity in the Church in Africa*. Kaduna, Nigeria: Baraka Press, 2006.

Manson, T. W. *Sayings of Jesus*. London: SCM Press, 1949.

Meredith, Martin. *The State of Africa: A History of Fifty Years of Independence*. London: Free Press, 2006.

Moibi, Kefa Onsando. *Biblical Teaching on Unity and Its Implications for National Unity in Kenya*. MA thesis, Nairobi Evangelical Graduate School of Theology (Kenya), 1997.

Nieves, Alvaro L., and Robert J. Priest, eds. *This Side of Heaven: Race, Ethnicity, and Christian Faith*. Oxford: Oxford University Press, 2007.

Ntamushobora, Faustin. *Transformation through the Different Other: A Rendezvous of Giving and Receiving*. Eugene, OR: Wipf & Stock, 2013.

Nyasani, Joseph M. "The Meaning and Implication of Ethnicity." In *Ethnicity, Conflict and the Future of African States*, edited by Aquiline Tarimo and Paulin Manwelo, 14–22. Nairobi: Paulines Publications Africa, 2009.

Ogachi, Oanda. "Economic Reform, Political Liberalization and Economic Ethnic Conflict in Kenya." *Africa Development / Afrique et Développement* 24, no. 1/2 (1999): 83–107.

Ojuka, Aloo, and William Ochieng, eds. *Politics and Leadership in Africa*. Kampala: East African Literature Bureau, 1975.

Oucho, John O. "Undercurrents of Post-Election Violence in Kenya: Issues in the Long-Term Agenda." In *Tensions and Reversals in Democratic Transitions: The Kenya 2007 General Elections*, edited by Karuti Kanyinga and Duncan Okello, 491–531. Nairobi: Society for International Development: Institute for Development Studies, University of Nairobi, 2010.

Robinson, Theodore H. *The Gospel of Matthew*. Moffat New Testament Commentary. London: Hodder & Stoughton, 1947.

Schaeffer-Duffy, Claire. "Building a Future of Hope." *National Catholic Reporter* 38, no. 25 (26 Apr. 2002): 24.

Schweizer, Eduard. *The Good News according to Matthew*. Atlanta: John Knox Press, 1975.

Talbert, Charles H. *Matthew*. Paideia Commentaries on the New Testament. Grand Rapids, MI: Baker Academic, 2010.

Tarimo, Aquiline, and Paulin Manwelo. *African Peacemaking and Governance*. Studies on Social Change in Africa. Nairobi: Acton, 2008.

———. *Ethnicity, Conflict and the Future of African States*. Nairobi: Paulines Publications Africa, 2009.

Tutu, Desmond. *No Future without Forgiveness*. 1st ed. New York: Doubleday, 1999.

Verkuyl, Johannes, and B. Lewis Smedes. *Break Down the Walls: A Christian Cry for Racial Justice*. Grand Rapids, MI: Eerdmans, 1973.

Wuerl, Donald W. "Christian Unity in an Age of Social Division." *Priest* 73, no. 1 (Jan. 2017): 10–21.

2

Interpersonal Forgiveness in the Early African Church

Conditional or Unconditional?[1]

Benjamin Straub
Dean of the School of Bible
Central Africa Baptist University, Kitwe, Zambia

Abstract

The last two decades have witnessed a significant increase in theological and philosophical interest in forgiveness. One contributing factor has been the tragic recent history of the African continent, which has become a testing ground for the formulation of theories of interpersonal forgiveness and their necessary application to bring healing into conflict and societal rupture. Alongside this, the continent has also experienced a reclaiming of the uniquely African contributions of the early church. These trends have led to several recent studies on interpersonal forgiveness in the early fathers, which claim to find a theology of interpersonal forgiveness that is conditioned upon the repentance of the wrongdoer. This study seeks to evaluate these recent claims by considering the writings of major early African church fathers, namely Clement of Alexandria, Tertullian, Origen, and Cyprian.

This study argues that the early African church did, in fact, teach a gracious and unconditional interpersonal forgiveness. This is demonstrated

---

1. Some of the material in this chapter has been adapted from my unpublished Masters Thesis, "'Forgive, If You Have Anything Against Anyone': A Biblical Account of Interpersonal Forgiveness," Central Baptist Theological Seminary, Minneapolis, Minnesota USA, 2012.

through close analysis of early African patristics texts, and through carefully distinguishing the fathers' teaching on interpersonal forgiveness from their teaching on divine or ecclesiastical forms of forgiveness. It also seeks to demonstrate that recent claims of conditional interpersonal forgiveness in the early fathers are based on a failure to maintain this essential distinction between God's forgiveness and humanity's, a distinction that is even found in the writings of the early African fathers. Given the great need for gracious and practical acts of forgiveness in modern Africa, this study has significant implications for today, both in recovering a strong and ancient African voice to speak to the African church and in allowing the early African fathers' theology of unconditional interpersonal forgiveness to guide today's church in Africa in leading the way toward reconciliation and healing in atrocity-torn societies.

Key words: interpersonal forgiveness, divine forgiveness, unconditional forgiveness, patristics, early church fathers, African Christianity.

Introduction

In the last century, few concepts have seen such an incredible flourishing of broad interdisciplinary attention like the concept of forgiveness. It is now in vogue to discuss matters relating to forgiveness in such varied academic fields as philosophy, psychology, counseling, political science, ethics, and theology. Yet discussions on forgiveness in theology, long its sole domain, seem to be overshadowed by the flurry of activity occurring in other quarters. Furthermore, while authors in various fields have pointed out the obvious development that this concept has experienced in recent times, few attempts have been made to offer a historical analysis of the development or to provide any in-depth examination into historical models of forgiveness. That is, until recently. In the last decade, several major works have been published which either are entirely devoted to tracing the development of historical models of forgiveness, or contain essays offering in-depth treatments of specific historical models. Since forgiveness was long seen as belonging to the domain of theology, these historical studies are inherently theological in nature and offer hope for a revived interest in forgiveness conceived theologically, while also providing opportunities for the reinvigoration of a robust theology of forgiveness. Of special interest to these studies are the conceptions of forgiveness offered by the earliest Christian documents, namely the New Testament and the first centuries of patristic writings, since these formative years shaped the contours of the discussion for centuries. This study will begin by briefly summarizing the works of two such authors who have greatly contributed to recent scholarship on historical models of forgiveness: David Konstan and Ilaria L. E. Ramelli.

Konstan: Forgiveness in the Early Church Fathers?

The first work which takes up a historical examination of the concept of forgiveness is a recent book by David Konstan, *Before Forgiveness: The Origins of a Moral Idea*. In this work, he examines the writings of the ancient Greeks and Romans, the Hebrew and Greek Scriptures along with the early church fathers, and the writings of late antiquity and the medieval period to determine whether the modern concept of forgiveness (which he argues includes repentance) was present in any meaningful way in these three eras. He finds that it "did not exist in classical antiquity . . . it is not fully present in the Hebrew Bible nor again in the New Testament or the early Jewish and Christian commentaries on the Holy Scriptures; it would still be centuries – many centuries – before the idea of interpersonal forgiveness, and the set of values and attitudes that necessarily accompany and help to define it, would emerge."[2]

Konstan is careful to state that he has a specific understanding of forgiveness in mind as he conducts his examination. He explains, "To the extent that forgiveness involves a change of heart or moral state, the abandonment of one's former ways, and sentiments such as remorse and penitence, it is all the more plausible that such an idea was absent in classical antiquity."[3] In the preface to his book he attributes his understanding of forgiveness as necessarily conditioned upon repentance to the book *Forgiveness: A Philosophical Exploration* and to discussions with its author, Charles Griswold. Griswold approaches the topic from a purely philosophical/ethical standpoint and argues that only a forgiveness based on repentance is morally sound and philosophically acceptable.[4] While much of the material that Konstan covers in the book lies beyond the scope of this study, his observations concerning the attitude of the ancient mind toward wrongdoing and reconciliation demonstrate keen insight and careful consideration of the various factors coming to bear on this uniquely social/relational behavior. He ably proves his thesis that forgiveness as

---

2. David Konstan, *Before Forgiveness: The Origins of a Moral Idea* (Cambridge: Cambridge University Press, 2010), ix.

3. David Konstan, "Before Forgiveness: Classical Antiquity, Early Christianity . . . and Beyond," unpublished paper, 12 March 2011, 4, accessed 10 February 2019, https://forum. evangelicaluniversalist.com/t/before-forgiveness-classical-antiquity-early-christianity/1460.

4. Charles L. Griswold, *Forgiveness: A Philosophical Exploration* (Cambridge: Cambridge University Press, 2007).

it is commonly understood today – necessarily conditioned upon repentance – is largely absent from the ancient mind, even in the New Testament or the early fathers. Yet, in spite of his astute observations of the character of early forgiveness, Konstan does not go so far as to say that forgiveness was, in fact, unconditional in the early fathers. Instead, he points to "that neglect of the conditions for human forgiveness that is characteristic, I believe, of all fathers of the church."[5] In fact, Konstan's commitment to the modern conditional view of forgiveness keeps him from seeing what his work actually proves – that interpersonal forgiveness in the church fathers is conceived of as unconditional and commanded regardless of whether the offender repents, as this study will seek to show.

Ramelli: Unconditional Forgiveness in the Early Church Fathers?

A second contribution to the discussion on forgiveness in the early church comes in two essays by Ilaria L. E. Ramelli: "Unconditional Forgiveness in Christianity? Some Reflections on Ancient Christian Sources" in *The Ethics of Forgiveness*, and "Forgiveness in Patristic Philosophy: The Importance of Repentance and the Centrality of Grace" in *Ancient Forgiveness: Classical, Judaic, and Christian*. In each of these essays Ramelli examines the writings of the early church fathers and comes to the firm conviction that "in Patristic authors and early Christianity, as well, there is plenty of evidence that forgiveness was not in the least considered as unconditional."[6]

Ramelli's work demonstrates extensive knowledge of a broad spectrum of patristic authors and penetrating insight into the intellectual currents which influenced their writings. However, there is a defect in her method which leads to her conclusion that interpersonal forgiveness was seen as necessarily conditional in the church fathers. In her chapter on forgiveness in ancient Christian sources in *Ancient Forgiveness*, Ramelli summarizes her earlier essay in *The Ethics of Forgiveness* and states that she there argues, "on the basis of massive evidence, that forgiveness is not unconditional either in the New Testament . . . or in early Christianity."[7] However, the majority of texts that

---

5. Konstan, *Before Forgiveness: Origins*, 139.

6. Ilaria L. E. Ramelli, "Unconditional Forgiveness in Christianity? Some Reflections on Ancient Christian Sources," in *The Ethics of Forgiveness*, ed. Christel Fricke (New York: Routledge, 2011), 35.

7. Ilaria L. E. Ramelli, "Forgiveness in Patristic Philosophy: The Importance of Repentance and the Centrality of Grace," in *Ancient Forgiveness: Classical, Judaic, and Christian*, ed. Charles L. Griswold and David Konstan (Cambridge: Cambridge University Press, 2012), 200, n. 18.

Ramelli cites in both essays, either from the New Testament or from the early fathers, are references to individuals seeking forgiveness from *God*, or to *God's* offer of forgiveness to humanity.[8] Yet she takes these texts as paradigmatic for all forgiveness and concludes that forgiveness can never be unconditional. Thus, this study will argue that her conclusions are based on the illegitimate conflation of God's forgiveness with interpersonal forgiveness, which must be properly distinguished in order to rightly understand either one.

The African Church Fathers on Forgiveness: A Reexamination

In spite of the great advances in our knowledge of the early church's teaching on forgiveness that these recent studies have achieved, when viewed from the perspective of modern Christianity in Africa a noticeable oversight begins to emerge. In both Konstan's book and Ramelli's essays, the authors have followed well-established scholarly habits of treating all the early fathers as participants in a single conversation and minimizing or overlooking the individual cultural and ethnic variations that one finds just under the surface of their texts and debates. This is not surprising and has been at times a helpful convention when such vast collections of texts and authors are engaged. But recent scholarship reexamining the various cultural and geographic influences that shaped early Christianity is beginning to challenge this longstanding convention, and slowly the African church fathers are reemerging as the unparalleled theological and ecclesiastical leaders of the church in its earliest centuries. The scholar at the forefront of this reevaluation of the African fathers was the late Thomas C. Oden, a leading proponent of what has been called "paleo-orthodoxy," an effort to return modern Christianity to its historic apostolic and patristic moorings. In his seminal work, *How Africa Shaped the Christian Mind: Rediscovering the African Seedbed of Western Christianity*, Oden argues, "Africa played a decisive role in the formation of Christian culture. Decisive intellectual achievements of Christianity were explored and understood first in Africa before they were recognized in Europe, and a millennium before they found their way to North America."[9] In reframing the historical context of early Christianity thus,

---

8. See for example Ramelli, "Forgiveness in Patristic Philosophy," and Konstan, *Before Forgiveness: Origins*, 125–145, for many quotations from early church fathers which teach that God's forgiveness of humankind is conditioned upon repentance. This study does not challenge those conclusions, and thus does not include any quotations from early African fathers where the explicit focus of the teaching is on God's forgiveness rather than on humanity's forgiveness.

9. Thomas C. Oden, *How Africa Shaped the Christian Mind: Rediscovering the African Seedbed of Western Christianity* (Downers Grove, IL: InterVarsity Press, 2007), 9.

he seeks to reestablish sound scholarship on the geographical and cultural milieus which profoundly shaped the thinking, values, and arguments of the earliest champions of apostolic orthodoxy. He goes on to explain, "My task is to show that the classic Christian mind is significantly shaped by the African imagination spawned on African soil. It bears the stamp of philosophical analyses, moral insight, discipline and scriptural interpretations that bloomed first in Africa before anywhere else. The seeds spread from Africa north."[10] For African Christian scholars and churches today, this restored recognition of the truly African influence that was exerted by these early champions offers a much-needed measure of historical rootedness and ancient Christian tradition from Africa for Africa. It affords the African church a chance to reevaluate its place in history and reclaim some of its ancient voice. This opportunity should be seized, and many avenues of investigation should be opened into the African cultural, educational, and worldview influences that shaped and informed the hermeneutics and theological reasoning of these ancient African fathers. This study seeks to take up that challenge by investigating the early African church's theology of interpersonal forgiveness.

As outlined above, recent studies focusing on the early church fathers (broadly undifferentiated) have argued that they taught a theology of interpersonal forgiveness that is necessarily conditioned on the repentance of the wrongdoer. In narrowing the focus specifically to the African church fathers, it is the thesis of this study that unconditional interpersonal forgiveness is in fact called for in their writings.[11] To substantiate this, the study will embark on a close examination of the writings of several key early African fathers, focusing especially on those texts where the writer in question is undoubtedly referring to interpersonal forgiveness as opposed to divine or ecclesiastical forgiveness. The reason for this focus will become apparent below as the strong distinction between God's forgiveness and interpersonal forgiveness

---

10. Oden, *How Africa Shaped*, 9–10.

11. Thomas Oden has offered a cogent defense of the validity of narrowing the focus from early church fathers in general to the early African church fathers specifically: "In the period of its greatest vitality, the first half of the first millennium, the African intellect blossomed so much that it was sought out and widely emulated by Christians of the northern and eastern Mediterranean shores. Origen, an African, was actively sought out by the teachers of Caesarea Palestina. . . . This point must be savored unhurriedly to sink in deeply: The Christians to the south of the Mediterranean were teaching the Christians to the north. Africans were informing and instructing and educating the very best of Syriac, Cappadocian and Greco-Roman teachers" (Oden, 29). It is thus beyond the scope of this study to show whether this African unconditional forgiveness had its echoes in the non-African fathers, but such evidence may also be found outside of Africa.

is examined and discussed. In order to limit the scope of the study, it will focus primarily on texts written by major African writers from AD 150 to 250. Finding unconditional interpersonal forgiveness in this period is especially significant since it is to this era of church history that modern writers most confidently appeal in order to prove conditional forgiveness.[12] This study will demonstrate that such a conclusion is largely drawn from an illegitimate conflation of God's forgiveness with interpersonal forgiveness. Ultimately this study will seek to demonstrate that the early African church has much to teach today's African church about how to forgive.[13] The meteoric rise of Christianity on the continent over the last century, coupled with the sad realities of ever-present war, religiously and/or tribally motivated violence, and even genocide create fertile ground for the evangelistic seeds of forgiveness to be sown. Yet despite many attempts to cultivate such a spirit of forgiveness, there remains a persistent resistance and even refusal to forgive in many African communities, even in those benefiting from otherwise vibrant Christian witness.[14] This study is offered in hope that by listening to the ancient African patristic voices, the church in Africa might be led into a more perfect commitment to historic apostolic orthodoxy, and more genuine expressions of Christian forgiveness. "African Christianity is entering into a maturing stage. It hungers for the strong meat of ancient African Christianity at this decisive stage . . . [Young Africans] grasp the need for a just political order, for social cohesion, for economic justice and for physical well-being. All these challenges can be better met by standing firmly within the historical community of faith that has been repeatedly tested by the experienced ancient African apostolate on African soil."[15] It is to such African church fathers and in such a spirit of historically rooted hope that this study now turns.

Early African Fathers' Teaching on Forgiveness

This study is limited to just four early African church fathers – Clement of Alexandria, Tertullian, Cyprian, and Origen – for three reasons: (1) their African heritage and influences can be easily demonstrated; (2) their writings

---

12. See fn. 7 above for examples.

13. Please see chapter 2 appendix on page 62 for further discussion on the term "early African church."

14. See the Conclusion for specific examples of both the need for and resistance to forgiveness in Africa.

15. Oden, *How Africa Shaped*, 106.

are voluminous and their influence on the shape of early Christianity is undisputed; and (3) their works are examined by Konstan and Ramelli in their efforts to prove early patristic conditional forgiveness. Clement of Alexandria was a teacher in the Catechetical School of Alexandria, Egypt, and the earliest of the fathers under consideration. Little is known of his birth and upbringing, and while he may or may not have been born in Egypt, he certainly did travel through much of the Mediterranean region before settling into his role as a teacher in Egypt. He was ordained while ministering there, and all of his extant major works were written during his time in Alexandria. Tertullian is of unquestionable African heritage, likely being of Berber descent. He was a teacher and lay theologian from Carthage in ancient Roman North Africa and is famous both as the first of the Latin fathers and as the first to introduce the Latin term *trinitas* into theological discourse. His writings were influential in the early Trinitarian debates and formulas that eventually coalesced in the Council of Nicaea (AD 325). Next comes Cyprian, the bishop of Carthage after the time of Tertullian, his fellow Berber, and one of his major formative influences.[16] He exercised leadership over the see of Carthage during a tumultuous time of church conflict following intense persecution (see below), and his doctrinal formulations and treatises carried significant influence on ecclesiology both during his lifetime and for many years after his martyrdom, having been executed by the Roman authorities for refusing to recant. And finally, there is the unquestioned giant of early African theologians, Origen.[17] Born in Alexandria and likely taught by Clement, he spent his early theological career in the same Catechetical School. Largely due to the generous patronage of his friend Ambrose, he became one of the most prolific writers the early church ever produced. His nearly two thousand writings impacted every doctrine and practice of the early church and continued to be studied for centuries after his death. Also after his death, many controversies arose over

---

16. For a defense of the African genuineness of both Tertullian and Cyprian and a summary of their impact on the doctrinal formulations of European Christianity, see Oden: "Whether Tertullian and Cyprian and Augustine learned everything from Rome can easily be answered based on impartial textual analysis. These Africans were being seriously read in Rome during their lifetimes when they were living in Africa because they were teaching in a way pertinent and useful to Rome and the awakening wider European ethos." Oden, 63.

17. On Origen's credentials as an African Christian: "There can be no doubt that Origen grew up in Africa, wrote much of his work in Africa and then transmitted his extensive African library and teaching to Caesarea Palestina. It is a strange and demeaning criterion to apply to Origen the odd assumption that because he was adept at many languages he was not very African. By his metaphors, the greatest biblical interpreter of early Christianity shows many indications of being indigenously African, whatever his specific ethnicity." Oden, 68.

the orthodoxy of his teachings, some of which were condemned as heretical by later popes and councils.[18] Despite this, his influence was unflagging, and he is generally acknowledged as one of the greatest early church fathers.

Clement of Alexandria: Seventy Times Seven

The first of these early African writers who offers clues as to the nature of interpersonal forgiveness is Clement of Alexandria (date of writings: AD 182–202), a teacher who many have supposed to have been a mentor to Origen. He wrote a series of treatises called *Stromateis* or *The Carpets* (i.e. Miscellanies) in which he co-opts the language of his opponents and, using their own terminology in many cases, seeks to describe the "gnostic," or perfect, Christian.[19] On interpersonal forgiveness he writes: "He never remembers those who have sinned against him but forgives them. Wherefore also he righteously prays, saying, 'Forgive us; for we also forgive.' For this also is one of the things which God wishes, to covet nothing, to hate no one. For all men are the work of one will" (*Stromata* 7.13.81).

Ramelli considers this passage and summarizes her interpretation of interpersonal forgiveness in Clement, saying that for him, "forgiveness depends on the offender's repentance and moral improvement, which is voluntary and indeed represents the best fruits of human free will."[20] However, the role of repentance is not mentioned in this short quote; thus her conclusion is based primarily on other passages where he discusses divine conditional forgiveness. There is, though, another place where Clement takes up the specific theme of interpersonal forgiveness in which he reveals that he does see it as unconditional:

---

18. There is not space in this study to examine the conflicted history of how the church has at various times both accepted and rejected Origen's hermeneutics and much of his theology, but Oden notes, "The heresy of Origenism, a movement that came after Origen's death, was condemned ecumenically for certain obviously skewed misinterpretations (e.g. preexistence of the soul, eternal creation, the stars have souls), yet the misinterpretations were largely fragmented statements of the broken pieces of the careful dialectic found in Origen's own writings. Hence it is no exaggeration to say that the greatest fourth-century Christian exegetes of East and West (Gregory Nazianzus, Gregory of Nyssa, Ambrose, Jerome, and Augustine) were all profoundly influenced by the writings of Origen. Even when Origen's detractors rejected his excesses, they continued to depend on his philological, linguistic and historical studies." Oden, 46.

19. In other words, one must be careful not to read Clement's comments on the gnostic Christian as an example of the ancient heresy of Gnosticism. Instead, he is co-opting their terms to show the true biblical nature of a perfect (gnostic) Christian, as opposed to their mystical heretical views.

20. Ramelli, "Forgiveness in Patristic Philosophy," 197.

> And he that earnestly strives to be assimilated to God, in the exercise of great absence of resentment, forgives seventy times seven times, as it were all his life through, and in all his course in this world (that being indicated by the enumeration of sevens) shows clemency to each and any one; if any during the whole time of his life in the flesh do the Gnostic wrong. For he not only deems it right that the good man should resign his property alone to others, being of the number of those who have done him wrong; but also wishes that the righteous man should ask of those judges forgiveness for the offences of those who have done him wrong. And with reason, if indeed it is only in that which is external and concerns the body, though it go to the extent of death even, that those who attempt to wrong him take advantage of him; none of which truly belong to the Gnostic. (*Stromata* 7.14.85)

Notice that he clearly states the extent of the perfect Christian's forgiveness: he "shows clemency to each and any one; if any during the whole time of his life in the flesh do the Gnostic wrong." This does not fit at all with a conditional understanding of interpersonal forgiveness.

Clement brings up one further point in this quote which deserves careful examination. He references Jesus's command in Matthew 18:22 to forgive in spite of repeated offenses, which is also echoed in Luke 17:3–4, a text which many modern defenders of conditional forgiveness hold up as incontrovertible proof of their position. For instance, Ramelli says of the passage, "Here forgiveness is expressly conditional: It depends on the offender's repentance and its clear manifestation to the offended person."[21] However, when examined logically, this use of Luke 17:3–4 to prove conditional forgiveness is invalid. The logic of the conditional forgiveness interpretation runs thus:

If he repents, forgive him.	If *a*, then *b*.
He does not repent,	Not *a*,
Therefore, do not forgive him.	Therefore not *b*.

On its surface, this argument seems to substantiate conditional forgiveness, which is why it is almost universally appealed to by defenders of the position.[22] However, the structure of the argument actually contains a classic logical

---

21. Ramelli, "Unconditional Forgiveness," 30.

22. For instance, Konstan makes the same appeal: *Before Forgiveness: Origins*, 122.

fallacy: *denying the antecedent.*[23] Simply put, given a simple if–then statement such as the one here, it is invalid to argue that a denial of the antecedent (the *if* clause) entails a denial of the consequent (the *then* clause). The statement does not address circumstances that fall outside of the antecedent; it only addresses circumstances that fall within it. Therefore, this statement cannot logically be used to address circumstances in which the offending party does not repent since that falls outside its purview. It only addresses instances of repentance; clues must be found elsewhere to determine what course of action to take in the case of the unrepentant.

Now, it is logically possible to argue that Christ (and thus Clement) actually meant "only if he repents," which would then, of course, substantiate Ramelli's argument.[24] However, close examination of the context of the command rules out this narrow reading. The irony that most fail to notice is that this verse, wherein Christ offers his strongest and clearest command to forgive (i.e. even if a person sins against you seven times in one day, forgive), is *the* passage most frequently used to excuse someone from forgiving! The context shows that the intent of this passage is not to delineate the necessary conditions for forgiveness, but to command forgiveness even in the face of blatant and repeated wrongs. Konstan's evaluation of the passage cedes this point, saying that "the emphasis here too would appear to be more on the moral requirement for the victim to be reconciled with the wrongdoer than on a change of heart on the part of the wrongdoer."[25]

Tertullian: The Necessity of Patience

Turning next to the writings of Tertullian (date of writings: AD 197–220), one finds that his repeated calls to patience, on which he wrote an entire treatise,

---

23. To illustrate, consider the following example: the statement "If it is raining, you should wear a coat" does not entail "If it is not raining, you should not wear a coat." The fact is, it may be snowing or fifty degrees below zero and you should still wear a coat, but these situations are simply not addressed in the original statement. That is why denying the antecedent is a logical fallacy.

24. "Only if" is a valid interpretation of "if," but *only if* it is clear from the context. For example, the statement "If you have beans, you can make bean soup" clearly means "only if you have beans." However, it must be either explicitly stated or unquestionably clear from the context, which in this case is quite the opposite.

25. Konstan, *Before Forgiveness: Origins*, 122.

serve to exhort his readers to remember that vengeance belongs to God.[26] Thus, believers should exhibit patience in the face of wrongdoing, since they have an eschatological hope that God will right the wrongs done to them. It becomes clear when one examines Tertullian's treatise *Of Patience* that he is calling his readers to unconditional interpersonal forgiveness. He writes, "For every injury, whether inflicted by tongue or hand, when it has lighted upon patience, will be dismissed with the same fate as some weapon launched against and blunted on a rock of most steadfast hardness. For it will wholly fall then and there with bootless and fruitless labour" (*Of Patience* 8).

Thus, he asserts that wrongs done to believers who exhibit patience as they ought will have no effect on them, implying that the believers are to forgive wrongdoers even as the wrongs are being done. He picks up the topic again a few sections later and makes the connection between patience and forgiveness even more explicit:

> As regards the rule of peace, which is so pleasing to God, who in the world that is prone to impatience will even once forgive his brother, I will not say "seven times," or "seventy-seven times?" Who that is contemplating a suit against his adversary will compose the matter by agreement, unless he first begin by lopping off chagrin, hardheartedness, and bitterness, which are in fact the poisonous outgrowths of impatience? How will you "remit, and remission shall be granted" you if the absence of patience makes you tenacious of a wrong? (*Of Patience* 12)

Thus, he rules out withholding forgiveness and becoming tenacious of a wrong, regardless of whether or not the wrongdoer has repented. He delineates what a lack of forgiveness looks like, condemns it, and then reminds his readers that they have been commanded to forgive, with no mention made of repentance.

One more quote from this treatise will suffice to show that Tertullian conceives of interpersonal forgiveness as being unconditional: "But, however, since Patience takes the lead in every species of salutary discipline, what wonder that she likewise ministers to Repentance (accustomed as Repentance is to come to the rescue of such as have fallen), when, on a disjunction of wedlock . . . she waits for, she yearns for, she persuades by her entreaties, repentance in all who are one day to enter salvation? How great a blessing she

---

26. For good overviews of the theology of Tertullian see Timothy David Barnes, *Tertullian: A Historical and Literary Study* (Oxford: Clarendon, 1971); Gerald Lewis Bray, *Holiness and the Will of God: Perspectives on the Theology of Tertullian* (Atlanta: John Knox Press, 1979); Robert E. Roberts, *The Theology of Tertullian* (London: Epworth, 1924).

confers on each!" (*Of Patience* 12). This quote is especially revealing since in it, Tertullian argues that patience, which he has already linked to forgiveness, precedes repentance and in some cases can actually lead to it! In other words, he argues that if the victim can patiently endure the wrong and forgive the wrongdoer, his or her very act of forgiveness can lead the wrongdoer to repent, clearly delineating a classic case of unconditional interpersonal forgiveness.

Forgiveness Tested: The Crisis of the Lapsed in the Early African Church

Turning now to evaluate the historical circumstances in which these African church leaders were writing, this time period was significant in the development of the theology of forgiveness due to the controversy over the lapsed. At the end of the second century and the beginning of the third, organized persecution of the fledgling church had become especially strong and many Christians succumbed to the pressure by officially recanting their faith, even in some cases offering sacrifices to pagan gods to prove their recantation and save their own lives. Once the intense persecution passed, many of these "former" Christians, who came to be known as the lapsed (*lapsi*, "fallen" in Latin), decided that they wanted to be readmitted into the church and sought ways to be forgiven for their apostasy. This caused a great debate over whether such sins could be forgiven, and, if they could, by whom and through what means.[27] Also during this time, the concept of repentance itself was being reconsidered, the primary focus shifting from an internal change of the heart to external manifestations of grief and sorrow or penitence.[28] Tertullian, Origen, and Cyprian were all very much engaged in these debates, often disagreeing with one another in strong terms. These developments caused the discussions concerning forgiveness and repentance to shift almost exclusively to the divine/ecclesiastical dimensions.

27. For information on the controversy over the lapsed see Christopher A. Hall, "Rejecting the Prodigal: The Early Church Debated Whether Apostate Christians Could Be Forgiven Again," *Christianity Today* 42 (26 Oct. 1998): 73–76; Frank Hudson Hallock, "Third Century Teaching on Sin and Repentance," *Anglican Theological Review* 4 (Oct. 1921): 128–142; Edward D. Junkin, "Commitment to the Fallen Brother: Cyprian and the Lapsed," *Austin Seminary Bulletin* 87 (Apr. 1972): 32–45; Johannes Roldanus, "No Easy Reconciliation: St. Cyprian on Conditions for Re-integration of the Lapsed," *Journal of Theology for Southern Africa* 92 (Sep. 1995): 23–31; William Tabbernee, "To Pardon or Not to Pardon? North African Montanism and the Forgiveness of Sins," in *Studia Patristica* 36 (Louvain: Peeters, 2001), 375–386.

28. For more on the debates concerning penance and repentance in the writings of Tertullian, Origen, and Cyprian see J. Patout Burns, "Confessing the Church: Cyprian on Penance," *Studia Patristica* 36 (Louvain: Peeters, 2001), 338–348; C. B. Daly, "Tertullian, Treatises on Penance: *On Penitence* and *On Purity*," *Theological Studies* 21 (Sep. 1960): 474–478; Ernest F. Latko, *Origen's Concept of Penance* (Laval, QC: Faculté de théologie, Université Laval, 1949).

Many are led astray by this strong emphasis on divine/ecclesiastical forgiveness into thinking that these early African fathers did not significantly address interpersonal forgiveness or else equated it with God's forgiveness and thus saw it as conditioned upon repentance/penance. Anthony Bash and Melanie Bash, for instance, argue that the early New Testament teaches unconditional forgiveness. But then after summarizing forgiveness in the fathers (focusing primarily on this controversy over the readmittance of the lapsed), they conclude that it is "undeniable that practices to do with forgiveness that are in the late New Testament in inchoate form (such as we see in John 20:23), and subsequently developed in the early church, detract from and even undermine the teaching of Jesus on forgiveness."[29] Konstan too, though he does not go so far as Anthony Bash and Melanie Bash, asserts that "Christian thinkers, in turn, were so focused on the trials of penitence that they too paid relatively little attention to what it might mean to forego resentment in the case of harm that is done intentionally: the injunction in the Gospels to forgive all debtors glosses over the question of voluntary and involuntary forfeiture and encourages a posture of loving consideration that is similar to God's and wins God's grace."[30]

Forgiveness in Scripture: The Lord's Prayer as a Common Patristic Theme

Despite the common consensus that the church fathers of the day, influenced by the controversy over the lapsed, taught a conditional model of both interpersonal and ecclesiastical forgiveness, there is evidence that even during this time the church continued to view interpersonal forgiveness as distinct from divine/ecclesiastical forgiveness. The former was offered unconditionally while the latter was conditioned upon repentance. While it will be readily admitted that concerns over divine/ecclesiastical forgiveness far exceeded concerns about interpersonal forgiveness for the writers of the day, a close examination of their writings shows that they did address the topic. Surprisingly, such examination also reveals that despite their numerous and quite vocal disagreements over the nature, extent, and availability of ecclesiastical forgiveness, these authors came to remarkably unanimous conclusions regarding interpersonal forgiveness. One helpful fact that allows this side-by-side examination of the writers' views

---

29. Anthony Bash and Melanie Bash, "Early Christian Thinking," in *Forgiveness in Context: Theology and Psychology in Creative Dialogue*, ed. Fraser Watts and Liz Gulliford (Edinburgh: T&T Clark, 2004), 49.

30. Konstan, *Before Forgiveness: Origins*, 140.

on interpersonal forgiveness is that three wrote extended treatises on the Lord's Prayer, one phrase of which directly addresses interpersonal forgiveness.[31]

Tertullian

Tertullian is the first African writer to devote an entire treatise to the topic of the Lord's Prayer, and his is the shortest with the least in-depth analysis. This is evident when he comes to the phrase in Matthew 6:12, "And forgive us our debts, as we also have forgiven our debtors" (*On Prayer* 7). He does little more than call Christians to forgiveness and lists a few passages which reinforce his call, primarily expounding the parable of the unforgiving servant in Matthew 18. The most significant aspect of his comments is that he makes no mention of repentance in this short section, except initially when referring to the first half of the clause which speaks of repentance directed toward God. This fact alone is not enough to conclude that he supports unconditional interpersonal forgiveness, but when read in light of his comments quoted above it does seem to prove rather than disprove the assertion.

Origen

Origen, a teacher in Alexandria best known for his significant contributions to early hermeneutics (date of writings: AD 203–250), devoted an extended treatise to the Lord's Prayer. The occasion came in response to a letter from his wealthy patron Ambrose who raised questions about the efficacy of prayer. In characteristic Origen style, he not only addresses the concerns of his patron but covers nearly every conceivable aspect of prayer, with one long section devoted to analyzing the Lord's Prayer.[32] Naturally, due to the length of his

---

31. For helpful discussions on these treatises see Lawrence S. Cunningham, "Origen's *On Prayer*: A Reflection and Appreciation," *Worship* 67 (Jul. 1993): 332–339; O. Wright Holmes, "Tertullian on Prayer," *Tyndale House Bulletin* 5–6 (Apr. 1960): 27–32; D. Richard Stuckwisch, "Principles of Christian Prayer in the Third Century: A Brief Look at Origen, Tertullian, and Cyprian with Some Comments on Their Meaning for Today," *Worship* 71 (Jan. 1997): 2–19.

32. For comprehensive treatments of Origen's biblical interpretation and theology see Charles Kannengiesser and William L. Petersen, eds., *Origen of Alexandria: His World and His Legacy* (Notre Dame: University of Notre Dame Press, 1988); Hugh T. Kerr, *The First Systematic Theologian: Origen of Alexandria* (Princeton: Princeton Theological Seminary, 1958); John Anthony McGuckin, ed., *The Westminster Handbook to Origen* (Louisville, KY: Westminster John Knox Press, 2004); John Clark Smith, *The Ancient Wisdom of Origen* (Lewisburg, PA: Bucknell University Press, 1992); Joseph Wilson Trigg, *Origen: The Bible and Philosophy in the Third-Century Church* (Atlanta: John Knox Press, 1983).

treatment, Origen has much more to say about forgiveness and its relationship to the prayer than either Tertullian or Cyprian.

Ramelli examines his treatment of forgiveness in *On Prayer* and elsewhere, and sees in it a fundamental dynamic of moral progress, concluding, "This conception of moral progress, again, points to a close link between Origen's conception of forgiveness and his soteriology and eschatology. It also is clear that for Origen forgiveness, either interpersonal or divine, is never unconditional, not even in the eventual *apokatastasis*."[33] Konstan agrees with Ramelli's evaluation, saying of Origen's passage on interpersonal forgiveness in the Lord's Prayer, "There is, then, a clear requirement for repentance, along with a parallel obligation on the part of the creditor – that is the person who has been wronged – to pardon the offense if the offender does repent. The emphasis, here as in other Christian treatments, is on the need for the offended party to forego vengeance so that she or he may, in turn, be shown mercy by God."[34] Yet in each of their treatments of Origen's comments on interpersonal forgiveness, they highlight his oft-repeated calls to repentance, most of which actually occur in the context of a sinner seeking the forgiveness of God, but do not fully examine his most explicit passage addressing interpersonal forgiveness or draw out all of its implications. To correct that oversight, large sections of it will be examined here to see whether conditional forgiveness best fits his comments.

Origen begins with the phrase from the Prayer "And forgive us our debts, as we also have forgiven our debtors" (Matt 6:12) by discussing the concept of debt and its relationship to sin, both against God and against a fellow human being. He then turns to address specific commands to interpersonal forgiveness:

> But if we refuse to become gentler towards those who have fallen
> in debt to us, our experience will be that of him who did not remit
> the hundred shillings to his fellow servant and of whom, according
> to the parable set down in the gospel, though already pardoned,
> the master exacts in severity what had already been remitted,
> saying to him: Wicked servant and slothful, was it not right for
> you to pity your fellow servant as I also pitied you? Cast him into

---

33. Ramelli, "Forgiveness in Patristic Philosophy," 202. While it is beyond the scope of this study to treat the subject, it should be noted that Origen's doctrine of *apokatastasis* is the basis for his doctrine of universal salvation. It refers to the idea that God will give everyone a chance to repent post mortem, which everyone will eventually do after having their various degrees of sin purged, thus leading to universal salvation. This idea is picked up by both Ramelli and Konstan and is defended by them in the works cited herein.

34. Konstan, *Before Forgiveness: Origins*, 136.

prison until he pay all that is owed. And the Lord continues: So shall the heavenly Father do to you also if you forgive not each his brother from your hearts. (*On Prayer* 18.7)

He makes no mention of repentance on the part of the wrongdoer. He simply warns against unforgiveness and exhorts the victim to forgive from the heart. After this passage is a phrase over which there is disagreement regarding the translation. In Origen's original Greek the phrase in question reads, "Λέγουσι μέντοιγε μετανοεῖν τοις εἰς ἡμᾶς ἡμαρτηκόσιν ἀφετέον."[35] Ramelli translates μέντοιγε as concessive, modifying λέγουσι, which she takes to be subjunctive, rendering it, "Therefore we *must forgive* [ἀφετέον] those who have sinned against us, *at least if they declare that they repent* [λέγουσι μέντοι γε μετανοεῖν]. And this, even if our debtor should do so many times."[36]

However, Origen's phrasing here is not as straightforward as Ramelli makes it out to be. First, λέγουσι can only be subjunctive if it is also passive, which the context would not allow here. Since the context requires it to be active, it is either indicative (statement) or a participle (several possible interpretations), thus calling into question Ramelli's translation. But it is also not likely to be indicative, because the force of the statement falls on the implied command in the predicate adjective ἀφετέον (it is forgiven). A further challenging factor is that the main verb is elliptical, linking the nominative predicate adjective to its participial agent or recipient (either ἡμαρτηκόσιν or λέγουσι). But the unclear question is what or who exactly must be forgiven? The interpretation that best accounts for the syntax and the context is to take λέγουσι as a dative substantival participle, marked as a dative of interest, showing the actor who benefits from the forgiveness ("For the ones who say they repent . . . it is forgiven").[37] Then ἡμαρτηκόσιν is functioning as the dative object of the indirect discourse infinitive μετανοεῖν.[38] Origen's choice of word order also supports this. Lastly, Liddell states that μέντοι is an adverbial particle which

---

35. Quoted from J. P. Migne and Theodor Hopfner, eds., *Patrologiae Cursus Completus: Patrologia Graecae*, vol. 11, Origen (Petit-Montrouge: Bibliotecae Cleri Universae, 1857), 528.

36. Ramelli, "Unconditional Forgiveness," 37; emphasis hers.

37. Taking λέγουσι as a participle also opens up the possibility of interpreting it as conditional, modifying the elliptical verb of the adjectival command, thus potentially justifying an "if" translation. Yet such an interpretation fails to account for the dative case of the participle since we would expect such an adverbial construction to be in the nominative case. For further explanation of this distinction see Martin Culy, "The Clue Is in the Case: Distinguishing Adjectival and Adverbial Participles," *Perspectives in Religious Studies* 30, no. 4 (2003): 441–453.

38. It is also significant to note that Origen chooses an indirect discourse construction to report the repentance. His focus is not on the act of repentance itself, but merely on the claim of repentance. This, of course, echoes Jesus's own comments in Luke 17, where the offender's

when used with an imperative (here the adjective bears imperatival force) strengthens the command, and when γε is added, the force is strengthened even more.[39] So it would be better construed as ascensive (certainly), rather than concessive (at least).

Thus, Oulton and Chadwick's older translation of the disputed passage is far more accurate than the one offered by Ramelli. Their translation reads, "Certainly, those who say that they repent of the sins that they have committed against us must be forgiven, even though the debtor does this frequently."[40] In this rendering, the emphasis falls on the absolute necessity of forgiveness in the face of repeated offenses, rather than on the necessity of repentance. This more accurately reflects the concerns both of Origen and of Jesus (seen in the Prayer and Luke 17), who both intend to command the practice of forgiveness rather than to lay out the conditions necessary for it to take place. It also accords better with what follows in the quotation from Origen.

He continues: "It is not we who are harsh towards the impenitent, but they who are wicked to themselves, for he that spurns instruction hates himself. Yet even in such cases, we should seek in every way that healing arise within him who is so completely perverted as not even to be conscious of his own ills but to be drunken with a drunkenness more fatal than from wine, from the darkening of evil" (*On Prayer* 28.7). Ramelli interprets this passage as Origen offering an alternative to forgiveness which the wronged party is to apply to the unrepentant party, but this is largely because she insists on seeing his earlier comments as upholding conditional forgiveness, which this study has challenged. It is better instead to see in this passage an assertion by Origen that it is not the individual's responsibility to withhold forgiveness from the unrepentant – in other words, to be harsh toward the offender. No, far from it; the wronged person is responsible to "seek in every way" to restore the wrongdoer and to encourage the wrongdoer to see his or her wrongdoing as sin. While unconditional forgiveness is not explicit yet, it does fit better with the overall tenor of Origen's remarks, and becomes even more apparent as he continues:

---

repeated sins call into question the genuineness of the repentance. Christ's command is to forgive graciously and generously even when the repentance is suspect, which Origen echoes here.

39. Henry George Liddell and Robert Scott, *An Intermediate Greek–English Lexicon: Founded upon the Seventh Edition of Liddell and Scott's Greek–English Lexicon* (Oxford: Clarendon, 1995), 498.

40. John Baille et al., eds., *The Library of Christian Classics*, vol. 2: *Alexandrian Christianity: Selected Translations of Clement and Origen*, trans. J. E. L. Oulton and Henry Chadwick (Philadelphia: Westminster Press, 1954), 308.

When Luke says Forgive us our Sins he means the same as Matthew since sins are constituted when we owe and do not pay, though he does not appear to lend support to him who would forgive only penitent debtors when he says that it is enacted by the Savior that we ought in prayer to add: for we ourselves also forgive everyone in debt to us. And it would seem that we have all authority to forgive the sins that have been committed against us as is clear from both clauses: as we also have forgiven our debtors; and for we ourselves also forgive everyone in debt to us. (*On Prayer* 28.8)

Ramelli's only comment on this passage is that Origen "observes that the meaning is the same" in both the Matthew and Luke passages.[41] However, she fails to point out that Origen explicitly states that Luke leaves no room for conditional interpersonal forgiveness, nor does she offer any explanation for how she interprets this passage. Throughout his treatment of the Lord's Prayer, Origen sought to examine both Synoptic passages and to glean insights from each, and here he comes to Luke's presentation of Christ's command for interpersonal forgiveness and highlights the universal nature of it, twice repeating the extent: we forgive *everyone* in debt to us. From this he concludes that the believer has all authority to forgive all sins committed against him or her, thus ruling out conditional forgiveness.[42]

Cyprian

The final African writer of this period to take up the theme of the Lord's Prayer and its commands to interpersonal forgiveness is Cyprian, bishop of Carthage (date of writings: AD 246–258). Kannengeisser notes that his comments are "more balanced than those of Tertullian [and] carefully pastoral in tone."[43] He is the strongest proponent of conditional ecclesiastical forgiveness in the controversies over the lapsed, and it is his proposed solutions which eventually resolve the crisis, but when one turns to examine his thoughts on interpersonal

---

41. Ramelli, "Forgiveness in Patristic Philosophy," 199.

42. This passage is returned to below to show how Origen goes on to highlight the distinction between divine and interpersonal forgiveness in order to resolve this apparent tension between God's forgiveness of some and humanity's forgiveness of all. The larger significance of that distinction is also explained below.

43. Charles Kannengiesser, *Handbook of Patristic Exegesis: The Bible in Ancient Christianity* (Leiden: Brill, 2006), 625.

forgiveness specifically, one finds that he too frames it as unconditional and not based on repentance.[44]

The first text where he addresses interpersonal forgiveness actually comes in a treatise to his son Quirinius written before his exposition of the Lord's Prayer:

> 22. That when we have received a wrong, we must remit and forgive it.

> In the Gospel, in the daily prayer: "Forgive us our debts, even as we forgive our debtors." Also according to Mark: "And when ye stand for prayer, forgive, if ye have aught against any one; that also your Father who is in heaven may forgive you your sins. But if ye do not forgive, neither will your Father which is in heaven forgive you your sins." Also in the same place: "In what measure ye mete, in that shall it be measured to you again." (*To Quirinius* 3.22)[45]

There is a noticeable lack of any mention of repentance in this call to forgiveness, and his use of the passage from Mark is significant since a careful reading of that verse shows that unconditional forgiveness is in view since it is commanded that one should forgive "anything" that one has against "anyone" at the moment of prayer. Thus, a straightforward reading of this passage necessitates seeing Cyprian calling his son to unconditionally forgive those who wrong him.

Then there are his comments in his treatise on the Lord's Prayer from Matthew 6:12:

> There remains no ground of excuse in the day of judgment when you will be judged according to your own sentence; and whatever you have done, that you also will suffer. For God commands us to be peacemakers, and in agreement, and of one mind in His house; and such as He makes us by a second birth, such He wishes us when new-born to continue, that we who have begun to be sons of God may abide in God's peace, and that, having one spirit, we should also have one heart and one mind. (*On the Lord's Prayer* 23)

---

44. For an overview of the theology of Cyprian and his use of Scripture see Michael Andrew Fahey, *Cyprian and the Bible: A Study in Third-Century Exegesis* (Tübingen: J. C. B. Mohr, 1971).

45. Cyprian follows this command for free and unconditional *interpersonal* forgiveness with a reminder only a couple of sections later (*To Quirinius* 3.28) that there are certain sins that *the church* cannot forgive. See below for a discussion on the significance of this distinction and references to other African authors who also maintain this key distinction.

Notice that his comment on Jesus's command to forgive is that there is no excuse to withhold forgiveness from a wrongdoer and that the goal of this forgiveness is that the believer might live in peace. He thus excludes conditional forgiveness and commands that believers forgive others, making no mention of whether or not the offender has repented.

God's Forgiveness and Humanity's: A Key Distinction

Having established that early African church fathers held to a robust conception of unconditional interpersonal forgiveness, one final question remains: How is it that they were able to balance unconditional forgiveness on the one hand with the clear calls to repentance and passages seeming to teach conditional forgiveness on the other? The answer lies in a fundamental distinction that is drawn by these early African writers which is often overlooked by modern interpreters examining these ancient conceptions of forgiveness. That is, they maintained that there is a fundamental and qualitative difference between forgiveness between humans and that offered to humanity by God.

Clement of Alexandria distinguishes between interpersonal and divine forgiveness when he associates forgiveness with the command that Christians be holy as God is holy:

> It was said by the Lord, "Be ye perfect as your father, perfectly," by forgiving sins, and forgetting injuries, and living in the habit of passionlessness. For as we call a physician perfect, and a philosopher perfect, so also, in my view, do we call a Gnostic perfect. But not one of those points, although of the greatest importance, is assumed in order to the likeness of God. For we do not say, as the Stoics do most impiously, that virtue in man and God is the same. Ought we not then to be perfect, as the Father wills? For it is utterly impossible for anyone to become perfect as God is. Now the Father wishes us to be perfect by living blamelessly, according to the obedience of the Gospel. (*Stromata* 7.13.88)

Tertullian also shows that he makes a clear distinction between interpersonal and divine forgiveness by arguing that the universal command to forgive applies only to sins committed against oneself. His concern is to show that it is possible to hold to unconditional interpersonal forgiveness and still maintain that there are certain sins which only God can forgive, since in the conflict over the lapsed, he disagrees with those who hold that the church has the power to forgive all sins.

> "But you remit, in order that remission may be granted you by God." The sins which are (thus) cleansed are such as a man may have committed against his brother, not against God. We profess, in short, in our prayer, that we will grant remission to our debtors; but it is not becoming to distend further, on the ground of the authority of such Scriptures, the cable of contention with alternate pull into diverse directions; so that one (Scripture) may seem to draw tight, another to relax, the reins of discipline – in uncertainty, as it were, – and the latter to debase the remedial aid of repentance through lenity, the former to refuse it through austerity. (*On Modesty* 2)

Tertullian follows this passage with an extended discussion of the "efficacious power" of repentance, but he is careful to connect it to forgiveness that comes from God. Later in his letter, he returns to this key distinction between God's forgiveness and humanity's and makes this distinction between unconditional interpersonal forgiveness and conditional ecclesiastically mediated divine forgiveness even more explicit:

> Hence the power of loosing and of binding committed to Peter had nothing to do with the capital sins of believers; and if the LORD had given him a precept that he must grant pardon to a brother sinning against *him* even "seventy times sevenfold," of course He would have commanded him to "bind" – that is, to "retain" – *nothing* subsequently, unless perchance such (sins) as one may have committed against *the Lord*, not against a *brother*. For the forgiveness of (sins) committed in the case of a *man* is a prejudgment against the remission of sins against *God*. (*On Modesty* 21)

Finally, Origen demonstrates that he distinguishes between human interpersonal forgiveness and divine/ecclesiastical forgiveness by arguing that individuals can forgive any sin committed against them, but when men stand in official roles for God, as in the leaders of the church, they fill the special function of mediating God's forgiveness to humanity and thus forgive conditionally, and even then, not all sins:[46]

---

46. This raises a question that is beyond the scope of this study: whether God uses human beings (priests) to mediate his absolution and forgiveness. Those arguments have been examined elsewhere, but the point remains that Origen clearly posits the distinction between God's

And it would seem that we have all authority to forgive the sins that have been committed against us as is clear from both clauses: as we also have forgiven our debtors; and for we ourselves also forgive everyone in debt to us. But it is when a man is inspired by Jesus as were the apostles, when he can be known from his fruits to have received the Spirit that is Holy and to have become spiritual through being led by the Spirit after the manner of a Son of God unto every reasonable duty, that he forgives whatsoever God has forgiven and holds those sins that are irremediable, and as the prophets served God in speaking not their own message but that of the divine Will, so he too serves the God who alone has authority to forgive. (*On Prayer* 28.8)

Returning to modern interpreters, both Ramelli and Konstan acknowledge this distinction, but do not leave sufficient room in their analyses to allow it to affect how they view interpersonal forgiveness. Ramelli acknowledges, "Only God knows human minds, and only God's forgiveness causes – not only presupposes – a change and improvement in the offender."[47] Konstan's conclusion is even stronger: "There is a deep gulf, reflected even at the level of vocabulary, between God's ability to cancel or obliterate sin, in the way one can abolish a debt, and human or interpersonal forgiveness, in which the reality of the offense – always a particular act – must in some sense persist into the present, neither abolished or forgotten."[48] And yet, for all the work they have done and the excellent insights they have offered, neither one takes the final step to conclude that interpersonal forgiveness as taught in these early fathers is actually unconditional, commanded whether or not the wrongdoer repents.

Unconditional Interpersonal Forgiveness in the African Fathers

Having examined the recent contributions by Ilaria Ramelli and David Konstan to the historical study of forgiveness, especially in the African patristic period, and compared their conclusions with a close reading of these fathers in context, it has been shown that, contra Konstan and Ramelli, the early African church held to an unconditional understanding of interpersonal forgiveness. Ramelli's arguments for conditional forgiveness were primarily influenced by conflating

---

forgiveness and humanity's forgiveness as a resolution to the tension between the conditional commands and the unconditional ones.

47. Ramelli, "Unconditional Forgiveness," 44.

48. Konstan, *Before Forgiveness: Origins*, 134.

God's forgiveness with interpersonal forgiveness, which has been shown even from the fathers' own writings to be illegitimate. When properly distinguished, God's forgiveness is seen as conditional whereas interpersonal forgiveness is rightly seen as unconditional. But what of Konstan's conclusions?

He has made a significant contribution to the discussion, but the problem lies in the definition of forgiveness that he offers at the beginning of each of his works cited herein. He so closely ties the idea of repentance to his definition of forgiveness that he is prevented from seeing any instances of forgiveness apart from repentance as forgiveness per se. This leads him to conclude that forgiveness is not present in the New Testament or the early church fathers, including those African fathers that he cites. However, his concluding evaluation of the concept in the fathers reveals possibly more than he intends and speaks directly to the thesis of this study:

> Human beings can forgive a debt in this sense: we simply cancel it, without reference to the attitude of the debtor, not to speak of remorse and repentance. What we cannot do is forgive another person's sin: that is the prerogative of God . . . I suggest that it was precisely this sense that forgiveness was the special province of God that inhibited the development of a doctrine of interpersonal forgiveness within the Christian tradition . . . The modern conception of forgiveness, with its insistence that the offender express remorse and a commitment to change her or his ways, may be understood as a secularization of the Jewish and Christian idea of divine forgiveness.[49]

However, what Konstan sees as an underdeveloped model of interpersonal forgiveness in the fathers is actually a fully developed one that is based on unconditional rather than conditional forgiveness. In all fairness to Konstan, it is not his project to examine ancient conceptions of interpersonal forgiveness and use them to correct modern notions. Rather he has started with the modern notion, which he rightly asserts is often predicated upon repentance, and looks back in time to prove that it is largely a modern notion and not one that existed in ancient times, which he has ably accomplished. This study has sought to do the opposite: to prove that in the minds of early African church fathers interpersonal forgiveness was not conditioned upon repentance, but was rather seen as a free and gracious releasing of the wrongdoer from any relational debt owed to the victim, and the decision to act toward the wrongdoer as if he or

---

49. Konstan, "Before Forgiveness: Classical Antiquity," 15.

she had not committed the offense, regardless of whether or not the wrongdoer had acknowledged the wrong and repented of it.

Unconditional Forgiveness: Africa's Great Need

If the African church fathers really do have a well-developed theology of interpersonal forgiveness, as this study has argued, then how relevant is it for the African church today? Have nineteen hundred years changed the landscape so much that their teaching is no longer needed? Have the great evils perpetrated across the continent in recent times eclipsed their simple notions of relational reconciliation? Is forgiveness of great moral evil even possible? Many victims of Africa's recent horrendous atrocities often legitimately wrestle with whether or not genuine forgiveness is possible in the face of wrongs done on such a massive scale. A poignant example of this was displayed recently on a Facebook page called "Humans of New York." This photojournalism social media page, originally created to document human-interest stories in New York City, in recent years has broadened its focus to document global human-interest stories as well. In October 2018 a series of miniature photo essays appeared, detailing the "recovery and reconciliation" that has occurred in the wake of the Rwandan genocide of 1994.[50] It focused on telling the stories of the survivors and saviors, and near the end of the series a couple of startling comments were made that vividly illustrate both the need for and the great difficulty of forgiveness. In one interview Paul Kagame, president of Rwanda reflects:

> There was a huge puzzle after the genocide. How do you pursue justice when the crime is so great? You can't lose one million people in one hundred days without an equal number of perpetrators. But we also can't imprison an entire nation. So forgiveness was the only path forward. Survivors were asked to forgive and forget . . . It was a huge burden to place on the survivors. And perhaps the burden was too great. One day during a memorial service, I was approached by a survivor. He was very emotional. "Why are you asking us to forgive?" he asked me. "Haven't we suffered enough? We weren't the cause of this problem. Why must we provide the solution?" These were very challenging questions. So I paused for a long time. Then I told him: "I'm very sorry. You are correct.

---

50. Brandon Stanton, post on "Humans of New York" Facebook page, 16 October 2018, accessed 6 February 2019, https://web.facebook.com/humansofnewyork/posts/2599594763447941.

I am asking too much of you. But I don't know what to ask the perpetrators. 'Sorry' won't bring back any lives. Only forgiveness can heal this nation. The burden rests with the survivors because they are the only ones with something to give."[51]

Despite Kagame's clear call for unbearably burdensome yet necessary forgiveness, clearly not all Rwandans are convinced.[52] In sharp contrast to Kagame's remarks, another post appeared on the very same day, giving the perspective of a woman who lost much of her family to the genocide:

And now we're being asked to forgive. Because our president tells us that reconciliation is the only path forward as a nation. And I know that he's right. So I'm trying my best. I'm spending time with Hutu people. I even found two Hutu elders to mentor my son. I want him to see that Hutus have good hearts. My son even calls them "Grandpa." So I understand the need for reconciliation. And I'm trying. Christianity has helped me a great deal. But true forgiveness is impossible. My entire family was murdered. How can I possibly forgive on behalf of those who can no longer speak for themselves? It's just not possible. But I will certainly pretend. Because I've seen where vengeance leads.[53]

And certainly, this woman cannot be alone in her conclusions. Even in the broader Christian community, such horrendous circumstances have come to be seen as beyond the reach of human forgiveness. Anthony Bash, whose own works have traced a clear trajectory from teaching unconditional forgiveness to teaching conditional forgiveness, reflects on the horrors of the

---

51. Paul Kagame, quoted in a post on "Humans of New York" Facebook page, 25 October 2018, accessed 6 February 2019, https://web.facebook.com/humansofnewyork/posts/2618742274866523.

52. Although some are. For an excellent recent account of one Rwandan community's struggle through post-genocide forgiveness, see Denise Uwimana, *From Red Earth: A Rwandan Story of Healing and Forgiveness* (Walden, NY: Plough, 2019). Cf. Meg Guillebaud, *After the Locusts: How Costly Forgiveness Is Restoring Rwanda's Stolen Years* (Oxford: Monarch, 2006).

53. Anonymous Rwandan woman, quoted in a post on "Humans of New York" Facebook page, 25 October 2018, accessed 6 February 2019, https://web.facebook.com/humansofnewyork/posts/2617254641681953. Comments on the post frequently mention either that forgiveness of genocide is neither necessary nor possible, or that forgiveness is possible because it is only for one's own healing (a therapeutic model of forgiveness), thus revealing that there is a common dilemma placed between conditional forgiveness on the one hand and therapeutic, self-focused forgiveness on the other. For an extended analysis examining the possibility of forgiveness offered on behalf of another (also in the context of genocide), see Simon Wiesenthal, *The Sunflower: On the Possibilities and Limits of Forgiveness* (New York: Schocken Books, 1998).

Rwandan genocide in a recent article and argues that any talk of unconditional forgiveness is inappropriate and impossible in such circumstances.[54] Where then is hope?

It would seem that many of those who offer counsel to victims of such atrocities have only two possible refrains: either "You must forgive!" (and what about the pain?) or "You cannot forgive!" (because there has been no repentance). What is sorely needed in Africa today is for forgiveness to be taught in a way that comes alongside and gently says, "You *can* forgive." Unfortunately, a conditional model of interpersonal forgiveness, which Konstan has shown to be prevalent in Christianity today, renders both the release of forgiveness and the healing of reconciliation contingent upon the actions of another, and thus renders it impossible in many cases. It is only unconditional forgiveness that retains the possibility of forgiveness even in cases where the offender cannot or will not express genuine repentance. It is only unconditional forgiveness, then, that can enter into the pain of broken Christian communities in Africa and offer a solution to victims who feel trapped and unable to forgive. And it is only when forgiveness starts with "you can" that it can ever reach the place of "you must." "Christians have a unique avenue for explaining the possibility of metaphysical forgiveness – union with Christ – and strong motivation to think of forgiveness as prevenient, and theists who rest in divine forgiveness have special reasons to think of interhuman forgiveness as a duty."[55] But who will teach this? Who will show the way?

---

54. Anthony Bash, "Forgiveness: A Reappraisal," *Studies in Christian Ethics* 24, no. 2 (2011): 136. Bash is not the only one to wrestle with how Rwandan genocide survivors can forgive. Chris Foreman recounts the time he was counseled by a Rwandan friend, "If you want to keep a gospel ministry in Rwanda, you have to forgive like a Rwandan." But later the same friend clarified: "But believe me, not all Rwandans are so ready to forgive. It takes time. That's why we Rwandese continue to talk about reconciliation sixteen years after the genocide. It is a very hard thing to do. In truth, we must learn to forgive like Christians – seventy times seven." Paul Gasigi, quoted in Chris Alan Foreman, *Forgive Like a Rwandan* (Colorado Springs, CO: Believers Press, 2015), 202. Earlier in the book (84–86), Foreman recounts Gasigi's story of the murder of his wife during the genocide and his subsequent forgiveness of a neighbor implicated in her death.

55. Jesse Couenhoven, "Forgiveness and Restoration: A Theological Exploration," *Journal of Religious Ethics* 90, no. 2 (2010): 170. His article addresses well a facet of the discussion that has been beyond the scope of this study: the fact that the Christian act of forgiveness is inextricably interwoven with the Christian's experience of divine forgiveness, a reality that resolves some of the perceived injustice inherent in interpersonal forgiveness.

Conclusion: Our Ancient Fathers Show Us the Way

We can be grateful that some modern African leaders are sounding the call and pointing the way toward forgiveness. Political leaders such as Paul Kagame and Nelson Mandela and religious leaders such as Desmond Tutu have warned of the dangers of unforgiveness and have led through the painful but necessary paths of forgiveness.[56] But as we have seen, many are yet to follow, perhaps because the political context of such calls tends to obscure the core Christian realities at stake. It is clear that the African church needs the ancient voices of its fathers as guides in these challenging times. "Among the benefits of reading early African Christian teaching are the courage to face complex tasks, reduced anxiety and the consolation of knowing that suffering can be transcended by hope."[57] On matters of interpersonal forgiveness the earliest African church fathers have known the suffering, and yet they still offer us hope. When violence, hatred, or brutality shatters the peace of African Christian communities, we need the strong clear voice of Cyprian the martyr, who shows us that we have no excuse to withhold forgiveness from anyone and that though the path through forgiveness may be dark and painful, it leads to a sure and certain peace. When we struggle to understand what true forgiveness is and what actions should attend it, we must wrestle with Clement's call to forgive "each and every one," even to the extent of asking the authorities for leniency for the perpetrator when appropriate. If one recoils at what feels like injustice in forgiveness before repentance, Clement also reminds us that this extravagant forgiveness is only possible for believers who have taken account of their lives, and recognized that nothing of real value can possibly be taken from believers who are secure in Christ, not even their very lives. When victims around us raise the painful plea "But how can I forgive?," we need the encouragement of Origen showing that Christians are free to forgive all sins that have been committed against them, warning us that there is grave danger for the believer who refuses to forgive, and reminding us that forgiveness then *is* possible, not because it is easy and cheap, but because it is so drastically different from the *sui generis* forgiveness that only God can offer to humanity. And when survivors of tribal violence or

---

56. Cf. B. J. de Klerk, "Nelson Mandela and Desmond Tutu: Living Icons of Reconciliation," *The Ecumenical Review* 55, no. 4 (Oct. 2003): 322–334; and Desmond Tutu, *No Future without Forgiveness* (New York: Doubleday, 1999). Tutu, an Anglican archbishop, was instrumental in leading South Africa through post-apartheid by helping to establish the Truth and Reconciliation Commission, which sought to mitigate national discord through official acts of confession to atrocities, forgiveness, and restitution. Though he has identified himself with liberation theology, one need not accept his other theological stances to agree with him that forgiveness is core to Christianity and sorely needed today.

57. Oden, *How Africa Shaped*, 134.

genocide struggle with legitimate issues of trust, justice, and reconciliation, we need the hope offered by Tertullian, that the grace of patient forgiveness opens the door to repentance, rather than being predicated upon it.

Bibliography

Baille, John, et al., eds. *The Library of Christian Classics*. Vol. 2, *Alexandrian Christianity: Selected Translations of Clement and Origen*. Translated by J. E. L. Oulton and Henry Chadwick. Philadelphia: Westminster Press, 1954.

Barnes, Timothy David. *Tertullian: A Historical and Literary Study*. Oxford: Clarendon, 1971.

Bash, Anthony. "Forgiveness: A Reappraisal." *Studies in Christian Ethics* 24, no. 2 (2011): 133–146.

Bash, Anthony, and Melanie Bash. "Early Christian Thinking." In *Forgiveness in Context: Theology and Psychology in Creative Dialogue*, edited by Fraser Watts and Liz Gulliford, 29–49. Edinburgh: T&T Clark, 2004.

Bray, Gerald Lewis. *Holiness and the Will of God: Perspectives on the Theology of Tertullian*. Atlanta: John Knox Press, 1979.

Burns, J. Patout. "Confessing the Church: Cyprian on Penance." In *Studia Patristica* 36, 338–348. Louvain: Peeters, 2001.

Couenhoven, Jesse. "Forgiveness and Restoration: A Theological Exploration." *Journal of Religious Ethics* 90, no. 2 (2010): 148–170.

Culy, Martin. "The Clue Is in the Case: Distinguishing Adjectival and Adverbial Participles." *Perspectives in Religious Studies* 30, no. 4 (2003): 441–453.

Cunningham, Lawrence S. "Origen's *On Prayer*: A Reflection and Appreciation." *Worship* 67 (Jul. 1993): 332–339.

Daly, C. B. "Tertullian, Treatises on Penance: *On Penitence* and *On Purity*." *Theological Studies* 21 (Sep. 1960): 474–478.

Deferrari, Roy J., ed. *The Fathers of the Church*. Vol. 36, *Saint Cyprian: Treatises*. Translated by Roy J. Deferrari. New York: Fathers of the Church, 1958.

———, ed. *The Fathers of the Church*. Vol. 51, *Saint Cyprian: Letters (1–81)*. Translated by Sister Rose Bernard Donna. Washington: Catholic University of America, 1964.

Ehrman, Bart D., Gordon D. Fee, and Michael W. Holmes. *The Text of the Fourth Gospel in the Writings of Origen*. Atlanta: Scholars Press, 1992.

Fahey, Michael Andrew. *Cyprian and the Bible: A Study in Third-Century Exegesis*. Tübingen: J. C. B. Mohr, 1971.

Foreman, Chris Alan. *Forgive Like a Rwandan*. Colorado Springs, CO: Believers Press, 2015.

Griswold, Charles L. *Forgiveness: A Philosophical Exploration*. Cambridge: Cambridge University Press, 2007.

Guillebaud, Meg. *After the Locusts: How Costly Forgiveness Is Restoring Rwanda's Stolen Years*. Oxford: Monarch, 2006.

Hall, Christopher A. "Rejecting the Prodigal: The Early Church Debated Whether Apostate Christians Could Be Forgiven Again." *Christianity Today* 42 (26 Oct. 1998): 73–76.

Hallock, Frank Hudson. "Third Century Teaching on Sin and Repentance." *Anglican Theological Review* 4 (Oct. 1921): 128–142.

Holmes, O. Wright. "Tertullian on Prayer." *Tyndale House Bulletin* 5–6 (Apr. 1960): 27–32.

Junkin, Edward D. "Commitment to the Fallen Brother: Cyprian and the Lapsed." *Austin Seminary Bulletin* 87 (Apr. 1972): 32–45.

Kannengiesser, Charles. *Handbook of Patristic Exegesis: The Bible in Ancient Christianity*. Leiden: Brill, 2006.

Kannengiesser, Charles, and William L. Petersen, eds. *Origen of Alexandria: His World and His Legacy*. Notre Dame: University of Notre Dame Press, 1988.

Kerr, Hugh T. *The First Systematic Theologian: Origen of Alexandria*. Princeton: Princeton Theological Seminary, 1958.

de Klerk, B. J. "Nelson Mandela and Desmond Tutu: Living Icons of Reconciliation." *The Ecumenical Review* 55, no. 4 (Oct. 2003): 322–334.

Konstan, David. "Before Forgiveness: Classical Antiquity, Early Christianity . . . and Beyond." Unpublished paper. 12 March 2011. Accessed 10 February 2019. https://forum.evangelicaluniversalist.com/t/before-forgiveness-classical-antiquity-early-christianity/1460.

———. *Before Forgiveness: The Origins of a Moral Idea*. Cambridge: Cambridge University Press, 2010.

Laporte, Jean. "Forgiveness of Sins in Origen." *Worship* 60 (Nov. 1986): 520–527.

Latko, Ernest F. *Origen's Concept of Penance*. Laval, QC: Faculté de théologie, Université Laval, 1949.

Liddell, Henry George, and Robert Scott. *An Intermediate Greek–English Lexicon: Founded upon the Seventh Edition of Liddell and Scott's Greek–English Lexicon*. Oxford: Clarendon, 1995.

McGuckin, John Anthony, ed. *The Westminster Handbook to Origen*. Louisville, KY: Westminster John Knox Press, 2004.

Migne, J. P., and Theodor Hopfner, eds. *Patrologiae Cursus Completus: Patrologia Graecae*. Vol. 11, *Origen*. Petit-Montrouge: Bibliotecae Cleri Universae, 1857.

Novak, Ralph Martin. *Christianity and the Roman Empire: Background Texts*. Harrisburg, PA: Trinity Press International, 2001.

Oden, Thomas C. *How Africa Shaped the Christian Mind: Rediscovering the African Seedbed of Western Christianity*. Downers Grove, IL: InterVarsity Press, 2007.

———, ed. *Ancient Christian Commentary on Scripture*. Vol. 1a, *Matthew 1–13*. Edited by Manlio Simonetti. Downers Grove, IL: InterVarsity Press, 2001.

————, ed. *Ancient Christian Commentary on Scripture*. Vol. 1b, *Matthew 14–28*. Edited by Manlio Simonetti. Downers Grove, IL: InterVarsity Press, 2002.

————, ed. *Ancient Christian Commentary on Scripture*. Vol. 2, *Mark*. Edited by Thomas C. Oden and Christopher Hall. Downers Grove, IL: InterVarsity Press, 1998.

————, ed. *Ancient Christian Commentary on Scripture*. Vol. 3, *Luke*. Edited by Arthur A. Just Jr. Downers Grove, IL: InterVarsity Press, 2003.

Ramelli, Ilaria L. E. "Forgiveness in Patristic Philosophy: The Importance of Repentance and the Centrality of Grace." In *Ancient Forgiveness: Classical, Judaic, and Christian*, edited by Charles L. Griswold and David Konstan, 195–215. Cambridge: Cambridge University Press, 2012.

————. "Unconditional Forgiveness in Christianity? Some Reflections on Ancient Christian Sources." In *The Ethics of Forgiveness*, edited by Christel Fricke, 30–48. New York: Routledge, 2011.

Roberts, Alexander, James Donaldson, and A. Cleveland Coxe. *The Ante-Nicene Fathers: Translations of the Writings of the Fathers Down to AD 325*. 10 vols. Grand Rapids, MI: Eerdmans, 1950.

Roberts, Robert E. *The Theology of Tertullian*. London: Epworth, 1924.

Roldanus, Johannes. "No Easy Reconciliation: St. Cyprian on Conditions for Reintegration of the Lapsed." *Journal of Theology for Southern Africa* 92 (Sep. 1995): 23–31.

Smith, John Clark. *The Ancient Wisdom of Origen*. Lewisburg, PA: Bucknell University Press, 1992.

Stuckwisch, D. Richard. "Principles of Christian Prayer in the Third Century: A Brief Look at Origen, Tertullian, and Cyprian with Some Comments on Their Meaning for Today." *Worship* 71 (Jan. 1997): 2–19.

Tabbernee, William. "To Pardon or Not to Pardon? North African Montanism and the Forgiveness of Sins." In *Studia Patristica* 36, 375–386. Louvain: Peeters, 2001.

Trigg, Joseph Wilson. *Origen: The Bible and Philosophy in the Third-Century Church*. Atlanta: John Knox Press, 1983.

Tutu, Desmond. *No Future without Forgiveness*. New York: Doubleday, 1999.

Uwimana, Denise. *From Red Earth: A Rwandan Story of Healing and Forgiveness*. Walden, NY: Plough, 2019.

Wiesenthal, Simon. *The Sunflower: On the Possibilities and Limits of Forgiveness*. New York: Schocken Books, 1998.

Chapter 2 Appendix

One should be cautious to note both the limitations and the ecumenical nature of the term "early African church" as it relates to the scope of this study. In the spirit of the early African church, this study (as well as Oden's work) does not limit itself to addressing one specific stream of modern Christianity, since these early African fathers predate all such subdivisions and thus cannot be properly said to be the forebears of any one form of modern Christianity, but in a very real sense are the forebears of all of them. But as Oden argues,

> The recovery of African Christianity seeks both its own unique identity and to be at the same time a full participant in the whole of world Christianity. The new yearning to recover ancient African texts seeks to correct a prevailing imbalance that has contributed to the African Christian crisis of identity. It seeks now to provide the sources and arguments through which Africans can affirm their distinct Africanness without denying their historic participation in the ecumenical whole.[58]

Furthermore, it is evident that Oden is quite hopeful in the ecumenical outcomes of his research, but he does issue cautions regarding the potential for such ecumenical outcomes, especially if they are expected to conform to the Western ecumenical ideals of the last century:

> Orthodox Africans are finding that the older (twentieth-century) forms of ecumenical organizations with their self-assured bureaucracies do not have an exclusive possession of the heartbeat of ecumenical reality. Many recent ventures in ecumenism have been tainted with unbiblical and ignoble illusions. The ideological momentum of late twentieth-century ecumenism is already experiencing a steep decline in support, confidence, and buoyancy. It is too long detached from its ancient ecumenical wellsprings. The deeper biblical wellsprings are now being recovered by a new African ecumenism of the Spirit. The actual living, organic unity of the body of believers in Christ is greater than the pretended unity of bureaucratic ecumenism.[59]

---

58. Oden, *How Africa Shaped*, 93.
59. Oden, 108–109.

Regardless of Oden's cautious hope, one need not accept his ecumenical aims to agree with the spirit of his hope. Even those committed to a clearly defined orthodoxy and skeptical of a form of ecumenism that would diminish doctrinal foundations can agree that any historical study that connects the church back to the apostolic traditions and moors it more securely to the ancient catholic faith can and should move the church today toward a more perfect unity of the Spirit.

3

Ethical Implications in the Use of E-Therapy in PTSD Contexts

Peter Mageto
Deputy Vice Chancellor
Africa University, Zimbabwe

and

Emily Kyalo
PhD Candidate in Clinical Psychology
Daystar University, Athi River, Kenya

Abstract

We live in a generation that is faced with a fast-moving landscape in data collection, use, and analysis due to improved and changing data-enabled technologies. The means of addressing such key life themes as forgiveness, peacemaking, and reconciliation are no longer bound by the traditions of the past. This is particularly evident in post-traumatic stress disorder (PTSD) situations in which people struggle with changes that affect their memories, emotions, and thoughts, resulting in avoidance. These four areas are being compromised in our time due to the fact that almost every sphere of life activity is being driven by technological advances.

In this chapter we consider the hallmarks of the Christian church, namely, forgiveness, peacemaking, and reconciliation, through an E-therapy approach. E-therapy is a new area of study in the African context that we explore through four ethical aspects: competence, record-keeping, managing crisis situations, and informed consent. These four ethical aspects serve as a foundation for adapting E-therapy in our search for forgiveness, peacemaking, and reconciliation among PTSD subjects and in their social-support systems for their well-being. In conclusion, we show the relevancy of E-therapy and the need for institutions of higher learning to retrain their teams, governments to create policies and regulations to guide E-therapy, and churches to embrace their core ministry mandate of forgiveness, peacemaking, and reconciliation.

Key words: E-therapy, memories, avoidance, physical and emotional reactions, competence, record-keeping, managing situations, and informed consent.

Introduction

Within Kenyan settings, the debate over E-therapy (electronic therapy) among therapists, professionals, and citizens has not yet settled on definitions, potential benefits, regulatory systems, ethical considerations, and competency standards. It is common knowledge that Kenyan people, both young and old, whether in rural or urban settings, have access to a number of digital devices, and this parallels technological advances in the country. The availability of these electronic devices has made E-therapy a subject that cannot be ignored, even though in practice and experience it is not ethically and legally available in the country and among the populace.

Information technology advances and specifically the upsurge in mobile usage has become an integral part of daily life in Kenya. Globally, 4.4 billion people make use of the Internet, and of these 3.5 billion are social media users. In Kenya alone, a total of 43.4 million people are Internet users. Various studies[1] conducted in different settings have shown that the advance of information technology influences people's daily lives. More importantly, some scholars[2] have argued that digital means such as email, virtual campuses, teleconferencing, Zoom, and Skype have been embraced as convenient avenues for business and decision-making. It is such avenues that have made it possible

---

1. A. Barak, "Psychosocial Applications on the Internet: A Discipline on the Threshold of a New Millennium," *Applied & Preventive Psychology* 8, no. 4 (1999): 231–245; Michelle Gayle Newman, "Technology in Psychotherapy: An Introduction," *Journal of Clinical Psychology* 60, no. 2 (2004): 141–145; J. E. Barnett and K. Sheetz. "Technological Advances and Telehealth: Ethics, Law, and the Practice of Psychotherapy," *Psychotherapy: Theory, Research, Practice, Training* 40, no. 1–2 (2003): 86–93.

2. S. L. Hopps, M. Pepin, and J. M. Boisvert, "The Effectiveness of Cognitive Behavioral Group Therapy for Loneliness via Inter-Relay Chat among People with Physical Disabilities," *Psychotherapy: Theory, Research & Practice* 40, nos. 1–2 (2003): 136–147.

for those struggling with traumatic issues to find information and/or treatment online. The ease of access to technological devices and the inexpensiveness of Internet access in Kenya has made it possible for individuals to seek online help. In addition, however, a number of users and those in the caring professions, such as clinicians, psychologists, counselors, and church ministers, have experienced an upsurge in fraudulent users offering E-therapy. Regardless of the efficacy of E-therapy, especially in African contexts, it provides us with the opportunity to consider positive and negative legal, regulatory, and ethical issues around the practice, since technological advancement will continue in our context.

The upsurge in mobile usage in Kenya has created scenarios that compel us to consider the use of electronically mediated communication, especially in the critical life-related issues of reconciliation, peacemaking, and forgiveness. It is very difficult for the church to engage with these noble issues, and yet they concern events that are traumatic for both perpetrators and victims. Where reconciliation, forgiveness, and peacemaking are concerned, both the perceived or real victim and the perpetrator are involved. More importantly, technological advances have become an avenue for addressing circumstances that lead to post-traumatic stress disorder (PTSD) experiences. Unfortunately, most people engaged in addressing PTSD have no prior training or experience, simply employing the availability of electronic devices. For this reason we see the need to address the place and role of E-therapy in the Kenyan context.

Within the Kenyan context, E-therapy occurs even though laws or guidelines to regulate the ethical issues relating to such services do not yet exist. E-therapy raises a number of ethical concerns that are of similar nature to those in other caring professions – namely, consent, privacy, professional credentials, skills capacity, and limitations regarding the extent to which a therapist should access a client.[3] In this research, we do not address ethical dilemmas in general practice, but we limit them to the operation of a particular context, namely, post-traumatic stress disorder (PTSD), which often arises from situations of stress, terror attacks, divorce, death, job loss, ethnic strife, war, accidents, wrong diagnosis, terminal illness – the list is endless. At times, however, to a greater or lesser extent, the honorable cause of forgiveness, peacemaking, and reconciliation is threatened by fraudulent E-therapists. As long as E-therapy continues to be practiced outside the realm of ethical values such as competence, record-keeping, managing situations, and informed

---

3. G. Corey, M. Corey, and M. Callanan, *Issues and Ethics in the Helping Professions*, 7th ed. (Pacific Grove, CA: Brooks/Cole, 2007), 169–191.

consent, seeking the desired results of holistic living as a result of forgiveness, peacemaking, and reconciliation will be a chasing after the wind.

Understanding the Terms

While we may not yet have a clear definition of E-therapy, as early as the 1940s records and publications[4] in the USA showed debate as to how the term "therapy" could be understood. Scholars[5] have tended to use terms such as "web-counseling," "online counseling," "computer-mediated psychotherapy," "education information," "advice," "Internet counseling," "email exchange," "chatting," "video via Skype, Zoom, hangout," and so on, as synonymous with E-therapy, cybertherapy, and/or Internet counseling. What is interesting in all these is that both social learning theory and cognitive behavior therapy are major contributors to E-therapy intervention strategies.[6] But this happens in a context where those who offer E-therapy do not keep in mind the seriousness and risks of providing E-therapy in Kenyan contexts.

Historically, there is evidence that various models[7] that nurture children and the elderly have been utilized.[8] This is an indication that in countries such as Australia, USA, and the United Kingdom, E-therapy-related services have been practiced for a while, unlike in countries in Africa, like Kenya.

---

4. See the works of J. F. Cogswell and D. P. Estavan, *Explorations in Computer-Assisted Counseling* (Santa Monica, CA: System Development Corp, 1965); J. Weizenbaum, "ELIZA: A Computer Program for the Study of Natural Language Communication between Man and Machine," *Communications of the ACM* (Association for Computer Machinery) 9, no. 1 (1966), https:DOI.org/10.1145/365153.365168.

5. For the related use of E-therapy terms, see the works of J. R. Alleman, "Online Counseling: The Internet and Mental Health Treatment," *Psychotherapy: Research, Practice, Training* 39, no. 2 (2002): 199–209; J. M. Grohol, "Best Practices in E-Therapy: Privacy and Security in E-Therapy," Psych Central, accessed 15 February 2019, https://psychcentral.com/lib/e-therapy/.

6. C. Barr Taylor, Kenneth O. Jobson, Andy Winselberg, and Liana Abascal, "The Use of the Internet to Provide Evidence-Based Integrated Treatment Programs for Mental Health," *Psychiatric Annals* 32, no. 11 (2002): 671–677.

7. Compare the works of E. H. Kaplan, "Telepsychotherapy: Psychotherapy by Telephone, Videophone and Computer Videoconferencing," *Journal of Psychotherapy Practice and Research*, 6 (1997): 227–237; Bette Bakke, James Mitchell, Steve Wonderlich, and Ron Erickson, "Administering Cognitive-Behavioral Therapy for Bulimia Nervosa via Telemedicine in Rural Settings," *International Journal of Eating Disorders* 30, no. 4 (2001): 454–457; S. Simpson, E. Morrow, M. Jones, J. Ferguson, and E. Bremen, "Tele-Hypnosis: The Provision of Specialized Therapeutic Treatments via Teleconferencing," *Journal of Telemedicine and Telecare*, 8, suppl. 2 (2002): 78–79. DOI: 10.1258/135763302320302136.

8. J. W. Bloom, "The Ethical Practice of Web Counseling," *British Journal of Guidance and Counseling* 26, no. 1 (1998): 53–59.

Various definitions have been offered of "E-therapy." Janaki Santhireevan defines it as therapy being provided through the Internet to those seeking mental health services.[9] Another perspective is provided by Grohol who notes that "E-therapy is used for relationship and life transition issues that are chronic."[10] Very similar to the definitions above, Jo-Anne M. Abbott, Britt Klein, and Lisa Ciechomsico define E-therapy as "the interaction between a consumer and a therapist via internet in association with the use of a structured web-based clinical treatment program."[11] They argue that E-counseling engages textual correspondence between a therapist and a consumer in real-time, though "it mimics the face-to-face supportive counseling approach for assistance with generic psychological issues."[12] Closely related to this is the definition that underscores a general view of online therapy "as any type of professional therapeutic interaction that makes use of the internet to connect qualified mental health professionals and their clients."[13] All these definitions indicate one constant: the Internet has to be utilized as a medium if E-therapy is to be practiced.

The definitions by the above scholars point to the fact that the debate on E-therapy is a continuing exercise, and for contexts like Kenya, and in matters related to forgiveness, peacemaking, and reconciliation among PTSD settings, more research and dissemination of information is required. At the same time, it is crucial to note that the understanding of E-therapy and all publications related to it have arisen from the West, which means that within the African context we still have room to embark on knowledge-sharing, as therapies in our advance and use of technology emerge.

Management of E-Therapy in PTSD Contexts

Often post-traumatic stress disorder is a result of a relapse following a traumatic event. In such occurrences, negating thoughts related to trauma, changing moods, and other external triggers tend to be experienced. A patient must

---

9. Janaki Santhiveeran, "E-Therapy: Scope, Concerns, Ethical Standards, and Feasibility," *Journal of Family Social Work* 8, no. 3 (2004): 38.

10. Grohol, "Best Practices in E-Therapy: Definition and Scope of E-Therapy," Psych Central.

11. Jo-Anne M. Abbot, Britt Klein, and Lisa Giechomsiki, "Best Practices in Online Therapy," *Journal of Technology in Human Services* 26, no. 2–4 (2008): 361.

12. Abbot, Klein, and Giechomsiki, "Best Practices," 361.

13. Aaron B. Rochlen, Jason S. Zack, and Cedric Speyer, "Online Therapy: Review of Relevant Definitions, Debates, and Current Empirical Support," *Journal of Clinical Psychology* 60, no. 3 (2004): 270.

meet eight DSM-5[14] criteria for the diagnosis of PTSD to be established. The first criterion is direct or indirect exposure (e.g. involving a family member) to a traumatic event, such as the death of another person or suicidal thoughts, a critical injury, or intimacy-related violence. Concerning the traumatic event, the patient must have symptoms in the following clusters: intrusion (with at least one symptom present), persistent neglect of all that may trigger the traumatic event (at least one symptom), negative attention in cognition and mood (at least two symptoms), and marked alterations in arousal and reactivity (at least one or two symptoms). Symptoms in all four clusters must start after the trauma and persist for at least one month.

Post-traumatic stress disorder is a mental health condition that occurs when one continues to relive and re-experience the terrifying or traumatic event. Such traumatizing events include the sudden loss of a loved one, a horrific car accident, a terrorist attack, domestic violence, natural disasters, or any other event that leaves an individual terrified and unable to cope or recover. The person may begin to experience flashbacks and nightmares, severe anxiety, uncontrolled thoughts about the traumatic event, and fears that later lead to psychological stress and disturbances.[15]

PTSD symptoms are grouped into four categories: intrusive memories, avoidance, negative changes in thought and mood, and changes in physical and emotional reactions. With intrusive memories, the client may experience recurrent, unwanted, and distressing memories of the traumatic event; may relive the incident, that is, experience flashbacks, as if it were reoccurring; have nightmares or terrifying dreams; and experience emotional distress or a physical reaction to issues or things that remind him or her of the traumatic event. Avoidance symptoms include blocking thoughts or deliberately not talking about the traumatic event, and staying away from places, activities, and people that may remind the client of the traumatic event.

There are many changes that might occur in form of thought and mood against oneself or in reaction to the surrounding world, such as feelings of hopelessness and memory lapses; often the client forgets that all these relate to the traumatic challenge because of pain. Often emptiness is felt by the client, and the client also is easily frightened, becomes more vigilant, unfortunately engages in self-destructive activities like drinking too much alcohol, suffers

---

14. American Psychiatric Association, *The Diagnostic and Statistical Manual of Mental Disorders*, 5th ed. (*DSM-5*) (Arlington: American Psychiatric Publishing, 2013), https://doi.org/10.1176/appi.books.9780890425596.

15. Arieh Shalev, Israel Liberzon, and Charles Marmar, "Post-Traumatic Stress Disorder," *New England Journal of Medicine* 376, no. 25 (2017): 2459–2469.

lack of sleep, has difficulties with concentration, is irritable, has anger outbursts, and feels guilt or shame.

It is in such contexts that E-therapy often takes place. In some contexts, it is important to check for manifestations of PTSD among those returning from war or peacekeeping missions, students/teachers who live and work in regions that are terror-stricken, or where rape and crimes of passion are frequently reported. During prolonged exposure patients are required to confront traumatic memories through repeated imagined exposure and to decrease avoidance by engaging in feared activities in a hierarchical manner. Often, this takes place whenever E-therapy is sought. Until we intentionally situate E-therapy, the likelihood of everyone engaging with their devices for their own sake is going to continue for a while in our context.

Setting the Context: Prospects and Challenges of E-Therapy

What happens in our Kenyan contexts when post-traumatic stress disorder (PTSD) triggers occur? It might be a rape case, ethnic conflict, a road accident, a terror attack, domestic violence, or sexual harassment. In such circumstances, often neither the victims nor the perpetrators have any idea where to go or who to consult, although a number might seek help from their relatives and/ or friends, or anyone who has a device that allows for E-therapy or computer-mediated therapy to occur. As a people, we are faced with many PTSD triggers, and the Kenyan context has become an avenue for E-therapy from both practitioners and quacks. How so? Imagine that you are online or in an e-group, and pop-up messages or videos are shared suggesting therapies that Kenyans (whether qualified or not) offer to combat certain disorders. You are swamped with prescriptions, with no idea as to the consequences of those prescriptions. It is because of this scenario that we consider the possible prospects for E-therapy and the challenges that E-therapy raises in our Kenyan contexts.

Prospects for E-Therapy

Technological advances are having a big effect on a number of African countries. The surging number of Internet users in the last few years in Kenya alone is evidence that increasing numbers of people have opportunities to engage in E-therapy as they seek help. Scholars in various settings in the West have identified several benefits for those who seek E-therapy services. Here we enumerate some of these prospects, and more specifically we contextualize them to show that if the same are embraced with clear ethical standards in

Kenyan contexts, E-therapy can be a means of progress, support, and treatment for our people.

First, E-therapy provides *an increased opportunity for both clients and therapists to conveniently offer and access services.* One of the struggles for those who have experienced PTSD is the question of how to access services easily and conveniently. It is becoming clear from settings in Western countries that E-therapy is a better alternative for reaching people who are hindered by limited mobility, time restrictions, or physical disability, or who feel stigmatized by the counseling process. In some Kenyan settings, PTSD clients face challenges related to familial responsibilities, physical or geographical challenges, poor access to transportation, and various disabilities, and for those in abusive relationships seeking treatment outside the home is difficult. In other words, considering that Kenya still has a large rural population, E-therapy is a potential means to offer clients the opportunity to access the services of a caregiver in an easily accessible manner without necessarily needing to make an appointment at a given time or place. Many Kenyans who live in regional and rural areas might easily be able to access E-therapy services, and especially those with mental health and domestic-related issues that sometimes are not brought to the fore as they tend to feel stigmatized and communities are not prepared to engage in such situations. More importantly, those faced with PTSD conditions may find it easier and more convenient to access E-therapeutic services when compared with time- and space-controlled appointments.

Second, E-therapy provides *disinhibition and internalization.* Every therapy seeks to help potential clients with a path to full restoration. In the Kenyan context, E-therapy provides an opportunity for clients to express themselves as they self-reflect.[16] E-therapy becomes a means by which a client has the opportunity to reflect, rehearse, rethink, write, rewrite, and reconsider potential solutions and resolutions by making revisions where necessary. In such contexts, the client creates a path with the E-therapist that can be discussed, reviewed, and reinforced at any given time. The opportunity for the client and therapist to revise the treatment path during the process is something that we cannot take for granted. It is an opportunity that face-to-face therapeutic services are not always likely to offer. In other words, the client is not left in a vacuum, as would happen in a face-to-face session in which physical separation does not allow the client easy follow-up conversations. Instead,

---

16. John Suler, "The Online Disinhibition Effect," originally published in *The Psychology of Cyberspace*, 2001, accessed 8 January 2019, http://truecenterpublishing.com/psycyber/disinhibit. html.

with disinhibition and internalization, a client is able to revisit messages or texts, and certain resolutions reached can be re-emphasized. This is essential especially when clients start the path to recovery; it is crucial that they start taking control of their therapy.

Third, *the personal reflection zone* is an opportunity especially for those who have gone through PTSD and who indeed may be in the midst of the church's work of forgiveness, peacemaking, and reconciliations. The personal reflection zone is an aspect that one-on-one therapy often does not guarantee. But E-therapy provides an opportunity whereby the written communications that occur between clients and therapists can be done as a means of owning the therapeutic process. Indeed, both the therapist and the client have an opportunity to enter that "zone of reflection."[17] In other settings where E-therapy has been exercised, the personal zone is often referred to as "therapeutic writing," which opens up a new venture for both the client and the therapist to meditatively and reflectively engage in, highlighting the challenges, issues, disagreements, and arguments, which for some may be a therapeutic process.[18] This is essential, keeping in mind that within an African setting orality is part of our tradition, but we now know that through technological advances, writing using electronic devices has taken root among our people. The ability to enter into the personal reflection zone provides the client with an opportunity to review feedback, and in PTSD contexts clients can ask questions, revisit clarifications, and ask more questions in their pursuit of full restoration.

Fourth, *the level of communication security is increased* and if there is need to refer the client to another therapist, electronic records are readily available and reliable since data may have been archived for potential benefits to humanity. E-therapy provides an opportunity compared to a face-to-face approach, as clients continue to seek assurance of the security of any online communication they engage in. This also provides opportunities to E-therapists to continuously engage in reviewing the latest digital advances, as they remain accountable and responsible to their potential clients seeking to use their services. In this way, therapists are compelled to uphold standards of accountability and responsibility to their clients since electronic correspondence is likely to remain available permanently.

---

17. Rochlen, Zack, and Speyer, "Online Therapy," 4.

18. Rochlen, Zack, and Speyer, 4.

Fifth, *hypertextuality and multimedia* are available for the client's reference. E-therapy provides ease of reference, in the sense that the availability of the Internet enables the therapist to suggest that the client refers to particular websites, videos, documents, or other relevant tools to enable therapy to take place. Hypertextuality and multimedia provide an opportunity for clients to quickly and easily access other possible resources to enhance their treatment. Once the therapist has the essential online skills, he or she can guide the client, enabling the client to participate in the healing process. E-therapy replaces the traditional office, surgery, or therapeutic-spaced clinics which often limit the therapist and the client to whatever resources are on the bookshelf; E-therapy is opening up opportunities for both client and therapist to access limitless resources. Such an opportunity enhances therapeutic services, and what has already been tested and accepted becomes a resource for collection, documentation, and interpretation of data.

Sixth, there is a *reduction of stigma and shyness* among clients. In PTSD contexts, victims tend to suffer from stigma and shyness even when opportunities are available for them to visit and consult a therapist face to face. The technological advances now make it possible for such victims to seek therapy in a more secure and confidential setting. This is one of the many advantages that E-therapy as a process provides to clients who may previously have hesitated to seek help. There is sometimes nothing more difficult than recounting one's past, and doing so in the presence of a stranger – hence the need for E-therapy. This is what some scholars have come to call "telepresence and transference,"[19] referring to that moment when a client feels safe to air his or her challenges without sharing a therapist's physical space. In most cases, such clients tend to have confidence to either chat or share audio without necessarily having the therapist around physically. We witness this among young people, the elderly, and with university students in particular.

According to research, among those eager to utilize E-therapy are those with bodyweight issues,[20] drinking problems,[21] and panic disorders.[22] In

---

19. J. Fink. *How to Use Computers and Cyberspace in the Clinical Practice of Psychotherapy* (Northvale, NJ: Aronson, 1999).

20. J. Harvey-Berino, S. Pintauro, B. Casey Gold, C. Moldovan, and E. Ramirez, "Does Using the Internet Facilitate the Maintenance of Weight Loss?," *International Journal of Obesity* 26, no. 9 (Sep. 2002): 1254–1260.

21. R. N. Cloud and P. L. Peacock, "Internet Screening and Interventions for Problem Drinking: Results from the http://www.carebetter.com," *Alcoholism Treatment Quarterly* 19, no. 2 (2001): 23–44.

22. B. Klein and J. C. Richards, "A Brief Internet-Based Treatment for Panic Disorder," *Behavioral & Cognitive Psychotherapy* 29, no. 1 (2001): 113–117.

some contexts, companies and institutions have embraced E-therapy to assist employees with various needs. In some instances, clients prefer E-therapy because they don't want to share an office or therapy room, or they feel uncertainty about the future and about potential repercussions that may arise as a result of seeking therapy. It is understood to be a good option for a client who is unable to address sensitive issues face to face.

Other clients find it comfortable to have an opportunity to operate from within their own space and at their own speed, without the hindrances that would be created by scheduled "therapeutic hours." In other words, such clients find it easy to compose emails, store them, revisit them, and rework them, and they can be sent at any time. This happens at the comfort of the client who does not have to worry about such social norms like dressing, timing, and verbal language that is required in the one-on-one counseling process.

Challenges of E-Therapy

Advances in technology not only provide positive opportunities for therapy, but they also pose challenges that must be addressed in our Kenyan context, where the populace has access to the Internet that allows for social media engagement without competence and ethical regulatory frameworks to ensure their safety and well-being. E-therapy in PTSD poses a number of challenges, and here we discuss some of them as well as proposing potential solutions. The lack of standard operating procedures and a regulatory framework renders potential clients and even the therapists themselves vulnerable.

First, *lack of sufficient Internet access* to support E-therapy services. Lack of sufficient Internet access among Kenyans may be the result of the rural populace, poor power supply, or lack of installation of masts in various regions. E-therapy services require good Internet access, and, more importantly, a sustained electricity supply for charging the electronic devices that are likely to be employed in E-therapy services. The Kenyan context remains rural, and access to education, especially the technical know-how for dealing with electronics, is still beyond the reach of many people. So, even where people have access to electronic devices, they still lack such basics as access to electricity to power their devices and the Internet to access E-therapy. Social media access also requires a certain amount of money to operate, and for low-income earners this will hinder E-therapy service access. It is common that for rural people who are faced with PTSD and desire to access E-therapy, their ideas of such a service are hindered since they can't access it. The unfortunate part is that some of those clients are able to afford data for air time but not data for the Internet. However, this would become a problem of the past if governments subsidized PTSD clients so that they could access the Internet easily and cheaply for treatment.

Second, *lack of human presence.* Traditionally, counseling has been understood to be based on human interaction that is determined by a geographical and physical space set-up.[23] The idea that therapy can be offered where a therapist and client are not in one space is new as technological advances provide possibilities that were not previously imagined. Indeed, that lack of human interaction is a major impediment when it comes to E-therapy, especially for Africans, since our socialization is people- and face-to-face-based. We have all heard of the idiom that presence is power, but now technological advances are taking that power away from the therapists and placing it more in the hands of the clients, as they determine the kinds of therapies they are seeking and from whom. Among most urban dwellers in Kenyan contexts there is an upsurge in seeking electronic services, as the human presence dies out slowly. A few years ago, people frequently gathered for social events, such as wedding gifting, fundraising, funerals, and dowry negotiations, but some of these activities are now being replaced by online interactions through video-conferencing, WhatsApp, Facebook, and other free video-calling means. The argument that the lack of human presence limits a therapeutic relationship needs to be researched, considered, and evidence adduced to ensure that the E-therapy model is not abandoned or condemned before considering its pros and cons.

Third, *the limitation in non-verbal cues and other facial expressions* limits diagnostic assessment. It is believed that face-to-face therapies allow both the therapist and the client to consider non-verbal cues such as eye contact, shaky hands, tired eyes, body language, and voice, but these opportunities are curtailed in E-therapy services.[24] The fact that E-therapy can to some extent utilize video conversations does not change the fact that certain social and non-verbal cues are lost. Consequently, therapists are likely to miss crucial client information expressed through non-verbal language. To ensure a successful E-therapy service, there is need for research to consider how electronic devices that are employed in E-therapy can be enhanced to allow the non-verbal cues to be read by the therapist so as to attain a high standard of client assessment.

---

23. Mary Finn Maples and Suni Han, "Cyber-Counseling in the United States and South Korea: Implications for Counseling College Students of the Millennial Generation and the Networked Generation," *Journal of Counseling & Development* 86, no. 2 (Spring 2008): 180.

24. Maples and Han, "Cyber-Counseling," 180.

Fourth, *E-therapy's inappropriateness*. Not all therapies suit every client. The opportunities that arise for new therapies may also be avenues for potential negative effects. For E-therapy in the Kenyan context, some high-risk groups – for example, those who suffer from some mental health problems, those with suicidal thoughts, victims of violence, stigmatized individuals, and/or victims of sexual abuse – may not be suited to one-to-one therapeutic services. The inappropriateness of E-therapy in such contexts requires potential therapists to evaluate critically the circumstances leading to a client requesting E-therapy services. Such an evaluation should provide checks and balances which will also protect the therapist from being exploited by the client. More importantly, in PTSD-related cases, critical scrutiny of potential clients must take center stage if we are to attain added value for clients through E-therapeutic services.

Fifth, *the security of the information transmitted* over the Internet or email server raises concerns both for the therapist and for the client. It is important to note that many potential clients may not be competent to understand how electronic data is transmitted and whether some of it is recorded or copied to other servers. The therapist should have a high level of knowledge regarding the security of transmitted information. This should then be provided to the potential client as an assurance that he or she can safely engage in an E-therapy service. Sometimes, the encryption of transmitted data does not necessarily mean that a third party cannot access such information. Consequently, the security of transmitted information must remain a key priority in helping potential clients make a decision as to whether or not to enroll in an E-therapy service. In cases where fraudulent therapists wish to exploit the innocence of potential clients, ethical and regulatory frameworks must be considered by professional groups and the government to guarantee client protection against exploitation.

Sixth, *technological skills and failures*. Technical skills and expertise have not yet been transferred to the larger population in the Kenyan context. Most Kenyan people who engage in electronic information transfer, whether in urban or rural settings, lack the technical skills that are required to safeguard the conversations that emerge from E-therapeutic services. Nevertheless, this has not hindered such clients from seeking E-therapy advice, counsel, or guidance. For example, the majority of E-therapy clients, whether receiving a service from a professional or a fraudulent therapist, have no idea what special software or hardware is required to enable them to get or share information confidentially. Neither are the therapists often aware of software that enhances confidentiality to avoid compromising E-therapy services. This in some way implies that within the Kenyan context, both the E-therapist and the potential client are in the same boat as far as technological skills are concerned. Consequently, government and human rights agencies must step up their efforts to ensure that E-therapies do not become a means of exploitation of innocent Kenyans.

Seventh, *cross-cultural considerations*. The Kenyan context provides cross-cultural considerations since the country is blessed with diverse ethnic groups that differ in culture, language, and beliefs. While technological advances seem to be held in common, the different appropriations based on people's language, culture, or beliefs raise concerns as far as E-therapy is concerned. For example, communication is central to any therapy. In E-therapy, communication might be impeded by differences between a therapist's and a client's language or ethnic culture. Technology does not necessarily attend to this on its own. Human beings behind E-therapy must ensure that for communication to take place, the E-therapy language used between a given therapist and the client is acceptable. Depending on the kind of language through which a service is rendered, E-therapy is likely to exclude individuals who may not speak that language. More importantly, some messages may be misunderstood or misinterpreted, and a simple assurance that a response to a message has satisfied the question that a client was posing leaves a lot to be desired. Those with no E-therapeutic knowledge and practice should be aware of evolving online therapies.[25]

A more important issue related to cross-cultural considerations is how well both the therapist and the client can share short messages or texts if they come from two different cultural backgrounds.[26] Within Kenyan contexts, with their diverse ethnic backgrounds, it is very difficult to imagine an E-therapy service that does not depend on a client/consumer language. The ethnic language diversity may at times be a hindrance for some, as potential E-therapists may not be familiar with a potential client's language. This is a challenge that cannot be ignored. There is a need for E-therapists to push for a technologically based harmonized language for ease of use of E-therapy services in cross-cultural settings. Without this, E-therapy will remain within the limits of clients and therapists who can relate only to their given languages and dialects. The potential of engaging a translator as a medium between a therapist and a client due to cross-cultural boundaries compromises the confidentiality which is the highest ethical consideration in therapist–client

---

25. John R. Suler, "The Future of Online Psychotherapy and Clinical Work," *Journal of Applied Psychoanalytic Studies* 4 (2002): 265–270, http://users.rider.edu/~suler/psycyber/futurether.html.

26. M. J. Mallen, D. L. Vogel, A. B. Rochlen, and S. X. Day, "Online Counseling: Reviewing the Literature from a Counseling Psychology Framework," *The Counseling Psychologist* 33, no. 6 (2005): 819–871.

relations. But more importantly, some words, whether in English or local dialects, do not necessarily mean the same thing for the client and the therapist. For this reason, E-therapists must engage with potential clients in a medium of communication that they are sure will provide sufficient service without compromising the client's needs.

Eighth, *lack of regulatory frameworks for E-therapy services*. Western countries have shown their determination to counter this aspect by providing legal regulatory frameworks to manage online services, and more specifically those that relate to E-therapy. However, while Kenyans continue to experience an upsurge in Internet usage, not much has been done regarding the legality and liability of online services, and more importantly E-therapy services. Specific standards and controls for online service therapies, and E-therapy in particular, must be championed in earnest to protect potential clients from fraudulent online therapists. We cannot afford only to market electronic devices and allow the free flow of information even to potential PTSD clients. We have every responsibility to ensure that those who offer E-therapy services have certified credentials. But we also acknowledge that within the Kenyan context, it is unclear who has qualifications as an E-therapist, and what procedures and processes, if any, are utilized not only to ensure that clients access qualified and credentialed E-therapists, but also to totally lock out potential fraudulent E-therapists who continue to propose online therapeutic services without basic qualifications and to access clients through manipulation and exploitation, thus creating more traumatic experiences.

Ethical Values for Effective E-Therapy

The struggle therapists face in the midst of PTSD and in a digitalized era is over the place of ethical values in E-therapy relations. As is well known, the duty of care is central to all therapeutic relationships, and the E-therapy relationship is no exception. Imagine the scenario where a human resource officer in an organization recommends a therapist to a struggling employee, without knowing that the therapeutic service is to be provided through E-therapy. Once the struggling employee has started the therapy, it is discovered that the therapist doesn't have E-therapeutic standards and procedures. This raises several ethical issues. But even when one knows that E-therapy will be the means of service delivery, one should understand the ethical values that accompany E-therapy services.

Different institutions and organizations have already recognized the need for added value and developed ethical values for effective E-therapy. For example, we can interact with specified ethical standards[27] in circumstances where professional therapists offer services using electronic modes. The British Association for Counselling and Psychotherapy (BACP) has ethical principles that guide an obligatory ethical role by considering relevant circumstances with care and accountability. Consequently, the duty of care must remain at the center of the E-therapy relationship, and in this research this can be understood under four key ethical values, namely, *competence, record-keeping, managing situations*, and *informed consent*.

Competence

The centrality of competence in caregiving professions cannot be overstated. And in an era of technological advances, the need to ensure that therapists have the requisite competencies, and especially E-therapists, must be emphasized. More importantly, the technological competence of all E-therapists must be assured before they engage in an E-therapy service.[28] It is important to note that technological competencies for therapists are an opportunity to consider the added value of E-therapeutic services. In the Kenyan context we are still far from such an engagement, as many therapists still have partial knowledge or competencies pertaining to hardware, software, encryption (keeping information secure after coding to ensure privacy), backup systems (files or data copied to a second medium and stored safely), firewalls (counselors utilize firewall protection externally or through web-based programs against unauthorized entry), password protection, virus protection (a security process to ensure that information is available only to those who have the right to access and utilize it), and third-party services. Even in cases of fraudulent E-therapists who pride themselves on having the latest fashionable gadgets, they still lack the competencies required for E-therapy services. What this implies is that E-therapy is not just for everyone, neither should it be declared a no-go zone; rather, it raises the bar and demands critical engagement by every therapist who desires to offer E-therapy, for such technological competencies are not easily attainable.

---

27. Compare the ethical standards developed by The National Board of Certified Counsellors (2007) and The British Association for Counselling and Psychotherapy (BACP), *Ethical Framework for Good Practice in Counselling and Psychotherapy* (Lutterworth: BACP, 2013).

28. Kate Anthony and DeeAnna Merz Nagel, *Therapy Online: A Practical Guide* (Thousand Oaks, CA: SAGE, 2010).

Competence in therapeutic professions embraces a number of skills that are not readily available through a single training session or one institution. Competence, therefore, demands qualifications based on education, training, experience, professional credentials, and supervision experience. For E-therapy, however, we may not have clarity on the specific qualifications determined for E-therapists, something that needs urgent attention by the respective professional bodies and governments so as to ensure the protection of clients from potential fraudulent E-therapists. It is important to keep in mind that potential clients may not then have the knowledge or skills to determine whether E-therapists have the requisite qualifications and credentials. It is for this reason that the American Counseling Association Ethical Standards compel counselors "to explain to clients the nature of all services provided. They inform clients about issues such as, but not limited to, the following: the goals, techniques, procedures, limitations, potential risks, and benefits of services; the counselor's qualifications, credentials, relevant experience and approach to counseling . . . the role of technology and other pertinent information."[29] Indeed, this is a good beginning for any E-therapist who wishes to consider E-therapy as a means to offer therapeutic services.

Another ethical issue of concern surrounding E-therapy in relation to competence is the right to privacy and confidentiality which is at the core of effective E-therapy. Confidentiality in any therapeutic relationship requires the therapist to protect private client communication. More specifically, confidentiality provides validation for clients seeking or receiving E-therapy. E-therapy at times can compromise confidentiality because of shared computers and possible email password exchanges in public places. Consequently, E-therapists have a responsibility to explain to their clients the potential limitations pertaining to confidentiality in the use of E-therapy or online counseling, and the provision of agreeable terms on the consent form by highlighting the privacy challenges and risks involved.[30] E-therapists must embrace requisite competencies to protect potential clients since online conversations are likely to be monitored or hacked.

29. American Counselling Association, "2014 ACA Code of Ethics," 4, retrieved from https://www.counseling.org/docs/default-source/ethics/2014-code-of-ethics.pdf?sfvrn=2d58522_4.

30. American Psychological Association, "Ethical Principles of Psychology and Code of Conduct," 2017, Code 4.02, http://www.apa.org/ethics/code2002.html.

Record-Keeping

The capturing and entering of a client's data and maintaining the same within a secure place must remain a concern of every therapist. Just as it is in the individual's interest to keep private and secure whatever is shared on social media, in E-therapy record-keeping is critical at all stages. More importantly, technological advances have made data recording and storage easier, but have also raised some ethical dilemmas and potential risks. The ethical issues related to privacy and confidentiality will continue to arise as long as record-keeping is part of E-therapy service delivery. We have witnessed record-keeping that is non-erasable appearing through such avenues as WikiLeaks, where sensitive data was recorded, stored, and released at will. It can be harmful if E-therapy clients who trusted a therapist discover or find their information leaked without their knowledge or consent. This is why both the practitioner and the recipient of the service must appreciate where certain information will be kept, whether or not it is in electronic form, and in some instances, whether it might exist in a non-erasable manner. Such electronic information, and especially that pertaining to PTSD clients, requires an intentional strategy that is part of the therapeutic process. At times, fraudulent E-therapists may compromise record-keeping, and this must not be allowed to happen, even though electronic devices and the Internet are easily accessible in Kenyan settings.

Within record-keeping is the issue of the safety and security of the information being shared through E-therapy. The assurance of a safe and secure communication environment and data storage is important for any E-therapy practitioner. We should be aware of critical security issues that often arise out of digitalized caring professions, especially E-therapy.[31] It is true that some blogs cannot assure clients of information security as shared online, hence the risk of exposure of clients' data. If a therapist decides to outsource information storage services because of server expenses, potential clients must be made aware that a third party is engaged in record-keeping, to enable them to make an informed decision as to whether to take up E-therapy services from such a therapist. But more closely related to this are the records that are kept or stored either on office PCs or laptops or mobile phones that are easily accessible through corporate control units or easy hacking from within and without. The safety and accessibility of any E-therapist client information must be assessed and evaluated continuously.

---

31. J. S. Zack, "The Technology of Online Counseling," in *Online Counseling: A Handbook for Mental Health Professionals*, ed. R. Kraus, G. Stricker, and C. Speyer (San Diego: Elsevier Academic, 2004), 93–121.

Record-keeping also provides another angle that is important for consideration. This is the capacity of both the client and the therapist to record the right thing, especially where and when you have spontaneous clarifications going on. Often, especially in PTSD contexts, you may experience an overly introverted or extroverted client whose record-keeping capacity may not be easily noticeable. For this reason, at times it gets even more complicated if both the client and the E- therapist lack computer or electronic literacy to manage the medium.[32] The level of electronic literacy should be considered not just for communication alone, but also for the capacity to gather, record, and keep safe the information provided. Therefore, record-keeping must be a high priority by both the therapist and the client in order to remove potential guesswork on what was previously discussed, thereby avoiding the possibility of exploitation from either one.

Managing Situations

One of the ethical issues that arises with E-therapy is whether E-therapists have the capacity to manage situations. Face-to-face therapies have proven for a while that during therapy, a client can experience a trigger that may necessitate a different management style or a potential referral. While being offered an E-therapy service, a client might become suicidal, and since there is no other therapist close to the client who can offer face-to-face help, often E-therapists are unable to deal with this challenge. Crisis intervention through E-therapy can be very tricky, and that is why any therapist planning to embrace E-therapy must ensure that all measures have been put in place to manage situations as they arise in the absence of a human being. Suicidal instances are not the only case in point; cultural clashes may occur between a client and a therapist, or differences in time zones and other related social systems may cause issues. Managing unexpected situations during E-therapy service delivery must be thought through before being implemented, otherwise it could shatter the lives of clients, and therapist practices may become liable for legal action.

Informed Consent

Informed consent is an ethical issue that focuses on human subjects. Voluntary informed consent is a prerequisite for E-therapy since it is a voluntary agreement

---

32. G. S. Stofle, *Choosing an Online Therapist* (Harrisburg, PA: White Hat Communications, 2001).

that exists between a client and an E-therapist. It should be understood that informed consent is more than a mere agreement form being signed. Accurate informed consent must be understood as a process. The process provides an opportunity for the client to receive from an E-therapist information about the potential risks, benefits, and confidential issues that may pertain to E-therapeutic services.

Just as with human subjects in therapeutic relations, clients have legal rights that may require being waived for the E-therapist to ask and provide E-therapy services. We note that the consent process requires the sharing of sufficient data with the client to enable him or her to make an informed decision about whether to embrace E-therapy services or not. In an E-therapy approach, the consent process can be very challenging. The first challenge is the limitations of language that may exist between the E-therapist and the client. Such language might be subjected to review by an expert to ascertain its viability since Kenyan contexts present with multiple languages. Above all, the client must be given enough time to process the information provided without any coercion before fully engaging in E-therapy.

Informed consent is characterized by competence, knowledge, voluntariness, and adequate information for a client to make a decision. It is critical that even if a client owns a high-quality electronic device and enjoys good Internet access, it should not be assumed that he or she has automatically consented to participate in E-therapy. Therefore, while an individual exercises autonomy by enrolling in E-therapeutic services, the E-therapist has an ethical responsibility to create an environment for the client to appreciate the potential challenges and limitations that E-therapy presents.

The most important elements to be considered in an E-therapy informed consent process are the purpose of E-therapy being sought, the procedures that will be followed, the possible alternatives available, the foreseeable risks and benefits, the length of time, the next of kin or a friend who may be contacted in case clarifications are needed, a statement indicating that participation in E-therapy is voluntary and may end at any time, what payments may be required, and how data will be collected, stored, and secured. All E-therapists must endeavor to ensure that the consent process of clients is not jeopardized in any way.

Toward the Future: Why E-Therapy Is a Must!

The technological advances in Kenya continue to raise ethical concerns, especially as professionals in different disciplines discover that online services are becoming intrinsic to our daily endeavors. The future of therapeutic professions cannot erase or wish away the role of E-therapy. It is for this reason that the following proposals need to be considered by the respective professional bodies, institutions of higher and tertiary education, government ministries, agencies, and their partners.

First, there is a need to enlist all professional organizations that offer therapeutic services in the country. Among these organizations, mechanisms need to be formulated so that those that offer individual E-therapeutic services in the country may be provided with a framework to determine and confirm any specific qualifications required. It is up to the professional organizations to develop strategies to ensure that a practicing E-therapist meets the basic criteria regarding qualifications, certification, and professional experience.

Second, all disciplines that provide therapeutic services may wish to consider recommending continuing education for practitioners in the area of E-therapy. Advances in technology demand that therapists continue to review and update their supervision, training, and practicing skills. This is important since no one is able to predict where and when E-therapy clients may call for help.

Third, therapists must come together to commit to develop ethical standards for practicing E-therapy in our contexts. It is crucial that psychologists, psychiatrists, counselors, and church ministers intentionally cultivate a collaborative approach that will urgently address the need to regulate E-therapy in Kenyan contexts. The fact that the populace has access to good electronic devices and fast Internet services does not necessarily mean they have the capacity and skills to provide E-therapy services.

Fourth, research remains central in determining the need and efficacy of E-therapy. Conducting ethical research among stakeholders, both potential clients and therapists, may help in evaluating the specific needs, standards, expectations, and potential regulations and guidelines that can be put in place to enhance E-therapy in Kenya. More importantly, research can pinpoint the potential risks and benefits of E-therapy being embraced on a large scale.

Fifth, institutions of higher learning and professional colleges in collaboration with professional organizations have an opportunity to provide leadership with regard to informing the Kenyan context and helping potential clients and therapists of E-therapy. Most therapists are graduates from such institutions, and therefore curriculum development, curriculum review, and tailor-made certification courses on E-therapy can be established accordingly.

Sixth, government agencies must work closely with professional organizations and licensing boards in the country through a dialogic approach so as to set up possible standard operating procedures that may help in regulating online therapeutic services. The government has the machinery to lead in calling all those who practice E-therapy to account through registration and licensing by the government. Any potential dangers that are likely to arise from an unregulated practice can be minimized if the government takes a positive approach in seeking to establish E-therapy as a professional practice in the country.

Seventh, there is a need to design a Kenyan model of care in which professionals who provide therapeutic services, such as psychologists, counselors, church ministers, clinicians, and medics, can pull together to attend to the needs of potential E-therapy clients. They can together design a model that allocates or assigns specific places or regions where primary care practitioners can be available to offer E-therapy to potential clients for the well-being of our people.

Conclusion

Technological advances do not necessarily mean a license to offer any service online. But at the same time, no one should assume that E-therapy can be appropriated by every client seeking online help. E-therapy in PTSD contexts should be safeguarded by other mechanisms to ensure that the client–therapist relationship is well maintained. Indeed, it is imperative that while a country like Kenya has embraced the Internet fully, some level of ethical regulatory operating standards needs to be developed and embraced to ensure that fraudulent E-therapists do not exploit innocent clients who are genuinely seeking help. It is paramount to keep in mind that there is no room to run away from the Internet; the only professional thing to do is to provide ethical regulatory procedures and operating procedures that ensure the protection of innocent citizens seeking therapeutic services.

Finally, it is our conviction that the public, professions, and practitioners require protection if E-therapy is to be ethically delivered in our settings. Consequently, where possible, as a country we should initiate legislation that can be enacted to ensure that the greater population that is likely to access E-therapy services is protected from potential fraudulent E-therapists. Such legislation will provide an avenue for the development of E-therapy standard operating procedures (SOPs), a regulatory framework in relation to training, competency skills, and credentialing and licensing of E-therapists. The future of E-therapy is promising, and all must be done to ensure its efficacy in Kenyan contexts.

Bibliography

Abbot, Jo-Anne M., Britt Klein, and Lisa Giechomsiki. "Best Practices in Online Therapy." *Journal of Technology in Human Services* 23, no. 2–4 (2008): 360–375.

Alleman, J. R. "Online Counseling: The Internet and Mental Health Treatment." *Psychotherapy: Research, Practice, Training* 39, no. 2 (2002): 199–209.

American Counselling Association. "2014 ACA: Code of Ethics." Retrieved from https://www.counseling.org/docs/default-source/ethics/2014-code-of ethics.pdf?sfvrsn=2d58522c_4.

American Psychiatric Association. *The Diagnostic and Statistical Manual of Mental Disorders*, 5th ed. (*DSM-5*). Arlington: American Psychiatric Publishing, 2013. https://doi.org/10.1176/appi.books.9780890425596.

American Psychological Association. "Ethical Principles of Psychology and Code of Conduct." 2017. http://www.apa.org/ethics/code2002.html.

Anthony, Kate, and DeeAnna Merz Nagel. *Therapy Online: A Practical Guide*. Thousand Oaks, CA: SAGE, 2010.

Bakke, Bette, James Mitchell, Steve Wonderlich, and Ron Erickson. "Administering Cognitive-Behavioral Therapy for Bulimia Nervosa via Telemedicine in Rural Settings." *International Journal of Eating Disorders* 30, no. 4 (2001): 454–457.

Barak, A. "Psychosocial Applications on the Internet: A Discipline on the Threshold of a New Millennium." *Applied & Preventive Psychology* 8, no. 4 (1999): 231–245.

Barnett, J. E., and K. Sheetz. "Technological Advances and Telehealth: Ethics, Law, and the Practice of Psychotherapy." *Psychotherapy: Theory, Research, Practice, Training* 40, no. 1–2 (2003): 86–93.

Bloom, J. W. "The Ethical Practice of Web Counseling." *British Journal of Guidance and Counseling* 26, no. 1 (1998): 53–59.

The British Association for Counseling and Psychotherapy (BACP). *Ethical Framework for Good Practice in Counselling and Psychotherapy*. Lutterworth: BACP, 2013.

Clinical Social Work Federation. "Social Workers Say No to Internet-Based Therapy." *EAP Association Exchange* 31, no. 5 (2001): 33.

Cloud, R. N., and P. L. Peacock. "Internet Screening and Interventions for Problem Drinking: Results from the http://www.carebetter.com." *Alcoholism Treatment Quarterly* 19, no. 2 (2001): 23–44.

Cogswell, J. F., and D. P. Estavan. *Explorations in Computer-Assisted Counseling*. Santa Monica, CA: System Development Corp, 1965.

Corey, G., M. Corey, and M. Callanan. *Issues and Ethics in the Helping Professions*. 7th ed. Pacific Grove, CA: Brooks/Cole, 2007.

Fink, J. *How to Use Computers and Cyberspace in the Clinical Practice of Psychotherapy*. Northvale, NJ: Aronson, 1999.

Grohol, J. M. "Best Practices in E-Therapy: Privacy and Security in E-Therapy." Last updated 2019. Psych Central. https://psychcentral.com/lib/e-therapy/.

Harvey-Berino, J., S. Pintauro, B. Casey Gold, C. Moldovan, and E. Ramirez. "Does Using the Internet Facilitate the Maintenance of Weight Loss?" *International Journal of Obesity* 26, no. 9 (Sep. 2002): 1254–1260.

Hopps, S. L., M. Pepin, and J. M. Boisvert. "The Effectiveness of Cognitive Behavioral Group Therapy for Loneliness via Inter-Relay Chat among People with Physical Disabilities." *Psychotherapy: Theory, Research & Practice* 40, no. 1–2 (2003): 136–147.

Kaplan, E. H. "Telepsychotherapy: Psychotherapy by Telephone, Videophone and Computer Videoconferencing." *Journal of Psychotherapy Practice and Research* 6, no. 3 (1997): 227–237.

Klein, B., and Richards, J. C. "A Brief Internet-Based Treatment for Panic Disorder." *Behavioral & Cognitive Psychotherapy* 29, no. 1 (2001): 113–117.

Mallen, M. J., D. L. Vogel, A. B. Rochlen, and S. X. Day. "Online Counseling: Reviewing the Literature from a Counseling Psychology Framework." *The Counseling Psychologist* 33, no. 6 (2005): 819–871.

Maples, Mary Finn, and Suni Han. "Cyber-Counseling in the United States and South Korea: Implications for Counseling College Students of the Millennial Generation and the Networked Generation." *Journal of Counseling & Development* 86, no. 2 (Spring 2008): 178–183.

Newman, Michelle Gayle. "Technology in Psychotherapy: An Introduction." *Journal of Clinical Psychology* 60, no. 2 (2004): 141–145.

Rochlen, Aaron B., Jason S. Zack, and Cedric Speyer. "Online Therapy: Review of Relevant Definitions, Debates, and Current Empirical Support." *Journal of Clinical Psychology* 60, no. 3 (2004): 269–283.

Santhiveeran, Janaki. "E-Therapy: Scope, Concerns, Ethical Standards, and Feasibility." *Journal of Family Social Work* 8, no. 3 (2004): 37–54.

Shalev, Arieh, Israel Liberzon, and Charles Marmar. "Post-Traumatic Stress Disorder." *New England Journal of Medicine* 376, no. 25 (2017): 2459–2469.

Simpson, S., E. Morrow, M. Jones, J. Ferguson, and E. Bremen. "Tele-Hypnosis: The Provision of Specialized Therapeutic Treatments via Teleconferencing." *Journal of Telemedicine and Telecare*, 8, suppl. 2 (2002): 78–79. DOI: 10.1258/135763302320302136.

Stofle, G. S. *Choosing an Online Therapist.* Harrisburg, PA: White Hat Communications, 2001.

Suler, John. "The Future of Online Psychotherapy and Clinical Work." *Journal of Applied Psychoanalytic Studies* 4 (2002): 265–270. http://users.rider.edu/~suler/psycyber/futurether.html.

———. "The Online Disinhibition Effect." Originally published in *The Psychology of Cyberspace.* 2001. Accessed 8 January 2019. http://truecenterpublishing.com/psycyber/disinhibit.html.

Taylor, C. Barr, Kenneth O. Jobson, Andy Winselberg, and Liana Abascal. "The Use of the Internet to Provide Evidence-Based Integrated Treatment Programs for Mental Health." *Psychiatric Annals* 32, no. 11 (2002): 671–677.

Weizenbaum, J. "ELIZA: A Computer Program for the Study of Natural Language Communication between Man and Machine." *Communications of the ACM* (Association for Computer Machinery) 9, no. 1 (1966). https:DOI.org/10.1145/365153.365168.

Zack, J. S. "The Technology of Online Counseling." In *Online Counseling: A Handbook for Mental Health Professionals*, edited by R. Kraus, G. Stricker, and C. Speyer, 93–121. 2nd ed. San Diego: Elsevier Academic, 2011.

Part 2

Peacemaking

4

Conflict and Peace

A Sociological Reading of Genesis 31:1–55 for Principles on Forgiveness, Peacemaking, and Reconciliation for the African Christian Context

Zebedi A. Muga
Lecturer, St Paul's University, Limuru, Kenya

Abstract

This research discusses the process of conflict resolution, forgiveness, peace, and reconciliation from the text of Genesis 31:1–55. It focuses on the interpersonal conflict between Jacob and Laban in that passage. It explores the escalation and de-escalation efforts adopted by the protagonists, Jacob and Laban, which led to forgiveness, peace, and resolution. The methodology used in this study is the sociological approach by Norman Gottwald, especially his emphasis on conflict models and social analysis. This method is used alongside a postcolonial approach and historical-critical analysis of the text. These approaches unearth the principles for the resolution of conflict in the modern context to achieve reconciliation, justice, and peace.

Key words: Conflict, covenant, escalation, de-escalation, Jacob, Laban, peace, violence.

Introduction

Conflicts pose serious threats to the stability and well-being of nations, communities, and individuals. In African societies and nations, conflicts have had devastating effects on the people. Conflicts are manifested in various ways. Acts of violence may be carried out against persons and their property, through wars, interethnic acts of aggression, individual physical aggression, or psychological and other means. These result in social suffering, psycho-physical devastation, loss of property, and loss of lives.

As a result, persons, communities, and nations are affected negatively through general insecurity and lack of freedom of movement, freedom of assembly, freedom of expression, freedom of worship, and freedom of conscience. Conflicts also hinder national, communal, and personal development, economic growth, education, and general national progress. They stifle individual freedoms, rights, and general well-being.

The Old Testament has many examples of conflict and processes of conflict resolution. However, Genesis 31:1–55 has been chosen for this research since it demonstrates a clear and progressive process of resolution of a potentially explosive conflict. It is therefore interesting due to its implications for the themes of forgiveness, peace, and reconciliation.

The conflict between two individuals, namely, Laban and Jacob, and the persons and communities connected with them are the focus of this text. This research explores the process of escalation and de-escalation of the conflict and their attempts to address it, and the interventions and principles used for the achievement of forgiveness, peace, and reconciliation. These can inform efforts for forgiveness, peace, and reconciliation in African contexts.

The approaches used in this study are sociological reading/exegesis of the text, the postcolonial method, and also the historical-critical method. The sociological approach by Gottwald[1] helps in unearthing the sociological issues underlying the text of Genesis 31:1–55. Since the text describes conflict, social exegesis enables the writer to highlight the principles for the process of peace, forgiveness, and reconciliation found in the biblical text. Gottwald emphasizes this method in terms of its conflict models and also the class issues analysis it proposes. This method links well with the postcolonial approach, which unravels current understandings of violence from a postcolonial perspective.

---

1. Norman Gottwald, *The Tribes of Yahweh: A Sociology of the Religion of Liberated Israel 1250–1050 BCE* (Sheffield: Sheffield Academic Press, 1979). He discusses the religion of Israel and the underlying sociological factors and how they affected them.

It analyses the issues of those at the periphery in postcolonial times, the underprivileged and those who are disadvantaged.

The historical-critical approach informs the exegesis of the biblical text with a view to exploring the various textual understandings of conflict and violence in terms of the history of the text. These approaches enable the writer to unravel biblical principles and approaches to mitigating the causes and preventing violent actions against persons and humanity in general.

The Biblical Text

Genesis 31:1–55 is in narrative form and is the story of a situation that threatened to escalate into conflict between Laban and Jacob. The basic text followed in this chapter is the Revised Standard Version (RSV) of the Bible. The passage has been assigned to the J, E, and P traditions[2] of the book of Genesis.[3] These are very old traditions of the pre-exilic and also exilic narratives of the forefathers of Israel, and in this case the narrator is dealing with the Jacob cycle of narratives (Gen 27–36).

The Social Setting and Textual Context

The narrative in this passage focuses on the conflict and tension between the families of Laban and Jacob. The text demonstrates an agricultural nomadic context and a society based on animal husbandry. This appears to have been their main economic activity. It also demonstrates a context of settled families engaging in economic activities and social relations – in other words, they are married and have children and those adopted into their families, as was the case for Jacob who was living and working for Laban to earn his living. It also demonstrates a religious context in which the subjects worship their own gods (they also have household gods, *teraphim*,[4] Gen 31:30). It is a situation in which families were prone to misunderstandings and also conflict due to

---

2. Julius Wellhausen set out in his Documentary Hypothesis four underlying traditions used in writing the Pentateuch. J the Yahwist tradition dated to the ninth century BCE; E the Elohistic tradition dated to the eighth century BCE; D the Deuteronomistic tradition dated to the sixth century; followed by P the Priestly tradition which dated to the fifth century, both exilic and post-exilic. G. H. Livingston, *The Pentateuch in Its Cultural Environment* (Grand Rapids, MI: Baker, 1995), 225–226.

3. See Hermann Gunkel, *Genesis* (Macon, GA: Mercer University Press, 1997), 331.

4. William Holladay, *A Concise Hebrew and Aramaic Lexicon of the Old Testament* (Leiden: Brill, 1988), 395.

the need for pasture or water for animals and other modes of wealth creation that disadvantaged certain persons or classes of persons.

The social relations in this text appear tenuous in terms of wealth creation, distribution, and also acquisition (31:1–2). There are also indications of socio-economic infractions such as exploitation: for example, Jacob accuses Laban of cheating him of his wages (31:7–8). Laban's daughters are also disgruntled about their inheritance status (31:14–16). It is noteworthy that the narrator keeps them voiceless, apart from two sections (Gen 31:14–16, 35), after which they are silent throughout the text.

The text of Genesis 31 fits within the wider division of Jacob narratives within Genesis (Gen 25:19 – 36:43). The pre-text of the immediate narrative is on Jacob's wealth (30:3) which becomes the source of conflict in chapter 31; the post-text, 33:3–13, is on Jacob's meeting with his brother Esau, another tension-packed narrative that hinges on the stolen blessing that led Jacob to flee from home.

The Literary Structure of Genesis 31:1–55

This passage can be structured as follows:

> A. The presentation of the causes of conflict (vv. 1–16);
>
> B. The escalation of the conflict situation (vv. 17–30);
>
> C. The de-escalation steps taken by Laban and Jacob (vv. 31–55).

The Presentation of the Causes of Conflict with Laban (31:1–16)

This section gives the first presentation or hints of the Laban–Jacob conflict. The sons of Laban accuse Jacob of having taken all the wealth that belonged to their father. This sends an alarm to Jacob and his household. He consults with his wives – that is, Laban's daughters – in a field, a private place. This claim creates a potential conflict between him and Laban's sons. His wives concur with him that the situation is not favorable, neither for them nor for him as their husband, and that their inheritance status is also not assured.

The second presentation of the conflict is the change in Laban's attitude to Jacob. Jacob notes that it is not as before. The text reads שלום כתמול עמו איננו והנה לבן את־פני יעקב וירא which translates literally as "Jacob looked at the face of Laban and behold it was not as three days formerly."[5]

---

5. "His face was not as before."

The NIV and the Hebrew Bible Tanakh (TNK) translate את־פנים (’*et panym*) with the words "attitude" and "manner" for face פנים (*Panym*) respectively, to describe the change that Jacob perceives in Laban's body language. This introduction sets the context for the conflict that runs through the narrative.

The Escalation of the Conflict Situation (31:17–30)

In this section, the narrative takes on a fast pace as events unfold. Jacob departs without informing Laban, which is construed as him running away with Laban's wealth, including his daughters. The situation is further aggravated by the knowledge that Laban's household gods, the תרפים (*teraphim*),[6] have also been stolen (it was believed that whoever had them would have the right to inheritance). With the magnitude of the situation as it stands – the belief that Jacob has stolen Laban's wealth – the perception that he is holding onto the gods further aggravates the situation. Laban and his kinsmen pursue Jacob for seven days. The section ends with the two groups in camps facing each other in a tense pitched battle position.

The De-Escalation Process for Peace and Reconciliation (31:31–55)

This section progresses through the tense situation. It indicates a situation de-escalated by the protagonists. Both Laban and Jacob adopt traditional and personal responses to de-escalate the situation, coupled with personal approaches and restraint enforced by the presence of "kinsmen." The Hebrew term used is לאחיו[7] (*Le Ahiv*) which indicates that the persons who accompany Laban are also related to Jacob. It is not clear who accompanies Jacob, but the narrator assumes that Jacob had men or those he adopted into his family. Since Laban is his uncle, those related to him are also considered his kinsfolk, the present group that has accompanied him to confront Jacob.

The rest of the narrative engages the reader in the covenant ברית נכרתה[8] and the covenant-making process between Laban and Jacob. This covenant-

---

6. Holladay, *Hebrew and Aramaic Lexicon*, 395, suggests idols (i.e. figurines or household gods).

7. The root word in Hebrew suggests "brother" or "full brother" (from the same parents) or "half-brother" (from different mothers), but it also suggests blood relatives, cousins, fellow-tribesman, or countryman (cf. Holladay, *Concise Hebrew and Aramaic Lexicon*, 8).

8. Literally, to cut a covenant. Animals were offered and the subjects passed between them. It was believed that the fate of the dead animals would befall any of the parties who broke this covenant.

making is accompanied by a covenant meal and setting up of covenant symbols, representing the agreements and solutions reached by the two parties for the sake of peace and reconciliation between them and their families.

An Anatomy of the Laban–Jacob Conflict

Table 4.1 shows the aspects of the growing conflict between Laban and Jacob that we see in this text. From this it can be seen that Laban is the main power-broker and wealth holder who feels threatened by the rise of a new wealth-holder, Jacob, who is also a foreigner, hence the treatment of Jacob as an outsider and intruder who is after Laban's wealth. Laban, as the power-holder, also feels threatened by the new and wealthy man.

Table 4.1

Power Structure	Laban	31:5–6, 29, 31
Wealth Creator/Owner	Laban	31:1, 14, 19, 23, 26, 41
Xenophobic Reaction	Laban's sons	31:1, 15
Personal Characteristics	Laban cheats and exploits	31:2, 7, 41

The other issue raised in this study is that wealth is defined by the social context, which appears to have been agricultural and subsistence farming. The geographical and topological factors appear to have suited a nomadic lifestyle, as indicated by the animals mentioned, such as sheep and goats, and also by the mountains and tents.

Jacob appears as an outsider, disadvantaged by the outsider tag. He is accused of stealing his benefactor's wealth, whereas it is actually his benefactor who has swindled him several times (cf. 31:41). It appears that Laban discovered that he could use Jacob to acquire or generate wealth, hence the xenophobic reaction by the local (family) community to his newfound wealth. It is also worth noting that the daughters feel excluded from the inheritance and see themselves as strangers. It is thought that they felt Laban had used them to exploit Jacob and to acquire his current wealth, hence Rachel's move to steal Laban's household gods. Thus the sociological context seems ripe for the reactions that occur within it, with all the disgruntled feelings that permeate the initial setting of the narrative.

Table 4.2

Status	Description	Response
Primary Situation	Laban and Jacob relate at servant–master level. Jacob begins to accumulate wealth.	Laban is comfortable with the status quo. Jacob is not comfortable. Sons of Laban begin to grumble. Laban's daughters grumble as well.
Escalation A	Report by Laban's sons. Changes in Laban's attitude to Jacob.	Fear, isolation, a tense situation erupts. Tense situation escalates.
Escalation B	Jacob flees with his family. Laban pursues Jacob with his kinsmen.	Fear of violence. Potential for all-out violence.
De-Escalation	Laban/Jacob/kinsmen sit at a covenant meal.	Resolved feelings and unresolved questions.

Step 1: Escalation of Situation A

In the first part of the narrative, Laban's sons indicate their displeasure at Jacob's newly acquired wealth, which they believe he has stolen from their father (v. 1). Jacob feels insecure and threatened by this new situation of how he is perceived by his host's family and especially the heirs to Laban's wealth. The toxic environment does not help matters but threatens to escalate further with the change in Laban's attitude to Jacob. This attitude appears to be markedly different from before (v. 2). Jacob decides to do a soul search and analysis with his immediate family (vv. 4–16). They make a decision to relocate and for him and his family to go back to his homeland in Canaan. This decision is prompted by Yahweh as well as by the immediate situation. Jacob is assured of divine prompting and presence as he prepares to move back to his father's home (vv. 17–18).

Step 2: Further Escalation B

Laban's reaction to the report that Jacob has left is telling. He is either moved by jealousy of Jacob's wealth or prompted by his sons and kinsmen, who move to pursue Jacob. It is significant that he receives a report three days after Jacob's departure. He pursues him for seven days, and when he reaches him, they adopt an adversarial posture. It is not clear whether they were face to face or shouting at each other across the valley. They appear to cross each other only when the situation de-escalates (vv. 27–30). The term "overtook," וישג (wa yaseg, "to reach or overtake"[9]), is common in biblical narratives of war and individual pursuit.

Step 3: De-Escalation Activities

The de-escalation activities in this section are preceded by the admission of fault. Jacob indicates to Laban the reasons for his fear and states his case (vv. 33–35). Laban searches for his property but misses the תרפים (teraphim), which is what he is really looking for. Note the use of trickery in telling the story. The teraphim – the gods – end up becoming unclean owing to Rachel having sat on them (the narrator notes that Jacob is unaware that Rachel stole the gods). If he approached Rachel, he himself would become unclean, and this prevents his finding the teraphim. The de-escalation process is also aided by witnesses, that is, the kinsfolk accompanying Laban, who are also related to Jacob (v. 37). The emphasis on relatedness and cords of connectedness – that is, Laban indicating his daughters and grandchildren – also serves to de-escalate the situation. In other words, whatever evil action Laban might have thought of, he is keenly aware that Jacob is his nephew, the son of his sister Rebecca; that Jacob's wives are his own daughters; and that Jacob's sons and daughter are his grandchildren. Such relationships de-escalate the almost volatile situation that faces him. As such, Laban is upbeat to ensure that his sons and other relations do not harm Jacob and his family.

The offer of peace signifies a further level of de-escalation. Both parties having proved their complaint in the presence of their kinsmen – particularly the failure of Laban to find evidence of infraction of his property and hospitality, and Jacob voicing his discontent about Laban's handling of his wages – they are now both open to guidance by the kinsfolk. There is the calling to a higher power, a witness to the proceedings of peacemaking. The crown of the whole process is the covenant-making, accompanied by sacrifice and eating. The protagonists then spend time together and leave only when sure there is no further infraction of hospitality and peacemaking (vv. 54–55).

---

9. Also means "catch up with." In the hiphil form it is figurative of battle terminology. Cf. Holladay, *Hebrew and Aramaic Lexicon*, 247.

Principles of Forgiveness, Peace, and Reconciliation

This narrative reveals the following principles which, if adapted and adopted by the people of Africa, could assist in resolving conflicts on the continent:

- Yahweh has a significant role in peacemaking and forgiveness: he was called upon as a witness to the process and to prevent further infractions of peace. Both parties encountered him and acknowledged him to be a higher power.
- Jacob read the situation and made a decision to move away with his wives. Could this be a form of situational analysis? Could it be used in the peace-building process today?
- It may be helpful to involve a third party, such as elders and mediators, similar to the role of the kinsmen.
- Elders and kinsmen reinforce restraint but they can also allow for the ventilation of pent-up feelings and intervene if the situation threatens to escalate.
- Coming together to solve the problem and analyzing the situation through retelling/narration of grievances is noteworthy.
- The use of covenants and tools and symbols for peacemaking is helpful – is it possible to adopt traditional tools for covenant-making and reconciliation efforts?
- Eating together in fellowship and efforts at mitigation of future issues are also important.

Conclusion

This study has explored the narrative of the conflict between Laban and Jacob and the reactions to this conflict and how they finally resolved it, thereby achieving forgiveness, peace, and reconciliation. It has also revealed the triggers and psycho-social factors that escalated the situation. It has been noted that the presence of witnesses (kinsmen) served to de-escalate the situation. Traditional methods of conflict resolution were used in the conflict process – that is, covenant-making and tools of resolution by Laban and Jacob. There were methods to ensure conflict did not recur. These are principles that can be learned by present societies in Africa for the resolution of conflict for both individuals and communities.

There are many parallels between the Laban–Jacob processes of de-escalation of conflict and those found in the traditional society. These helped solve conflicts and created forgiveness and peace. The church today can institute such de-escalation systems to solve current individual, communal, and national conflicts. The church can also create tools for covenant-making to ensure the viability of such de-escalation processes.

Bibliography

Brueggemann, Walter. *Genesis*. Interpretation: A Bible Commentary for Teaching and Preaching. Atlanta: John Knox, 1982.

Gottwald, N. *The Tribes of Yahweh: A Sociology of Religion of Liberated Israel 1250–1050 BCE*. Sheffield: Sheffield Academic Press, 1999.

Gunkel, Hermann. *Genesis*. Macon, GA: Mercer University Press, 1997.

Harrison, R. K. *The Book of Genesis*. Grand Rapids, MI: Eerdmans, 1995.

Herbert, A. S. *Genesis 12–50*. London: SCM, 1962.

Holladay, W. *A Concise Hebrew and Aramaic Lexicon of the Old Testament*. Leiden: Brill, 1988.

Livingston, G. H. *The Pentateuch in Its Cultural Environment*. Grand Rapids, MI: Baker, 1974.

Marks, J. H. *Genesis*. Interpreter's Bible. Edited by Charles Laymon. Nashville: Abingdon Press, 1979.

Pritchard, James B., ed. *The Ancient Near East: An Anthology of Texts and Pictures*. Vol. 2. Princeton, NJ: Princeton University Press, 1975.

5

God's Masterpiece

Ephesians 2:11–22 as Inspiration for the Church's Involvement in Peacemaking and Reconciliation with People with Albinism in Tanzania

Timothy J. Monger

Emmanuel International Tanzania Country Director/Part-Time Lecturer
St Paul College, Mwanza, Tanzania

and

Marco Methuselah

Lecturer, St Paul College, Mwanza

Abstract

Persons with albinism (PWA) in Tanzania are frequently exploited and discriminated against, and their lives are in constant danger of attack. This is particularly prevalent in the Lake Zone in the northwestern part of the country. It is commonly believed, on the one hand, that PWA are not fully human and are a curse on their families, but, on the other, that their body parts can be a source of good luck for good health or gaining wealth or position. Thus, PWA experience social exclusion and the loss of opportunities while also living in fear for their personal safety. Efforts have been made in recent years, particularly by NGOs, to tackle the plight of PWA so as to bring social change. The church has unfortunately not been at the forefront in addressing this social evil, the roots of which lie deeply embedded in culture and traditional beliefs and therefore can be removed only through the transformative work of the gospel. This chapter explores how the church can be involved in peacemaking and reconciliation with PWA by using Ephesians 2:11–22 in the context of the whole letter to the Ephesians and its purpose. In this passage, Gentiles are brought together with Jews, with Christ himself being their peace, and in him the two become a new humanity, embodying God's plan for the world. In light of this passage and on the basis of insights gained from interviews with PWA, the role of the contemporary church in Tanzania is considered in relation to PWA who are frequently thought of as, like Gentiles, "outsiders," either by others or by themselves.

Key words: albino, albinism, church, Ephesians 2, peacemaking, reconciliation, Tanzania, witchcraft.

Introduction

When Amidu Didas of Ukerewe Island tried to become a musician and record a song, he was thrown out of the local music studio. Teleza Finias exclaims, "When I was born, my father said I wasn't his daughter." "People wouldn't let me get water from the wells," says Elias Sostines.[1] And Emmanuel Festo "has spent much of his life learning to live with what he lost one night when he was six. Four men with machetes hacked off most of his left arm, most of the fingers on his right hand, part of his jaw, and four front teeth, intending to sell them."[2] Why have these four experienced these things? Because they have albinism. Sadly, this is all too common for persons with albinism (PWA).

"Albinism is a rare . . . genetic condition that limits the body's ability to process melanin, reducing or eliminating pigmentation in the skin, eyes, and hair," leaving the person with low vision and without adequate skin protection against the sun's ultraviolet rays. It occurs if both parents carry the recessive

---

1. Alex Marshall, "Feared, Ostracised and Murdered: How Music Saved the Tanzania Albinism Collective," *The Guardian*, 13 August 2017, accessed 10 January 2019, https://www.theguardian.com/music/2017/aug/13/albinos-tanzania-albinism-collective-album-womad-ian-brennan.

2. Susan Ager, "For Them, Being Pale Can Bring Scorn, Threats, and Worse," *National Geographic* 231, no. 6 (June 2017), accessed 10 January 2019, https://www.nationalgeographic.com/magazine/2017/06/albinism-health-genetics-society/.

albinism gene. Worldwide, 1 in 18,000 people have albinism, but in Tanzania the figure stands much higher, at 1 in 1,400.[3]

Sadly, as illustrated above, PWA in Tanzania[4] are frequently exploited and discriminated against, and they are in constant danger of attack, particularly since killings of PWA began in 2006–7. It is commonly believed that PWA are not fully human[5] and are a curse on their families. Children with albinism (CWA) are frequently denied provisions, hidden away, or abandoned by their families. Fathers and/or other family members, misunderstanding the reason for albinism, often blame the mothers for bringing a CWA into the world and bad luck upon the family.

Also, the body parts of PWA (such as fingers, limbs, tongues, and hair) are widely seen as a source of good luck for gaining good health, success, and wealth. Usually, family members are implicated in the attacks on PWA. Thus, PWA experience social exclusion and the loss of opportunities as well as living in fear for their personal safety.

In Sukumaland, part of the Tanzania Lake Zone, where PWA attacks and killings are most prevalent, the roots of this problem have been shown to lie deeply embedded in culture, traditional beliefs, and witchcraft.[6] Methuselah has explored the Sukuma worldview, which he sees as built on causation and fortune-seeking, believing that the world is governed through a complex interaction between God, powers, spirits, and their ancestors,[7] in which Wasukuma, living in fear of these powers and ancestors, seek to please them so that their ancestors will continue to act for them. Intrinsically connected to this is the belief in witchcraft in which a person may visit a diviner who makes a potion from PWA body parts as a way to gain favorable access to such powers and spirits. As one fisherman said, "We can't just go into the lake without some

---

3. "What is Albinism?," Standing Voice, accessed 10 January 2019, www.standingvoice. org/albinism.

4. The problem is wider than Tanzania; see "Reported Attacks of Persons with Albinism," Under the Same Sun, accessed 3 April 2019, http://www.underthesamesun.com/sites/default/ files/Attacks%20of%20PWA%20-%20extended%20version_0.pdf.

5. They are sometimes referred to as "ghosts" (zeruzeru in Swahili).

6. See Julia Gabriel Mutungi, "The Killing of Albinos in Sukumaland, Tanzania: A Challenge to the Church's Mission in the Evangelical Lutheran Church in Tanzania – East of Lake Victoria Diocese" (master's thesis, School of Mission and Theology, Stavanger, Norway, 2013), 30–37.

7. Marco Methuselah, "A Theological Response to the Belief on the Albinos in Some Parts of Tanzania" (master's thesis, Africa International University, 2015), 20–55. See also Joseph Healey and Donald Sybertz, Towards an African Narrative Theology (Mary Knoll, NY: Orbis, 1996), 291.

kind of guidance or protection. Some of us believe in God, but the ones who believe in witch doctors get more than those who believe in God!"[8]

Furthermore, often in African worldviews, sacrifice is demanded by an ancestor, and so the sacrifice of the life of PWA can be seen not as killing, but as good and necessary.

Given that the Mwanza region has three thousand registered witchdoctors, more than any other region, and with an estimated 80 percent of the population consulting traditional healers (many of whom are diviners), it is not hard to see why the problem is so widespread.

Efforts have been made in recent years, particularly by NGOs such as Standing Voice and Under the Same Sun (UTSS), to tackle the issue of the plight of PWA in Tanzania. Unfortunately, the church has not been at the forefront in addressing this social evil, but is lagging behind in taking up its responsibility.

Peter Ash, UTSS founder, asked in a church in Mwanza, "Will all those with albinism please stand up?" And then he added, "Often when I ask this question, it is just the members of our staff who stand up, which means the church is part of the discrimination."[9]

Sadly, we must concur. Christians themselves are often syncretistic and visit the witchdoctor/diviner on Monday after having sung "God is able" on Sunday.[10] Often deep within the culture is a sense that "God is far away, but the diviner is close by."[11] What is apparent is that in many places a Christian veneer has simply been laid over the traditional belief systems, which explains why Christianity has not developed deeper roots and brought a deeper and wider transformation.

It is our belief that since the roots of this social evil lie deeply embedded in culture and traditional beliefs, which also include spiritual powers and witchcraft, justice for PWA can be realized only through the transformative work of the gospel. Therefore, the church must take its place, a place beautifully unveiled in the book of Ephesians.

Thus, by using Ephesians 2:11–22 in the context of the whole letter to the Ephesians, this chapter explores how the Tanzanian church can be involved in peacemaking and reconciliation for PWA. This exploration also harnesses the

---

8. Quoted in Ager, "For Them."

9. This interaction was witnessed in person on 4 May 2014.

10. One of the authors was once asked by a Pentecostal believer from DR Congo, "Why do Tanzanian Christians go to the witchdoctor so much?"

11. Ager, "For Them," quoting retired Tanzanian sociology professor Simeon Mesaki.

views of PWA, mothers of PWA, and those who work with PWA. Although there are other roles for the church, the scope of this chapter is limited to using Ephesians, and Ephesians 2 in particular, as a catalyst for the church's involvement in a way the authors believe the Tanzanian church has generally failed to grasp. So to Ephesians we now turn.

The Letter to the Ephesians and Peacemaking and Reconciliation
Occasion and Purpose of the Letter

Ephesians was likely written by Paul as a circular letter to Christians in and within the vicinity of Ephesus. Ephesus was the leading city of Asia Minor, with influence over the province's politics, commerce, and religious atmosphere. It was cosmopolitan, with many Jews,[12] and with Jew and Gentile tensions apparently present in the city (e.g. Acts 19:23–41). It was known for its religious pluralism and belief in spirits, powers, and magic (cf. Acts 19:11–30). Most significant to the city was the presence of the goddess Artemis, the guardian of the city, whose huge temple lay just outside the city. She was seen as a powerful deity who wielded power over fertility, gave protection from harm, and was able to break the curses of fate. Arnold has made a strong case for seeing a fear of the powers and magic as forming a significant part of the backdrop to the letter.[13] As we will see, this will be important for our purposes concerning albinism and witchcraft.

It seems most plausible that the recipients were a mixed community of mainly Gentiles and probably at least some Jews, who may have been experiencing fear of the powers that sought to rule over them, destroy, and divide, as evidenced by the Jew and Gentile hostilities. In light of this, the author tells the readers how God is reconciling all things in Christ who is above the powers (1:10, 20–22) and is using the church, his new united humanity, as a preview of what he will do for the whole of creation. Thus, the church, being seated with Christ above these powers, should live out this calling, by walking together in love in the power of the Spirit and standing against these powers which seek to destroy the unity of the Spirit and thwart God's plan. Ephesians, then, is the story the church should live in, the drama it is called to perform.[14]

---

12. Josephus, *Antiquities* 14.225–228.

13. Clinton E. Arnold, *Ephesians*, Zondervan Exegetical Commentary on the New Testament (Grand Rapids, MI: Zondervan, 2010), 30–31.

14. For more on Ephesians as drama, see Timothy G. Gombis, *The Drama of Ephesians: Participating in the Triumph of God* (Downers Grove, IL: InterVarsity Press, 2010), 15–36.

Ephesians 2:11–22: Literary Context and Exegesis

Literary Context of Ephesians 2:11–22

Paul begins in 1:3–14 with a Trinitarian *berakah*, blessing God for the spiritual blessings which he has showered on believers ("us"),[15] now with status as adopted "children of God" which enables them to perform their role. The blessings are located in the heavenly realms, the very place inhabited by evil spiritual powers whose rule resulted in fear for those living in Asia Minor. The implication is that the believers need no longer fear those powers but instead can allow these blessings to penetrate and transform their lives. These blessings include the unveiling of his cosmic plan to bring all things together in Christ (1:10). This is a new arrangement for the uniting of the whole cosmos in Christ. The assumption is that everything which evil and spiritual forces have fractured is being brought back together in Christ – that is, under the headship of Christ (1:22; 4:15; 5:23; cf. Col 1:19–20).[16] This plan of reuniting all things in Christ is the key theme that launches the rest of the letter (1:22; 2:14–16; 3:2–6, 10–11; 4:3, 15–16; 5:2, 21). Paul will later explain how the church fits into this plan.

In 1:15–23, Paul prays that the recipients might enter into these spiritual blessings and in particular, as God enables them to see his incomparably great power *available* to them – power which he used to raise Christ, seat him above all the (hostile) powers, and appoint him as head over everything for the church – that they as the church might receive from Christ all the empowering resources they need to fulfill their role in God's plan of 1:10.

Paul turns in 2:1–10 to show the church's path toward appropriating the opening blessings (cf. 1:3–14) and being part of this plan by how God has displayed his power in the lives of the readers. They were all previously "dead" and under the control of evil powers. *But God*, because of his great love for "us," *exerting his power*, has made "us" alive together with Christ and caused "us" to *share* in Christ's resurrection and exaltation above the powers (cf. 1:20), something which displays "us" as God's work of art,[17] his new creation in Christ Jesus for good works.[18]

---

15. Paul carefully employs the use of the pronouns "we"/"you" throughout this letter, to express at times ("we") the inclusivity of Christ's work, and at other times ("you") its particular significance to the readers.

16. See Charles H. Talbert, *Ephesians and Colossians*, Paideia Commentary (Grand Rapids, MI: Baker Academic, 2007), 47.

17. The Greek word is ποίημα which carries the idea of something made by an expert craftsman or designer.

18. The nature of these "good works" will be picked up later in relation to 2:15.

Exegesis of Ephesians 2:11–22

In 2:11–22[19] Paul now applies and extends what he has just said about the reconciliation God has achieved between himself and believers to the mutual relationships of believers, specifically how in Christ he has overcome the hostility between Jews and Gentiles.[20]

In 2:11–13 Paul begins to retell the story of the Gentile Christians. He commences in verse 11 with Διὸ ("Therefore"). Does this refer to 2:1–10 or to 2:10? Although commentators seem to spend little time considering the options, instead simply stating that what follows is in light of 2:1–10,[21] it seems better to us to see both in view. Therefore, 2:11–22 both is in light of their being made alive in Christ and unpacks the significance of their being God's corporate work of art or masterpiece. Paul now turns to address the Gentiles within the church and urges them to remember their story,[22] particularly their pre-Christian plight. First, he references the hostile and derogatory terminology the Jews used of them. They were called "the uncircumcision"[23] – in essence, "the non-covenant ones."[24] Next, he proceeds to show five disadvantages these Gentiles by birth had by being outside the covenant: (1) they were apart from Christ (i.e. not connected to the Jewish Messiah who would bring deliverance), (2) excluded from citizenship in Israel (God's treasured possession), and so (3) outside the covenants of promise (Abrahamic, Sinaitic, Davidic, new covenants), and (4) thus without hope for the future (which comes through the Messiah, the people of Israel, and the covenants), and finally (5) without

---

19. The structure of 2:11–22 is as follows: 2:11–13 – the Gentiles' former hopeless position; 2:14–18 – how Christ has achieved this change of position for the Gentile Christians and the meaning of this in relation to all Christians; 2:19–22 – summing up and applying the meaning of the Gentiles' new position.

20. In many ways, 2:11–22 is a parallel passage to 2:1–10: 2:1–10 tells the story of all Christians whereas 2:11–22 tells the same story as applied to Gentile Christians. See Charles A. Ray Jr, "Removing the Wall (Eph. 2:1–22)," *The Theological Educator* 54 (Fall 1996), 55.

21. See e.g. Arnold, *Ephesians*, 153; Ernest Best, *Ephesians*, International Critical Commentary (London: Bloomsbury T&T Clark, 1998), 237–238; Harold Hoehner, *Ephesians* (Grand Rapids, MI: Baker Academic, 2002), 353; or Andrew T. Lincoln, *Ephesians*, Word Biblical Commentary 42 (Dallas: Word, 1990), 135.

22. One of the questions is whether this passage is attempting to deal with Gentile superiority or even inferiority. Whatever one thinks, it appears that at issue is an appropriate self-understanding by the Gentile believers, particularly since Paul does not pick up an issue with which to address Jewish believers. However, even if this is true, the main aim is to ensure there is harmony within the community where each one experiences equal valuing by others.

23. They were also called "dogs" (cf. Phil 3:2).

24. Paul anticipates where he is going with his additions "in the flesh" and "by the hand" (v. 11) whereby these previous designations for both Jew and Gentile no longer have significance.

God in the world. The author has poignantly revealed the bleak and powerless previous state of the readers (cf. 2:1–3).

But then Paul swiftly exclaims, "But now in Christ Jesus you who were formerly far off have become near by the blood of Christ" (v. 13), that is, all these former disadvantages are done away with "in Christ." "Now" (νυνὶ) implies that "the fullness of the times" (1:10) has come, the time when Gentiles are welcomed and included and brought into union with Christ Jesus by his blood and through faith.[25] This is Paul's main point of this passage, which he will substantiate in verses 14–18 and apply and develop in verses 19–22. "Far" and "near" most likely pick up the proclamation of salvation of Isaiah 57:19, which offered peace to exiled Jews and Jews remaining in the land, but now is applied to Gentiles and Jews.[26] Thus, the sacrificial death of Christ ("by the blood of Christ") is the means of the Gentiles' being brought near to God (cf. 1:7) and has created a new reality for them (cf. Isa 56:3–5), both fulfilling Isaiah 56:6–8 and the "house of prayer for all nations" and transcending the possibilities offered to them in Judaism as proselytes.

Paul immediately offers this stunning explanation in 2:14–16 of how these Gentiles can be "near": "For [Christ] himself is *our* peace" (v. 14, emphasis added)! In a dramatic change from second person plural to first person plural, Paul shows the unity Christ has achieved between Jew and Gentile as the following phrase, "who has made both [groups] one," makes clear. They have peace, not in an agreement, but in a person! εἰρήνη ("peace")[27] often refers to political peace, which fits the Ephesian context where hostilities have ended between Jew and Gentile.[28] But Paul has been drawing on Isaiah (esp. 57:19) where the concept of peace (*shalom*), meaning "wholeness" or "well-being," includes relational and political dimensions and is brought about in the era of the Messiah. Thus, Isaiah's vision of eschatological peace when the Gentiles would join Israel in worship in the temple on Mount Zion (Isa 2:2–4), including the celebration of God's reign and presence (Isa 52:7–10), has now been realized

---

25. For the eschatological ingathering of the nations, see e.g. Isa 2:2–5; 45:22–23; 49:6; 56:6–7; Zech 8:20–23; 9:10.

26. See Lincoln, *Ephesians*, 131, 138.

27. *Peace* is the dominant concept here, being mentioned four times in 2:14–18.

28. From a Jewish point of view, humanity was divided into two, Jews and Gentiles (i.e. non-Jews). So this unity is worldwide unity.

in Jesus (cf. Isa 9:6; 11:1–9). This unity[29] between Jew and Gentile has been achieved in his death by his tearing down the dividing wall of hostility between the two. But to what does this wall refer? The Old Testament law or the wall in the temple that separated Jew and Gentile and was the cause of much enmity? Commentators are divided here.[30] Although there is a lot of temple imagery in this passage, overall it more likely refers to the Mosaic law as a whole (cf. "circumcision" v. 11 and "law of commandments" v. 15a) and its perceived hostile boundary-marking commandments, although the abolition of the latter also makes provision for the abolition of the former.

Paul does not stop there, as if merely the cessation of hostilities was sufficient, but continues with Christ's greater purpose (ἵνα)[31] – Paul's main point in verses 14–18 – that Christ might create a whole new people, "a new humanity," with the result of making peace, whereby hostility and alienation give way to full reconciliation in one body. What does this new humanity mean and look like? It is a new human race, no longer in Adam (cf. Gen 1:26–28; 2:7) but a new creation in Christ (cf. Rom 5:12–21; 2 Cor 5:17; Gal 6:15), which now takes its identity from Christ himself and bears his likeness. Therefore, the old ethnic identities of Jew and Gentile, and for that matter any identities of race, gender, and background, have no further significance or rank in this new people (cf. Gal 3:28). Moreover, given that Paul uses the verb κτίζω[32] ("to create," v. 15), this most likely picks up and explains "For we are God's workmanship created in Christ Jesus to do good works" (2:10). Commentators do not seem to make this connection[33] but just interpret 2:10 individually, thus weakening the link between 2:1–10 and 2:11–22. But this seems to miss the flow of Paul's argument. It seems better to see this new

---

29. Paul may have in mind the huge riot in Ephesus to which Jewish and Gentile tensions contributed (Acts 19:23–41). His great vision is that this church will not add to racial tensions in the city, but, as God's new humanity, will rise above old divisions and be an instrument of God's healing and peace.

30. E.g. Arnold, *Ephesians*, 159–160; and Lincoln, *Ephesians*, 141–142. See also Craig McMahan, "The Wall Is Gone," *Review and Expositor* 93 (1996): 262; and Bruce W. Fong, "Addressing the Issue of Racial Reconciliation according to the Principles of Eph 2:11–22," *Journal of the Evangelical Theological Society* 38, no. 4 (Dec. 1995): 573–574.

31. The purpose comes in two parts through two subjunctives: "that in him he might *create* a new humanity" (v. 15) and "in one body *reconcile* both of them" (v. 16); emphasis added.

32. This verb occurs in 2:10, 15; 4:24. Paul is surely anticipating vv. 14–18 with his phrase in 2:10, "[we *together* were] created in Christ Jesus," adding weight to the thought that God's work of art is a new humanity.

33. E.g. see the otherwise excellent commentaries by Arnold, *Ephesians*, 164; F. F. Bruce, *The Epistles to the Colossians, to Philemon, and to the Ephesians* (Grand Rapids, MI: Eerdmans, 1984), 299; or Lincoln, *Ephesians*, 143–144.

humanity as God's corporate "work of art" or "masterpiece" (2:10), the first part of God's bringing all things together in Christ (1:10). And the works that God has prepared in advance that "we should walk in" (2:10) are none other than walking together and living out being God's new united people (for the rulers and principalities to see, 3:10[34]), which Paul will unpack in chapters 4–6. This point will be developed more in the application to albinism in the next section, but for now we can say we believe that the Tanzanian church has yet to grasp the power of being God's corporate work of art and that its corporate life is missional. The result of creating this new humanity was "establishing peace" between Jew and Gentile and so the solution has fixed the problem of hostility and distance (2:12–14).

In verse 16, Paul picks up the second part of Christ's purpose which was to effect reconciliation – namely, to bring Jew and Gentile fully together in one body – and emphasizes that the first part has indeed achieved Christ's aim of reconciliation "in one body."[35] The means of this reconciliation was the cross which put to death (literally and figuratively) in Christ their hostility toward one another. In his death, Jesus thus experienced hostility in order to end "our" hostility to one another.

So in summary – somewhat in a chiastic fashion with verses 13–14 – Paul in 2:17–18 comes back to say that when Christ came he preached peace to the Gentiles who were far off and to the Jews who were near (cf. Isa 57:19), because through him both have access in one Spirit to the Father. This also shows that both Jews and Gentiles needed to be reconciled to God, and Christ's death achieved both. It was not the case that the Gentiles needed simply to come to the position of Jews as if to be Judaized. No, what was needed was a whole new humanity. Bantum is right when he says, "In this overcoming Jesus knits two particular peoples within himself and thus the atoning work of Christ creates something new among those peoples."[36] Paul marvelously draws the whole argument together with the Trinitarian picture of both Gentiles and Jews coming through Christ in the one Spirit to worship the Father as one body! In so doing he has united the horizontal reconciliation (2:11–17) with the vertical reconciliation (2:1–10). Through Jesus's work on the cross all the

---

34. Works of art are meant to be displayed!

35. This phrase may have a double meaning of "in the church as one body" and "in Christ's own physical body."

36. Brian Bantum, "To Those Who Were Distant and Those Who Were Near: Atonement, Identity, and Identification," *Ex Auditu* 26 (2010): 138. He also notes, "The Day of the Atonement [which lies behind this passage] was about a reconciliation of Israel's personhood" (142).

barriers to God for all have been removed and now, in the new age, Jews and Gentiles alike have equal and free access to *the Father*.

In the final paragraph (2:19–22), Paul, with his "Consequently then," begins to sum up his whole argument before reaching his climax when he beautifully unveils what this new entity of Jews and Gentiles together is. First, he applies what he has just said about the readers' new nearness to God and peaceful relationship with Jewish believers to say that the readers are no longer "strangers and foreigners" (cf. v. 12) – that is, they are no longer "Gentiles." Rather, they are "fellow citizens with the saints[37] and members of the household of God."[38] What they previously lacked they now share in fully and equally. The one new humanity/the one body (2:15–16) is now reinterpreted as the household of God. Thus, these readers, along with all Christians, are part of the family of God (cf. "adopted to be sons," 1:5) where they are now brother and sister, instead of divided as enemies, with the same Father. These members of God's household are then likened to the building itself, in which they are the building materials, "having been built on the foundation of the apostles and prophets,[39] Christ Jesus himself being the cornerstone" (v. 20). The main point is clear for the readers: the building of which they are a part has a strong and sure foundation, being built on the gospel of Christ, and can never fall. In many ways, Paul is restating what he has said in verses 14–16, not least in the final phrase "with Christ Jesus himself as the cornerstone," which picks up "he is our peace . . . in his flesh . . . in him." If all things are being brought together in Christ (1:10), then naturally he would be the cornerstone[40] of the new building. Here Paul seems to be drawing on the cornerstone of Isaiah 28:16. There Yahweh is building Zion, laying a tested stone, a cornerstone, which is to be built upon by trust. The cornerstone was the most important part of the foundation. It was a large stone that "bore much of the weight of the building and tied [two adjacent] walls together,"[41] here tying Jew and Gentile

---

37. Either Jewish Christians or Christians in general.

38. In the Greek "members of the household of God" is οἰκεῖοι τοῦ θεοῦ, where οἰκεῖοι includes the sense of belonging in which the members form a closely knit community.

39. Given that both the readers and Jesus Christ are described as materials of the building, it is best to take "the foundation of the apostles and prophets" as appositional, meaning "the foundation which is the apostles and prophets." But as one can hardly separate Jesus and his work on the cross, so one can hardly separate these leaders and their foundational work of proclaiming the work of Jesus Christ on the cross, which has been stressed in vv. 14–18 as the bedrock of this new unity.

40. Since the context is about the foundation of the building it is most likely ἀκρπγωνιαίου should be translated as "cornerstone" rather than "capstone."

41. Arnold, *Ephesians*, 171.

together. Christ is the new stone God has placed in Zion, the foundation for the new people of God in a new order (cf. Isa 2:2–4).

And so Paul continues, "in [Jesus] the whole building being joined together grows into a holy temple in the Lord, in whom you also are being built together into the dwelling of God by the Spirit" (vv. 21–22). Having spoken of the foundation of the building, he now describes the superstructure and finally the occupancy. First, the whole building is being joined together in Jesus, very much like the work of a cornerstone. And we learn that this building grows into a holy temple in the Lord, expounding the thought of verse 18 where they both have access to the Father in the presence of the Spirit. Paul draws on the image of the Jerusalem temple, which was the focal point of every aspect of the national life of Israel, being a political, religious, and cultural center. It was a place of community, of feasting and celebration, worship, prayer, and hope. It was seen as the joining of heaven and earth, the symbol of the dwelling of God himself. Interestingly, this new temple is unfinished:[42] it is one that continually grows as more people are added. Here the author transforms this image of temple into the church, which is to be a holy temple in the Lord, given over to the Lord and his purposes. Paul brings this temple image to bear specifically on the readers by adding, "in whom [i.e. Christ] you also are being built together": these Gentiles Christians are now being built together with their Jewish believers into its superstructure (a first fulfillment of 1:10; cf. also 1 Pet 2:4–6). This image of the temple does not stop here with the new people as the bricks, but concludes with this newly joined-together people becoming a home for God. This is how 1:23 gets worked out: God, by filling the ever-growing temple with his presence, fills all things. Now by his Spirit God indwells his people corporately, who are this new temple which has no interior barrier or walls (cf. vv. 14–15). This temple truly is, by the indwelling of the Spirit, the joining of heaven and earth: the sign and instrument for God's bringing all things together in and under Christ! This temple also shows God's reconciling vertically and horizontally. He has indeed overcome the powers and is "near" to them (cf. vv. 13, 18).

So in conclusion, we see the church is God's new creation in Christ, a new humanity, which turns out to be a new temple, which displays rich and unbroken community with both God and one another. This temple is still being built as more people are made alive in Christ. Believing Gentiles could not now have a more privileged position! As Lincoln says, "[Believers'] new privileged

---

42. Arnold, 171–172.

position in the church owes everything to Christ."[43] This passage is designed to lead the readers to a fresh appreciation of Christ's powerful reconciling work – now they are with hope in the world and with God – so much so that they continue to grow into this new community where God's healing, power, and presence are made known to the world.[44]

The Rest of Ephesians: Chapters 3–6

In chapter 3, Paul emphasizes the role of the church as this new united people (cf. 2:15) in God's eternal purposes (picking up 1:10) of disclosing God's manifold wisdom to the world's principalities and powers; namely, that these powers which seek to destroy and divide have lost (3:10).[45] As Ernest Best says, "The reconciliation of Jews and Gentiles in the church is a kind of pilot scheme for a much greater reconciliation in which the powers will in turn be embraced."[46] Then Paul prays that the Father would strengthen the church so that as it grasps God's power it might become all that God intends, being the new humanity, the inhabited temple of God, thus participating in God's reconciling purposes.

At this point, the center of the letter (4:1), Paul urges the recipients, based on God's calling of them and his power available to them described in chapters 1–3, to walk worthily of this calling, which is chiefly to maintain the unity of the Spirit (the one new humanity of Jew and Gentile together) and to grow this unity until together they as the body of Christ fully reach the likeness of Christ (4:1–16, picking up 1:23 and 3:10, participating in Christ's triumph over the powers, 4:8). In 4:17 – 5:20 he fleshes out what this looks like for the church in practical daily living with Christ-reflecting virtues for new-age living that contribute to the unity and growth as well as the mission of the church (5:3–7, 8–14; cf. 1:10, 23; 2:10; 4:10). This happens as they, the temple, are filled with the Spirit who is the power for walking ethically and worshipping (5:15–20; cf. 2:21–22), as well as for living out being God's new humanity in their households (5:21 – 6:9). Finally, Paul now urges the recipients to guard the vision for living out their calling as God's people by being strong in the Lord and his mighty power so as to withstand the schemes of the devil, who

---

43. Lincoln, *Ephesians*, 162.

44. See Lincoln, 165.

45. Gombis says, "God demonstrates his power by his ability to create his one new people and to make them flourish in the midst of enemy territory, thus confounding the evil powers" (Gombis, *Drama*, 116).

46. Best, *Ephesians*, 326.

works to wreck that vision through "the rulers, the authorities, the powers of this dark world and the spiritual forces of evil in the heavenly realms" to pull apart the church (6:10–20; cf. 1:9–10; 3:10). Paul thus returns to the themes of "power" and "strength" with which he began in 1:19 and continued until 3:20. This vision, inaugurated by Christ's victory and enthronement as Lord over the powers (1:20–22; 4:8–10), is under threat by these powers who are trying to oppose the church's involvement in God's worldwide plan in Christ (1:9–10; 3:10). Thus, they need not Artemis's but God's protection.

Letting Ephesians Loose in the Church as Its Inspiration for Peacemaking and Reconciliation with PWA

As we have seen, Ephesians offers the church a truly awe-inspiring and far-reaching vision for its life as God's people. Indeed, the vision is to share in God's cosmic plan of bringing together everything which evil has fractured, pulled apart, and damaged so that it all fits together and works as a cohesive whole under the lordship of Christ (1:9–10). As Lincoln so aptly says, "If the church in Ephesians 2 stands for the overcoming of that fundamental division of humanity into either Jew or Gentile, it stands for the overcoming of all divisions caused by tradition, class, color, nation, or groups of nations. Anything less would be a denial of that nature of the Church which this writer takes as axiomatic."[47]

This plan, therefore, of course includes PWA finding their place, accepted as precious in society, and making their contribution to the running of God's world. When this happens, God's manifold wisdom will be disclosed to the principalities and powers – a wisdom that among other things will display the value, significance, and contribution of PWA, informing these powers of their limitation and weakness.

Sadly, the church in Tanzania has often failed to appreciate this vision and its role in it, instead settling for a sub-existence. In so doing, it simply accepts the status quo, unwittingly colludes with the powers and spiritual forces, and wonders why it has little impact in society. It is time for the church in Tanzania to grasp this vision and role in God's story, realizing that Ephesians is its script, to bring healing to what the spiritual forces seek to divide and harm, which includes PWA.[48]

---

47. Lincoln, *Ephesians*, 161–162.
48. Cf. Gombis, *Drama*, 62.

In this regard, prayer is important (1:15–23), that the church's eyes might be enlightened so that it may understand the current plight of PWA, realizing that Christ is above all the powers, including the power of witchcraft. No longer do members need to fear or submit to such powers: this is good news to Tanzanian Christians, many of whom still fear such powers. Rather, God's mighty power in Christ is available to them (who are also seated with Christ above the powers) as they fulfill their role as the church in the world.

Ephesians 2:1–10 reminds church members of two profound things. First, we all share a common history, one of being dead in our sins, being under the power of the ruler of this age (and by implication under the power of spirits and other powers), and deserving of God's wrath. Second, we have all equally been given new life in Christ based on God's love, mercy, and grace. There is no room for any of us to view ourselves as superior to our brothers and sisters in Christ, including our brothers and sisters who are PWA. We are all in the same boat! This passage concludes with our seeing that God wants to lift us up as his workmanship and has great things for us to do. Though we saw that the focus is on the corporate nature of this workmanship, this cannot be at the exclusion of the individual. Christian PWA are God's works of art (cf. 2 Cor 5:17).[49] And the church will not be able to be all that God intends and participate in his mission (cf. 1:10) if our self-understanding remains rooted in our former identities.

Applying Ephesians 2:11–22 to the Church with PWA

Now let us begin drawing out the application of our main passage, Ephesians 2:11–22. It is vital churches take seriously that our reconciliation with God (2:1–10) lays the ground for and necessitates our reconciliation with one another as members of the same family (2:11–22); otherwise the former is not complete!

In preparation for this, the authors conducted research among thirty-one people who have albinism, have children with albinism, or work with people with albinism, in order to gain their perspectives. Participants included those within and outside the church. Surveys were carried out, which first considered their experience of albinism with family members, society, and church, and its effect on them. Second, participants were asked questions about how they

---

49. If it is common to emphasize that all people are created in the image of God, this passage focuses on *new creation*, with our being new creations, being remade and bearing the likeness of Christ (cf. Eph 4:13).

believe the church as a community can be an example of transformation and encouragement to create a better Tanzania. Finally, Christian participants were invited to reflect on how Ephesians 2:11–22 can be used to inspire the church in its work among PWA.

1. The Importance of the Church's Understanding of the Plight of PWA (2:11–13)

In 2:11–12, Paul spoke to the Gentile believers about their need to remember their former situation so they could appreciate their new blessings in Christ. Today, it is not Christian PWA who need to remember what it was/is like – they know it only too well. It is other church members! Many respondents mentioned that the church needs to understand better what life is like for PWA in Tanzania. Two specific comments are worth noting. First, just as the Gentiles were referred to in derogatory terms, so also PWA are frequently called unpleasant and hurtful names, such as *zeruzeru* or *dili dili*.[50] In essence they have their identity defined by others in terms of the color of their skin or their disability, an identity that they often cannot help but imbibe themselves.[51] Similarly, those PWA who are students but who, because of their poor eyesight, cannot see the blackboard are incorrectly labeled "stupid." They can even hear the taunt as they walk along the road: "Walking money!"[52] Churches therefore need to think carefully about the language they use about PWA in general and Christian PWA in particular, to ensure that it reflects who they are in Christ and so builds up the whole Christian community. Churches should help Christian PWA grow into their new identity in Christ, an identity that is full of healing and guarantees a wonderful inheritance, rather than hindering them from experiencing their full blessings in Christ (cf. 1:3–14).

Second, all respondents who are PWA or mothers of CWA explained they had experienced exclusion in some form. The Gentile readers of Ephesians were excluded from citizenship in Israel, the covenants of the promise, and hope. So also PWA are frequently denied the rights of citizenship, which include the right to education, to work opportunities, and to live peaceful lives, so much so that they are without promise or hope. The most common social exclusion

---

50. The Swahili word for a person with albinism is *zeruzeru*, and *dili dili* is a deal that brings money.

51. "I feel bad," "I am a problem," "I am a person at the bottom," "I am not a full person" were some of the self-designations from participants.

52. This refers to the value of their body parts for witchdoctors.

experienced by PWA is from their own families. One respondent mentioned they lost their relationship with their father. Another was told by a family member that they did not want an albino in the family. The family is the place where more than anywhere else we are supposed to find our acceptance and belonging, our nurturing and our security, and the place from which we are launched out into the world. Churches should realize that for a person to have been deprived of these, and worse still, maybe to have been abandoned by his or her family, leaves that person truly at a disadvantage with regard to succeeding in life (cf. 2:12). In essence, PWA are frequently considered as "Gentiles" and feel themselves to be "outsiders." The church needs "to enter" the world of PWA (cf. John 1:14) and as far as possible understand the lives of PWA or loving families with PWA as an essential step in sharing in Christ's mission of bringing wholeness to the world.

Next, the church should consider how 2:13 ("But now in Christ Jesus you who once were far away have been brought near by the blood of Christ") can be heard loud and clear by all Christian PWA, not only in words but also through the loving actions of the church. We must not underestimate the power of experiencing this nearness for those who for their whole lives have been told to go away or have been abandoned. This role has evangelistic, pastoral, and community dimensions. Respondents spoke of the opportunity for the church to offer trauma counseling and prayer for inner healing so that PWA can enter into this nearness with God in Christ. And one respondent who is a Christian PWA wanted the church to explain apparent inconsistencies in the Bible concerning people with disabilities, citing the Old Testament law where persons with disabilities were barred from serving in the temple (i.e. they were kept at a "distance"). There is an opportunity for the church to teach the whole counsel of God, particularly the Bible as the unfolding story of God's redemption. Interestingly, Isaiah 56:4–5, which probably lies in the background of Ephesians 2, says,

> To the eunuchs[53] who keep my Sabbaths,
>   who choose what pleases me
>   and hold fast to my covenant –
> to them I will give within my temple and its walls
>   a memorial and a name
>   better than sons and daughters;

---

53. Eunuchs, by their being maimed, were previously excluded from the temple (Deut 23:1) but in the new messianic age are fully welcomed in, since what counts for wholeness is not outer appearance but inner devotion.

> I will give them an everlasting name
>> that will endure forever.

What an encouragement to PWA and other people with disabilities!

2. Understanding the Corporate Peace (2:14–18)

Verse 14 begins with, "For he himself is our peace." The church should reflect on this and allow it to sink deep into its being: that Jesus Christ is the essence of the harmony among all members of the church. To know peace with our brothers and sisters with albinism can only truly be found in Jesus. Jesus cannot be avoided in the search for peace, as many try unsuccessfully to do. Therefore, for the church to fail to be active in assisting PWA to appropriate this peace is to deny the work of Christ on the cross. We should appreciate that the peace created by Christ results in a completely new entity. It is not just a case of adding PWA into existing church entities and structures; these entities and structures themselves need to be made anew in Christ. All of us need to be changed and made whole in order to be fit for this new entity. One of the challenges in Africa is that, for instance, the entities of tribe, family, gender, and hierarchy often seem to be untouchable and even defended by the church. In this way the church castrates itself and aligns itself with the powers that maintain differences and discrimination.[54] Instead, churches need to reflect on their corporate life so that it exhibits the life of the kingdom of God.

A good example is Beacon Mission Christian Centre in Mwanza which has a ministry to CWA. One Sunday, during a church lunch after the service, the pastor announced, "Today there is no high table, no middle table, no low table. We are all at the high table. You are free to sit anywhere." People lined up together for the same food: CWA, ordinary church members, elders, pastors, and special guests. They all mixed together as they ate the same food at the same table. This was a powerful demonstration of the equality of the church, and was a tremendous healing experience for those CWA and PWA who for all their lives had been downtrodden and excluded; that day they were lifted up, treated as fully human,[55] and integrated in the sight of all. And for the church itself, it was a reshaping of identities into a unified whole. It is time for church leaders to heed Jesus's words in Matthew 23:6 to the position-seeking

---

54. E.g. Rwanda, where, in the 1994 genocide, for many Christians their basic identity came from their tribe rather than from their being in Christ, and thus they failed to stand up for their Christian brothers and sisters of the opposite tribe.

55. Indeed they experienced the *new humanity* and no longer being viewed as "ghosts."

Pharisees and to take an axe to unhealthy African traditions, so that the church becomes what Jesus achieved for it in his death. Church leaders should take up *their own servant role* of equipping and building up the whole body of Christ (Eph 4:11–13).

If churches are serious about experiencing this communal peace, they need to understand what the walls of hostility are and be active in tearing them down.[56] We would encourage churches to listen to PWA and give them an opportunity to share redemptively about the hostility they have experienced. And just as Jesus experienced hostility which resulted in his death to overcome the hostility between Jew and Gentile, so church members need to be willing to face hostility themselves on behalf of PWA, by standing with them and being advocates for them, thereby demonstrating to PWA and others the reality of the new communal love in Christ. One advocate of PWA said, "People do not understand why I defend the rights of persons with albinism if I do not have albinism or a child or relative with albinism. I have been on a boat and a bus where people stared at us because I was with children with albinism; some of them moved away from our seats and others called them names." In response to having received many threats, this person said, "At first I felt angry and lost because I did not understand why people would treat PWA as less human. Later I felt more empowered and I was determined to help change the public perception about albinism."

Churches need to grasp deeply the words "For through him we both have access to the Father by one Spirit" (Eph 2:18). Three implications are noteworthy. First, implicitly there is the understanding that we are all equally children of God (cf. 1:4–5). Therefore, if God has chosen our brothers and sisters with albinism, for us to fail to treat them with high respect is also to fail to honor the One who chose them. Second, for PWA, many of whom have lost relationships with or been excluded by their families, and often their fathers in particular, the good news here is that they have a new belonging with full access to a new Father. Churches will need to assist PWA to come into the joy of having a new Father, given what they have experienced. This should include offering PWA seats at the front of the congregation as a simple but powerful symbol of the good access they now possess; this will also help them to participate better, given their poor eyesight. Helping them get large-print Bibles also enables them to have good access to their Father. Third, the whole

---

56. Bertram L. Melbourne, "Ephesians 2:13–16: Are the Barriers Still Broken Down?," *The Journal of Religious Thought* 57/58, no. 2/1–2 (2001–2005): 116–117, makes this point well in terms of race.

church can appreciate and demonstrate that in Christ and by the Spirit God is now close and there is no longer any need to visit the diviner, which will increase peace for PWA.

3. Building the Family of God as God's New Humanity, His Masterpiece (2:19–22)

It is vital that churches in Tanzania do not just reluctantly or mentally accept this new peace, but positively and actively embrace it, so that it becomes an experienced reality. In many ways, this paragraph is the icing on the cake of Ephesians 2:11–22 in which Paul drives his point home and applies it to the church. First, the church must become a new home for PWA where they truly belong, find and give love, and support and share in the responsibilities of God's household. In this regard, it is paramount that church members appreciate their fundamental identity as children of God and thus members of the family of God, and that their first loyalty is to it, rather than to a natural family, tribe, nation, social background, color, or anything else. This is a big challenge to the Tanzanian, and indeed the African, church. But if the church can grasp its identity, all that PWA have missed out on, such as family, love, and protection, can be provided for them by the church. Therefore, the church must work at *being a community*, not just offering a time and place for services. Practically, PWA suggest that the church should build relationships with them through acknowledging the presence of PWA, praying for and encouraging PWA, helping PWA to know God and love themselves, visiting PWA in their homes and schools to understand their needs, assisting PWA to get glasses, hats, full-covering clothing, and sun cream, and helping them to find employment and education opportunities. Churches should also be willing to offer PWA safe housing when necessary, possibly with other church members, thus displaying the "new family."

Second, the church should be active in seeking to grow as this integrated family. Paul wonderfully uses a plethora of images to show the glory of the church. It is clear that the building is the temple (v. 21), which is also the household/family of God (v. 19), which is none other than the new humanity (v. 15) and God's masterpiece (v. 10). It is a shame that so many churches refer to the church building, rather than the church community, as the house of God and the sanctuary. This is not only biblically incorrect, but it also means the church is failing to reflect on its identity and calling. The church must realize that as a people it is God's masterpiece or work of art, and thus a new way of being human, and that until there are PWA faces shining out from its life together, that masterpiece will never be finished nor its full beauty seen. Efforts should be taken to build this temple, PWA with non-PWA, brick upon brick (v. 22). PWA recommend utilizing their gifts, such as by giving them ministry and leadership opportunities to serve alongside non-PWA. They are keen to point out that there should be no special favors, but such opportunities should be given only to the gifted. Unfortunately, however, all too often the gifts of PWA are simply overlooked and "the riches of his glorious inheritance in his holy people"[57] (1:18) are unrealized. Churches may wish to explore the African concept of *ubuntu* in the context of PWA and non-PWA reconciliation and growing together.[58]

The image of (PWA and non-PWA) bricks being laid together to form a temple is a potent demonstration of God's plan to bring all of creation together (cf. 1:10). It is important to remember that the Old Testament temple was supposed to be a place to which the Gentiles would be drawn and where they would be welcomed as fellow worshippers, as evidenced by Jesus's words, "My house will be called a house of prayer for all nations" (Mark 11:17; cf. Isa 56:7), meaning a place where all nations can pray together. PWA and those who work with them recognize the value of this and that it is a part of the church's being a light to the world (cf. Eph 3:10). For this reason, they also suggest that churches offer seminars, conducted by PWA and non-PWA together, to educate society about albinism, and to show what PWA are capable of and that love has conquered social norms. They also believe that when the church acts in this way, by being a model society whose foundation is Christ and where everyone is a full citizen (cf. v. 19), other PWA may be encouraged to come to Christ, as might other groups of people who normally feel excluded, such as those with other disabilities or with HIV/AIDS. It will be a masterpiece displayed for all to see.

Third, since the ultimate purpose of this temple is to be the dwelling place of God (v. 22), when churches embody the character of God – love, peace, grace, acceptance – they may experience the presence of God more fully. As church members, across social divides, allow themselves to be built together to

---

57. This phrase refers to God's wonderful inheritance which is his people, comprising both Jews and Gentiles and both PWA and non-PWA; thus to ignore one group is to perceive his inheritance as limited.

58. Desmond Tutu says, "*Ubuntu* is the essence of being human. A person is a person through other persons. We are made for togetherness, to live in a delicate network of interdependence." Quoted in Robert Kaggwa, "Is Reconciliation the New Model for Mission? Reflections on the Rwandan Genocide and Conflicts in the Great Lakes Region of Africa," *Studies in World Christianity* 9, no. 2 (2003): 257.

become a dwelling in which God lives by his Spirit, they will all meet God in a powerful way, worshipping him as one body, and thus all experience his healing transformation. As Plantinga Pauw says, "Christians are invited into this new space,"[59] a space where forgiveness can be asked for, peace and reconciliation enjoyed, and God adored together. The church will indeed be a united family and a temple filled with the presence and glory of God (cf. 1 Kgs 8:10–11).

The Rest of Ephesians in Relation to Peacemaking with PWA

In briefly considering the contribution of the remainder of Ephesians, we mention four points. (1) Ephesians 3:10–11 places the preceding discussion on the church as God's new humanity firmly on the world stage of God's activities, and so churches need to be encouraged that being reconciling communities for PWA is of cosmic significance. (2) We would encourage churches to pray the prayer of Ephesians 3:14–21 in their gatherings, with reconciliation of peoples in mind. (3) Churches should be aware that being united with PWA takes hard and indeed daily work to maintain the unity of the Spirit, but the opportunity to move toward it is worth it: "so that the body of Christ may be built up until we all reach unity in the faith and in the knowledge of the Son of God and become mature, attaining to the whole measure of the fullness of Christ" (4:12–13). It takes the whole body of Christ, PWA and non-PWA, to bear the likeness of Christ. (4) Churches should be aware that even after they have started to go down this road, the enemy will seek to destroy them and their unity with PWA; thus they should be ready to take their stand together against his schemes (6:10–20).

Conclusion

This research has shown how Ephesians 2:11–22 and its place within the letter can inspire Tanzanian churches to become peacemaking and reconciling communities for PWA, who can be fully embraced as equal members with non-PWA. Such communities are possible because Jesus has triumphed over spiritual forces and the power of witchcraft that hold many Tanzanians in fear and bondage, resulting in division and discrimination. Now, Tanzanian Christians, PWA and non-PWA, as they are seated together with Christ, above these defeated powers, can enjoy rich and profound fellowship as brothers

---

59. Amy Plantinga Pauw, "Theological Meditations on Ephesians 2:11–22," *Theology Today* 62 (2005): 81.

and sisters, knowing that "unity is power."[60] In so doing, they will display themselves as *God's magnificent corporate masterpiece* and radiate to society the multicolored wisdom of God, who has stunningly confounded the powers and brought a peace that no one and no organization could achieve or even imagine possible.

Bibliography

Ager, Susan. "For Them, Being Pale Can Bring Scorn, Threats, and Worse." *National Geographic* 231, no. 6 (June 2017). Accessed 10 January 2019. https://www.nationalgeographic.com/magazine/2017/06/albinism-health-genetics-society/.

Arnold, Clinton E. *Ephesians*. Zondervan Exegetical Commentary on the New Testament. Grand Rapids, MI: Zondervan, 2010.

Bantum, Brian. "To Those Who Were Distant and Those Who Were Near: Atonement, Identity, and Identification." *Ex Auditu* 26 (2010): 128–144.

Best, Ernest. *Ephesians*. International Critical Commentary. London: Bloomsbury T&T Clark, 1998.

Bruce, F. F. *The Epistles to the Colossians, to Philemon, and to the Ephesians*. Grand Rapids, MI: Eerdmans, 1984.

Fong, Bruce W. "Addressing the Issue of Racial Reconciliation according to the Principles of Eph 2:11–22." *Journal of the Evangelical Theological Society* 38, no. 4 (Dec. 1995): 565–580.

Gombis, Timothy G. *The Drama of Ephesians: Participating in the Triumph of God*. Downers Grove, IL: InterVarsity Press, 2010.

Healey, Joseph, and Donald Sybertz. *Towards an African Narrative Theology*. Mary Knoll, NY: Orbis, 1996.

Hoehner, Harold. *Ephesians*. Grand Rapids, MI: Baker Academic, 2002.

Kaggwa, Robert. "Is Reconciliation the New Model for Mission? Reflections on the Rwandan Genocide and Conflicts in the Great Lakes Region of Africa." *Studies in World Christianity* 9, no. 2 (2003): 244–264.

Lincoln, Andrew T. *Ephesians*. Word Biblical Commentary 42. Dallas: Word, 1990.

Marshall, Alex. "Feared, Ostracised and Murdered: How Music Saved the Tanzania Albinism Collective." *The Guardian*, 13 August 2017. Accessed 10 January 2019. https://www.theguardian.com/music/2017/aug/13/albinos-tanzania-albinism-collective-album-womad-ian-brennan.

McMahan, Craig. "The Wall Is Gone!" *Review and Expositor* 93 (1996): 261–266.

Melbourne, Bertram L. "Ephesians 2:13–16: Are the Barriers Still Broken Down?" *The Journal of Religious Thought* 57/58, no. 2/1–2 (2001–2005): 107–117.

---

60. This is the English translation of the Swahili proverb *umoja ni nguvu*.

Methuselah, Marco. "A Theological Response to the Belief on the Albinos in Some Parts of Tanzania." Master's thesis, Africa International University, 2015.

Mutungi, Julia Gabriel. "The Killing of Albinos in Sukumaland, Tanzania: A Challenge to the Church's Mission in the Evangelical Lutheran Church in Tanzania – East of Lake Victoria Diocese." Master's thesis, School of Theology and Mission (a university owned by the Norwegian Mission Society), Stavanger, Norway, 2013.

Plantinga Pauw, Amy. "Theological Meditations on Ephesians 2:11–22." *Theology Today* 62 (2005): 78–83.

Ray, Charles A., Jr. "Removing the Wall (Eph. 2:1–22)." *The Theological Educator* 54 (Fall 1996): 53–59.

Talbert, Charles H. *Ephesians and Colossians*. Paideia Commentary. Grand Rapids, MI: Baker Academic, 2007.

"What Is Albinism?" Standing Voice. Accessed 10 January 2019. www.standingvoice.org/albinism.

6

Re-Reading Spanish Medieval *Convivencia*

Lessons for Christian–Muslim Relations among Borana People of Marsabit, Kenya

Judy Wang'ombe and Harun Wang'ombe
PhD Candidates, Africa International University, Nairobi

Abstract

The population of Borana people in Marsabit County, Kenya, comprises Muslims and Christians who have coexisted with minimal conflict. Interfaith relations and peaceful coexistence are essential for the stability of society and the healthy expression of one's faith. There are lessons from historical encounters between Islam and Christianity that can be applied in the contemporary context to promote mutual understanding. Yet more significantly are the biblical/theological insights that can be gleaned to suggest means of enhancing peaceful coexistence between Muslims and Christians in Marsabit County. This chapter begins by recollecting the significant historical realities of the Spanish medieval coexistence (*convivencia*) of Jews, Christians, and Muslims which began about AD 711 and spanned a period of more than seven hundred years. It was experienced in two major epochs, one under Islamic rule and the other under Christian rule, during which there was relative peace among the three religions. However, a change of attitude toward each other and a desire for the religion in power to dominate the others disrupted this experience, which to the present day is looked upon with nostalgia. This chapter then derives significant lessons from this history for the contemporary situation among the Borana people, as a case in Africa, into how *convivencia* might be possible if we avoid some of the pitfalls encountered in the Spanish experience. A Christian response toward peaceful coexistence in the Marsabit context is also suggested.

Key words: *Convivencia*, Reconquista, Christian–Muslim relations, Borana, coexistence.

Introduction

This paper is about peaceful coexistence between Christians and Muslims. It alludes to the historical *convivencia* and outlines some key lessons that can be learned in a bid to sustain positive Muslim–Christian relations[1] in Marsabit County, Kenya. Such lessons are intertwined with biblical references that allude to peaceful coexistence.

In discussing *convivencia*, Wheatcroft cautions that we should not perceive it as a "fixed and settled entity."[2] Yet, even though it also had unpleasant experiences, such coexistence in a religiously heterogeneous community deserves our reflection. As Cluett claims, it was the greatest achievement of religious integration in Spain that can be a model of peace for countries plagued with religious conflicts.[3]

Religious antagonism in Marsabit County, Kenya, has not been witnessed on a large scale as it has in other places where Muslims and Christians coexist. This chapter suggests ways of enhancing peaceful coexistence in Marsabit County, especially among the Borana people. The focus on the Borana community is largely because it forms the largest part of the population in the county which consists of both Christians and Muslims. Both Muslims and Christians have a sizeable population in this community, with 90 percent being Islam and 5–8 percent Christian.[4] According to the 2009 national population

---

1. "Relations" refers to formalized and structured engagements between the two religions, usually at the institutional level.

2. Andrew Wheatcroft, *Infidels: A History of Conflict between Christendom and Islam* (New York: Random House, 2005), 73.

3. John Cluett, "Convivencia: A Model for Peace between Christians, Muslims and Jewish Cultures," August 2015, 2, https://www.researchgate.net/publication/280717941_Convivencia_A_Model_for_Peace_Between_Christians_Muslims_and_Jewish_Cultures.

4. Orville Boyd Jenkins, "People Profile: The Borana of Ethiopia and Kenya," Strategy Leader, 2015, accessed 5 January 2018, http://strategyleader.org/profiles/borana.html.

census, Borana in Kenya numbered 161,399,[5] which was projected to reach 191,000 in 2018, with 80 percent Muslim and 8 percent Christian. Two percent of Christians are evangelical, the rest being Catholic.[6]

The analysis of *convivencia* will be based on a religio-cultural framework of peace in view of what is taught in the Bible and the Qur'an. The first part of the chapter describes the Spanish *convivencia* and its important aspects, while the second part scans the religio-historical background of the Borana people, considering the value of cultural underpinnings that have essentially boosted peaceful coexistence in the recent past. The third section considers contemporary religious coexistence in Marsabit, and how lessons derived from Spanish *convivencia* can give insight into strengthening Muslim–Christian relations. This final section also outlines biblical/theological references that address peaceful coexistence.

Spanish Medieval *Convivencia*

The term *convivencia*[7] was coined to describe the way Jews, Christians, and Muslims coexisted in medieval Spain. Both Wheatcroft[8] and Rashid[9] trace the term to Américo Castro's discussion of the Spanish identity (1885–1972). Spanish historians have used the term to describe the relationship between Jews, Christians, and Muslims during two consecutive epochs of their nation's history between the years 711 and 1492. Even though it is variously perceived, *convivencia* was, for most of its time, marked by stable relationships among the three religions. *Convivencia* evokes an aura of tolerance, coexistence, and open-mindedness. However, this did not characterize the entire period. It was during the medieval era that the Inquisition[10] and the Crusades occurred (1095–1492) to taint the picture of Christendom. The Christian martyrs of Cordoba under the Islamic rule cannot be forgotten either. Kenneth Wolf

---

5. According to the Kenya National Bureau of Statistics (KNBS), as quoted by Karol Czuba "Ethnic Politics in Marsabit," 2018, 3.

6. "Oromo, Borana in Kenya," Joshua Project, https://joshuaproject.net/people_groups/19651/KE.

7. Cluett, "Convivencia," 2.

8. Wheatcroft, *Infidels*, 73.

9. Bibi Tasleema Rashid, "Convivencia: The Burden of Spain?" (master's thesis, Palacký University in Olomouc, 2011), 20, https://theses.cz/id/66ersg?lang=en.

10. The Inquisition was a tribunal started in 1478 by Ferdinand II of Oregon and Isabella I of Castile to curb heresy against the Catholic Church, and in which disloyalty to the Church was cruelly punished.

alludes to the suffering meted out on Christians in Cordoba when he writes that "forty-eight Christians were decapitated for religious offenses against Islam."[11] The victorious Christians of Reconquista decreed a radical policy of mass conversion that ended with the ethnic cleansing of all the descendants of the "Moors."[12] During this time, there were also episodes of mistrust and religious suspicion among the Christians, Jews, and Muslims. The focus of this chapter, however, is on the fact that there was coexistence, tolerance, and open-mindedness between the different religious groups in Spain for most of the *convivencia* period. The fact that Muslims and Christians can coexist peacefully is, therefore, not a fallacy in light of the current violence by militant Muslims. While the religion in power was tempted to disadvantage the others, there was evident flexibility that allowed substantial freedom among them. Whenever the Muslim state refrained from enforcing some of the *dhimmi* demands, and Christian rulers did not force conversion of Muslims and Jews, a strong sense of coexistence was experienced.[13]

Convivencia can, therefore, be a model for peace in those countries that are plagued by religious wars, and an example to foster interfaith harmony.[14] It is deemed sound and appropriate to revisit *convivencia* for insights for peaceful coexistence in our time.

Two Periods of Convivencia

According to Andrew Wheatcroft, there were two periods of *convivencia*.[15] The first period covers the Muslim Umayyad Conquest (711 to 1238), while the second refers to Christian Reconquista from 1238 to 1492, when the last rule of Islam in Grenada fell.[16] In the first period Christians, Jews, and Muslims lived together under the Muslim rule of Moorish Islam.[17] Non-Muslims were given

---

11. Kenneth Wolf, *Christian Martyrs in Muslim Spain* (Cambridge: Cambridge University Press, 1988), 5.

12. Wheatcroft, *Infidels*, 73.

13. Wolf, *Christian Martyrs*, 71.

14. Cluett, "Convivencia," 2.

15. Wheatcroft, *Infidels*, 73.

16. Rashid, "Convivencia," 20.

17. Moors were Berber Muslims from Morocco in North Africa, so called by Christians. They occupied Spain in Cordoba after the fall of Roman rule in AD 711.

the *dhimmitude*[18] privilege of continuing in their respective religions as long as they paid the required *jizya* (poll tax) annually. Non-Muslims were given good positions in the government, especially under the more tolerant Umayyads. The Almoravids and later the Almohads (1170s) were fundamentalist Berbers invited by the Moors to counter the expansion of the Catholics from the north of Spain.[19] The Almoravids and Almohads were intolerant of non-Muslims and this ruined the *convivencia* experienced previously. The second period of *convivencia* was under Christian rule in Spain. It began in 1238 and ended in 1492 when Jews were expelled from Spain. Key rulers in this second era were the fifteenth-century Christian monarchs Ferdinand and Isabella. These rulers chose to purify Christendom by eliminating Jews and requiring Muslims to convert to Christianity. This attitude broke the spirit of *convivencia* as Christianity was elevated above other religions and adopted policies of systematic suppression of the others.

Unsustained Convivencia: An Accident of Conquest?

As already mentioned, the first period of *convivencia* ceased when militant Islam took over leadership in Al-Andalus in the eleventh and twelfth centuries under the Almoravids and Almohads respectively.[20] These rulers were said to have been open-minded toward philosophy and arts, but they strongly advocated against religious contact with non-Muslims. This broke the *convivencia* experience in medieval Spain.[21]

It was not only Muslims who displayed a fundamentalist view in trying to purify religion; Christians are recorded to have done the same. The thirteenth century gave a final blow to *convivencia* in Spain when the Castile Christian kingdom reconquered Spain. In 1492 the Catholic monarchs Ferdinand and Isabella sought to homogenize Spain into a Christian state. Jews were eventually expelled from Spain on the premise that they would "corrupt the re-Christianized peninsula."[22] The Catholic monarchs did not expel Muslims at first because they believed they would be gradually converted and become

---

18. *Dhimmitude* is a state of treatment of non-Muslims living in a Muslim state, in which they are given conditional protection. They are subjugated to an inferior citizenship of "protection" with a prescribed state of relationship with the Muslims.

19. Rashid, "Convivencia," 16.

20. Wheatcroft, *Infidels*, 68.

21. Rashid, "Convivencia," 30–31.

22. Wheatcroft, *Infidels*, 116.

"useful" citizens of Spain.[23] Muslims were later given the choice to convert to Christianity or otherwise be expelled, forcing many to seek refuge in North Africa.[24]

Even though *convivencia* was not sustained, it is possible to derive lessons from it that are beneficial for other religiously diverse societies. Muslims and Christians are increasingly neighbors to each other all over the world through migration and missionary pursuits. Marsabit County in northern Kenya is not exempt from this. The largest inhabitants of this county are the Borana people, who have both Islamic and Christian representation. The following sections attempt to give a picture of this coexistence specifically, starting with their brief history.

A Brief History of the Borana People

The Borana people of Marsabit County are part of a large Oromo group, whose population is more in Ethiopia than in Kenya. The Borana people have embraced Islam and Christianity although a number still adhere to the traditional religion, giving the picture of "triple heritage," a term coined by Ali Mazrui.[25] Before Borana were either Muslims or Christians, they adhered strongly to their traditional religion. They were monotheistic, acknowledging one God, *Waaqa*, who created all things. One aspect of *Waaqa* is that he loved the Borana people and gave them laws and traditions to govern their lives.[26] The advent of Islam and Christianity is therefore worth noting.

Islam came earlier than Christianity in Marsabit, and prior to the colonialists. One businessman interviewed for this research asserts that Islam came before World War I.[27] Trimingham's account of Islam in East Africa excludes the Borana (whom he classifies as Galla) on the basis that they belong to the "Islam of the Eastern Horn."[28] P. T. W. Baxter describes how Islam was

---

23. Wheatcroft, 118.

24. Wheatcroft, 126.

25. John Azumah, *The Legacy of Arab-Islam in Africa: A Quest for Inter-Religious Dialogue* (Oxford: Oneworld, 2001), 181.

26. P. T. W. Baxter, "Acceptance and Rejection of Islam among the Boran of the Northern Frontier District of Kenya," in *Islam in Tropical Africa*, ed. I. M. Lewis (London: Oxford University Press, 1966), 238.

27. Ndi, personal interview with author, Marsabit town, 2018.

28. J. Spencer Trimingham, *Islam in East Africa: The Report of a Survey Undertaken in 1961* (London: Edinburgh House, 1982), 29.

accepted and rejected by Borana of the Northern Frontier District in Kenya.[29] His discussion is about Borana people who stayed in Isiolo County, while this chapter is concerned with those of Marsabit. It can be reasonably estimated that the Borana adapted Islam within the past hundred years[30] through their long-time interaction with the Somali.[31]

Azumah reports that the Galla and Somali people were exported to the Islamic world as slaves before Islamization especially of the Somali people.[32] The interactions of Arabs and the two communities go back in history and were significant for their Islamization. Marsabit forest is home to a number of wild animals such as cheetahs, buffalos, and "mighty elephants."[33] The elephants bear some of the largest tusks and hence are a major attraction for ivory dealers. Arab and Somali ivory dealers may have taken some of the Borana people as porters to carry their ivory to the Coast. Pouwels also affirms that ivory and other animal byproducts were mostly supplied by "Oromo and Aweera hunters" in the coastal trade between 1500 and 1800.[34] The Arab and Somali traders did not come primarily as Muslim missionaries, so it was "unintentional" that the Borana embraced Islam, seeing the affluent lifestyles of these traders who eventually made Marsabit their home. Their progeny are prominent business people whose influence continues to impact many parts of contemporary Marsabit.

Christianity among the Borana People

The first Christian missionaries arrived in Marsabit town in January 1931. They belonged to the Bible Church Missionary Society (BCMS). Borana people are known to be courteous. This is evident from Waaqo's report that when these first missionaries shared the gospel with the Borana, they said it was good, although they did not embrace it. The Burji people were more open and ready

---

29. Baxter, "Acceptance," 232.

30. Halkano A. Wario, "Networking the Nomads: A Study of Tablīghī Jamāʿat among the Borana of Northern Kenya" (PhD diss., University of Bayreuth, 2012), https://epub.uni-bayreuth.de/1689.

31. Esther Mombo and Samson Mwaluda, "Relationship and Challenge in Kenya and East Africa," *Transformation* 17, no. 1 (2000): 36–41.

32. Azumah, *Legacy of Arab-Islam*, 42.

33. Mervyn Maciel, *Bwana Karani* (Braunton: Merlin, 1985), 79.

34. Randall L. Pouwels, "The East African Coast, c. 780 to 1900 C.E.," in *The History of Islam in Africa*, ed. Nehemia Levtzion and Randall L. Pouwels (Athens, OH: Ohio University Press, 2000), 259.

to accept Christianity than the Borana.[35] The Roman Catholic mission followed in 1963 and it has expanded to almost all parts of Marsabit County. At present, the county has several Protestant churches, including Seventh-Day Adventists. Islam was readily accepted because it allowed the Borana people to continue with their traditional beliefs and practices. Christianity, on the other hand, was perceived to be opposed to cultural practices, which are highly esteemed. Waaqo confirms this, giving examples of Borana people who became Christians and were ostracized for abandoning the traditions of their fathers.[36]

Contemporary Coexistence among the Borana People

There has been a notable situation of peaceful coexistence in Marsabit County between Muslims and Christians. No prominent interreligious tension has been experienced in most of the region, although challenges have been encountered when visiting Islamic preachers have attacked Christianity.[37] Attacks on churches were witnessed in 2018 when a local Maalim was arrested on allegations of terrorism.[38] The main tensions that have been experienced are inter-tribal clashes, especially between the Gabra and the Borana tribes. One of the worst such conflicts was the infamous Turbi massacre in 2004, but others have continued to the present time. Religion will continue to play a key role in inter-tribal relations, and if inter-tribal conflicts turn religious, they will become too complex to resolve.

Socio-Cultural Aspects of Coexistence

Peaceful coexistence between Muslims and Christians among the Borana in Marsabit has largely been due to the traditional concept of peace termed *nagaa Borana* (literally "peace of Borana"). Waaqo believes that the most important word for the Borana people is *nagaa* (peace).[39] The word is included in the

---

35. Jillo Naomi Waaqo, "The Church and the Booran of Northern Kenya: An Analysis and Evaluation of the Traditional Booran Culture and Religion with a View to the Contextualization of the Gospel" (master's thesis, Norwegian School of Theology, 2000).

36. Waaqo, "Church and the Booran," 66.

37. Paul Tablino, *Christianity among the Nomads: The Catholic Church in Northern Kenya* (Nairobi: Paulines Publications Africa, 2004), 132.

38. "The Proto-Cathedral of Marsabit Attacked," Agenzia Fides, 22 January 2018, http://www.fides.org/en/news/63607-AFRICA_KENYA_The_proto_Cathedral_of_Marsabit_attacked.

39. Waaqo, "The Church and the Booran," 39.

exchange of greetings and pervades Borana social life, from salutations to wishes for the well-being of the entire community.

Borana do not believe in being at war among themselves, regardless of their religious affiliation, and any alliance with the "enemy" (*nyapa*) is jointly resisted. Baxter confirms that he has no record of the Borana people anywhere in the north fighting each other.[40] Furthermore, killing a fellow Borana is perceived to be a "heinous sin and an offense against God."[41] Nevertheless, an accusation of alliance with the enemy can be punishable by death. A case in point was the participation of a mob (regardless of religion) in attacking and killing a Borana chief who was accused of betraying the community and siding with the "enemies."[42] Cultural solidarity is of prime importance as they observe the *sera Borana* (law of Borana) and the *aada Borana* (culture/tradition of Borana). Fayo mentions that the Borana community value their structural and cultural cohesion for the sake of *nagaa Borana* (peace of Borana). Any threat to this peace is dealt with through "reparative and restorative justice."[43] Anyone perceived to be damaging the "peace of Borana" is likely to suffer the pain of banishment that may affect that person's whole clan.[44] Engulfing the concept of the "peace of Borana" (*nagaa Borana*) is the *gadaa* system of governance among the Borana, which encompasses the religious, cultural, and political features of Borana communities and determines the rules (*sera*) and traditions (*addaa*) of the Borana people. Borana people in Marsabit have tried to maintain the *gadaa* system even though in a diluted form because of the distance from their Ethiopian heritage. However, the *gadaa* system is helpful in sustaining coexistence among the Oromo Muslims and Christians in Ethiopia.[45]

Another key element in Borana Muslim–Christian coexistence is intermarriage. Many Christian girls have been married to Muslim men with the consent of their parents. Marriage is seen as joining two families together,

---

40. Baxter, "Acceptance," 236.

41. Baxter, 247.

42. *Daily Nation*, 16 December 2018.

43. Godana Denge Fayo, "Coping with Scarcity in Northern Kenya: The Role of Pastoralist Borana Gada Indigenous Justice Institutions in Conflicts Prevention and Resolutions for Range Resources Management" (master's thesis, Graduate School of Development Studies, the Netherlands, November 2011).

44. Fayo, "Coping with Scarcity," 36.

45. Samuel Yonas Deressa, *Cultural Ethics and Inter-Religious Coexistence and the Ethiopian Context: The Case of Karayyu Oromo* (Addis Ababa: Mekana Yesus Seminary, 2011), 65. See Mohammed Girma's article "Muslim–Christian Relations in Ethiopia: Exploring the Price Tag," where he discusses aspects that contribute to social harmony in Ethiopia (*CMCS Research Briefings* 9 [Summer 2017], 6–8).

hence the Muslim–Christian relationship is enhanced. Without ignoring the theological challenges some of these cultural practices will bring, there is need to harness their strengths to ensure interreligious peace in the region.

The Current Socio-Political Arena in Marsabit County

With the current devolved units of governance in Kenya, Marsabit County has a mixed leadership consisting, at the time of writing, of a Muslim governor who is a Borana, and an Anglican deputy governor from a minority Burji tribe. It is worth noting that the former governor (2013–18), a Gabra by tribe, was a Roman Catholic. The senator is from the Rendille tribe and is a Muslim (converted from Catholicism). The majority of the County leaders are Muslims. Christian leaders are in the minority and they mostly feel ignored when leading prayers during government meetings, against the norm. Even though conflicts in the region have never taken a religious dimension, Christians do feel pressure and discrimination in the midst of the growth of Islam. Zirulnick quotes Martin, the then bishop of the Anglican Church, saying, "Most of our church leaders feel Muslims are trying to take over government. There is the belief that Islam is pursuing the Islamization of Kenya."[46] This view continues to be shared by many Christians, requiring an appropriate response from the Marsabit Muslims to safeguard peaceful relations.

Interreligious Conflicts in Marsabit County

Somali and Borana have been in conflict since the early 1800s. Trimingham discusses the 1848 massacre of Galla chiefs by Somali people.[47] Somali raiders frustrated the Borana people, yet it is not apparent if this was an interreligious conflict. Interreligious conflicts between Muslims and Christians among the Borana people have been witnessed in the towns of Moyale and Sololo in Marsabit County, and Merti town in Isiolo county. These seem to be isolated and sporadic, spurred by incidents that vexed the Muslims, causing them to react in a violent way. Many of the above conflicts involved Borana-speaking non-Borana people such as the Burji, Garre, and Gabra.[48] Instead, the regular

---

46. Ariel Zirulnick, "In Kenya, Religious Coexistence Feels Pressure of Stronger Muslim Identity," *The Christian Science Monitor*, 29 March 2005, 4, https://www.csmonitor.com/World/Africa/2015/0329/In-Kenya-religious-coexistence-feels-pressure-of-stronger-Muslim-identity.

47. Spencer Trimingham, *Islam in East Africa* (New York: New York Books for Libraries, 1980), 30.

48. Proper Borana or Borana *gutu*.

conflicts witnessed in Marsabit have largely been due to non-religious factors like ethnicity, competition for scarce resources, and cattle rustling.[49] Militant Islam is creeping into Marsabit at a fast yet seemingly invisible rate. In early 2014, claims that people were being inducted into Al-Shabaab[50] started with a report by Ali Abdi that a female local primary school teacher and a student were among them.[51] Allegations concerning many other people have continued since then, with one prominent sheik taken to court on terrorism charges.[52] Christians are feeling insecure because of Islamism, which has made guarding church meetings necessary.

Theology of Coexistence in the Qur'an and the Bible

This section gives a brief examination of the teachings in both the Old and the New Testament on the relationships between Christians and non-Christians. Islamic doctrine will also be reviewed regarding Muslim relationships with Christians. Coexistence describes the ability of two religious traditions to live together in harmony or even cooperation. Majid states that Islam has continued to be accused of incompatibility with interreligious coexistence.[53] However, using texts from the Qur'an, such as Surah 4:1 and 49:13, Majid argues that the Qur'an negates distinctions based on racial, linguistic, and national grounds, and also identifies diversity as a sign of God and hence as something to be respected. Many have interpreted Surah 5:256 to mean that Islam is against the use of force to demand allegiance to religion, and that "any Islamic state is also obliged by *Shariah* to provide welfare and support

49. Wolde Wesa, "Effects of Climate Change on Inter-Ethnic Conflicts in Marsabit Central District, Kenya" (master's thesis, St Paul's University, Kenya, 2012), 33.

50. Al-Shabaab is a militant Islamic group based in Somalia that is aligned with Al-Qaeda. It has conducted terrorist attacks in parts of East Africa and seeks to establish Islamic rule in the region.

51. Ali Abdi, "Report Says Female Teacher, Student Join Al Shabaab Militants," Standard Digital News: Kenya, 9 January 2012, https://www.standardmedia.co.ke/article/2000049661/report-says-female-teacher-student-join-al-shabaab-militants.

52. Cyrus Ombati, "Police Repulsed Youths from the Station, which Ignited Violent Protests," 15 January 2018, https://www.standardmedia.co.ke/article/2001265955/police-repulsed-youths-from-the-station-which-ignited-violent-protests.

53. Abdul Majid, "Peaceful Co-Existence of Various Cultures and Religions: An Islamic Perspective with Special Reference to Spain," Metanexus, 28 May 2008, 1, https://www.metanexus.net/peaceful-co-existence-various-cultures-and-religions-islamic-perspective-special-reference/.

to the followers of other divine religions equal to the Muslims."[54] Coexistence between Muslims and non-Muslims is seen by some Muslim scholars as a legal obligation in Islam.[55] In Christianity, God demands that we all love each other as neighbors, regardless of religious affiliation. Christians are to love not only those who love them but even their enemies.[56] Christians are also called to live at peace with each other and do all they can to ensure it.[57] Indeed, blessed are the peacemakers, for they will be called children of God.[58] God's children are expected to enhance peaceful existence in society. Peace during conflict is possible only by forgiveness and is truly meaningful only through reconciliation. The Esau–Jacob conflict, which had lasted since their youth, was resolved and reconciliation realized in their old age.[59] The themes of conflict, forgiveness, and reconciliation are evident in the Esau–Jacob encounter. These themes provide a valid theoretical background for discussing a theology of coexistence between Muslims and Christians as espoused in the following section.

Conflict

As fraternal twins, Esau and Jacob's conflict began right in the womb of their mother Rebekah.[60] God foreknew the emergence of this conflict when he told Rebekah that the twins were "two nations," "two peoples," who would be separated, and that one would be stronger than the other. Jacob the younger grasped the heel of Esau, hence the meaning of his name (one who grasps the heel of his brother). They differed in many ways, especially in their sources of livelihood. Esau was an outdoors person, whereas Jacob liked staying "among the tents."[61]

---

54. Mansour Leghaei, "Living in Harmony: Islamic Perspective," 2015, www.al-islam. org; Shittu Balogun Abdulazeez, "Peaceful Co-Existence in a Multi-Religious Society: Islam and Christianity Perspectives," *International Journal of Islamic Thought* 2 (2013), https://www. researchgate.net/publication/316158024_Peaceful_Co-Existence_in_a_Multi-Religious_ Society_Islam_and_Christianity_Perspectives.

55. Thābet Aḥmad Abū al-Ḥāj et al., "Peaceful Coexistence between Muslims and Christians: The Case of Jerusalem," *International Journal of Humanities, Social Sciences and Education (IJHSSE)* 2, no. 4 (2015): 120.

56. Lev 19:18; Matt 5:43–45; Mark 12:30–31.

57. Rom 12:18; 14:19; 1 Tim 2:2; Heb 12:14.

58. Matt 5:9.

59. Gen 32–33.

60. Gen 25:23–26.

61. Gen 25:27.

Sibling rivalry escalated with parental favoritism that saw Jacob flee for his life after decisively taking the birthright from Esau. In light of this rivalry, this chapter considers the tense coexistence between Muslims and Christians in Marsabit. The chapter also seeks to derive biblical insights for peaceful relations.

Forgiveness and Reconciliation

Genesis 32–33 is a narrative of forgiveness and reconciliation that can provide rich insights for peaceful coexistence between Muslims and Christians. Esau was bitter with Jacob after having been exploited and given up his inheritance in exchange for a meal.[62] Further, Jacob wrestled Esau's blessing from their father Isaac's hand. Because of all this, "Esau held a grudge against Jacob."[63] However, with all these warranted accusations against Jacob, Esau was willing to forgive him. Esau not only forgave such offenses, but he also embraced Jacob again as his brother.[64] Muslims and Christians should recognize their brotherhood as God's creations, but also as people of faith, and seek to forgive and embrace each other in peace. The classical teachings of both Islam and Christianity are to a large extent believed to encourage peaceful coexistence, and even though some divergent interpretations exist, they are a minority voice, especially in Muslim Borana society. But what lessons can we learn from the medieval Spanish *convivencia* to enhance interfaith relations?

Lessons from the Spanish *Convivencia* for Marsabit County

The truth of the matter is that *convivencia* was not experienced in a perfect environment devoid of negativity. Yet it is crucial to note that there was a working relationship between Muslims, Jews, and Christians that bore valuable fruit in Spain. Thus in this section we will note some features that enabled coexistence in Spain and draw lessons that can benefit Marsabit County from a contextual theological perspective. In discussing these lessons from the historical *convivencia*, we also give biblical application.

---

62. Gen 25:29–34.
63. Gen 27:41.
64. Gen 33:4.

Socio-Cultural Aspects of Coexistence

The different religious groups in medieval Spain adopted some similar outward socio-cultural forms that made them difficult to differentiate. Yet in spite of such outward similarities, they remained distinct and maintained individual customary laws.[65] Many people in Spain adopted each other's style of dress as they did in Palermo, Sicily. O'Shea reports that Christian women went to church "bearing all the adornments of Muslim women, including jewelry, henna on the fingers and perfumes."[66] Similarly, many Borana Muslim and Christian women in Marsabit dress alike. A Borana lady also wears a light shawl or wraparound that is tied over her head and shoulder, called *garbasa*. Muslim and Christian men also dress in similar ways except for the religious tunics worn by Muslim men, usually on Fridays. A people's cultural appearance and disposition are very influential to cognitive perceptions of relationships, a factor that determines Muslim–Christian coexistence even today. Dress and other cultural adornments that do not draw distinctions between religions should be promoted for a more interconnected society.

Another social-cultural characteristic was the architectural design of buildings. Architectural ideas were integrated from the Muslim Arabs' and the Christians' art. The Great Mosque of Cordoba stood as a magnificent witness to this interchange and appreciation of each other's artistic ideas. The structure and function of this mosque were essentially Eastern, which was assimilated with the Visigoth way of shaping the columns and arches of buildings.[67] Christian and Muslim houses have distinctive features and are designed in similar ways. However, this should be extended to places of worship, which do not have to be rigid in design. Some Catholic churches among the Borana people have adopted the designs of mosques or other Islamic features, which can serve to improve views between the two religions.[68]

Language was another cultural aspect that had the propensity to buttress *convivencia*. Many Christians adopted Arabic as a trade language and relinquished Latin during the Islamic reign. Castilian, on the other hand, gradually became the "language of authority" together with Arabic.[69] Muslims and Christians among the Borana people of Marsabit do not have language

---

65. Wheatcroft, *Infidels*, 67.

66. Stephen O'Shea, *Sea of Faith: Islam and Christianity in the Medieval Mediterranean World* (New York: Walker, 2006), 135.

67. Wheatcroft, *Infidels*, 67.

68. The Roman Catholic Church in Merti, Isiolo County, among Waso Borana, has been designed to closely resemble a mosque architecturally.

69. Rashid, "Convivencia," 19.

barriers. In spite of certain Arabic words being used exclusively by Muslims, one can hardly tell someone's religious affiliation from his or her language. The growing tendency to do away with Borana names among some Muslims is likely to widen the "us versus them divide," which is unhelpful in promoting relations.

Biblical Application

The theme of modest dressing is crucial to both Muslims and Christians as mentioned distinctively in their respective texts. Muslims are advised to "guard their modesty."[70] Christian women are admonished to adorn themselves in modest apparel.[71] The theme of modesty hence is common to Islam and Christianity and can be a reason to emphasize uniformity in dress, as discussed in the previous paragraph.

Dialogue

Hugh Goddard mentions that in the second half of the medieval era, an attempt was made to engage in dialogue with a rational perspective. Petrus Alfonsi, a Spanish Jewish convert to Christianity, wrote a dialogue between a Christian and a Jew that also included an account of Muhammad and Islam. His work is described as one of the "best informed and most rational statements . . . in the twelfth century."[72] Others, like Peter the Venerable, undertook the task of making Muslim materials available in Spain.[73] Peter's aim was to encourage others to recognize the need to understand Muslims and avoid castigating Islam ignorantly.

Had a culture of dialogue been cultivated in Spain, it would ostensibly have sustained *convivencia*. Coexistence in Marsabit County can be sustained if such a culture is embraced. Hans Küng is reported to have stated, "There will be no peace among the nations without peace among the religions. There will be no peace among the religions without dialogue among the religions."[74] Religious leaders are encouraged to meet and dialogue without prejudice.

---

70. Surah 24:30–31.

71. 1 Tim 2:9.

72. Hugh Goddard, *A History of Christian–Muslim Relations* (Chicago: New Amsterdam Books, 2000), 92.

73. Goddard, *A History*, 93.

74. Thomas Scheffler, "Interreligious Dialogue and Peacebuilding," *Die Friedens-Warte* 82, nos. 2/3, Religion, Krieg und Frieden (2007): 173–187.

It is God who designs where we all live and even those we are to live with, for the purpose of seeking and finding him.[75] *Convivencia* involved a profound appreciation of others in recognition of the fact that each has a valuable contribution for mutual benefit. Muslims lament discrimination by Christians generally in Kenya.[76] Dialogue should be all-inclusive to help address any feelings of discrimination and to enable all to contribute to the well-being of Borana society in Marsabit.

Biblical Application

Dialoguing in religious circles is encouraged in 1 Peter 3:15, where Christians are exhorted to be ready always to give an answer to every person who inquires about their faith. It is to be inferred from this verse that dialogue is helpful so that people from different religions can understand each other's religious stand and not judge unnecessarily. Jesus made use of dialogue with those ignorant of him or even living in sinfulness. This was the case for the Samaritan woman (John 4), Zacchaeus (Luke 19), and his disciples (Matt 16), among others, to bring his message of love to humankind.

Economic Aspects of Coexistence

Trade was key in sustaining the *convivencia* in medieval Spain. Muslims engaged in business following in the footsteps of their prophet Muhammad, who was a merchant. Various kinds of trade ventures caused Muslims and Christians to interact with each other (and also the Jews). Business in Marsabit central business area is made up of both Christian and Muslim entrepreneurs from all the tribes in the county. Both Muslims and Christians have particularly ventured into *miraa* (khat) business for economic viability.[77] Other prominent businesses where Christians and Muslims work together are the animal trade, transport, and food supplies. In spite of situations where there are religious groupings for business purposes, there are strong interactions and people are hired into these businesses across religions.

---

75. Acts 17:25–28.

76. Hassan Kinyua Omari, "Facts and Issues of Christian–Muslim Co-Existence," in *Christian–Muslim Co-Existence in Eastern Africa*, eds. Fritz Stenger, Joseph Wandera, and Paul Hannon (Nairobi: Paulines Publications Africa, 2008), 35.

77. Omari, "Facts and Issues," 45.

Biblical Application

The economic aspect of Muslims and Christians working together should be encouraged in Marsabit County, as seen in some indirect inferences from the Bible. One example is that of Jesus paying his taxes[78] and encouraging his disciples to give to Caesar what belonged to him.[79]

Intellectual Exchange as an Aspect of Coexistence

O'Shea examines the intellectual and cultural coexistence during the eleventh and twelfth centuries. Of relevance for this chapter is his discussion of the *convivencia* experienced in Toledo, central Spain. He states that it was in the twelfth and thirteenth centuries that Toledo became a center of learning and "polyglot scholarship."[80] Toledo was at this time an environment where Muslims, Jews, and Christians coexisted under Christian rule. Muslim and Christian scholars sought to understand each other's faith through translating and reading each other's materials. It has been noted that many Muslims and Christians in sub-Saharan Africa today acknowledge that they know relatively little about each other's faith.[81] Are religious leaders in Marsabit County willing to read the vast materials available from different religious sources? Can Christian leaders enroll in institutions offering Islamic studies to gain a greater understanding of Islam? These are pertinent questions that should be pondered if sustainable coexistence is to be realized in the county. Learning is a fundamental point of contact, formally and informally, for greater understanding of one another. Much criticism and prejudice is based on the lack of dedication to identify with each other's perspectives.

Archbishop Raymond of Toledo, described as having been "astonishingly open-minded," oversaw the translation of Arabic documents into Latin in the twelfth century.[82] A key Muslim leader who also facilitated *convivencia* was Abd ar-Rahman III. The two leaders were open-minded enough to embrace ideas and knowledge from each other's religion. Libraries were established in various cities in Spain, and many learned people flocked there for academic

---

78. Matt 17:24–27.

79. Mark 12:17.

80. O'Shea, *Sea of Faith*, 145.

81. Pew Research Center, "Tolerance and Tension: Islam and Christianity in Sub-Saharan Africa." Accessed 23 February 2019, http://www.pewforum.org/2010/04/15/executive-summary-islam-and-christianity-in-sub-saharan-africa/.

82. O'Shea, *Sea of Faith*, 148; Goddard, *A History*, 98.

interest.[83] There is need for humility among the religious leaders in Marsabit County to acknowledge that both Christians and Muslims can contribute immensely toward a holistic development of the county. There should be deliberate collaboration by leaders of the county government, regardless of their religion, to serve as an example for sustained peace.

Education as a Means of Sustaining Peaceful Coexistence

The quest for knowledge, described above as part of the intellectual exchange between scholars of Islam and Christianity, went beyond religious divisions, as scholars willingly shared and translated this knowledge into a readable language. Education today should similarly transcend religious partitions and pursue mutual benefit. Primary and secondary schools have been founded by Muslims in Marsabit County. They have been performing relatively well and thus attract both Muslim and Christian students. Similarly, there are Christian-based schools where both Muslims and Christians learn without coercion into each other's faith. These can be used as avenues of mutual understanding especially among the youth, to be models for future generations.

Non-Purist Position by Religious Leaders

Convivencia was curtailed in both Muslim and Christian eras when purist leaders emerged who wanted to keep their religion free from contamination. Al-Shabaab will continue to take major strides in Marsabit unless Muslim leaders acknowledge its destructive character and stop its advance. Christians and Christian leaders should also avoid exclusivist views and a purist approach to social needs, or there will not be sustained coexistence in Marsabit. Nevertheless, the onus is on the majority population of Islam to promote regard and provide equal space for the minority through the county leadership.

Conclusion

It is reasonable to conclude that Spanish *convivencia* was valuable while it lasted. A purist attitude that failed to appreciate the beliefs and practices of other faiths led to its demise. Thus Marsabit *convivencia* can be sustained if people have the right mindset toward others and their religions. Religious and local leaders are key players in promoting and sustaining peace between religions. Muslims

---

83. Omari, "Facts and Issues," 30.

and Christians should seek to understand each other's faith to avoid prejudice, and provide only constructive opinions in an environment of friendship and respect. As explained, this perspective of Islamic and Christian theology has to be strengthened and encouraged in shaping relations between the two faith communities. All peace-loving inhabitants of Marsabit should shun purist and judgmental attitudes that breed division among people who have a great deal to share in their humanity. The pursuit of inclusion spelled out in the Kenyan constitution needs to be enhanced to promote equal opportunities for all across religions. As already expressed in this chapter, many Christians in Marsabit have felt excluded by the new county government structures and job opportunities, compared with Muslims.

Another conclusion that can be derived from Spanish *convivencia* is that women were not party to the intellectual exchange, apart from in their way of dressing. There is no mention of women among the scholars involved in the great translation work during *convivencia*. It is, however, noteworthy that women and children are the ones who bear the greatest burden during conflict. Women should therefore be fully included in advocating for peace and religious dialogue in Marsabit.

Bibliography

Abdi, Ali. "Report Says Female Teacher, Student Join Al Shabaab Militants." *Standard Digital News: Kenya*. 9 January 2012. Accessed 19 August 2018. https://www.standardmedia.co.ke/article/2000049661/report-says-female-teacher-student-join-al-shabaab-militants.

Abdulazeez, Shittu Balogun. "Peaceful Co-Existence in a Multi-Religious Society: Islam and Christianity Perspectives." *International Journal of Islamic Thought* 2 (2013). https://www.researchgate.net/publication/316158024_Peaceful_Co-Existence_in_a_Multi-Religious_Society_Islam_and_Christianity_Perspectives.

Akdogan, Fatih. "Gulen-Inspired Schools and Their Contribution to Christian–Muslim Relations in Nairobi, Kenya." Master's thesis, St Paul's University, Limuru, 2013.

al-Ḥāj, Thābet Aḥmad Abū, Zulkifli Bin Mohd Yusoff, Nayel Musa Shaker Al-Omran, and Munirah Abdul Razak. "Peaceful Coexistence between Muslims and Christians: The Case of Jerusalem." *International Journal of Humanities Social Sciences and Education* (*IJHSSE*) 2, no. 4 (Apr. 2015): 119–133.

Azumah, John Alembillah. *The Legacy of Arab-Islam in Africa: A Quest for Inter-Religious Dialogue*. Oxford: Oneworld, 2001.

Baxter, P. T. W. "Acceptance and Rejection of Islam among the Boran of the Northern Frontier District of Kenya." In *Islam in Tropical Africa*, edited by I. M. Lewis, 233–240. London: Oxford University Press, 1966.

Cluett, John. "Convivencia: A Model for Peace between Christians, Muslims and Jewish Cultures." August 2015. Accessed 21 November 2018. https://www.researchgate.net/publication/280717941_Convivencia_A_Model_for_Peace_Between_Christians_Muslims_and_Jewish_Cultures.

Czuba, Karol. "Ethnic Politics in Marsabit." September 2018. Accessed 9 July 2020. https://www.researchgate.net/publication/318456646.

Deressa, Samuel Yonas. *Cultural Ethics and Inter-Religious Coexistence and the Ethiopian Context: The Case of Karayyu Oromo*. Addis Ababa: Mekana Yesus Seminary, 2011.

Fayo, Godana Denge. "Coping with Scarcity in Northern Kenya: The Role of Pastoralist Borana Gada Indigenous Justice Institutions in Conflicts Prevention and Resolutions for Range Resources Management." Master's thesis, Graduate School of Development Studies, Netherlands, November 2011.

Girma, Mohammed. "Muslim–Christian Relations in Ethiopia: Exploring the Price Tag." *CMCS Research Briefings* 9 (Summer 2017): 6–8.

Goddard, Hugh. *A History of Christian–Muslim Relations*. Chicago: New Amsterdam Books, 2000.

Jenkins, Orville Boyd. "People Profile: The Borana of Ethiopia and Kenya." Strategy Leader. 2015. Accessed 5 January 2018. http://strategyleader.org/profiles/borana.html.

Kim, Caleb Chul-Soo. *Islam among the Swahili in East Africa*. Nairobi: Acton, 2016.

Leghaei, Mansour. "Living in Harmony: Islamic Perspective," 2015. Accessed 9 July 2020. www.al-islam.org.

Lewis, I. M., ed. *Islam in Tropical Africa*. 2nd. ed. Bloomington, IN/London: International Africa Institute in association with Indiana University Press, 1980.

Maciel, Mervyn. *Bwana Karani*. Braunton: Merlin, 1985.

Majid, Abdul. "Peaceful Co-Existence of Various Cultures and Religions: An Islamic Perspective with Special Reference to Spain." Metanexus. 28 May 2008. Accessed 10 November 2018. https://www.metanexus.net/peaceful-co-existence-various-cultures-and-religions-islamic-perspective-special-reference/.

Mombo, Esther, and Samson M. Mwaluda. "Relationship and Challenge in Kenya and East Africa." *Transformation* 17, no. 1 (2000): 36–41. http://www.jstor.org/stable/43054960.

Omari, Hassan Kinyua. "Facts and Issues of Christian–Muslim Co-Existence." In *Christian–Muslim Co-Existence in Eastern Africa*, edited by Fritz Stenger, Joseph Wandera, and Paul Hannon, 33–40. Nairobi: Paulines Publications Africa, 2008.

Ombati, Cyrus. "Police Repulsed Youths from the Station, which Ignited Violent Protests." 15 January 2018. https://www.standardmedia.co.ke/article/2001265955/police-repulsed-youths-from-the-station-which-ignited-violent-protests.

"Oromo, Borana in Kenya." Joshua Project. https://joshuaproject.net/people_groups/19651/KE.

O'Shea, Stephen. *Sea of Faith: Islam and Christianity in the Medieval Mediterranean World*. New York: Walker, 2006.

Pew Research Center. "Tolerance and Tension: Islam and Christianity in Sub-Saharan Africa." Accessed 23 February 2019. http://www.pewforum.org/2010/04/executive-summary-islam-and-christianity-in-sub-saharan-africa/.

Pouwels, Randall L. "The East African Coast, c. 780 to 1900 C.E." In *The History of Islam in Africa*, edited by Nehemia Levtzion and Randall L. Pouwels, 251–271. Athens, OH: Ohio University Press, 2000.

"The Proto-Cathedral of Marsabit Attacked." Agenzia Fides. 22 January 2018. http://www.fides.org/en/news/63607-AFRICA_KENYA_The_proto_Cathedral_of_Marsabit_attacked.

Rashid, Bibi Tasleema. "Convivencia: The Burden of Spain?" Master's thesis, Palacký University in Olomouc, 2011. Accessed 10 January 2019. https://theses.cz/id/66ersg?lang=en.

Scheffler, Thomas. "Interreligious Dialogue and Peacebuilding." *Die Friedens-Warte* 82, no. 2/3, Religion, Krieg und Frieden (2007): 173–187.

Sperling, David C. "The Coastal Hinterland and Interior of East Africa." In *The History of Islam in Africa*, edited by Nehemia Levtzion and Randall L. Pouwels, 273–302. Athens, OH: Ohio University Press, 2000.

Tablino, Paul. *Christianity among the Nomads: The Catholic Church in Northern Kenya*. Nairobi: Paulines Publications Africa, 2004.

Trimingham, J. Spencer. *Islam in East Africa: The Report of a Survey Undertaken in 1961*. London: Edinburgh House Press, 1962.

———. *Islam in East Africa*. New York: New York Books for Libraries, 1980.

Waaqo, Jillo Naomi. "The Church and the Booran of Northern Kenya: An Analysis and Evaluation of the Traditional Booran Culture and Religion with a View to the Contextualization of the Gospel." Master's thesis, Norwegian School of Theology, 2000.

Wario, Halkano A. "Networking the Nomads: A Study of Tablīghī Jamāʿat among the Borana of Northern Kenya." PhD diss., University of Bayreuth, 2012. Accessed 6 December 2017. https://epub.uni-bayreuth.de/1689.

Wega, John Perminus. "The Contribution of Miraa (Khat) Business to Christian–Muslim Encounters in Meru North District Kenya." Master's thesis, St Paul's University, Limuru, 2008.

Wesa, Wolde. "Effects of Climate Change on Inter-Ethnic Conflicts in Marsabit Central District, Kenya." Master's thesis, St Paul's University, Kenya, 2012.

Wheatcroft, Andrew. *Infidels: A History of Conflict between Christendom and Islam*. New York: Random House, 2005.

Wolf, Kenneth. *Christian Martyrs in Muslim Spain*. Cambridge: Cambridge University Press, 1988.

Zirulnick, Ariel. "In Kenya, Religious Coexistence feels Pressure of Stronger Muslim Identity." *The Christian Science Monitor*, 29 March 2005. Accessed 5 November 2018. https://www.csmonitor.com/World/Africa/2015/0329/In-Kenya-religious-coexistence-feels-pressure-of-stronger-Muslim-identity.

7

John Wesley and the "Catholic Spirit"

An Early Methodist's Vision for Peace

Benson Phiri
Academic Dean, Nazarene Theological College of Central Africa

and

Gregory Crofford
Dean, School of Religion and Christian Ministry
Africa Nazarene University

Abstract

John Wesley (1703–91) was the co-founder of Methodism. While the theme of peace is found throughout his writings, it receives special attention in homilies addressing the Sermon on the Mount (Matt 5–7) as well as in comments in his *Explanatory Notes upon the New Testament* (1755). Also of note is his 1750 sermon "Catholic Spirit," from which his well-known dictum is taken: "If your heart is as my heart, give me your hand." From these selected primary sources, this chapter will trace the outlines of Wesley's views on peace.

Theory is one thing; practice is another. The chapter closes with a study of two contentious episodes from John Wesley's life, as described in the journals of both John and Charles Wesley and Henry Rack's *Reasonable Enthusiast: John Wesley and the Rise of Methodism* (2002), among others. An assessment of the degree to which Wesley lived up to his ideals about peace will be given.

Though Wesley did not always conform to his own irenic vision, the chapter concludes that he never abandoned his hope for peaceful relationships between Christian communities and in society at large. The study closes with a brief comparison of Wesley's ideals and the African concept of *ubuntu*.

Key words: peace, peacemaker, catholic spirit, free grace, predestination.

Introduction

John Wesley (1703–91) is best known as the co-founder of Methodism. In his 1742 treatise "The Character of a Methodist," Wesley underscores his preference for peaceful coexistence between a broad range of Christian traditions. The basis of this harmony is love. For Wesley, a Methodist "is one who has the love of God shed abroad in his heart by the Holy Ghost given unto him; one who loves the Lord his God with all his heart, and with all his soul, and with all his mind, and with all his strength. God is the joy of all his heart and the desire of his soul."[1]

Yet for John Wesley, the desire for peace extended beyond the ecclesiastical realm. For the Methodist – indeed, for all who professed faith in Christ – peace was more than a doctrine. It was intended to be a way of life. It begins with the peace that Christ established between humanity and God. In turn, this reconciliation impacts how the Christian reacts in the face of persecution. Peacemaking is one area (among others) where Wesley proved himself to be "more concerned with life than theory."[2]

The study that follows begins with an examination of key writings from John Wesley regarding peace. Afterwards, a discussion of two episodes in Wesley's life (one failure and one success) will serve as a reminder that peacemaking is always a challenge to put into practice but is well worth the effort. A brief comparison of Wesley's peacemaking principles with the African concept of *ubuntu* brings the study to a close.

---

1. John Wesley, *The Character of a Methodist* (Nashville: United Methodist Publishing House, 1992), 35.

2. T. Crichton Mitchell, *Meet Mr. Wesley: An Intimate Sketch of John Wesley* (Kansas City, MO: Beacon Hill, 1981), 139.

John Wesley on Peace
Homilies on the Sermon on the Mount

John Wesley's teaching on peace from the Sermon on the Mount hinges on Matthew 5:9: "Blessed are the peacemakers: for they shall be called the children of God" (KJV). He presents the ideas of "peace" and "peacemaking" as the central focus of the Gospels as well as of holy living. Reflecting on Matthew 5:8–9, Wesley comments: "Thus far our Lord has been more directly employed in teaching the religion of the heart. He has shown what Christians are to be. He proceeds to show what they are to do also: how inward holiness is to exert itself in our outward conversation."[3] Wesley helps his audience to understand that peace and holiness cannot be divorced from each other. He is of the idea that a person who is truly holy is the instrument of peace that God uses in the world. Based on his understanding of holiness as "loving God with our whole being and our neighbor as ourselves," Wesley shows great optimism that a Christian will translate his or her "heart purity" (v. 8) into the practice of peacemaking in the world where he or she lives.

John Wesley sees a peacemaker as a person "full of genuine humility, so unaffectedly serious, so mild and gentle, so free from all selfish design, so devoted to God, and such an active lover of men."[4] He indicates that the word "peacemaker" literally "implies those lovers of God and man who utterly detest and abhor all strife and debate, all variance and contention; and accordingly labor with all their might either to prevent this fire of hell from being kindled, or when it is kindled from breaking out, or when it is broke out from spreading any farther."[5] Thus peacemaking goes beyond what peacekeepers do in countries where there is war. In such war-torn areas, peacekeeping armies are sent to help bring peace where there is already chaos. In contrast, Wesley understands a peacemaker as someone whose attitude and passion is tuned for peace. In fact, while a peacemaker will make efforts to bring peace in chaotic situations, he or she also takes proactive measures to prevent chaos occurring, and looks for ways to improve the peace that already exists. The motivation to act for peacemakers is not the eruption of chaos but the love of peace that makes them work prior to the eruption of chaos or animosity. Wesley observes:

> [Peacemakers] endeavor to calm the stormy spirits of men, to quiet their turbulent passions, to soften the minds of contending

---

3. Frank Baker, ed., *The Works of John Wesley*, bicentennial ed., 35 vols. projected (Nashville: Abingdon, 1984 to present), 1:517; hereafter, *Works*.

4. *Works*, 1:520.

5. *Works*, 1:517.

parties, and if possible reconcile them to each other. They use all innocent arts, and employ all their strength, all the talents which God has given them, as well to preserve peace where it is as to restore it where it is not. It is the joy of their heart to promote, to confirm, to increase mutual goodwill among men, but more especially among the children of God, however distinguished by things of smaller importance; that as they have all "one Lord, one faith," as they are all "called in one hope of their calling," so they may all "walk worthy of the vocation wherewith they are called": "with all lowliness and meekness, with long-suffering, forbearing one another in love; endeavoring to keep the unity of the Spirit in the bond of peace."[6]

Thus peacemakers are not simply reactive to chaotic situations but rather proactive so as to prevent them occurring. Wesley also understands that conflict can never be prevented or curtailed completely, so it is the duty of Christians to use all their skills and abilities to bring about peace among contending parties. Wesley further recognizes that peacemakers endeavor to bring reconciliation among those in conflict as a way of ensuring lasting peace. Reconciliation results in one thing: peace; though reconciliation with God goes further, bringing enduring peace. The peace from the Lord is not transient but lasting, and those who receive it become conduits of the same (Rom 5:1; Eph 2:14).[7]

The peacemaker, "according to the measure of grace which he has received . . . uses all diligence either to reprove the gross sinner, to reclaim those who run on headlong in the broad way of destruction . . . [and] to bring back or heal them that are lame and turned out of the way."[8] In so doing, the peacemaker helps a sinner to have peace with God. A peacemaker is happy to see that there is friendship, love, and mutual understanding where previously there was enmity. Peacemaking involves helping those who are already looking for peace, or working toward achieving it, to find it: peacemakers are

> zealous to confirm those who are already striving to enter in at the strait gate; to strengthen those that stand, that they may "run with patience the race which is set before them"; to "build up in their

---

6. *Works*, 1:520.

7. Similarly, John Wesley taught the "assurance of the Holy Spirit," which, among other aspects, included a clear conscience before God. See Kenneth J. Collins, *The Theology of John Wesley: Holy Love and the Shape of Grace* (Nashville: Abingdon, 2007), 129.

8. *Works*, 1:519.

most holy faith" those that know in whom they have believed; to exhort them to stir up the gift of God which is in them, that daily "growing in grace," so an entrance may be ministered unto them abundantly into the everlasting kingdom of our Lord and Savior Jesus Christ.[9]

Peacemakers are thus engaged continuously in creating avenues for unadulterated peace.

Wesley understands peacemaking as enduring love toward others. It involves committing oneself to the work of touching other people's lives, seeking to improve their welfare. He indicates that peacemakers try by all means to see that there is peace in the world. They are not at peace themselves until they make peace for those who do not have it. He says, "They use all innocent arts, and employ all their strength, all the talents which God has given them, as well to preserve peace where it is as to restore it where it is not."[10]

There is no partiality in peacemaking. Peacemakers labor for the common good of all people. For Wesley, a "peacemaker" is

one that as he hath opportunity "doth good unto all men," one that being filled with the love of God and of all mankind cannot confine the expressions of it to his own family, or friends, or acquaintance, or party; or to those of his own opinions; no, nor those who are partakers of like precious faith; but steps over all these narrow bounds that he may do good to every man; that he may some way or other manifest his love to neighbors and strangers, friends and enemies.[11]

Peacemaking involves compassion. As Wesley understands it, "A peacemaker does good, to the uttermost of his power, even to the bodies of all men . . . And all this he does, not so as unto man, but remembering him that hath said, 'Inasmuch as ye have done it unto one of the least of these my brethren, ye have done it unto me.'"[12] In other words, peacemaking is the full manifestation of brotherly love that Christ commanded of his disciples before his death: "By this everyone will know that you are my disciples, if you love one another" (John 13:35). Wesley helps his audience to understand that those who strive to make peace for others do not labor in vain: there is a reward

---

9. *Works*, 1:519–520.
10. *Works*, 1:518.
11. *Works*, 1:518.
12. *Works*, 1:519.

for them. He remarks: "Blessed are they who are continually employed in the work of faith and the labor of love; 'for they shall be the children of God' . . . [who] shall acknowledge them as sons before angels and men; and 'if sons, then heirs; heirs of God, and joint heirs with Christ.'"[13]

From Wesley's sermon on Matthew 5:8–12 we learn, first, that holiness is the basis for one's involvement in peacemaking. God uses holy people as his instruments for peace in the world. Second, peacemaking goes beyond ceasefires. It involves taking proactive measures to prevent chaos occurring, healing the brokenhearted, and reconciling those who are at loggerheads. Third, peacemaking involves making a deliberate effort to improve people's lives for the sake of promoting peace. Finally, the motivation for peacemakers is love of peace and the joy that fills their hearts when they see others live in peace.

Explanatory Notes on the New Testament (Sermon on the Mount and other New Testament passages)

The word "peace" is used variously in both the Old and New Testaments. Daniel Arichea notes: "The word 'peace' together with its derivatives is one of those terms which more often than not is translated literally and consistently in many translations."[14] While the Old Testament uses the term "peace" (Hebrew *shalom*) to mean "wholeness, total health, and total welfare," the New Testament enriches the term further.[15] Peace is used in the New Testament to mean "(1) peace as the absence of war or chaos; (2) peace as a right relationship with God or with Christ; (3) peace as a good relationship among people; (4) peace as an individual virtue or state, that is, tranquility or serenity; and (5) peace as part of a greeting formula."[16] Interestingly, Wesley does not follow through all the New Testament nuances of the term. Rather, he focuses on the term "peace" in the context of relationships. Wesley underscores the essence of peace and its relationship to holy living.

One of the most important passages in the New Testament on peace is John 14:27. Here Christ communicates to his disciples that he is able to give them genuine peace. Wesley, on the basis of this verse, contends that peace is about having a right relationship with God. This peace can be accessed only by

---

13. *Works*, 1:520.

14. Daniel C. Arichea, "Peace in the New Testament," *The Bible Translator* 38, no. 2 (1 Apr. 1987): 201, accessed 13 January 2019, https://doi.org/10.1177/026009438703800201.

15. Arichea, "Peace," 201.

16. Arichea, 201.

an individual who is in good standing with the Lord. Wesley thus maintains that the peace that Christ generates and gives is not "unsatisfying, unsettled, transient; but [fills] the soul with constant, even tranquility."[17] Christ gives the peace that proceeds only from him, which is genuine and not illusive. Contrary to what Christ is able to give, Wesley says that the world can give only what is poor, cosmetic, and shallow, a very thin plating over a depth of restlessness. The legitimate peace that only Christ can give satisfies the soul. Wesley exclaims, "how serenely may we pass through the most turbulent scenes of life when all is quiet and harmonious within! Thou hast made peace through the blood of thy cross."[18] The reconciling power of the blood of Christ is the only means of bringing peace between God and humanity. Genuine peace, according to Wesley, is possible only through a right relationship with God. Since only Christ can do this, "may we give all diligence to preserve the inestimable gift inviolate, till it issue in everlasting peace!"[19] Wesley continues: "How desirable, in a world of anxiety and care, to possess this peace. And how should all who have it not, seek that which the world can neither give nor take away!"[20] This is peace born out of God's assurance that Christ is with us (John 14:27).

On the basis of Romans 14:17–18, where Paul says that the kingdom of God is not about food or drink but about righteousness, peace, and joy in the Holy Spirit, Wesley also argues that peace is a characteristic of the kingdom of God. It is a necessary byproduct of a relationship with God. Wesley comments: "True religion does not consist in external observances. But in righteousness – the image of God stamped on the heart; the love of God and man, accompanied with the peace that passeth all understanding, and joy in the Holy Ghost."[21] Wesley highlights God's kingdom as the main thing, and it hinges not on external matters, but on our relationship with God and with others. Since it is so easy to neglect the weightier matters of the kingdom of God, these verses are a ready reminder to "keep the main thing the main thing." Peripheral matters should never be allowed to make one lose focus on the greater kingdom view. We experience both peace and joy because of God's Holy Spirit within us. In other words, our place with God is secure, and that brings real emotional stability and confidence.

---

17. "Wesley's Explanatory Notes Bible Commentary," Bible Study Tools, accessed 13 January 2019, http://www.biblestudytools.com/commentaries/wesleys-explanatory-notes/.

18. "Wesley's Explanatory Notes."

19. "Wesley's Explanatory Notes."

20. "Wesley's Explanatory Notes."

21. "Wesley's Explanatory Notes."

As seen earlier, peace is also about having a right relationship between people. A significant degree of our Christian life is found simply in how we treat other people and the quality of our relationships with them. On Philippians 4:6 Wesley comments that thanksgiving is "the surest mark of a soul free from care, and of prayer joined with true resignation. This is always followed by peace. Peace and thanksgiving are both coupled together."[22] The peace of God is always expressed and enjoyed in good relationships. Wesley adds color to the Philippians 4:7:

> *And the peace of God* – that calm, heavenly repose, that tranquility of spirit, which God only can give. *Which surpasseth all understanding* – which none can comprehend, save he that receiveth it. *Shall keep* – Shall guard, as a garrison does a city. *Your hearts* – your affections, your minds, your understandings, and all the various workings of them; through the Spirit and power of Christ Jesus, in the knowledge and love of God. Without a guard set on these likewise, the purity and vigor of our affections cannot long be preserved.[23]

Hebrews 12:14 presents an exhortation to follow peace with all holiness. The exhortation concerns our neighbors and God. Wesley considers the pursuit of peace as a prerequisite to living a life of holiness. Since holiness, as conceived by Wesley, is built into relationships, it is impossible to realize it when animosity between people prevails. The effect of righteousness is always peace. If you are holy, you will be at peace and will pursue peace. Wesley makes this sound like an imperative so that it carries urgency. To exercise a wholesome influence as a peacemaker, one needs to understand this as an imperative. Making or pursuing peace also implies avoidance of all that breaches the bond of peace.

On James 3:18 Wesley further adds that those who engage in the pursuit of peace receive the blessing of peace and happiness. At the same time, the pursuit of righteousness or holiness issues in peace: "the principle productive of this righteousness is sown, like good seed, in the peace of a believer's mind, and brings forth a plentiful harvest of happiness, for them that make peace."[24] Eternal life, which is the fruit of Christ's righteousness, will be enjoyed by all those who genuinely pursue peace and holy living.

---

22. "Wesley's Explanatory Notes."
23. "Wesley's Explanatory Notes."
24. "Wesley's Explanatory Notes."

On 1 Peter 3:11, Wesley continues the idea of pursuing peace. He says, "pursue peace . . . even when it seems to flee from you."[25] Living peacefully with all people is sometimes a matter of diligent search, and if there is any reason to believe that peace is slipping away, there is a need to pursue it. Practical measures are here prescribed to uphold and preserve peace in relationships.

We therefore draw from Wesley the following affirmations:

1. Peace is about a right relationship with God. It is both a state and an accomplishment that proceed from that relationship.

2. Peace is about being in a healthy relationship with other people. It involves a continuous pursuit of such a state.

3. Peace as an individual virtue involves serenity and tranquility of heart. This is achieved only when one is in a right relationship with God.

"Catholic Spirit"

John Wesley's 1750 sermon "Catholic Spirit" is key in further comprehending his idea of peace. The sermon addresses the kind of attitude one needs to have in order to live at peace with all people. Bearing in mind the horizontal axis of relationships, "Catholic Spirit" is an address on the ideal disposition that Christians must have toward those who hold different views on certain doctrines. Wesley takes his time to elucidate what a catholic spirit is and what it is not. Kevin Watson says that "Catholic Spirit" is one of the Standard Sermons of Wesley that constituted essential Methodist doctrine.[26] By "catholic spirit" Wesley meant an all-embracing attitude, a tolerant and humble attitude toward others. Fascinatingly, the catholic spirit does not mean indifference to the opinions of others, nor is it an endeavor to prove one's religion as the only truth.

Having a "catholic spirit," according to Wesley, is to possess solid convictions on one's faith, yet leave room for dialogue with fellow Christians who may disagree on certain "opinions," as Wesley calls them. However, this does not negate the place of convincing each other as to the truth. Wesley writes: "Although every man necessarily believes that every particular opinion

---

25. "Wesley's Explanatory Notes."

26. Kevin M. Watson, "(Mis)Understanding Wesley's Catholic Spirit," *Vital Piety* (blog), 26 July 2012, accessed 11 February 2019, https://vitalpiety.com/2012/07/26/misunderstanding-wesleys-catholic-spirit/. For a print edition of Wesley's fifty-two standard sermons, see Nathanael Burwash, *Wesley's Doctrinal Standards, Part 1: The Sermons with Introductions, Analysis, and Notes* (1881; repr., Salem, OH: Schmul, 1988), https://archive.org/details/doctrinalstand00wesluoft.

which he holds is true (for to believe any opinion is not true, is the same thing as not to hold it) yet can no man be assured that all his own opinions taken together are true. Nay, every thinking man is assured they are not . . . He knows in general that he himself is mistaken; although in what particulars he mistakes he does not, perhaps cannot, know."[27]

Most certainly, Wesley does not advocate unsettledness of thought. He supports neither indecisiveness nor relativism. At the same time, he rejects rigid and inflexible attitudes that do not leave room for theological conversation with those of a different view. While it is right to be firm in one's beliefs, to truly possess a catholic spirit is to leave room for correction and even improvement. Wesley advises: "A man of a truly catholic spirit has not now his religion to seek. He is fixed as the sun in his judgment concerning the main branches of Christian doctrine. 'Tis true he is always ready to hear and weigh whatsoever can be offered against his principles. But as this does not show any wavering in his own mind, so neither does it occasion any."[28]

"Though we can't think alike, may we not love alike?"[29] This is the most quotable statement in this sermon. Kevin Watson interprets the phrase to mean that "doctrinal agreement is unimportant compared to loving one another."[30] It also implies that we may have liberty to think in differing ways but when it comes to love, we must love the same. For Wesley, commitment to particular emphases within Christian doctrines was no warrant to disregard other members within the Christian family. Differences in perceptions, interpretations, and practices are inevitable, but the identity or essential attributes of Christians ought to bring them together. The context of the quote provides further light:

> But although a difference in opinions or modes of worship may prevent an entire external union, yet need it prevent our union in affection? Though we can't think alike, may we not love alike? May we not be of one heart, though we are not of one opinion? Without all doubt we may. Herein all the children of God may unite, notwithstanding these smaller differences. These remaining as they are, they may forward one another in love and in good works.[31]

---

27. *Works*, 2:83–84.

28. *Works*, 2:93.

29. *Works*, 2:82.

30. Watson, "(Mis)Understanding Wesley's Catholic Spirit."

31. John Wesley and Albert Cook Outler, *The Works of John Wesley, Volumes 1–4* (Nashville: Abingdon, 1984).

Disagreement over doctrinal matters should never keep persons from recognizing others as fellow Christians. Does this encourage unresolved differences among Christians? Certainly not, because those who truly love will find ways to win over those who are in error and will be humble enough to accept any correction when found in the wrong. Wesley argues that no one thinks of their opinions as being wrong, yet there is indeed a possibility of our being wrong in our opinions, and this possibility calls everyone to humility.

From this sermon, we learn that a truly catholic spirit is about

1. Having the mind that was in Christ: a humility and a healthy attitude toward those with differing views and opinions;

2. Loving God and neighbor, and cultivating a love that counteracts the sinful mind, draws out the heart in affectionate connection to God, and graciously opens us up to the need for peace with God and others;

3. Loving peace for its own sake.

The Imperfect Practice of the "Catholic Spirit"

Having seen the broad outline of John Wesley's thought regarding peacemaking, this investigation turns to two episodes from Wesley's early ministry to answer the question: How well did Wesley follow his own counsel? From these episodes, it will be shown that, despite his theories, when it came to pursuing peaceful relationships Wesley's practice was uneven. This will be demonstrated by first examining his controversial 1739 interaction with George Whitefield over the question of predestination. A description of his successful peacemaking when faced by a mob in 1743 in the village of Wednesbury will then be given.

The "Free Grace" Controversy

John Wesley and George Whitefield (1714–70) were friends of long acquaintance, stemming back to their time at Oxford, where both were members of the "Holy Club."[32] In the months following his celebrated "heartwarming" in May 1738, Wesley found a cold hearing in Church of England pulpits for his preaching of the doctrine of justification by faith. So it was that, at George Whitefield's invitation, he began field preaching in the coal-mining area of

---

32. See Richard P. Heitzenrater, *Wesley and the People Called Methodists*, 2nd ed. (Nashville: Abingdon, 2013), 54–64.

Kingswood, near Bristol.[33] On Whitefield's prior work, Henry Rack observes: "Even allowing for retrospective exaggerations, there is little doubt that before his departure for Georgia Whitefield had lifted the movement for awakening from an eccentricity of a few friends into something more extensive and public. If he alienated the respectable, he soon found an appeal to the less sophisticated when he went into the open air . . . He was certainly moved by the Kingswood colliers' situation as 'sheep without a shepherd.'"[34]

What this admirable collaboration masked was a fundamental doctrinal disagreement over the doctrine of predestination. Rack contends that the controversy arose "virtually as soon as he [Wesley] started work in Bristol" and gained momentum as some individuals who joined the Methodist societies agitated in favor of the doctrine, perhaps as a result of Whitefield's earlier preaching on the topic.[35] What is clear is that Wesley, following the casting of lots for divine guidance on 26 April 1739, subsequently moved to publish "Free Grace," a frontal attack on Calvin's doctrine of predestination.[36]

"Free Grace" was by any measure polemical. As Wesley announced the gospel to all comers, the doctrine of universal grace – that is, that Jesus died for all – undergirded his appeal. The sermon took as its text Romans 8:32: "He that spared not his own Son, but delivered him up for us all, how shall he not with him also freely give us all things?" (KJV). Wesley maintained that God's grace is "free in all," by which he ruled out any meritorious action on the part of humanity: "Whatever good is in man, or is done by man, God is the author and doer of it."[37] Salvation comes from God alone. Yet Wesley went further, insisting not only that God's activity in salvation is God's work alone, but that the *possibility* of salvation exists because God's grace is extended to all. It is not only "free in all" but also "free for all." For the remainder of the sermon, Wesley rails against what he calls "the horrible decree," a reference to Calvin's *Institutes* 3.23.7. This is Calvin's teaching that God not only "foresaw the fall of the first man, and in him the ruin of his descendants, but also meted it out in accordance with his own decision."[38]

---

33. Henry D. Rack, *Reasonable Enthusiast: John Wesley and the Rise of Methodism*, 3rd ed. (London: Epworth, 2002), 192.

34. Rack, *Reasonable Enthusiast*, 192–193.

35. Rack, 198.

36. See Albert Outler's introductory comment to "Free Grace" in *Works*, 3:542.

37. *Works*, 3:545. This is a nascent version of Wesley's later, more fully developed doctrine of prevenient grace.

38. John T. McNeill, ed., *Calvin's Institutes of the Christian Religion*, 2 vols. (Louisville, KY/ London: Westminster John Knox, 1960), 2:955–956.

Wesley laid out his multiple objections to the doctrine. For our purposes, analyzing the *tone* of the sermon, an excerpt from paragraph 26 is representative: "This is the blasphemy clearly contained in the 'horrible decree' of predestination. And here I fix my foot. On this I join issue with every asserter of it. You represent God as worse than the devil – more false, more cruel, more unjust."[39] Later, Wesley hypothetically advises the devil that, if predestination is true, then the devil's work is pointless: "Thou fool, why dost thou roar about any longer? Lying in wait for souls is as needless and useless as our preaching . . . Thou canst only entice; but his unchangeable decree to leave thousands of souls in death compels them to continue in sin till they drop into everlasting burnings."[40]

Whitefield had heard of John and Charles Wesley's harsh dealings with predestinarians in the Methodist societies. Further, Whitefield had urged John Wesley to let the matter of predestination drop, suggesting that the latter was not acting with a "catholic spirit."[41] When Wesley ignored Whitefield's advice and both preached and published against predestination, a breach opened up between the two. In a public treatise dated 24 December 1740, Whitefield responded to Wesley's "Free Grace." The letter reads as a point-by-point refutation of Wesley's sermon. However, Whitefield's surprise that it had come from the pen of a friend is evident in the introduction, where he concludes: "But to hear the Whispers of the Enemy, reviving from the Mouth, and Pen, of the Reverend and learned Mr. Wesley, gives me Room to apprehend, That there is none, in Time, can plead Exemption from sinning."[42]

The consequences of this theological battle were unfortunate, causing a split between the two principal leaders of the revival, a rift not quickly healed.[43] Albert Outler maintains that the sermon is "noteworthy as the signal of a major schism in the ranks of English evangelicals, the consequences of which have outlasted the lives of the antagonists."[44] If the themes presented in Wesley's later

---

39. *Works*, 3:556.

40. *Works*, 3:557.

41. Allan Coppedge, *Shaping the Wesleyan Message: John Wesley in Theological Debate* (1987; repr., Nappanee, IN: Francis Asbury/Evangel, 2003), 39.

42. George Whitefield, "Free Grace Indeed! A Letter to the Reverend Mr. John Wesley, Relating to His Sermon against Absolute Election; Published under the Title of Free Grace," 1741, Oxford Text Archive, accessed 11 February 2019, https://ota.bodleian.ox.ac.uk/repository/xmlui/handle/20.500.12024/N03939. This quote maintains the use of upper-case letters and other punctuation found in the original.

43. Kenneth J. Collins, *John Wesley: A Theological Journey* (Nashville: Abingdon, 2003), 104.

44. *Works*, 3:542.

writings on peace are the benchmark by which to judge his actions – including the sentiments contained in "Catholic Spirit" – then it must be admitted that in this episode Wesley failed abysmally. "Free Grace" was never included in his collected *Sermons*, and when it later appeared in his *Works* it was classed with his controversial writings.[45]

The October 1743 Riot in Wednesbury

While John Wesley arguably fanned the flame of theological discord between himself and George Whitefield in 1739, he fared much better in a second episode that occurred just four years later. Methodism was expanding rapidly, taking Wesley, his brother, Charles, and other Methodist preachers by horseback into remote corners of the kingdom, preaching and organizing converts into societies. Both John and Charles record in their separate journals harrowing events that transpired in Wednesbury, a market town in the West Midlands of England. It was here that the elder Wesley showed himself to be an adept peacemaker, calming crowds by the force of his presence and soothing words.

John Wesley's journal entry for 20 October 1743 is nearly six pages long.[46] For several hours, Wesley was hurried along (sometimes dragged) by the crowd as they took him from magistrate to magistrate, lodging complaints against him and the Methodists. At a key early juncture, Wesley and his hosts prayed for the mob who were menacingly surrounding the house to disperse, and God granted their prayer. However, an hour later the mob were back. This time, he invited their leaders one by one inside the house, where he spoke softly to them and won them over. Wesley noted: "After a few sentences interchanged between us, the lion was become a lamb."[47] Even when he was forced to go to the magistrate, surrounded by the rabble, he kept engaging them in conversation: "I continued speaking all the time to those within hearing, feeling no pain or weakness."[48]

Wesley noted that his voice gave out, but his demeanor had won over the head of the mob. "'Sir, I will spend my life for you. Follow *me*, and not one soul here shall touch a hair of your head.' Two or three of his fellows confirmed his words and got close to me immediately."[49] Later, when the harrowing several

---

45. *Works*, 3:542.
46. *Works*, 19:344–349.
47. *Works*, 19:344.
48. *Works*, 19:345.
49. *Works*, 19:346.

hours were over, he noted: "When I came back to Francis Ward's I found many of our brethren waiting upon God. Many also whom I had never seen before came to rejoice with us."[50] Though Wesley later discovered that it was the justices themselves who had some days before put up a notice calling upon the population to apprehend "Methodist preachers" and bring them before the Justices of the Peace, Mr Lane, one of the two justices who had signed the notice, refused to act when Wesley actually appeared before him. The mob's only complaint against Wesley was that "the Methodists sang psalms all day and required folks to rise at 5 a.m.," to which Lane replied: "Go home and be quiet."[51] Charles, meeting up with his brother later, noted in his journal the following day: "My brother came, delivered out of the mouth of the lion! He *looked* like a soldier of Christ. His clothes were torn to tatters."[52] Charles's subsequent interviews with those who were eyewitnesses confirmed that his brother had been threatened with drowning and hanging, and the strategies he had mustered that resulted in a peaceful outcome. Charles recorded: "In the intervals of tumult, he spoke, the brethren assured me, with as much composure and correctness as he used to do in their Societies. The Spirit of glory rested on him. As many as he spoke to, or but laid his hand on, he turned into friends."[53]

Why in this instance did John Wesley succeed as a peacemaker? First, he relied upon prayer, both individual and corporate. Second, Wesley understood that "a soft answer turneth away wrath" (Prov 15:1 KJV). As he remained level-headed, the crowds came to mirror his demeanor. Finally, he had an ability to quickly size up a crowd and identify its leaders. In winning them over, he helped defuse an explosive situation. Henry Rack concludes: "Unless he was exaggerating their murderous intent, one may perhaps suppose that his calm or charisma unnerved them; and sometimes mob leaders suddenly became his protectors."[54] These were peacemaking techniques that were effective in a volatile situation.

However, the Methodists also engaged in longer-term peacemaking. In the seventh point of a ten-point summary of Wesley's moral practice, Ronald Stone identifies "active peacemaking through preaching, preparation of tracts,

50. *Works*, 19:348.

51. *Works*, 19:345.

52. S. T. Kimbrough, Jr., and Kenneth G. C. Newport, eds., *The Manuscript Journal of the Reverend Charles Wesley, M.A.*, 2 vols. (Nashville: Abingdon/Kingswood, 2007), 2:374.

53. Kimbrough and Newport, *Manuscript Journal*, 2:376.

54. Rack, *Reasonable Enthusiast*, 272.

publication of books, criticism of war, letter writing, preaching, and witnessing to soldiers."[55] In a difficult situation, Wesley was able to promote peace between himself and his accusers because his daily habit as the leader of the Methodists was already long established: that of promoting peace in society at large, whether peace through reconciliation with God or peace between individuals. Yet despite his success in Wednesbury, he knew that peacemaking is often unwelcome. Stone concludes: "The process of peacemaking, Wesley recognizes, leads to persecution. Persecution is the inevitable fruit of serious religion. All Christians should expect persecution for their pursuit of righteousness. Particularly, they are persecuted for being peacemakers."[56]

Wesley's Peace Principles and *Ubuntu*

Africa has suffered all kinds of unsettling issues: slavery, colonialism, apartheid, genocide, wars, ethnic conflicts, and many other forms of violence. The need for peace is thus critical for all those who have been born in and live in Africa. For some, Africa continues to experience the antithesis of peace due to external forces at work on the continent. However, this chapter has argued that peace cannot be found when the hearts of people are detached from the fountain of peace, Jesus Christ. Paul insists: "For he himself is our peace, who has made the two groups one and has destroyed the barrier, the dividing wall of hostility" (Eph 2:14). If Jew and Gentile can become one, then there is no barrier that cannot be removed in Christ. It can never be denied that the gospel has positive injunctions for Christians to participate actively in peacemaking in every aspect of life.

In Africa, peace means not just the absence of war, violence, disease, poverty, hunger, inequality, or terror. It goes beyond such phenomena. Peacemaking means going beyond creating theories and formulas, developing movements, or just improving communications between people. Rather, peace is a state of being. It is embedded in the African conception of community. Thus, from an African perspective, peace or peacemaking has been linked with concepts such as *ubuntu* and its various renditions. William Flippin observes: "The philosophy of Ubuntu derives from a Nguni word, *ubuntu*, meaning 'the quality

---

55. Ronald H. Stone, *John Wesley's Life and Ethics* (Nashville: Abingdon, 2001), 227.
56. Stone, *John Wesley's Life*, 115.

of being human.'"[57] It recognizes the importance of others in one's being and actions. "Ubuntu manifests itself through various human acts, clearly visible in social, political, and economic situations, as well as among family."[58] The *ubuntu* concept highlights the "essential unity of humanity." It thrives on constant reference to the principles of empathy, compassion, generosity, cooperation, cohabitation, tolerance, and respect in efforts to resolve common problems. This culturally located social schema of *ubuntu* is thus the thread that holds African people and communities together. More than that, it is a reflection of the quality of being that manifests itself in right actions toward others.

In the same way, John Wesley's explication of peace or peacemaking underscores that one's being is critical and is directly related to one's actions toward others. As pointed out, Wesley understood a peacemaker to be a person "full of genuine humility, so unaffectedly serious, so mild and gentle, so free from all selfish design, so devoted to God, and such an active lover of men."[59] This description resonates with the four *ubuntu* stages of the peacemaking process: "acknowledging guilt; showing remorse and repenting; asking for and giving forgiveness; and paying compensation or reparations as a prelude to reconciliation."[60] All lovers of God will not only acknowledge wrongdoing but will go all the way, even to making reparations. As in *ubuntu*, an understanding that an individual owes his or her selfhood to others will certainly result in detesting and abhorring all disagreement, all strife and debate, and all contention that does not support the spirit of peace. Even with this brief description, it is apparent that Wesley's understanding of a peacemaker as a lover of God and humankind generally suits the African concept of *ubuntu*.

Conclusion

In the Sermon on the Mount, especially Jesus's affirmation of peacemakers (Matt 5:9), John Wesley found a timeless template for peace. Reinforcing this with other New Testament passages that recommend the pursuit of peace with both God and others, Wesley ascribed to the vision of a "catholic spirit," a call

---

57. William E. Flippin Jr., "Ubuntu: Applying African Philosophy in Building Community," *The Huffington Post*, 2 May 2012, accessed 28 August 2019, https://www.huffpost.com/entry/ubuntu-applying-african-p_b_1243904.

58. Flippin, "Ubuntu."

59. Wesley and Outler, *Works of John Wesley*, 520.

60. Tim Murithi, "An African Perspective on Peace Education: Ubuntu Lessons in Reconciliation," *International Review of Education / Internationale Zeitschrift für Erziehungswissenschaft / Revue Internationale de l'Education* 55, no. 2/3 (2009): 221.

to embrace others in love regardless of theological differences. In practice, Wesley did not always live up to his own ideal. Despite his failings, however, he provides a model of calm persistence in the face of hostility, a love of peace that is comparable to the African concept of *ubuntu* and is highly commendable in our own time.

Bibliography

Arichea, Daniel C. "Peace in the New Testament." *The Bible Translator* 38, no. 2 (1 Apr. 1987): 201–206. Accessed 11 February 2019. https://doi.org/10.1177/026009438703800201.

Baker, Frank, ed. *The Works of John Wesley*. Bicentennial edition. 35 volumes projected. Nashville: Abingdon, 1984–.

Burwash, Nathanael. *Wesley's Doctrinal Standards, Part 1: The Sermons with Introductions, Analysis, and Notes*. 1881. Reprint, Salem, OH: Schmul, 1988.

Collins, Kenneth J. *John Wesley: A Theological Journey*. Nashville: Abingdon, 2003.

———. *The Theology of John Wesley: Holy Love and the Shape of Grace*. Nashville: Abingdon, 2007.

Coppedge, Allan. *Shaping the Wesleyan Message: John Wesley in Theological Debate*. 1987. Reprint, Nappanee, IN: Francis Asbury/Evangel, 2003.

Cubie, David L. "Early Methodism: A Paradigm for Non-Violence: An Exercise in 'Vision Ethics.'" *Wesleyan Theological Journal* 37, no. 1 (Spring 2002): 86–105.

Flippin, William E., Jr. "Ubuntu: Applying African Philosophy in Building Community." *The Huffington Post*. 2 May 2012. Accessed 28 August 2019. https://www.huffpost.com/entry/ubuntu-applying-african-p_b_1243904.

Heitzenrater, Richard P. *Wesley and the People Called Methodists*. 2nd ed. Nashville: Abingdon, 2013.

Kimbrough, S. T., Jr., and Kenneth G. C. Newport, eds. *The Manuscript Journal of the Reverend Charles Wesley, M.A.* 2 vols. Nashville: Abingdon/Kingswood, 2007.

Long, D. Stephen. *John Wesley's Moral Theology: The Quest for God and Goodness*. Nashville: Abingdon/Kingswood, 2005.

Marquardt, Manfred. *John Wesley's Social Ethics: Praxis and Principle*. Translated by John E. Steely and W. Stephen Gunter. Eugene, OR: Wipf & Stock, 2000.

McNeill, John T., ed. *Calvin's Institutes of the Christian Religion*. 2 vols. Louisville, KY/London: Westminster John Knox, 1960.

Mitchell, T. Crichton. *Meet Mr. Wesley: An Intimate Sketch of John Wesley*. Kansas City, MO: Beacon Hill, 1981.

Murithi, Tim. "An African Perspective on Peace Education: Ubuntu Lessons in Reconciliation." *International Review of Education / Internationale Zeitschrift für Erziehungswissenschaft / Revue Internationale de l'Education* 55, no. 2/3 (2009): 221–233.

Rack, Henry D. *Reasonable Enthusiast: John Wesley and the Rise of Methodism*. 3rd ed. London: Epworth, 2002.

Schwenk, James L. *Catholic Spirit: Wesley, Whitefield, and the Quest for Evangelical Unity in Eighteenth Century British Methodism*. Lanham, MD: Scarecrow, 2008.

Stone, Ronald H. *John Wesley's Life and Ethics*. Nashville: Abingdon, 2001.

Watson, Kevin M. "(Mis) Understanding Wesley's Catholic Spirit." *Vital Piety* (blog). 26 July 2012. Accessed 11 February 2019. https://vitalpiety.com/2012/07/26/misunderstanding-wesleys-catholic-spirit/.

"Wesley's Explanatory Notes Bible Commentary." Bible Study Tools. Accessed 13 January 2019. http://www.biblestudytools.com/commentaries/wesleys-explanatory-notes.

Wesley, John. *The Character of a Methodist*. Nashville: United Methodist Publishing House, 1992.

Wesley, John, and Albert Cook Outler. *The Works of John Wesley, Volumes 1–4*. Nashville: Abingdon, 1984.

Whitefield, George. "Free Grace Indeed! A Letter to the Reverend Mr. John Wesley, Relating to His Sermon against Absolute Elections; Published under the Title of Free Grace." Oxford Text Archive. Accessed 11 February 2019. https://ota.bodleian.ox.ac.uk/repository/xmlui/handle/20.500.12024/N03939.

8

The Church and Ethnopolitical Conflict in Kenya, 1982–2013[1]

David Tarus

Executive Director, Association for Christian Theological Education in Africa (ACTEA)

Abstract

This chapter examines the role of the church in addressing the problem of ethnopolitical conflict in Kenya from 1982 to 2013. Though ethnocentrism within the Kenyan Christian community goes beyond the years cited to the colonial period and the years immediately following independence, the intensity of the problem after 1982 calls for special attention. The single event that marked political change in Kenya was the 1982 attempted coup. Although this was not successful, the coup heightened opposition against Moi's rule and thus 1982 marks the beginning of Kenya's recent history, a history in which three phases may be identified in the relationship between church and state: a united church (1982–2002); a divided church (2002–2008); and a recovering church (2008 onwards). The thesis of this chapter is that the church in Kenya generally exhibited robust sociopolitical engagement in the 1980s and 1990s but lost its prophetic voice from 2002 to 2008, mainly because of ethnocentrism and the co-option and compromise of the clergy by the government and the opposition. The chapter, which is based on archival and library materials, broadly examines the roles the mainstream Protestant, evangelical, and Roman Catholic churches, and their umbrella organizations, the National Council of

---

[1]. This chapter appears as chapter 2 in *A Different Way of Being: Towards a Reformed Theology of Ethnopolitical Cohesion for the Kenyan Context* (Carlisle: Langham Monographs, 2019), by the same author.

Churches of Kenya (NCCK), the Evangelical Fellowship of Kenya (EFK) – now called the Evangelical Alliance of Kenya (EAK) – and the Kenya Catholic Episcopal Conference (KCEC) – now called Kenya Conference of Catholic Bishops (KCCB) – played in their quest for social cohesion. In so doing, the chapter highlights the failures of Kenyan churches in addressing the problem of ethnopolitical conflict.

Key words: ethnopolitical, cohesion, ethnicity, tribalism, conflict, church, Kenya, evangelical.

Ethnopolitical Conflict and the Church in Kenya: A Unified Voice (1982–2002)

The period 1982–2002 saw a Kenyan church that was generally unified against social injustice, including tribalism. In most cases the church spoke with one voice. Protestant bishops joined together to push for justice, democracy, and ethnic cohesion, especially during the years preceding the introduction of a multiparty political system in Kenya. Reverend Bishop Timothy Njoya of the Presbyterian Church of East Africa (PCEA), Bishop Zablon Nthamburi of the Methodist Church in Kenya (MCK), and Bishops John Henry Okullu and Alexander Kipsang Muge, and Archbishops Manasses Kuria and David Gitari of the Church Province of Kenya (CPK), were instrumental in pushing for social justice, cohesion, and democracy in Kenya.[2] The bishops used the media (television and radio), publications, and their pulpits for this purpose.[3] Bishop Gitari summarized this sociopolitical engagement and the risks it involved: "Bishop Okullu was very vocal. Bishop Muge was very vocal. Timothy Njoya was very vocal. I spoke out at every occasion. There was great reluctance by the government to enter into dialogue with church leaders. Live broadcasts of church services were stopped. Only churches [that] praised the

---

2. "The Outspoken Clergyman," *The Weekly Review*, 1994, 5–6; "Okullu Ready for 1994," *The Weekly Review*, 1994, 3–5; "Njoya At It Again," *The Weekly Review*, 1990, 3–6; "Okullu's Volley: Bishop Calls for Multi-Party System," *The Weekly Review*, 1990, 6–9.

3. Such include, among others, the NCCK newspaper *Target/Lengo* and the various talkshows on the state-owned Voice of Kenya (VOK) (later renamed Kenya Broadcasting Corporation). Gitari observes that he delivered six live talks on VOK after the assassination of J. M. Kariuki in 1975 (David Gitari, *Troubled but Not Destroyed: The Autobiography of Archbishop David Gitari* [Vancouver: Isaac, 2014], 33–34).

government were allowed on the air. There was a lot of stiffening of the part of the government."[4]

Reverend Njoya led in preaching fiery sermons against Moi's one-party regime. In a New Year (1 January 1990) sermon preached at St Andrews PCEA in Nairobi, Njoya audaciously compared Kenya's one-party rule to the monolithic communist regimes in Eastern Europe, saying that it would one day collapse just as Nicolae Ceausescu's regime had collapsed in Romania.[5] Thus Njoya avowed that Kenya had no option but to embrace multipartyism. In addition, he condemned patronage and tribalism, which had derailed Kenya's progress.[6]

Bishop Okullu preached a comparable sermon at St Stephen's Cathedral in Kisumu.[7] Okullu explained why he opposed a single-party system of government: "I am infinitely suspicious of one-party system of government being capable of safeguarding and promoting human rights, because it is there to promote a colonization of the mind and to assist its leaders in staying in power for life. One-party government only encourages idolization of leaders and the party and non-accountability to the people."[8]

The bishops' courageous sermons had two major effects. First the sermons rallied the Kenya African National Union (KANU) government against Njoya, Gitari, Kuria, Okullu, and Muge, the five most vocal clergymen.[9] These five clerics had been outspoken since the 1980s, resisting the *mlolongo* (queue-voting) system of the KANU regime and urging Christians to set a good example of neighborliness. In the *mlolongo* system, voters would line up behind their preferred candidate and then the presiding officer would do a head count before declaring the winner. In most cases, the candidate with the shortest line got declared the winner. Bishop Manasses Kuria termed the voting system "unchristian, undemocratic, and embarrassing," while Bishop Muge referred to it as totalitarian.[10] Bishop Okullu said the queue system "produced some of

---

4. Margaret Crouch, *A Vision of Christian Mission: Reflections on the Great Commission in Kenya* (Nairobi: NCCK, 1993), 95–96.

5. "Njoya At It Again," 3.

6. "Njoya At It Again," 6.

7. "Clerics Kick Up Storm," *The Weekly Review*, 1990, 5–6; Jemima Atieno Oluoch, *The Christian Political Theology of Dr. John Henry Okullu* (Nairobi: Uzima, 2006), 20.

8. Henry Okullu, "Some Theological and Ethical Considerations in African Context," in *An African Call for Life: Contribution to the World Council of Churches Sixth Assembly Theme "Jesus Christ: The Life of the World"* (Geneva: WCC, 1983), 103.

9. "The Question of Opposition," *The Weekly Review*, 1990, 8.

10. "The Queue-Voting Furore," *The Weekly Review*, 1990, 19.

the most blatant and cruel vote rigging and cheating that has been practiced in Kenya."[11] Leaders of the National Council of Churches of Kenya (NCCK) urged KANU "to find an alternative method" of voting, otherwise they would ask Kenyan Christians to refrain from taking part in elections.[12]

Because of their resistance, the bishops were condemned. Bishop Okullu was branded a "prophet of doom who should be shunned by every peace-loving Kenyan,"[13] while Timothy Njoya was referred to as a "tribalist bent on causing chaos in Kenya."[14] Gitari said that he "was in several instances referred to as a tribalist, a political activist, a champion of political groupings, a member of *Mwakenya* (the underground political movement) and a messenger of foreign masters."[15] These criticisms did not deter the clerics from critiquing the KANU regime.

Second, the sermons rallied the opposition against the KANU government and bolstered the push for multiparty democracy. The members of parliament opposed to the KANU regime, the civil society, and the church united to oppose the dictatorial trends of the KANU regime and to push for multiparty politics. Even the then US Ambassador, Smith Hempstone, agreed with the clerics that Kenya must accede to multiparty democracy.[16] Several politicians, including Kenneth Matiba, Paul Muite, Philip Gachoka, Charles Rubia, and Bishops Henry Okullu and David Gitari, held night meetings to strategize how to plan campaigns for multiparty democracy.[17] These meetings resulted in several rallies and street protests.

In response, the KANU regime marshaled its forces to stop the protests. For instance, on 7 July 1997 hundreds of demonstrators who had met at Uhuru Park grounds in Nairobi were brutally assaulted, including those who sought refuge at All Saints Cathedral, a church adjacent to the park.[18] Several clerics

---

11. Oluoch, *Christian Political Theology*, 17.

12. Oluoch, 85–86.

13. "A Dissenting Patriot," *The Weekly Review*, 1990, 15.

14. "A Heated Debate," *The Weekly Review*, 1990, 23; "Njoya At It Again," 6.

15. Gitari, *Troubled*, 240.

16. Smith Hempstone, *Rogue Ambassador: An African Memoir* (Sewanee, TN: University of the South Press, 1997); Kamau Ngotho, "The Day Democracy Visited and Stayed," *The Daily Nation*, 2000, 5.

17. Gitari, *Troubled*, 256.

18. The Uhuru Park grounds have been a venue for many other political rallies. The 7 July 1990 meeting, and subsequent meetings every 7 July, referred to as Saba Saba (Seven Seven), borrowing from Tanzania's revolution day which falls on the same day, inspired great struggles for justice in Kenya. For more on the Saba Saba struggles, see "A Strike for Freedom," *The Weekly Review*, 1992, 3–6; "Show of Force," *The Weekly Review*, 1997, 4–6.

including Timothy Njoya and the provost of the cathedral, Rev. Peter Njoka, were beaten up. The clergy and the opposition condemned the brutality as a sign of the government's infringement of religious freedom, suppression of its citizens, and disregard for the sanctity of human life.[19] Following the incident, Archbishop Gitari called for a "cleansing" service of the cathedral. Thousands of people attended the televised meeting. Gitari preached from Daniel 5, warning President Moi that God's hand would soon write "Mene, Mene, Tekel, Parsin" on the wall of State House if he continued to hinder reforms.[20]

However, not all Protestant bishops accepted multiparty democracy. Bishop Lawi Imathiu of MCK and Bishop Muge of CPK issued a joint press statement supporting one-party rule.[21] They contended that the multiparty system would precipitate ethnic conflict in Kenya. Interestingly, Bishop Imathiu had served as a nominated Member of Parliament during Kenyatta's presidency (1974–9), and the MCK had benefited greatly from both Kenyatta and Moi's governments. This historical reality might have informed Imathiu's non-confrontational stance against the Moi regime.[22]

However, even though Imathiu and Muge did not support multipartyism, they, especially Muge, condemned ethnocentrism in Kenya. Bishop Muge, who at the time was the chairman of NCCK's Justice, Peace, and Reconciliation Committee, paid a heavy price for his opposition to KANU.[23] On 12 August 1990, Peter Habenga Okondo, the Labor Minister, issued a warning to both Bishop Okullu and Bishop Muge that they "would see fire and may not come out alive" if they went to Busia district for a church service.[24] Bishop Muge defied him and attended the service at St Stephen's Church in Busia on Sunday, 14 August 1990. On his way to Eldoret, Muge was killed in a road accident. Muge joined the list of other prominent persons mysteriously killed in Kenya.

According to Margaret Crouch, Muge died "a champion of justice, peace, and human rights," and "a true nationalist, a martyr to the truth."[25] He was not afraid to speak his mind against tribalism in all areas, including the church and NCCK. At one time he wrote, "The NCCK in Kenya is like a rotten apple. To

---

19. "A Strike for Freedom," 6; "A Blessing for the Mothers," *The Weekly Review*, 1992, 17.

20. Gitari, *Troubled*, 260.

21. "A Heated Debate," 23.

22. Henry Okullu, *Quest for Justice: An Autobiography of Bishop Henry Okullu* (Kisumu: Shalom, 1997), 128.

23. His courageous actions are recorded in Nicholas Otieno, *Beyond the Silence of Death: The Life and Theology of Bishop Alexander Muge* (Nairobi: NCCK, 1993).

24. Okullu, *Quest*, 120.

25. Crouch, *A Vision*, 158.

the best of my knowledge, the NCCK has nothing to lecture our nation because all the evils which eat our nation, such as tribalism, favoritism, nepotism, and other-isms, have found shape in NCCK."[26]

Comparable to the activist-oriented Protestant churches, the Roman Catholic Church also united in pushing for socio-economic justice, democracy, and social cohesion in Kenya. Under the leadership of Cardinal Mourice Michael Otunga, Archbishop Rafael Ndingi Mwana a'Nzeki, Archbishop Zacchaeus Okoth, and Archbishop John Njue, the Roman Catholic Church produced several pastoral letters highly critical of the government and KANU.[27] For example, in February 1992, the Roman Catholic bishops issued a joint statement saying, in part, "The continuation of Kanu rule is a hazard to the genuine evolution of democracy in Kenya as evidenced by the brutal tribal clashes West of Nakuru."[28] On 22 March 1992, eighteen Roman Catholic bishops issued another pastoral letter accusing the government of complicity in the violent ethnic clashes prevalent in parts of western Kenya since October 1991 where more than sixty-five people had died and thousands been rendered homeless.[29]

Individual bishops issued similar calls. Bishop Ndingi Mwana a'Nzeki condemned the Meteitei ethnic strife of 1992 saying, "These tragic happenings are orchestrated by irresponsible statements made in Kapsabet, Kapkatet, Kericho, and Narok."[30] Bishop Manasses Kuria declared that all peace-loving Kenyans should resist politicians who capitalized on ethnicity for personal gain; "anything that is likely to cause disharmony, strife and chaos is evil; it is even satanic" and must be stopped.[31] Likewise, Bishop Cornelius Korir of the Roman Catholic Diocese of Eldoret and Bishop Longinus Atundo of the Bungoma Diocese condemned ethnic-based violence in the Rift Valley and Western provinces.[32]

Thus, during this pro-liberation struggle, the church in Kenya generally worked together across denominational divides. The NCCK and the Catholic

26. "A Controversial Churchman," *The Weekly Review*, 1985, 5–7.

27. See Paul Gifford, *Christianity, Politics and Public Life in Kenya* (London: Hurst, 2009), 36–39; "The Church Factor: The NCCK Tries to Unite the Opposition Parties," *The Weekly Review*, 1992, 5.

28. "New Radicalism in Pastoral Letter," *The Weekly Review*, 1992, 11.

29. "Moving into the Political Arena," *The Weekly Review*, 1992, 20.

30. "The Nandi Clashes," *The Nairobi Law Monthly* (1991): 19.

31. Njehu Gatabaki, "Peace: Interview of the Most Rev. Manasses Kuria," *Finance*, 1991, 37.

32. "Fresh Outbreak of Violence," *The Weekly Review*, 1992, 16; "Lawlessness Must End," *The Weekly Review*, 1992, 19.

Church formed the National Ecumenical Civic Education Program (NECEP) to provide civic education to Kenyan voters and politicians under the chairmanship of Bishop Henry Okullu.[33] In addition to civic education, NECEP coordinated two interparty symposiums in May and June 1992 "to discuss national issues, particularly the spate of ethnic clashes" prevailing throughout the country.[34] NECEP joined forces with other concerned citizens to form the National Election Monitoring Unit (NEMU), with the idea of monitoring the General Election scheduled for 29 December 1992 to ensure that peace, order, and democracy prevailed.[35]

The courage of the leaders extended to the corridors of power. The Catholic Church and the NCCK, under the leadership of the chairman of the Kenya Episcopal Conference, Archbishop Zacchaeus Okoth, and the Very Rev. George Wanjau, respectively, took a strongly worded joint statement to State House titled "People Have Lost Confidence in You," addressed to President Moi and condemning the violence of 1992.[36] The statement is here quoted in part:

> What [brings] us here is nothing less than the life or death of Kenya, the question of the lives and future of hundreds of families who have been treated inhumanly, butchered, slaughtered. The scenes are truly heartbreaking. No human being can be left unmoved. Anyone who carries responsibility before the nation, even more before our God and Father, must be forced to stop the bloodshed and human misery at once . . . Unless you change your present policies, Kenya will not be Kanu but a cemetery for thousands of its sons and daughters . . . Why do you not commit your administration officers, your police, and army to capturing these men? . . . Why have leading government ministers who made provocative statements and ordered non-Kalenjins out of Rift Valley province at public meetings in Kapsabet, Kaptagat, and Narok in September 1991, not been prosecuted or censured in any way? Your Excellency, you cannot deny what we have seen . . .

---

33. Henry Okullu, "Render unto Caesar," in *A Vision of Christian Mission: Reflections on the Great Commission in Kenya*, ed. Margaret Crouch (Nairobi: NCCK, 1993), 151.

34. "The Church Factor," 3; "United by a Common Cause," *The Weekly Review*, 1992, 16.

35. Okullu, "Render unto Caesar," 152.

36. "People Have Lost Confidence in You," *The Weekly Review*, 1992, 21; "A Severe Dressing Down for the President," *The Weekly Review*, 1992, 20.

whether you like it or not the truth is that the people have lost confidence in you and those close to you.[37]

The bishops went ahead to make public the details of the joint statement, and this greatly angered President Moi, who termed it a "violation of secrecy and trust."[38] But for Archbishop Manasses Kuria, "the statement concerned a grave matter of public national interest" and thus the bishops' actions were "a divine right and most patriotic."[39] For Linus Mwangi of the PCEA, "anything whispered in secret would be shouted on the rooftops."[40] However, not all bishops supported the publicity of the statement. Others, like Bishop John Njue of the Embu Catholic Diocese, Bishop Longinus Atundo of the Bungoma Diocese, and Rev. Stephen Njenga of the CPK Kasarani, Nairobi, condemned the leak as unethical and a breach of trust.[41]

Only a few, mainly evangelical churches, such as the Africa Inland Church (AIC), the Deliverance Church (DC), and the Redeemed Gospel Church (RGC), did not want to be part of the pro-liberation movements. They protested the so-called social-oriented NCCK, especially its engagement in politics, while preferring the gospel-oriented Evangelical Fellowship of Kenya (EFK), the national umbrella body formed in 1975 to serve the interests of evangelical churches in Kenya.[42] However, several authors contend that it was not NCCK's sociopolitical engagement that drove evangelical churches out of the NCCK; other reasons were predominant.

First, evangelical churches were pro-establishment while NCCK was pro-opposition.[43] Bishop Arthur Kitonga of the RGC urged Kenyan Christians "to preach obedience to the government and the established political order," while Bishop Japhet Omucheyi of the Overcoming Faith Church of Kenya and Fr. Juma Pesa of the Holy Ghost Coptic Church urged Christians "to desist from involving themselves in politics."[44] Bishop Birech of AIC told Margaret Crouch that the AIC preferred to critique the government "in love" as opposed

---

37. "People Have Lost Confidence in You," 21.

38. "Violation of Secrecy and Trust," *The Weekly Review*, 1992, 21.

39. "Violation of Secrecy," 21.

40. "Violation of Secrecy," 21.

41. "Violation of Secrecy," 21–22.

42. "Self-Appointed Honest Broker," *The Weekly Review*, 1992, 6. See also Okullu, *Quest*, 120.

43. See Oluoch, *Christian Political Theology*, 33; "The Church Factor," 3–5; "A Partisan Role in Politics," *The Weekly Review*, 1992, 12.

44. "Self-Appointed Honest Broker," 6.

to "shouting it from the rooftops" as the NCCK did.[45] Thus these churches did not take an active approach to critique the state as the NCCK did.

Second, ethnicity shaped the political leanings of evangelical churches. For instance, the AIC, which has a significant Kalenjin and Kamba presence, supported President Moi, a Kalenjin. A columnist noted, "The complete antithesis of the likes of Kuria, Okullu, and Nzeki are the AIC's Bishop Ezekiel Birech [a Kalenjin] and the Rev. Jones Kaleli [a Kamba], as is evident from the sermons they deliver at the televised religious services attended by President Moi every Sunday."[46] This ethnic factor was not unique to evangelical churches. As the next section will show, ethnicity shaped the political choices of Anglican and Catholic Christians, greatly intensifying during President Kibaki's presidency, especially from 2002 to 2008.

Third, biblical and missional reasons shaped the evangelical position on social engagement. Evangelicals argued that the church, as Paul teaches in Romans 13, is called to pray and to support the government and not to oppose it.[47] Also, since power comes from God, no one should resist those in leadership. Thus opposing the ruling government was equal to opposing God. Therefore, they argued that civil disobedience, protests, and other forms of agitation were uncharacteristic of biblically centered Christians. On the missional front, evangelical churches perceived their calling to be that of saving souls, which for them must be clearly distinguished from sociopolitical engagement.[48] The primary task of the church was to win souls, not to engage in politics.

Fourth, self-interest and the desire for state patronage shaped evangelicals' political leanings. Many church leaders argued that the growth of the church and its programs depended on the support of the government. Thus resistance and agitation against the government hindered outreach and mission work. A happy and peaceful government equaled a happy and peaceful church. Thus

---

45. Crouch, *A Vision*, 139.

46. "Self-Appointed Honest Broker," 7.

47. Gifford, *Christianity, Politics*, 217.

48. Damaris Seleina Parsitau, "From Prophetic Voices to Lack of Voice: Christian Churches in Kenya and the Dynamics of Voice and Voicelesness in a Multi-Religious Space," *Studia Historiae Ecclesiasticae* 38 (2012): 251. See also Oluoch, *Christian Political Theology*, 32. On this point, Okullu ("Render unto Caesar," 148) observes, "Some churches have left the Council over these issues [political engagement] . . . These church leaders tend to be more conservative evangelicals who see the Gospel message as for only saving souls. In some of these churches it is largely a question of the leadership. The AIC, for example, is one of the largest Protestant churches in Kenya. Many ordinary folk in that church expressed sorrow that the church pulled out of the Council. They are convicted that NCCK is doing the right thing, and that conviction extends to the political arena as well as ecumenical. It is the church leadership that is not enlightened enough to interpret these issues."

the government must be supported. Therefore evangelicals supported the government, and in return the government supported evangelical churches and their programs. For example, President Moi allocated several tracts of land to the AIC and the Africa Brotherhood Church (ABC) for the building of churches, schools, and hospitals.[49] Several Pentecostal churches also received large sums of money from the president.[50]

The breakaway evangelical churches joined the Evangelical Fellowship of Kenya (EFK). EFK and NCCK differ in their social engagement. The prevailing notion at that time was that EFK was gospel-oriented while NCCK was social-oriented. This is not to say that NCCK did not have the gospel at heart. On the contrary, they affirmed that social engagement, evangelism, and missions are intertwined. Thus it was this kind of sociopolitical theology which drove NCCK's public engagement. While the NCCK participated in pro-reform movements, the EFK stayed away from them. In fact, the EFK, under the leadership of Rev. Jonah Chesengeny and Rev. Isaac Simbiri, condemned the NCCK as "arrogant and anti-government."[51] According to Rev. Arthur Kitonga, the NCCK's public engagement was an example of a serious loss of spiritual vision.[52]

The NCCK condemned hate-speech utterances which were prevalent during the pre-election campaigns of 1992. Under the leadership of Rev. George Wanjau of PCEA, the NCCK's taskforce named and condemned several politicians known for instigating ethnic violence.[53] Also during the meeting, the chairman of the NCCK's Justice, Peace and Reconciliation Commission, Bishop Henry Okullu, strongly criticized the opposition parties for their failure to unite together for the sake of the Kenyan people: "Our people," he said, "are asking, what has gone wrong? Where shall our true liberators come from? Must we be condemned to walk in the darkness of oppression for yet another decade? Must we move from dictatorship to anarchy?"[54]

Since it was clear NCCK was more in tune with the opposition than with the KANU government, the NCCK bore the heat of Moi's presidency to the

---

49. See Gifford, *Christianity, Politics,* 220–221.

50. Gifford, 215–220.

51. "A Partisan Role in Politics," 12. See another critique of the NCCK and the Roman Catholic Church because of their pro-opposition stance in "A Poor Pastoral Strategy," *The Weekly Review,* 1994, 3.

52. "A Partisan Role in Politics," 12. See also "Self-Appointed Honest Broker," 6.

53. "A Report on Ethnic Violence," *The Weekly Review,* 1992, 14. See also "Stop This Heinous Atrocity," *The Weekly Review,* 1992, 10–11.

54. "United by a Common Cause," 16.

extent that it was almost deregistered.[55] Soon after the interparty symposium the NCCK published a document, "A Kairos for Kenya," similar to one their counterparts in South Africa had published calling for the end of apartheid.[56] "A Kairos for Kenya" called for political reforms and the necessity of a "Kenya We Want" national convention.[57]

During the 1997 national elections, the NCCK, the Roman Catholic Church, and the Institute for Education of Democracy formed an election monitoring group to monitor the elections. The Joint Election Monitoring group, as it was named, published a report on the elections titled "Report on the 1997 General Elections in Kenya."[58] Jacqueline Klopp asserts that the NCCK was the first ever church-based organization to "document the nature, dynamics, and human consequences of the [ethnic] violence [in Kenya]."[59]

On Tuesday, 27 January 1998, two hundred Catholic priests, nuns, and brothers from the Nakuru Diocese, under the leadership of Bishop Peter Kairu, presented a protest letter to the Rift Valley provincial commissioner, Mr. Nicholas Mberia, in which they condemned the government of Kenya for its complicity in the ethnic strife.[60] The statement from the Catholic bishops is here quoted in part:

> It is against this background, and out of our steadfast love and genuine concern for this nation, that we are compelled to make the following appeals to the president: (1) To fulfil the pledges that he made to Kenyans as he sought their votes, to unite the country and to bring lasting peace in his last tenure of office, as his legacy; (2) To put an end to the violence immediately, because we know that he is able if he so wishes; (3) To dismiss from his

---

55. "A Partisan Role in Politics," 12.

56. With a foreword by John W. de Gruchy, the South African document ("The Kairos Document") was signed by 156 individuals representing twenty denominations and focused on calling the church and state to engage in social-political reforms in South Africa. The Kenyan document was focused on conquering one-party dictatorship. Drawing from the South African experience, the NCCK contended that the government of Kenya oppressed the people just as apartheid oppressed the people of South Africa.

57. NCCK, "A Kairos for Kenya: NCCK Reflections on the KANU Review Committee Report and KANU Special Delegates' Conference Resolutions on It" (Nairobi, 1991).

58. Institute for Education in Democracy, *Report on the 1997 General Elections in Kenya* (Nairobi: Institute for Education in Democracy, Catholic Justice and Peace Commission, National Council of Churches of Kenya, 1998).

59. Jacqueline M. Klopp, "The NCCK and the Struggle against 'Ethnic Clashes' in Kenya," in *Religion and Politics in Kenya*, ed. Ben Knighton (New York: Palgrave Macmillan, 2009), 193.

60. See "Oh, Not Again!," *The Weekly Review*, 1998, 6.

cabinet those well-known ministers who have hitherto uttered inflammatory statements that have always led to ethnic violence. There must be firm action if he wants to put an end to impunity and enhance respect for the law; (4) To respect and accept defeat from certain areas and from certain communities, which did not vote for him in the recently concluded general election, in the same way that they have accepted the presidential results; (5) To concretely assure Kenyans that ethnic violence will not spread to other areas as is now feared; (6) To respect the oath of office that he took barely three weeks ago even if he is not eligible for re-election in the next general elections.[61]

More than just condemn the violence, the Church did something to help the victims of the ethnic strife, who numbered about 200,000 people.[62] The Roman Catholic Church established several camps for the internally displaced in several parts of the country, including Thessalia in Kericho, Kamwaura and Elburgon in Nakuru, and Burnt Forest in Eldoret.[63] Similarly, NCCK sponsored camps in Eldoret town, Soi, and Turbo, while the Quakers had camps in Chwele and Bungoma.[64]

Though the church united in its condemnation of ethnopolitical conflict in the 1990s, it often failed to exemplify ethnic cohesion. A few examples illustrate this failure. First, there were reports of impartiality in the relief efforts offered to victims of ethnic violence. Bishop Ndingi of the Catholic Diocese of Nakuru allegedly concentrated relief work on the mostly Kikuyu Nakuru District, while neglecting the predominantly Kalenjin Kericho District.[65]

The second example is the election of bishops. The election of Bishop Stephen Kewasis, a Pokot, to replace Bishop Alexander Muge, a Nandi, of the CPK Eldoret Diocese is a good example of a church election decided on the basis of ethnicity. The Nandi Christians of the Anglican Diocese of Eldoret rejected the election of Kewasis simply because he was not a Nandi, though Kewasis finally became the bishop through a court verdict.[66] In Kajiado, the Maasai rejected the election of Rev. Bernard Njoroge, a Kikuyu, as first bishop

---

61. "A Call to End the Violence: Excerpts from a Statement by Catholic Bishops on the Security Situation in Laikipia and Njoro," *The Weekly Review*, 1998, 7.

62. See "Oh, Not Again!," 4.

63. "Oh, Not Again!," 5.

64. "Oh, Not Again!," 5.

65. "Self-Appointed Honest Broker," 6.

66. "A Stormy Enthronement," *The Weekly Review*, 1992, 18.

of the newly created Kajiado Diocese, threatening "that fresh tribal clashes would erupt in Kajiado if Njoroge attempted to discharge his duties as bishop in the new diocese."[67] The Maasai Anglican Christians rejected Bishop Njoroge because "he is a stranger in the diocese."[68] After two years of resistance, the Maasai Christians finally got one of their own, Rev. Jeremiah Taama, as the bishop.[69]

Another example is the creation of several dioceses in the CPK church. Ethnicity dominated the creation of Katakwa Diocese in Busia District. For more than five years, the Teso-dominated Katakwa region fought a dramatic and protracted battle to break away from the Luhya-dominated Nambale Diocese of Bishop Isaak Namango. Finally, the CPK leadership under Archbishop Manasses Kuria granted the Teso Christians their own diocese of Katakwa on 1 January 1991 under the leadership of Bishop Eliud Okiring.[70] This ethnicization of ecclesiastical leadership in the Anglican Church affected its credibility. It also provided precedence in the church for aggrieved Christians from a particular community to use ethnicity to create a new diocese for themselves from any of the existing dioceses that encompassed disparate ethnic communities within their jurisdiction.

The Anglican bishops also divided along ethnic lines in their support of political leaders.[71] Archbishop Manasses Kuria preferred to support FORD-Asili chairman Kenneth Matiba, a fellow Kikuyu, for the presidency, while Henry Okullu, the bishop of Maseno South, openly supported FORD Kenya's Oginga Odinga, a fellow Luo.[72] The Rev. Elijah Yego of the Eldoret Diocese, a man who had earlier opposed the election of Bishop Stephen Kewasis because he was not a Nandi, supported President Daniel Arap Moi, a fellow Kalenjin. Reverend Yego called all non-Kalenjins to vote for Moi "or be prepared for eviction from the district if he loses."[73] Ironically, Rev. Yego had previously, in

---

67. "Election Controversy Deepens," *The Weekly Review*, 1993, 14. See also "Ethnicity in the CPK," *The Weekly Review*, 1993, 12–14.

68. "Election Controversy Deepens," 14.

69. Although Rev. Jeremiah Taama is not a Maasai but a Kamba, he was nevertheless considered a Maasai because he had lived among the Maasai for many years and spoke the language very well.

70. "A Stormy Enthronement," 18; "Katakwans to Do It Their Way," *The Weekly Review*, 1990, 13–15.

71. "Of Clergymen and Tribalism," *The Weekly Review*, 1992, 12–13.

72. "Of Clergymen and Tribalism," 12.

73. "Of Clergymen and Tribalism," 12.

March 1992, condemned the government for "not doing enough to quell the fighting in which the Luo have been the main victims."[74]

The above account shows that the Kenyan church actively engaged in political and social reforms in the 1990s. However, the church was not completely free of ethnic-based conflict. The next time period (2001–08) marked the demise of the prophetic voice of the church in Kenya mainly because of ethnocentrism. The next section therefore examines ethnopolitical conflict and the church in Kenya from 2001 to 2008.

Ethnopolitical Conflict and the Church in Kenya: A Divided Voice (2002–2008)

Ethnic divisions and conflict within the church in Kenya intensified from 2002 to 2008. The period began with great hope for the country as it marked the end of President Moi's twenty-four-year rule. However, his successor, President Mwai Kibaki, though he had campaigned on the platform of ethnic unity, failed to unify the country. Kibaki's government continued to polarize the country along ethnic lines. In the same manner, churches during this time, whether mainline, evangelical, or Pentecostal, were greatly divided.

The first division occurred during the struggle for constitutional review. For many years the opposition, civil societies, and the church had been pushing for a constitutional review. In 2001, President Moi allowed them some latitude to constitute a forum for constitutional change. This caused a massive rift between the major church organizations. On the one hand, the Forum for Restoration of Democracy (FORD) and NCCK wanted a review process that engaged Kenyans from all sectors, from the civil society to professional bodies to the clergy. On the other hand, evangelicals and a few opposition members such as Raila Odinga wanted a parliamentary-led review process. The NCCK under the leadership of the General Secretary, Rev. Mutava Musyimi, proposed a merger between NCCK and the Parliamentary review team. The group, referred to as "Ufungamano Initiative" (after the Ufungamano House, a Christian ecumenical guest house that was a venue for most of the meetings), would lead the constitutional review process. The evangelicals, under the leadership of Archbishop Samson Gaitho, the Bishop of the African Independent Pentecostal Church, went to court because they wanted to be included in the team.[75] Archbishop Gaitho bolstered his point by noting that

---

74. "Ethnic Strife," *The Weekly Review*, 1992, 5.
75. Wahome Thuku, "Churches in Threat of Merger," *The Daily Nation*, 5.

the NCCK represented "fewer than 40 bodies" while the evangelicals comprised "more than 800 registered denominations."[76]

Reverend Musyimi defended the Ufungamano Initiative arguing that they were not being partisan.[77] Similarly, Archbishop Gitari responded to the evangelicals, describing them as "probably confused because their theology is faulty."[78] Gitari argued that evangelicals were aloof during the campaign for multiparty democracy in the early 1990s, and when Kenyans were struggling for constitutional review, "they only wanted to support the government, whether it was right or wrong."[79] He added, "They kept away from us and even held rallies against Ufungamano; now that the war is almost won, it's not sincere of them to appear at the eleventh hour with all manner of conditions."[80]

This rift between churches did not go unnoticed. In an editorial cartoon in *The Daily Nation* of 7 May 2001, the cartoonist drew two goats dressed in a manner likely to suggest that they were prelates, complete with a miter. Chained to each other but pulling in different directions, each was endeavoring to reach a pot of water labeled "constitutional reforms," although the pot was out of reach. This derision of the church highlighted the zero-sum game of each camp's attempts to block the other from working toward constitutional reform. The constitutional reforms did not continue until after the election of December 2002.

After the election, the Kibaki presidency constituted the Kenya Review Act Chapter 3A, which established the Kenya Review Commission under the chairmanship of Professor Yash Pal Ghai, and mandated it to carry on the constitutional review process. The Commission held its meetings at the Bomas of Kenya in Nairobi from 2002 to 2005, producing the Draft Constitution (Bomas Draft), which was debated at the Kenya Constitutional Conference at Bomas and later organized as the Proposed New Constitution to be voted with a "Yes" or "No" in a national referendum in 2005.

During the campaigns for the referendum, the church divided along ethnic, denominational, and party lines. For instance, a group of Catholic bishops from the Central Province under the leadership of Cardinal John Njue, also from the Central Province (Embu), defended President Kibaki's presidency, arguably

---

76. Thuku, "Churches in Threat of Merger," 5.

77. "Musyimi Clears Air over Team Selection," *The Daily Nation*, 2001, 4.

78. Chege wa Gachamba, "Gitari Tells Off Churches Group," *The Daily Nation*, 2001, 1.

79. Gachamba, "Gitari Tells Off Churches Group," 3–4.

80. Gachamba, 5.

because he was Catholic and from the Central Province.[81] Their support came at a time when Kibaki was facing resistance from the opposition because of his rejection of *majimbo* (regionalism). Thus Cardinal Njue's rejection of *majimbo*, though he claimed to be informed by national cohesion, was interpreted as support for Kibaki.[82] Accordingly, Njue was accused of being a "central Kenya mouthpiece" and a "Kibaki sympathizer."[83] Another Catholic bishop, Archbishop Zacchaeus Okoth of Kisumu, distanced himself from Cardinal Njue's position by openly supporting the opposition. Here too, Kenyans saw ethnicity as informing Okoth's view because he was from Nyanza, and was a Luo, the community of the opposition leader, Raila Odinga.

As to the matter of the Bomas Draft constitution, Cardinal Njue encouraged Kenyan Catholics to vote "with their conscience."[84] The other denominations, except the Anglican Church of Kenya (ACK) (formerly known as the Church Province of Kenya), which also encouraged its members to "vote with their conscience," openly campaigned against it because it permitted abortion under certain circumstances and it favored Islam by recognizing the formation of Kadhi courts operated through taxpayers' money. Njue's word had great authority not only because he was in charge of the Catholic Church at the time, but also because he was a Constitution of Kenya Review Commission national delegate at the Bomas of Kenya representing the Catholic Church. Kenyans voted to reject the Bomas Draft constitution on 21 November 2005.[85] It can be argued that Njue's recommendations to the Catholics played a part in this defeat. On this note, Chacha states, "the defeat of the new constitution was overwhelmingly not only along ethnic lines but religious too, undoubtedly on

---

81. Gifford, *Christianity, Politics*, 40; Emeka Mayaka Gekara, "Religious Leaders Regain Their Voice," *The Daily Nation*, 2009, 19; Emeka Mayaka Gekara, "Cardinal Njue's Leadership Faces Litmus Test as Church Voices Differ," *The Daily Nation*, 2009, 15.

82. Njue is reported to have said: "I have no apologies to make on the *majimbo* stand. I stood for what I thought was right at the time and what was important for national unity." See Gekara, "Cardinal Njue's Leadership," 15.

83. Gekara, 15.

84. Parsitau, "From Prophetic Voices," 256; Gifford, *Christianity, Politics*, 59.

85. A banana was the symbol for "Yes" and an orange, a symbol for "No." When Kenyans voted No to the Draft Constitution, their decision inspired the formation of the Orange Democratic Movement (ODM) under the leadership of Raila Odinga. Later, the ODM campaigned vigorously against the Party of National Unity (PNU), leading to a much-contested election in 2007 and the subsequent violence.

the side of Kibaki, who was continually viewed by the Catholics as a prominent member."[86]

Similarly, the government and the opposition co-opted some clergy to their sides. President Kibaki appointed Rev. Mutava Musyimi, the NCCK undersecretary and hitherto a tough critic of the Moi regime, as the head of the Steering Committee on Anticorruption (he went on to contest and win a parliamentary seat in the president's party soon after resigning from NCCK). Gifford observes that "the NCCK under Musyimi changed its stance from 'principled opposition' during the Moi administration to 'principled cooperation' towards Kibaki's."[87] Raila Odinga of the newly formed Orange Democratic Movement (ODM) brought Bishop Margaret Wanjiru, a prominent televangelist with a larger following, to most of his political rallies. Wanjiru later contested a parliamentary seat for the ODM party and won. Several clerics also sought elective positions in government, but the majority of them lost. Thus the church failed because of the co-option and the compromise of the clergy by the government and the opposition.[88]

The years 2006 and 2007 also intensified partisanship in the church to the point where "Caesar and God spoon-fed each other," as Chacha observes.[89] The church divided along tribal and party lines. The church's lack of voice and its clear ethnic division disappointed the Kenyan people. Frequent newspaper columns and letters to the editor written during this time clearly show the disappointment. Editorials appeared with titles such as "The Church Is Not Our Voice Anymore";[90] "No Longer the Beacon of Morality";[91] "Heal Yourself First, Dear Clerics";[92] "Kenya Badly in Need of New Leaders";[93] "House of God Divided";[94] "When the Shepherds Led Their Flocks Astray";[95] "How Clergy

---

86. Kerata Chacha, "Pastors or Bastards? The Dynamics of Religion and Politics in the 2007 General Elections in Kenya." In *Tensions and Reversals in Democratic Transitions: The Kenya 2007 General Elections* (Nairobi: Society for International Development, 2010), 114.

87. Gifford, *Christianity, Politics*, 43.

88. Parsitau, "From Prophetic Voices," 251–252.

89. Chacha, "Pastors or Bastards?," 114.

90. Adam Oloo, "The Church Is Not Our Voice Anymore," *The East African Standard*, 2006.

91. G. Ogola, "No Longer the Beacon of Morality," *The East African Standard*, 2006.

92. "Heal Yourself First, Dear Clerics," *The Daily Nation*, 2006.

93. Kwendo Opanga, "Kenya Badly in Need of New Leaders," *The Daily Nation*, 2008, 14.

94. Mildred Ngesa, "House of God Divided But It Can Still Help Nurture Hope," *The Daily Nation*, 2008, 13.

95. "When the Shepherds Led Their Flocks Astray," *The Daily Nation*, 2008, 10.

Took Battle to Grim Reaper";[96] "Church Embedded Long before Elections";[97] "Ethnicity in the Church Comes of Age";[98] "Church's Worrying Slide to Silence";[99] "Political Bishops Betraying the People";[100] "Kenyan 'Prophets' Who Won No Respect";[101] "Did Church Leaders Fail Kenyans?"[102] One author commented that church leaders used their pulpits "to beat drums of ethnic hatred, which fueled the post-election chaos."[103] Another writer said, "They preached poison from the pulpits, these men and women of God! They asked their communities to arm themselves and attack their fellow Kenyans. Yes, the clergy set community against community and brother against brother."[104]

In the wake of the 2007/2008 post-election chaos, the clergy urged people to embrace peace, but they were ignored. In fact, more than ten churches nationwide were burnt down.[105] The burning to death of thirty-five women and children who had sought shelter in an Assemblies of God church in Eldoret embodied the force of this national acrimony against the church. By being partisan, the church had lost its prophetic voice and could not be trusted to provide moral and spiritual direction.

Ethnopolitical Conflict and the Church in Kenya: On the Road to Recovery? (2008–2013)

Soon after the 2007 General Election, the church discovered that it had lost its prophetic stand and had no authority to offer moral and spiritual guidance to the people of Kenya. The recovery of its prophetic place began with a formal apology from the NCCK on 15 February 2008 entitled "Hope for Kenya." The NCCK apology is here quoted in part:

---

96. Tom Osanjo, "How Clergy Took Battle to Grim Reaper," *The Daily Nation*, 2008, 22.

97. "Church Embedded Long before Elections," *The East African Standard*, 2008.

98. Erick Wamanji, "Ethnicity and the Church Comes of Age," *The East African Standard*, 2008.

99. Dennis Onyango, "Church's Worrying Slide to Silence," *The East African Standard*, 2008.

100. Elias Mokua Nyatete, "Political Bishops Betraying the People," *The East African Standard*, 2008.

101. E. Ogutu, "Kenyan 'Prophets' Who Won No Respect," *The East African Standard*, 5 March 2008.

102. "Did Church Leaders Fail Kenyans?," *The Daily Nation*, 2008.

103. Gekara, "Cardinal Njue's Leadership," 15.

104. Opanga, "Kenya Badly in Need of New Leaders," 14.

105. Chacha, "Pastors or Bastards?," 126.

We regret that we as church leaders were unable to effectively confront these issues because we were partisan. Our efforts to forestall the current crisis were not effective because we as the membership of NCCK did not speak with one voice. We were divided in the way we saw the management of the elections; we identified with our people based on ethnicity; and after the elections, we are divided on how to deal with the crisis. As a result, we together with other church leaders have displayed partisan values in situations that called for national interests. The church has remained disunited and its voice swallowed in the cacophony of those of other vested interests. We call on church leaders to recapture their strategic position as the moral authority of the nation. We have put in place measures to enable us to overcome the divisive forces, and set off on a new beginning. As the church, we will do our best in helping achieve the rebirth of a new Kenya.[106]

Another apology from the NCCK came in August 2008 at the NCCK General Assembly at Kabarak University, a meeting attended by more than 1,300 clerics. Reverend Canon Peter Karanja convened the meeting to give the clerics "a chance to reflect, repent, pray together and be transformed in the power of the Holy Spirit to become agents of healing and reconciliation to the nation."[107] During the meeting, the "Clergymen admitted to blessing warriors to engage in violence and inviting politicians to disseminate hate messages that incited people against members of various communities."[108] The confession was in line with the theme of the meeting, which was "the truth shall set you free."

The Catholic bishops became the second religious group to confess. Their public confession came in March 2008. Cardinal Njue offered a formal apology at the Holy Family Basilica in Nairobi at a thanksgiving service offered for the establishment of a grand coalition government. Cardinal Njue said, "We [the Catholic Church] did not listen to the voice of the shepherd, who is Jesus Christ. We failed to love one another. We sinned by failing to love one another."[109] Similarly, at a meeting to welcome the Pope's representative

106. NCCK Executive Press, "Hope for Kenya," 13 February 2008, Rescue Kenya, https://rescuekenya.wordpress.com/2008/02/21/ncck-executive-committee-press-statement-13-feb-2008/.

107. "Clergymen Own Up to Partisan Role in Post-Election Chaos," *The Daily Nation,* 23 August 2008, https://www.nation.co.ke/news/1056-462380-koien2z/index.html.

108. "Clergymen Own Up to Partisan Role in Post-Election Chaos."

109. As quoted in Chacha, "Pastors or Bastards?," 129.

in Kenya, Archbishop Alain Paul Lebeaupin, Cardinal Njue confessed, "We may have taken sides, we may have gone wrong, but we have to turn around now. Let us embrace the idea of a coalition government because it is through it that we can ensure the government does not serve the interests of a single individual or community."[110]

Several other churches and organizations joined the NCCK and the Catholic bishops in apologizing to the country and calling for national healing. For instance, during a prayer meeting for the Sachang'wan fire tragedy victims in which more than 111 people lost their lives, religious leaders sought forgiveness for "leaving the people of Kenya dispersed like lost sheep without a shepherd" during the 2007 General Election.[111] Similarly, the Evangelical Alliance of Kenya was instrumental in the formation of a lobby group to mediate national cohesion and healing following the post-election chaos. The group met three times with the former UN Secretary General Kofi Annan in an attempt to broker a national accord.[112]

After the post-election chaos, the new Grand Coalition government appointed a commission of experts to draft a new constitution. When Members of Parliament could not get the required signatures to amend the 150 contentious clauses, the proposed constitution was passed as it was. The Attorney General presented it to be voted on with either a Yes or a No in a referendum on 4 August 2010. The church at this time united with the ODM party to campaign against it. The issue of Kadhi courts and abortion triggered the church's rejection of the proposed constitution. All church bodies (NCCK, the Evangelical Alliance of Kenya [EAK], and the Kenya Catholic Episcopal Conference [KCEC]) urged their member churches to reject it. On 30 July 2010 the Christian leaders issued a joint statement urging their members "to exercise their democratic right to vote, and to display their patriotism for our country and convincingly vote NO to this flawed proposed constitution."[113] Again, on 31 July 2010, the Kenya Episcopal Conference issued a statement signed by all twenty-five Roman Catholic bishops rejecting the proposed constitution because it permitted abortion.[114]

However, not all leaders supported the "No" campaign. Retired Archbishop Gitari urged Anglican Christians to vote "Yes" because the proposed

---

110. Oliver Mathenge, "Clerics Push for Faster Healing," *The Daily Nation*, 2009, 6.

111. Gekara, "Religious Leaders Regain Their Voice," 19.

112. Chacha, "Pastors or Bastards?," 129.

113. Gitari, *Troubled*, 284–285.

114. Gitari, 285.

constitution was far better than the Lancaster House constitution Kenya had used since independence.[115] Gitari gained the support of Bishop Peter Njoka, the Anglican Bishop of Nairobi, and Bishop Lawi Imathiu of the Methodist Church. At the end of the campaign, the "Yes" camp won. Kenya promulgated a new constitution on 27 August 2010. Even though the "No" side had been defeated, the unity of the church was clearly manifest during this time. For the first time in several years, the church had risen above ethnic divides. Indeed, the church could be said to be "on the road to recovery." Even the Kenyan bishops who had lost their moral ground to talk to Kenyans regained respect in national issues. For instance, the Kenya Conference of Catholic Bishops issued a pastoral letter urging Kenyans to "to embrace peace and co-existence."[116] The Maseno West Anglican bishop urged Kenyans to "stand up and say no to the culture of negative ethnicity, land grabbing, hate speech, and impunity because the country cannot continue to live in the past."[117]

Conclusion

This chapter has argued that the church in Kenya commanded great influence in the 1990s but lost its prophetic voice in the years 2002 to 2008, mainly because of ethnocentrism and the co-option and compromise of the clergy by the government and the opposition. Mainline Protestant churches, especially the CPK and PCEA, under the auspices of the NCCK, called for justice, democracy, and ethnopolitical cohesion. Similarly, the Roman Catholic Church actively engaged in the sociopolitical transformation of Kenya. However, evangelical churches, especially the AIC, RGC, and DC, under the umbrella organization the EFK (now EAK), steered away from social-political engagement. After the post-election skirmishes which followed this period, and the church's subsequent apologies to the Kenyan people, the church could be said to be on the road to recovery. Or is it?

---

115. Gitari, 287–289.

116. "Kenya Bishops Call for Unity as Country Awaits Pope Francis," *Vatican Radio*, 11 September 2015, http://en.radiovaticana.va/news/2015/11/09/kenya_bishops_call_for_unity_as_country_awaits_pope_francis/1185353.

117. Erick Juma, "Crack Whip on Hate Mongers," *People Daily*, 2016, 9.

Bibliography

"A Blessing for the Mothers." *The Weekly Review*, 1992.

"A Call to End the Violence: Excerpts from a Statement by Catholic Bishops on the Security Situation in Laikipia and Njoro." *The Weekly Review*, 1998.

Chacha, Babere Kerata. "Pastors or Bastards? The Dynamics of Religion and Politics in the 2007 General Elections in Kenya." In *Tensions and Reversals in Democratic Transitions: The Kenya 2007 General Elections*, 101–135. Nairobi: Society for International Development, 2010.

"Church Embedded Long before Elections." *The East African Standard*, 2008.

"The Church Factor: The NCCK Tries to Unite the Opposition Parties." *The Weekly Review*, 1992.

"Clergymen Own Up to Partisan Role in Post-Election Chaos." *The Daily Nation*, 23 August 2008. https://www.nation.co.ke/news/1056-462380-koien2z/index.html.

"Clerics Kick Up Storm." *The Weekly Review*, 1990.

"A Controversial Churchman." *The Weekly Review*, 1985.

Crouch, Margaret. *A Vision of Christian Mission: Reflections on the Great Commission in Kenya*. Nairobi: NCCK, 1993.

"Did Church Leaders Fail Kenyans?" *The Daily Nation*, 2008.

"A Dissenting Patriot." *The Weekly Review*, 1990.

"Election Controversy Deepens." *The Weekly Review*, 1993.

"Ethnicity in the CPK." *The Weekly Review*, 1993.

"Ethnic Strife." *The Weekly Review*, 1992.

"Fresh Outbreak of Violence." *The Weekly Review*, 1992.

Gachamba, Chege wa. "Gitari Tells Off Churches Group." *The Daily Nation*, 2001.

Gatabaki, Njehu. "Peace: Interview of the Most Rev. Manasses Kuria." *Finance*, 1991.

Gekara, Emeka Mayaka. "Cardinal Njue's Leadership Faces Litmus Test as Church Voices Differ." *The Daily Nation*, 2009.

———. "Religious Leaders Regain Their Voice." *The Daily Nation*, 2009.

Gifford, Paul. *Christianity, Politics and Public Life in Kenya*. London: Hurst, 2009.

Gitari, David. *Troubled but Not Destroyed: The Autobiography of Archbishop David Gitari*. Vancouver: Isaac, 2014.

"Heal Yourself First, Dear Clerics." *The Daily Nation*, 2006.

"A Heated Debate." *The Weekly Review*, 1990.

Hempstone, Smith. *Rogue Ambassador: An African Memoir*. Sewanee, TN: University of the South Press, 1997.

Institute for Education in Democracy. *Report on the 1997 General Elections in Kenya*. Nairobi: Institute for Education in Democracy, Catholic Justice and Peace Commission, National Council of Churches of Kenya, 1998.

Juma, Erick. "Crack Whip on Hate Mongers." *People Daily*, 2016.

Kairos Theologians (Group). *The Kairos Document: Challenge to the Church: A Theological Comment on the Political Crisis in South Africa*. Grand Rapids, MI: Eerdmans, 1986.

"Katakwans to Do It Their Way." *The Weekly Review*, 1990.

"Kenya Bishops Call for Unity as Country Awaits Pope Francis." Vatican Radio. 11 September 2015. http://en.radiovaticana.va/news/2015/11/09/kenya_bishops_call_for_unity_as_country_awaits_pope_francis/1185353.

Klopp, Jacqueline M. "The NCCK and the Struggle against 'Ethnic Clashes' in Kenya." In *Religion and Politics in Kenya*, edited by Ben Knighton, 183–199. New York: Palgrave Macmillan, 2009.

"Lawlessness Must End." *The Weekly Review*, 1992.

Mathenge, Oliver. "Clerics Push for Faster Healing." *The Daily Nation*, 2009.

"Moving into the Political Arena." *The Weekly Review*, 1992.

"Musyimi Clears Air over Team Selection." *The Daily Nation*, 2001.

"The Nandi Clashes." *The Nairobi Law Monthly*, 1991.

NCCK. "A Kairos for Kenya: NCCK Reflection on the KANU Review Committee Report and KANU Special Delegates' Conference Resolutions on It." Nairobi, 1991.

NCCK Executive Press. "Hope for Kenya." 13 February 2008. Rescue Kenya. https://rescuekenya.wordpress.com/2008/02/21/ncck-executive-committee-press-statement-13-feb-2008/.

"New Radicalism in Pastoral Letter." *The Weekly Review*, 1992.

Ngesa, Mildred. "House of God Divided but It Can Still Help Nurture Hope." *The Daily Nation*, 2008.

Ngotho, Kamau. "The Day Democracy Visited and Stayed." *The Daily Nation*, 2000.

"Njoya At It Again." *The Weekly Review*, 1990.

Nyatete, Elias Mokua. "Political Bishops Betraying the People." *The East African Standard*, 2008.

"Of Clergymen and Tribalism." *The Weekly Review*, 1992.

Ogola, G. "No Longer the Beacon of Morality." *The East African Standard*, 2006.

Ogutu, E. "Kenyan 'Prophets' Who Won No Respect." *The East African Standard*, 5 March 2008.

"Oh, Not Again!" *The Weekly Review*, 1998.

Okullu, Henry. "Render unto Caesar." In *A Vision of Christian Mission: Reflections on the Great Commission in Kenya*, edited by Margaret Crouch, 147–154. Nairobi: NCCK, 1993.

———. "Some Theological and Ethical Considerations in African Context." In *An African Call for Life: Contribution to the World Council of Churches Sixth Assembly Theme "Jesus Christ: The Life of the World,"* edited by M. ma Mpolo, R. Stober, and E. V. Appiah, 97–112. Geneva: WCC, 1983.

———. *Quest for Justice: An Autobiography of Bishop Henry Okullu*. Kisumu: Shalom, 1997.

"Okullu Ready for 1994." *The Weekly Review*, 1994.

"Okullu's Volley: Bishop Calls for Multi-Party System." *The Weekly Review*, 1990.

Oloo, Adam. "The Church Is Not Our Voice Anymore." *The East African Standard*, 2006.

Oluoch, Jemima Atieno. *The Christian Political Theology of Dr. John Henry Okullu.* Nairobi: Uzima, 2006.

Onyango, Dennis. "Church's Worrying Slide to Silence." *The East African Standard*, 2008.

Opanga, Kwendo. "Kenya Badly in Need of New Leaders." *The Daily Nation*, 2008.

Osanjo, Tom. "How Clergy Took Battle to Grim Reaper." *The Daily Nation*, 2008.

Otieno, Nicholas. *Beyond the Silence of Death: The Life and Theology of Bishop Alexander Muge.* Nairobi: NCCK, 1993.

"The Outspoken Clergyman." *The Weekly Review*, 1994.

Parsitau, Damaris Seleina. "From Prophetic Voices to Lack of Voice: Christian Churches in Kenya and the Dynamics of Voice and Voicelesness in a Multi-Religious Space." *Studia Historiae Ecclesiasticae* 38 (2012): 243–268.

"A Partisan Role in Politics." *The Weekly Review*, 1992.

"People Have Lost Confidence in You." *The Weekly Review*, 1992.

"A Poor Pastoral Strategy." *The Weekly Review*, 1994.

"The Question of Opposition." *The Weekly Review*, 1990.

"The Queue-Voting Furore." *The Weekly Review*, 1990.

"A Report on Ethnic Violence." *The Weekly Review*, 1992.

"Self-Appointed Honest Broker." *The Weekly Review*, 1992.

"A Severe Dressing Down for the President." *The Weekly Review*, 1992.

"Show of Force." *The Weekly Review*, 1997.

"Stop This Heinous Atrocity." *The Weekly Review*, 1992.

"A Stormy Enthronement." *The Weekly Review*, 1992.

"A Strike for Freedom." *The Weekly Review*, 1992.

Thuku, Wahome. "Churches in Threat of Merger." *The Daily Nation*, 2001.

"United by a Common Cause." *The Weekly Review*, 1992.

"Violation of Secrecy and Trust." *The Weekly Review*, 1992.

Wamanji, Erick. "Ethnicity and the Church Comes of Age." *The East African Standard*, 2008.

"When the Shepherds Led their Flocks Astray." *The Daily Nation*, 2008.

Part 3

Reconciliation

9

The Consequences of Taking Advantage of a Brother's Misfortune

Situational Irony in the Use of the Hebrew Concept שׁתה (*Shatah*) in Obadiah 16

Peter Kamande Thuo
Bible Translation Consultant and Part-Time Lecturer

Abstract

The presence of God is supposed to be a place of reconciliation between brothers as well as where they stand together to face a common enemy.[1] The key to understanding God's judgment in Obadiah against the people of Edom, and by extension of the other nations, is to appreciate the use of situational irony in the use of the Hebrew verb שׁתה (transliterated as *shatah*, which has the lexical meaning "to drink") in Obadiah 16. The argument made in this research is that both literal and metaphorical senses of שׁתה paint a picture of the abstract concept of divine wrath. An eclectic theoretical approach between Frame Semantics and Relevance Theory is used in this work to advance this argument by formulating the frame of שׁתה and also by addressing exegetical issues that arise in the context of Obadiah 16, with the suggested solutions

---

1. See Ps 133:1; John 17:11.

expected to meet expectations of relevance.[2] In its application, this research seeks to sound a warning to the African church where believers tend to turn to their ethnic alignments when it comes to addressing political and societal challenges. After providing a brief historical and contextual setting of Obadiah 16 and examining the theoretical framework of this work, the chapter explores the uses of the verb שתה with its implied referent(s) and object(s) before concluding with an application.

Key words: Obadiah, situational irony, literal meaning, metaphorical meaning, שתה, eclectic theoretical approach, Frame Semantics, Relevance Theory, ad hoc concept.

A Brief Historical and Contextual Setting of Obadiah 16

The people of Edom are said to have had a hand in the attack and capture of the city of Jerusalem by the Babylonians in 587 BC as well as in making life difficult for the remnants of that city even after the attack.[3] Now the time was ripe for God to turn the tables on the people of Edom and make them suffer for what they had done to his chosen people, a judgment that is extended to neighboring nations who were also enemies to the nation of Israel.[4] Most English Bibles tend to agree on two main divisions for the book of Obadiah.[5] The first section, which runs from verse 1 to verse 14, talks of the punishment which was coming upon the people of Edom for their offenses against the people of Judah. The remaining section, which runs from verse 15 to verse 21, talks about the eschatological events of the Day of the Lord in which Israel will be restored and other nations judged. This second major section, which is the focus of this chapter, is treated by some English translations as one section,[6] while others subdivide it into two, namely, verses 15–16, which talk of God's judgment to the nations, and verses 17–21, which foretell the restoration of

---

2. Charles Fillmore, "Frame Semantics," in *Linguistics in the Morning Calm*, The Linguistic Society of Korea, edited by Han'guk Ŏnŏ Hakhoe (Seoul: Hanshin, 1982); Dan Sperber and Deirdre Wilson, *Relevance, Communication and Cognition*, 2nd ed. (Oxford: Basil Blackwell, 1995).

3. John Barton, *Joel and Obadiah: A Commentary*, Old Testament Library (Louisville: Westminster John Knox, 2001), 120; Obad 10–14.

4. Obad 15–16, 19–20.

5. Cf. English Standard Version (ESV), the Contemporary English Version (CEV), the Good News Bible (GNB), the New Living Translation (NLT), and the New English Translation (NET).

6. See NLT and NET.

the people of Israel.[7] In this work, verses 15–16 are treated as a unit. The next section provides the theoretical underpinning of this work.

Theoretical Framework

Situational irony is implied in what is argued in this chapter, as both literal and metaphorical uses of the verb שתה in Obadiah 16 paint a picture of the consequences that will take place at the coming of the Day of the Lord. Situational irony, also referred to as irony of events, points to a situation that is contrary to what the reader expects, or to what is deemed appropriate.[8] The literal meaning of a word has to do with its plain meaning, or what is referred to as its truth condition, while the metaphorical meaning has to do with the use of a word in a way that is suggestive of another, with the compared concepts sharing some sort of resemblance.[9] One factor that influences the meaning of any lexical unit is its underlying cognitive frame since "frames provide the fundamental representation of knowledge in human cognition."[10] A cognitive frame is a detailed knowledge structure or schema that "represents a schematisation of experience (a knowledge structure), which is represented at the conceptual level and held in long-term memory, and which relates by elements and entities associated with a particular culturally-embedded scene, situation or event from human experience."[11] Frames as knowledge structures are shaped by how particular societies view the world and hence include beliefs, values, and emotions.[12] Frame Semantics will help to highlight the contextual knowledge as well as related encyclopedic entries that are evoked

---

7. ESV subdivides it as vv. 15–18 and vv. 19–21, while CEV and GNB subdivide it into vv. 15–16 and vv. 17–21.

8. Leland Ryken, *How Bible Stories Work: A Guided Study of Biblical Narrative* (Ashland, OH: Weaver Book Company), 2015.

9. George Lakoff and Mark Johnson, *Metaphors We Live By* (Chicago/London: University of Chicago Press, 1980), 6; Janet M. Soskice, *Metaphor and Religious Language* (Oxford: Oxford University Press, 1985), 15; Antonio Barcelona, "Introduction: The Cognitive Theory of Metaphor and Metonymy," in *Metaphor and Metonymy at the Crossroads: A Cognitive Perspective*, edited by Antonio Barcelona (Berlin: Mouton de Gruyter, 2000), 3.

10. L. W. Barsalou, "Frames, Concepts, and Conceptual Fields," in *Frames, Fields, and Contrasts: New Essays in Semantic and Lexical Organization*, edited by Adrienne Lehrer and Eva F. Kittay (Hillsdale, NJ: Lawrence Erlbaum Associates, 1992), 21.

11. Vyvyan Evans and Melanie Green, *Cognitive Linguistics: An Introduction* (Edinburgh: Edinburgh University Press, 2006), 211.

12. Ana R. López, "Applying Frame Semantics to Translation: A Practical Example," *Translator's Journal* 47, no. 3 (2002): 312.

by the concept שתה.[13] The general assumption of Relevance Theory (RT) is that the more cognitive effects an utterance has and the less the mental effort used to process it, the more relevant it becomes to an individual.[14] RT makes two general claims with respect to how our minds process information and how we communicate. The first claim, referred to as the Cognition Principle of Relevance, is that human cognition is geared toward maximization of relevance; and the second claim, referred to as the Communicative Principle of Relevance, is that utterances raise anticipations of relevance to their addressees. This theory, which states that the linguistic meaning of an utterance is only a hint to the speaker's intentions, will prove useful in addressing textual issues that arise in Obadiah 16, which include lexical adjustment processes of narrowing (restricting the category) and broadening (extending the category), solving cases of ambiguity, assigning referents to referential expressions, supplying contextual assumptions, and deriving implications with the solutions expected to meet expectations of relevance.[15] Since RT is a cognition-based communication theory, it will go a long way to addressing both the cognitive and the communication processes involved in the understanding and use of the ad hoc concept שתה*.[16] An ad hoc concept is an occasion-specific concept that involves an interaction between the encoded concept, contextual information, and the expectation of relevance.[17] The next section explores the literal and metaphorical uses of the ad hoc concept שתה*.

The Literal and Metaphorical Uses of שתה

The following is the Hebrew text of Obadiah 16 and its free translation with the three occurrences of שתה underlined.

כִּי כַּאֲשֶׁר שְׁתִיתֶם עַל־הַר קָדְשִׁי יִשְׁתּוּ כָל־הַגּוֹיִם תָּמִיד וְשָׁתוּ וְלָעוּ וְהָיוּ כְּלוֹא הָיוּ

For just as <u>you have drunk</u> on my holy mountain,
so all the nations <u>will drink</u> continually.

---

13. John I. Saeed, *Semantics*, 2nd ed. (Oxford: Blackwell, 2003), 343; Evans and Green, *Cognitive Linguistics*, 216.

14. Sperber and Wilson, *Relevance, Communication and Cognition*, 158, 260, 263–266.

15. Sperber and Wilson, 158–162, 260, 263–266.

16. The asterisk is used with concepts to indicate that the word has gone through the process of either narrowing or broadening.

17. Sperber and Wilson, *Relevance, Communication and Cognition*, 231–237; Deirdre Wilson and Robyn Carston, "A Unitary Approach to Lexical Pragmatics: Relevance, Inference and Ad Hoc Concepts," in *Pragmatics*, edited by Noel Burton-Roberts (Basingstoke: Palgrave-Macmillan, 2007), 230.

<u>They will drink</u>, and they will gulp down;
they will be as though they had never been.
(New English Translation)

Are the uses of the concept שתה in Obadiah 16, especially its first occurrence, literal, metaphorical, or both? The RT approach to metaphors allows for both literal and metaphorical interpretations of the same concept, with the literal meaning accommodating the metaphorical one as well. This loose use of words results in the creation of new ad hoc (occasion-specific) concepts through an inferential process using both linguistic and contextual clues, concepts which are broader or more general than their encoded lexical meaning.[18] According to this theoretical framework, a hearer does not make a distinction in the interpretation process between words used literally and those used metaphorically, for as Wilson argues, "There is a continuum of cases of broadening, ranging from strictly literal use, through various shades of approximation to hyperbole and metaphor, with no sharp cut-off point between them."[19] To illustrate this lack of a sharp cut-off point, he uses the sentence "The audience slept through the lecture," which can be interpreted literally to mean that the audience was asleep throughout the lecture; as an approximation by arguing for a slightly weaker claim that the audience was on the point of falling asleep; metaphorically as making a still weaker claim of a physical state of drowsiness; and metaphorically as making an even weaker claim that the audience was extremely bored with the lecture.[20] The choice between these different possible interpretations is context-dependent. Similarly, the ad hoc concept שתה* in Obadiah 16 is used literally to claim that the people of Edom did indeed hold a "merry party" on the mountain of God that involved drinking alcohol, and at the same time it is used metaphorically to bring out the irony that what they were really drinking was not the wine of celebration but God's wrath.[21] Since there is no cut-off point that would involve different interpretive mechanisms, these two interpretations are accommodated in the ad hoc concept שתה*. The following subsections discuss the referent of the personal pronoun -תֶּם as well as its implied object(s).

---

18. Deirdre Wilson, "Parallels and Differences in the Treatment of Metaphor in Relevance Theory and Cognitive Linguistics," *Studies in Pragmatics* 11 (2009): 43.

19. Wilson, "Parallels and Differences," 44.

20. Wilson, 46.

21. Thomas E. McComiskey, *The Minor Prophets: An Exegetical and Expository Commentary* (Grand Rapids, MI: Baker, 1992), 536.

The Referent(s) of the Personal Pronoun -תֶּם

What is the referent implied by the second person plural pronoun -תֶּם attached to the first occurrence of the *qal* perfect form of the verb שׁתה? There are those who argue that the relative particle כַּאֲשֶׁר compares the situation between the people of Judah, who were made to drink the cup of divine judgment, and the nations who are now to drink of it.[22] One of the reasons given in support of this interpretation is the shift in the second personal pronoun from singular to plural, which is taken to justify the change in the people being addressed. It is important to note that such an alternation between singular and plural is not unusual especially when a nation is in view.[23] This change can be attributed to stylistic use of the grammatical person in poetry where prior to verse 16 the second person singular is necessitated by the choice to refer to the general group as an entity whereas in verse 16 the second person plural form is necessitated to identify the individuals within the group.[24]

Another argument advanced to support the people of Judah as the referents of the pronoun -תֶּם is that since in Obadiah 2–15 there is no distinction made between Edom and the other nations, the referent pronoun -תֶּם does not refer to the Edomites alone.[25] However, going by the fact that in verse 1 the subjects of the first person common plural of the cohortative verb נָקוּמָה "let us arise" are the nations who are urged to form a military alliance against the people of Edom, then, contrary to this argument, a distinction is made between Edom and the other nations.

Another reason given is that picturing other nations celebrating the downfall of Edom is reading too much into the text.[26] But is it really? Judging from the fact that these other nations are the ones invited to fight the people of Edom, it is not unreasonable to expect these very nations to rejoice at the downfall of the nation of Edom, with the predicative adjectival passive participle בָּזוּי "will be despised" in Obadiah 2 allowing for such an interpretation. It is only from verse 15 that the tables are turned on these other nations.

One more reason which is given to rule out the possibility of the people of Edom being the subjects of the verb שׁתה is that a metaphorical interpretation

---

22. Irvin Busenitz, *Joel and Obadiah*, Mentor Commentary (Fearn, Ross-shire: Christian Focus, 2002), 266.

23. Busenitz, *Joel and Obadiah*, 266.

24. McComiskey, *Minor Prophets*, 535.

25. Paul R. Raabe, *Obadiah: A New Translation with Introduction and Commentary*, Anchor Bible (New York: Doubleday, 1996), 203; Johan Renkema, *Obadiah*, trans. Brian Doyle, Historical Commentary on the Old Testament (Leuven: Peeters, 2003), 40.

26. Raabe, *Obadiah*, 203.

of the verb שתה does not allow the personal pronoun to refer to the people of Edom.[27] Since I have argued for an interpretation that takes both literal and metaphorical interpretations of the verb שתה on board, this argument is inconsequential. The main problem with interpreting the first occurrence of שתה as referring to the people of Judah is the abrupt transition from the people of Edom in the preceding context.[28] It is not convincing to introduce the people of Judah as new participants with a pronoun since in Hebrew discourse new participants are introduced by the use of a proper noun or a descriptive phrase and then referred back to by use of personal pronouns, not the other way round.[29] An example is in Obadiah 1 where the people of Edom are introduced using a proper noun and then mainly referred to later in the entire book by the use of the second person singular pronoun. Another example is in verse 6 of the same book where (the people of) Esau are first mentioned using a proper noun and then referred to in the following verses using third person pronoun referents. This also applies to (the people of) Jacob who are introduced by a proper noun in verse 10 and then in verse 11 are referred back to using the third person singular pronoun. According to the Communicative Principle of Relevance, a communicator attempts to formulate his or her utterance in such a way as to guide the addressees to access the intended assumptions and into drawing the intended conclusion(s), and in the process spend the least possible effort.[30] The same principle guarantees that the first interpretation that is consistent with this principle is the only one that is intended by the speaker. The referent(s) of the pronoun תֶם- who can be easily accessed from short-term memory are the people of Edom, since they are the ones mentioned in the immediate context.

The Implied Objects of שתה

What are the implied objects of the three occurrences of שתה in Obadiah 16? To address this issue there is a need to draw the underlying cognitive frame of שתה.[31] There are a number of potential objects that the first occurrence of the verb שתה can take. They are water (in the context both of quenching thirst

---

27. Raabe, 203.

28. Renkema, *Obadiah*, 190.

29. Thomas J. Finley, *Joel, Amos, Obadiah: An Exegetical Commentary* (repr., Peabody, MA: Biblical Studies Press, 2003), 327.

30. Sperber and Wilson, *Relevance, Communication and Cognition*, 155–162, 271.

31. Barsalou, "Frames, Concepts," 21.

and of being a mark of generosity to identify a potential bride), (fermented) wine (which if taken to excess makes one lose control, and which also should not be taken by those set apart to serve God since they would become ritually unclean), milk (which is used for nourishment), as well as urine (to refer to the devastating effects of the siege against Jerusalem by the Assyrians).[32] In light of the demands of RT, the context of the book of Obadiah rules out water, milk, and urine as being the likely objects of the first occurrence of the verb שתה since it is not about the people of Edom quenching their thirst, being refreshed, or even being under siege. Therefore, the most probable object for the first occurrence of the verb שתה is wine.

The verb שתה is also used figuratively in a number of ways. It is used with the object "blood" to refer to the water which David's men risked their lives to bring to their king, symbolizing their sacrifice, and also to represent an act of slaughter.[33] The challenge with this interpretation is that the people of Edom are accused of having done this action when the people of Israel were escaping and not on God's holy mountain.[34] Another likely object is poison, which symbolizes the sufferings Job was going through because of his righteousness.[35] Another object is "water from one's own cistern," which symbolizes enjoyment of sexual relations with one's spouse.[36] Evil and slander as abstract objects of שתה are given in the context of a person committing evil and slander with the same ease with which he or she drinks water.[37] The object "violence" is compared to sending a message through a fool, which can have injurious consequences.[38] Evil, slander, and violence are ruled out in the context of the book of Obadiah since they would require more processing effort. The most likely object for these remaining two occurrences of שתה is the cup of God's wrath.[39] The common noun כוס "cup" is one of the encyclopedic entries related to the concept שתה referring to a vessel that is used for drinking wine.[40]

---

32. F. Brown, S. Driver, and C. Briggs, *The Brown–Driver–Briggs Hebrew and English Lexicon (BDB)* (Peabody, MA: Hendrickson, 2007), 1059bf; cf. Num 20:11; Gen 19:33; 24:14; Judg 13:4, 7, 14; Ezek 25:4; 2 Kgs 18:27; Isa 36:12.

33. 1 Chr 11:19; Num 23:24; Isa 49:26; Deut 32:42.

34. Obad 14.

35. Job 6:4.

36. Prov 5:15.

37. Job 15:16; 34:7.

38. Prov 26:6.

39. Renkema, *Obadiah*, 191; Busenitz, *Joel and Obadiah*, 266; Isa 51:17, 22; Jer 25:16, 26–27; 49:12; 51:7; Ezek 23:32–34; Obad 16; Job 21:20; Pss 11:6; 75:8; Lam 4:21; Hab 2:16.

40. Busenitz, *Joel and Obadiah*, 468a; Gen 40:11, 13, 21; Prov 23:31; Jer 35:5.

Metaphorically, כּוֹס is also used to refer to a person's allotted destiny whether bad or good.[41] In Obadiah 16 it has a negative denotation to metaphorically symbolize God's judgment, with Babylon being referred to as a golden cup used to punish other nations including the city of Jerusalem.[42] This cup of God's wrath is deep and wide, symbolizing that it is full of God's anger and rage, with those who partake of it staggering from its effects which are horrible and disastrous.[43] Therefore the figurative use of the cup of wine is used in Obadiah 16 as a picture of God's anger against the people of Edom for having treated their brothers, the people of Israel, with cruelty. The same figure is also used in the New Testament to symbolize Christ's suffering and God's anger.[44] The encyclopedic entry for the concept יַיִן "wine" refers to a common drink for refreshment which mostly formed part of regular meals as well as feasts.[45] There are related entries that are stored and retrieved as an extension of the ad hoc concept שׁתה*.[46] In the context of Obadiah 16, the ad hoc concept שׁתה* is broadened to refer to excessive drinking of wine which the people of Edom most likely did in the name of their heathen gods as they rejoiced over the downfall of Jerusalem.[47] A related concept within this same ad hoc concept is the entry "drunkenness," which results from an excessive use of alcoholic drink, with its effects compared to the state of those who are under God's wrath. There are other instances where celebration parties involving the drinking of wine are held by raiding parties, with the prophecy that such nations will be punished for their disrespect for human life.[48] Other uses of wine include consoling mourners and sustaining those who are faint, which are ruled out here in light of the principle of relevance since the people of Edom are accused of doing the opposite.[49]

The encyclopedic entry list of the negative effects of wine, which points to the effects of God's wrath, is long and includes "staggering, confusion, insensibility . . . sleep," and disgraceful acts including treading in one's own vomit and exposing one's nakedness, which was considered shameful; it can

---

41. Pss 11:6; 16:5.
42. Hab 2:16; Jer 49:12; 51:7; Lam 4:21; Ps 75:8.
43. Isa 51:17, 22; Jer 25:15; Ezek 23:32, 33.
44. Mark 14:36; John 18:11; Rev 14:10; 16:19.
45. *BDB*, 406b, c; Gen 27:25; Judg 19:19; Amos 5:11; Eccl 9:7; Isa 5:12; Esth 5:6.
46. Sperber and Wilson, *Relevance, Communication and Cognition*, 86.
47. Deut 32:38; Ps 104:14–15.
48. 1 Sam 30:16; Joel 3:3; Lam 2:7.
49. Jer 16:7; 2 Sam 16:2; Obad 10–14.

also be used to lure someone to his or her death.[50] Even though, as discussed above, the most likely object for the first occurrence of שתה is (fermented) wine, it is important to point out that there is implied irony in taking this interpretation. According to God, what the people of Edom really drank, in the name of celebrating their triumph, was the wine not of celebration but of divine wrath.[51] Their joyful celebrations turned out to be short-lived, giving way to drunkenness and its effects, which were associated with the "cup of wrath" of the Lord.[52]

Therefore, the ad hoc concept שׁתה* in Obadiah 16 has both literal and metaphorical senses. On the one hand, it is literal, since it refers to someone who has swallowed some alcoholic substance; but, on the other hand, it is metaphorical, in that it has some figurative use. There is no cut-off point that would involve different interpretive mechanisms for the literal and metaphorical uses; they are blended together within the same context.

Application

African Christians have been accused of living dichotomized lives such that their faith seems to have minimal effect on their everyday lives.[53] Indeed, they have not been immune to accusations of participating in divisive, politically driven ethnic tensions/violence over power and resources, with such fights even occurring in places of worship.[54] Just as the Edomites invited God's wrath for using their ethnic identity to take advantage of their brothers the Israelites, so too do Christians who relegate their faith for the sake of selfish ethnic alignments with the goal of taking advantage of their brothers and sisters. The situational irony is that any such "advantage" is but a means toward inviting God's punishment rather than his blessing. The will of God in this matter is for Christians to resist the temptations that come with negative ethnic diversity, for every person is created with dignity and thus deserves equal treatment

---

50. Raabe, *Obadiah*, 211; cf. Gen 9:21, 24; 19:32–38; Exod 20:26; Lev 10:9; Deut 21:20; Isa 19:14; 20:4; 24:20; 28:7–8; 47:3; Ezek 16:22; Ps 107:27; Lam 1:8; Job 12:25; 1 Sam 25:36–37; 2 Sam 6:20; Prov 23:20, 31–33, 35; 34:4–5; 1 Sam 1:12–16; Hab 2:15; 2 Sam 13:28; 1 Kgs 16:9–10; 20:16; Nah 3:5.

51. McComiskey, *Minor Prophets*, 536.

52. Lam 4:21; Richard J. Coggins and S. Paul Re'emi, *Israel among the Nations* (Grand Rapids, MI: Eerdmans, 1985), 91.

53. Elizabeth Mburu, *African Hermeneutics* (Carlisle: Langham Publishers, 2019), 3.

54. Mary G. Wosyanju, "The Role of the Church in Combating Negative Ethnicity in Kenya: A Survey of Mainline Churches in Eldoret, Kenya," *African Journal of Education, Science and Technology* (Dec. 2013), https://www.researchgate.net/publication/311671416.

when it comes to accessing resources.[55] Justice, peace, and reconciliation are to be practiced equitably, including those who might seem disadvantaged or marginalized for one reason or another.[56] Therefore, the church in Africa needs to be at the forefront in rejecting ill-motivated ethnic group activities or beliefs which are against the will of God, for as the apostle Paul reminds us, we are one body called to one hope, through our Lord Jesus Christ.[57]

Bibliography

Barcelona, Antonio. "Introduction: The Cognitive Theory of Metaphor and Metonymy." In *Metaphor and Metonymy at the Crossroads: A Cognitive Perspective*, edited by Antonio Barcelona, 1–28. Berlin: Mouton de Gruyter, 2000.

Barsalou, L. W. "Frames, Concepts, and Conceptual Fields." In *Frames, Fields, and Contrasts: New Essays in Semantic and Lexical Organization*, edited by Adrienne Lehrer and Eva F. Kittay, 21–74. Hillsdale, NJ: Lawrence Erlbaum Associates, 1992.

Barton, John. *Joel and Obadiah: A Commentary*. Old Testament Library. Louisville: Westminster John Knox, 2001.

Brown, F., S. Driver, and C. Briggs. *The Brown–Driver–Briggs Hebrew and English Lexicon*. Peabody, MA: Hendrickson, 2007.

Busenitz, Irvin A. *Joel and Obadiah*. Mentor Commentary. Fearn, Ross-shire: Christian Focus, 2002.

Coggins, Richard J., and S. Paul Reʾemi. *Israel among the Nations*. Grand Rapids, MI: Eerdmans, 1985.

Evans, Vyvyan, and Melanie Green. *Cognitive Linguistics: An Introduction*. Edinburgh: Edinburgh University Press, 2006.

Fillmore, Charles. "Frame Semantics." In *Linguistics in the Morning Calm*, The Linguistic Society of Korea, edited by Hanʾguk Ŏnŏ Hakhoe, 111–138. Seoul: Hanshin, 1982.

Finley, Thomas J. *Joel, Amos, Obadiah: An Exegetical Commentary*. Reprint, Peabody, MA: Biblical Studies Press, 2003.

Lakoff, George, and Mark Johnson. *Metaphors We Live By*. Chicago/London: University of Chicago Press, 1980.

López, Ana R. "Applying Frame Semantics to Translation: A Practical Example." *Translator's Journal* 47, no. 3 (2002): 312–350.

Mburu, Elizabeth. *African Hermeneutics*. Carlisle: Langham Publishers, 2019.

McComiskey, Thomas Edward. *The Minor Prophets: An Exegetical and Expository Commentary*. Grand Rapids, MI: Baker, 1992.

---

55. Rev 5:9; 7:9; Gen 1:26–27.
56. Amos 5:25; cf. Mic 6:8; Acts 2:6; Eph 2:14–16; 5:19; 6:15; Rom 12:17–18; 14:19.
57. Eph 4:4–6.

Raabe, Paul R. *Obadiah: A New Translation with Introduction and Commentary*. Anchor Bible. New York: Doubleday, 1996.

Renkema, Johan. *Obadiah*. Translated by Brian Doyle. Historical Commentary on the Old Testament. Leuven: Peeters, 2003.

Ryken, Leland. *How Bible Stories Work: A Guided Study of Biblical Narrative*. Ashland, OH: Weaver Book Company, 2015.

Saeed, John I. *Semantics*. 2nd ed. Oxford: Blackwell, 2003.

Soskice, Janet Martin. *Metaphor and Religious Language*. Oxford: Oxford University Press, 1985.

Sperber, Dan, and Deirdre Wilson. *Relevance, Communication and Cognition*. 2nd ed. Oxford: Basil Blackwell, 1995.

Waltke, Bruce K., and M. O'Connor. *An Introduction to Biblical Hebrew Syntax*. Winona Lake, IN: Eisenbrauns, 1990.

Wilson, Deirdre. "Parallels and Differences in the Treatment of Metaphor in Relevance Theory and Cognitive Linguistics." *Studies in Pragmatics* 11 (2009): 42–60.

Wilson, Deirdre, and Robyn Carston. "A Unitary Approach to Lexical Pragmatics: Relevance, Inference and Ad Hoc Concepts." In *Pragmatics*, edited by Noel Burton-Roberts, 230–259. Basingstoke: Palgrave-Macmillan, 2007.

Wosyanju, Mary G. "The Role of the Church in Combating Negative Ethnicity in Kenya: A Survey of Mainline Churches in Eldoret, Kenya." *African Journal of Education, Science and Technology* (Dec. 2013). https://www.researchgate.net/publication/311671416.

10

Some New Testament Invitations to Ethnic Reconciliation

John 4:4–42; Luke 10:29–37; Romans; Ephesians 2:11–22[1]

Craig Keener

*F. M. and Ada Thompson Professor of Biblical Studies at Asbury
Theological Seminary, Wilmore, Kentucky, USA*

Abstract

Ethnic conflicts and prejudices were endemic in antiquity as today, and
surmounting them was at the heart of early Christian mission. Indeed,
New Testament writers repeatedly call attention to ethnic-reconciliation
implications of the gospel itself. This chapter reflects on some key examples
of New Testament teaching on this subject, including Jesus's ministry to the
Samaritan woman (John 4), his illustration of a good Samaritan (Luke 10),
Paul's application of the good news of salvation to Jew and Gentile in Romans,
and the Pauline vision of the new temple (Eph 2).

Key words: Luke 10, John 4, Ephesians 2, spiritual temple, new temple, ethnic
reconciliation, ethnic conflict, ethnic prejudice.

---

1. Reprinted with minor editing from Craig Keener, "Some New Testament Invitations to
Ethnic Reconciliation," *Evangelical Quarterly* 75, no. 3 (2003): 195–213.

Introduction

Most parts of the world currently experience some forms of ethnic conflict. Because prejudices from these conflicts inevitably affect Christians, they invite Christian theological reflection on ethnic reconciliation, which in turn invites an examination of biblical teaching on the subject.

Although the ethnic and national groups in competition in the first century largely differ from those in question today, the earliest Christian exhortations to ethnic reconciliation remain relevant for contemporary discussion. Jewish–Gentile and Jewish–Samaritan prejudices were deep-seated and often theologically justified, and we should not think that the early churches themselves always managed to surmount them (see e.g. Acts 11:3; 15:1, 5). Nevertheless, some widely held, central Christian convictions did challenge such intense prejudices, suggesting their value for combating analogous prejudices today which can claim less salvation-historical justification.

This chapter samples the approach of several streams of New Testament thought that challenge such prejudices. Although one could also draw on much of the rest of the New Testament (such as the theme of Gentiles in Matthew or the Gentile mission's development in Acts), we will restrict our samples to two texts regarding the Samaritans (John 4:4–42; Luke 10:29–37); Jewish–Gentile relations in one of Paul's undisputed letters (Romans); and finally the teaching of a new temple in Ephesians 2:19–22 (which I also accept as Pauline).

Samaritans in John 4

In John 17, Jesus prayed that his disciples would be one, even as he and the Father were one (17:21–22). But even a first-time reader of John's gospel would already understand that the kind of unity Jesus demanded included unity between sheep of both Jesus's folds (10:16), which probably implies Jews and Gentiles.[2] Although Jesus's ministry apparently included only a few opportunities for contact with Gentiles (cf. 12:20–21; Matt 8:5; Mark 7:26), John is able to focus at greater length on Samaritans, who figure prominently in John 4:4–42. Shortly after the claim that Jesus's mission is for "the world" (3:16), Jesus is recognized by the Samaritans as "Savior of the world" (4:42) – a world which therefore inevitably includes them.

---

2. Other views include Samaritans (e.g. Edwin D. Freed, "Samaritan Influence in the Gospel of John," *Catholic Biblical Quarterly* 30 [4 Oct. 1968]: 580–587) or Diaspora Jews (e.g. John A. T. Robinson, "The Destination and Purpose of St. John's Gospel," *New Testament Studies* 6 [2 Jan. 1960]: 127–128), but Gentiles is the most common view here.

Some scholars argue that John's audience or that of its traditions originally included Samaritans (cf. Acts 15:3).[3] If, as seems likely, John's ideal audience is a predominantly Jewish Christian community in Asia Minor rather than in Syria-Palestine,[4] this proposal seems unlikely, at least on the level of the finished gospel.[5] A Samaritan Diaspora did exist, though in contrast to the Jewish Diaspora they probably would not constitute a large focus for early Christian mission.[6] More likely, John writes for a Diaspora Jewish audience with much more experience in incorporating Gentiles than in incorporating Samaritans. They could nevertheless find in Jesus's ministry to the Samaritan woman appropriate models for their own ministry to outsiders of various kinds, including ethnic outsiders who might be open to their message.

In John's narrative, Jesus crossed at least three barriers to reach his first Samaritan contact. One was a directly cultural and ethnic barrier, but the other two also relate to it in terms of the complications they created: his dialogue-partner's gender and her perceived moral status.[7]

The Gender Barrier

The gender barrier is explicit in the text: the disciples were shocked that Jesus was speaking with a "woman" (John 4:27). Some modern interpreters object that cross-gender conversation must have occurred in various rural settings

---

3. Cf. Edwin D. Freed, "Did John Write His Gospel Partly to Win Samaritan Converts?," *Novum Testamentum* 12 (3 Jul. 1970): 241–256; Edwin D. Freed, "Samaritan Influence"; James D. Purvis, "The Fourth Gospel and the Samaritans," *Novum Testamentum* 17 (3 Jul. 1975): 161–198; George Wesley Buchanan, "The Samaritan Origin of the Gospel of John," in *Religions in Antiquity: Essays in Memory of Erwin Ramsdell Goodenough*, ed. Jacob Neusner, SHR, NumenSup 14 (Leiden: Brill, 1968), 149–175.

4. In favor of the traditional Asian audience, see e.g. Stephen S. Smalley, *John: Evangelist and Interpreter* (Exeter: Paternoster, 1978), 148–149.

5. Cf. Margaret Pamment, "Is There Convincing Evidence of Samaritan Influence on the Fourth Gospel?," *Zeitschrift für die neutestamentliche Wissenschaft* 73 (1982): 221–230.

6. On the Samaritan Diaspora, see e.g. *Corpus Papyrorum Iudaicarum* 3:103, §513; 3:105, §514; Alf Thomas Kraabel, "New Evidence of the Samaritan Diaspora Has Been Found on Delos," *Biblical Archaeologist* 47 (1984): 44–46; Pieter W. van der Horst, "De Samaritaanse diaspora in de oudheid," *Nederlands Theologisch Tijdschrift* 42 (1988): 134–144; in Thessalonica, Irina Levinskaya, *The Book of Acts in Its Diaspora Setting*, vol. 5 of *The Book of Acts in Its First Century Setting* (Grand Rapids, MI: Eerdmans; Carlisle: Paternoster, 1996), 156.

7. I have abbreviated and adapted much of the material on John 4 from my commentary on John published by Hendrickson.

(cf. Ruth 2:8) despite the scruples of some more conservative pietists.[8] But for a stranger to engage in private cross-gender conversation would have at least troubled many conservative observers: according to extant opinions of early Jewish sages, Jewish men were to avoid unnecessary conversation with women.[9] Thus among six activities later listed as unbecoming for a scholar is conversing with a woman,[10] and in theory the strict opined that a wife could be divorced without her marriage settlement if she spoke with a man in the street (m. Ket. 7:6).

The oldest tradition especially attributed this custom to the dangers of sexually ambiguous situations that could lead to further sin (Sir. 9:9; 42:12). In time, however, sages also worried about the interpretation of onlookers: if one talked with even one's sister or wife in public, someone who did not know that the woman was a relative might get the wrong impression.[11] Many would suspect a wife of adultery if she were found in private with a man other than her husband.[12] Traditional Greek culture likewise normally viewed it as "shameful" for a wife to be seen talking with a young man.[13] The most traditional Romans also regarded wives speaking publicly with others' husbands as a horrible matter reflecting possible flirtatious designs and subverting the moral order of the state.[14] Even today in traditional Middle Eastern societies, "Social intercourse between unrelated men and women is almost equivalent to sexual intercourse."[15] Jesus thus crossed a barrier of culturally accepted gender roles to reach this Samaritan woman and her people.

---

8. Robert Gordon Maccini, *Her Testimony Is True: Women as Witnesses according to John*, JSNTS 125 (Sheffield: Sheffield Academic Press, 1996), 132. His claim that Samaritans may have excluded women from the public sphere less than Jews (133–138), even if true, was probably not something John could have expected his audience to catch without him making it explicit.

9. E.g. m. Ab. 1:5; tos. Shab. 1:14; b. Erub. 53b.

10. B. Ber. 43b, bar.

11. E.g. b. Ber. 43b. See in more detail C. S. Keener, *Paul, Women and Wives* (Peabody, MA: Hendrickson, 1992), 161–162, although the balance there may be overly negative.

12. E.g. p. A.Z. 2:3, §1; Sot. 1:1, §7. This would apply even more so to a Jewish woman left alone with a Gentile (m. A.Z. 2:1); Samaritan women, though better than Gentiles, were presumably likewise suspect.

13. E.g. Eurip. *Electra* 343–344, though there are two men.

14. Livy 34.2.9, 18 (195 BCE). A more progressive speaker argues that this behavior is acceptable under some circumstances (34.5.7–10).

15. Carol Delaney, "Seeds of Honor, Fields of Shame," in *Honor and Shame and the Unity of the Mediterranean*, ed. David D. Gilmore, AAA 22 (Washington, DC: American Anthropological Association, 1987), 43.

The Moral Barrier

Because women often came to draw water together, that this woman came alone warrants attention.[16] The time of day (4:6) may underline this point further. Everyone recognized that noon would be hot,[17] explaining why Jesus needed to sit down and why he would be thirsty.[18] Thus at midday one would temporarily break from most agricultural work;[19] from hearing legal cases;[20] from hunting;[21] from allowing animals to graze;[22] and sometimes from battles.[23] The time of day, hence intensity of heat, also probably reminds John's audience that this was not the time when most of the women would come to draw – hence lead the reader to consider why this woman had to come alone at that time.[24]

That she came alone probably implies that she was not welcome among the other women. Despite some Jewish polemic to the contrary, the Samaritans were intensely religious,[25] and like other ancient Near Eastern and Mediterranean peoples, they took seriously a woman's immorality. Even Gentiles (whose standards for male sexual behavior diverged considerably from Judaism's) regarded women's sexual purity as essential, sometimes preferring death to defilement.[26] All ancient Mediterranean cultures disapproved of adultery, that

---

16. The sharing of common water supplies usually facilitates interaction among local Middle Eastern women (Dale F. Eickelman, *The Middle East: An Anthropological Approach*, 2nd ed. [Englewood Cliffs, NJ: Prentice Hall, 1989], 163).

17. E.g. Soph. *Antig.* 416; Ap. Rhod. 2.739; 4.1312–1313; Ovid *Metam.* 1.591–592; Jos. & Asen. 3:2/3:3.

18. Cf. Philostratus *Heroikos* 11.7; 15.6; 16.3; also I. Howard Marshall, "Historical Criticism," in *New Testament Interpretation: Essays on Principles and Methods*, ed. I. Howard Marshall (Grand Rapids, MI: Eerdmans, 1977), 126.

19. Columella *Trees* 12.1; Longus 2.4.

20. Sus. 7 (= Dan 13:7 LXX); Aul. Gel. 17.2.10.

21. Ovid *Metam.* 3.143–154.

22. Virg. *Georg.* 3.331–334; Longus 1.8, 25.

23. Livy 44.35.20; 44.36.1–2.

24. Raymond E. Brown, *The Gospel according to John*, 2 vols., Anchor Bible 29 and 29A (Garden City, NY: Doubleday, 1966–70), 1:169.

25. See e.g. S. Dar, "Three *Menorot* from Western Samaria," *Israel Exploration Journal* 34, no. 2–3 (1984): 177–179, on the strictness of rural Samaria. Cf. further John Bowman, *Samaritan Documents Relating to Their History, Religion and Life*, POTTS 2 (Pittsburgh: Pickwick, 1977), 299.

26. Among men, see Diod. Sic. 12.24.3–4; Livy 3.44.4–3.48.9; among women, see Diod. Sic. 15.54.3; Livy 1.58.12; in premarital situations, see e.g. Hom. *Od.* 6.287–288.

is, the wife's unfaithfulness to her husband and a man's seduction of another's wife.[27]

The text does not clearly indicate this woman's adultery, but most ancient readers would view her negatively. From their perspective, as many as five successive husbands had found some reason to divorce her (if they knew the Palestinian custom that normally only the husband could initiate divorce), and, most plainly, she was now living with a man to whom she was not married (4:17–18). In Sychar this story must have been widely known; the townspeople seem to know of her past (4:29).

Within the narrative world, the woman herself would be aware of what her coming alone at noon might indicate to Jesus, and how he might have viewed her. Thus she, like most of Jesus's dialogue partners in this gospel, misunderstands him on a purely natural level (e.g. 3:4; 6:52; 8:33). The situation in which Jesus confronts the woman would have appeared morally ambiguous to his contemporaries; an uninformed reader's assumption – and that of the woman within the narrative world – could have been that Jesus intended to consort with her.

The conversation's location reinforces this ambiguity. That Jesus meets the woman at "Jacob's well" (4:6) alludes to a different well in Mesopotamia where Jacob met the matriarch Rachel and provided water for her (Gen 29:10),[28] just as Jesus promises to provide living water (4:10). In Genesis, the Jacob scene also recalls the earlier well scene where Abraham's steward finds a wife for Isaac (Gen 24:11–49); John 4 provides numerous formal parallels with this passage.[29] Paralleling these patriarchs, Moses meets Zipporah at a well, and like Jesus in this passage, sits down there, exhausted from his travel (Exod 2:15; John 4:6).[30] It is possible that Josephus depends on a more widely known Jewish tradition when he indicates that the time at which Moses sat at the well was "noon" (Jos. *Ant.* 2.257).

That dialogues at wells could lead to marriage in unrelated traditions suggests that even less biblically literate readers might have noticed the

---

27. E.g. Plut. *Bride* 42, 46; *Mor.* 144B–F; Dio Cass. 77.16.5; Apul. *Metam.* 6.22; Athen. *Deipn.* 4.167e. For more detail, see C. S. Keener, "Adultery, Divorce," in *Dictionary of New Testament Background*, ed. C. A. Evans and S. E. Porter (Downers Grove, IL: InterVarsity Press, 2000), 6–16.

28. The two wells were conflated in tradition (Martin McNamara, *Targum and Testament* [Grand Rapids, MI: Eerdmans, 1972], 145–146).

29. See Norman R. Bonneau, "The Woman at the Well: John 4 and Genesis 24," *The Bible Today* 67 (Oct. 1973): 1254; T. Francis Glasson, *Moses in the Fourth Gospel*, SBT (Naperville, IL: Alec R. Allenson, 1963), 57.

30. Bonneau, "Woman at the Well," 1255.

ambiguity.[31] Of course, not all such conversations invited suspicion of motives; thirsty people did not hesitate to ask strangers for water.[32] Nevertheless, it was possible for men and women interacting at wells to understand their interaction in terms specified by Genesis 24.[33] But if the Samaritan woman in our passage interprets the encounter in even partly conjugal or sexual terms, the narrative quickly indicates that this is not how Jesus intends it.

Given cultural constraints, the gender barrier described above would take on still more serious overtones in this morally ambiguous setting. Jewish teachers warned against social intercourse with those practicing overtly sinful lifestyles. Jewish tradition developed the biblical prohibition against social intercourse with those whose behavior was overtly sinful (e.g. Prov 13:20; 14:7; 28:7).[34] Some Greek moralists issued similar warnings.[35] Jesus thus crossed a perceived moral barrier to speak with this woman.

The Ethnic Barrier

Most significantly for this narrative, Jesus crossed an ethnic barrier, for "Jews avoid dealing with Samaritans" (4:9, author's translation). The opposition between the two peoples was proverbial: one widely circulated book of Jewish wisdom announced that God hated "the foolish people" who lived in Samaria (Sir. 50:25–26).[36] Later rabbis rejected most kinds of testimony from

---

31. E.g. Arrian *Alex*. 2.3.4.

32. E.g. b. Kid. 9a; Ovid *Metam*. 5.446, 448–450; 6.340–341, 343–365; Eurip. *Cycl*. 96–98.

33. See the later account in Lam. Rab. 1:1, §19.

34. E.g. Sir 6:7–12; 12:13–18; Ep. Arist. 130; m. Ab. 1:6–7; 2:9; Sifre Deut. 286.11.4; Ps-Phocyl. 134.

35. E.g. *Gnomologium Vaticanum* 460 (in Abraham J. Malherbe, *Moral Exhortation: A Greco-Roman Sourcebook*, LEC 4 [Philadelphia: Westminster, 1986], 110); Crates *Ep*. 12; Socratics *Ep*. 24; Diod. Sic. 12.12.3; 12.14.1; Diog. Laert. 1.60.

36. The text specifies Shechem, the leading Samaritan city, and in the LXX replaces the Hebrew's "Mount Seir" with "Mountain of Samaria." Cf. Joachim Jeremias, *Jerusalem in the Time of Jesus* (Philadelphia: Fortress; London: SCM, 1969), 352–358, for a catalogue of examples of hatred between many Jews and Samaritans.

Samaritans.[37] They also recounted theological conflict stories where Jewish teachers naturally triumphed.[38]

Like many ethnic conflicts in today's world, these conflicts were deeply rooted in history, although in recent centuries the Jewish side of the conflict had often held the upper hand. These conflicts affected the way Jewish people viewed Samaritans: thus, for example, Samaria was founded by those who rejected Jeremiah's call to repentance (4 Bar. 8).

Conservative Palestinian Jews steeped in this history (as well as many of their Diaspora counterparts) may have regarded as offensive Jesus sending his disciples to buy food in a Samaritan city (4:8).[39] One prominent late first-century teacher insisted that whoever eats bread from Samaritans is as if he eats pork.[40] Before this ruling, however, even Pharisees probably would have permitted buying Samaritan grain, provided one then tithed on it.[41] More certainly, however, Jesus's request for water from the "unclean" woman's vessel would have disturbed them (4:7).[42] Strict Jewish men would avoid drinking after *any* woman who *might* be unclean,[43] and viewed Samaritan women as

---

37. M. Git. 1:5; p. Git. 1:4, §2; as also from women (Jos. *Ant.* 4.219; Sifra VDDeho. pq. 7.45.1.1; cf. Justin. *Inst.* 2.10.6); slaves (Jos. *Ant.* 4.219; cf. Prop. *Eleg.* 3.6.20); and other groups. But on many such issues later rabbinic opinion as to the degree of Samaritans' Jewishness varied according to rabbi, period, and issue, though none of them viewed the Samaritans in a positive light.

38. E.g. Lam. Rab. 1.1.14–15; Koh. Rab. 10:8, §1. On Samaritan–Jewish relations, see generally James D. Purvis, "The Samaritans and Judaism," in *Early Judaism and Its Modern Interpreters*, ed. Robert A. Kraft and George W. E. Nickelsburg, SBLBMI 2 (Atlanta: Scholars, 1986), 81–98; Ferdinand Dexinger, "Limits of Tolerance in Judaism: The Samaritan Example," in *Jewish and Christian Self-Definition*, ed. E. P. Sanders, 3 vols. (Philadelphia: Fortress, 1980–82), 2:88–114.

39. So e.g. Richard N. Longenecker, *Paul, Apostle of Liberty* (Grand Rapids, MI: Baker, 1976), 141 n. 76, citing principles applicable to *am haaretz* in general.

40. M. Shebiith 8:10; according to p. A.Z. 5:11, §2, the sages accepted this opinion of R. Eliezer. Amoraim permitted some Samaritan food and drink, but prohibited much of it (p. A.Z. 5:4, §3).

41. Tos. Demai 5:24 (from R. Eliezer's generation); untithed food was obviously unclean whatever its source (e.g. m. Demai, *passim*; Gen. Rab. 60:8; Lam. Rab. 1:3, §28). But whatever the Samaritans imported from Judea was clean and could be bought from them (tos. Demai 1:11).

42. Many regarded Samaritan drinking vessels as unclean (m. Kelim, *passim*; C. K. Barrett, *The Gospel according to St John: An Introduction with Commentary and Notes on the Greek Text*, 2nd ed. [Philadelphia: Westminster, 1978], 232).

43. Cf. Jos. *Ant.* 3.261; m. Toh. 5:8; tos. Shab. 1:14; Judith Romney Wegner, *Chattel or Person? The Status of Women in the Mishnah* (New York: Oxford, 1988), 162–165. Some Jewish groups, however, including the Sadducees, appear to have rejected Pharisaic strictness on the issue (see Tal Ilan, *Jewish Women in Greco-Roman Palestine* [Tübingen: J. C. B. Mohr; Peabody, MA: Hendrickson, 1996], 100–105, 227).

unclean from infancy.[44] Some went so far as to declare that if a Samaritan woman (or a Gentile) were in a town, one should regard all the spittle there as unclean (because it might derive from them).[45]

What is most significant about the interaction, however, is that while Jesus's own people accuse him of being a "Samaritan" (8:48) or a "Galilean" (7:40–52), the Samaritan woman recognizes Jesus as a "Jew" (4:9), and he agrees (4:22). Subsequent history no less than this narrative warns that hostile voices on both sides of ethnic barriers may regard one who crosses them as a traitor to their cause. John's teaching on the unity of Jesus's followers (10:16; 17:21–23), however, suggests that Jesus's act of crossing such barriers provides a model for Johannine Christians.

Samaritans in Luke 10

Luke seems to exhibit special interest in Samaritans. In Luke 9:51–56, Jesus condemns the disciples' desire to summon judgment on Samaritans, following the model of Elijah (9:54; 2 Kgs 1:10, 12). The model of Elijah and Elisha, emphasized in Luke's programmatic scene (Luke 4:25–27), may also be implicit in the account of the Samaritan man with leprosy in Luke 17:11–19, although this is less clear. Whereas God used Elisha to heal Naaman the Gentile with leprosy (2 Kgs 5:9–15), a story Luke knows quite well (Luke 4:27), those with leprosy in Israelite Samaria were not cleansed (2 Kgs 7:3; Luke 4:27). In Luke 17:16–18, however, it is only the outsider Samaritan with leprosy who returns to give Jesus thanks for cleansing him. Luke might portray this leprosy sufferer through the prism of Naaman's healing through Elisha (though Luke portrays Jesus as one greater than Elijah and Elisha – cf. Luke 1:17; 9:8, 19, 30). Most significantly, the first explicit expansion of the Way outside Judea in Acts includes (and focuses on) Philip's Samaritan mission (Acts 8:8–25; cf. 1:8; 9:31; 15:3).

For our present purposes, however, one Lukan sample will suffice. In Luke 10:30–37, Jesus teaches that relationships with Samaritans, proverbial enemies already introduced in the previous chapter (9:52–53), are relevant for soteriology (10:25–29). When a legal scholar confronted Jesus with a

---

44. M. Nid. 4:1; tos. Nid. 5:1.
45. M. Toh. 5:8.

standard question, how to have eternal life,[46] Jesus responded with a good rabbinic counter-question: How do you interpret the law?[47] He commends his interlocutor's reply (which appeals in part to Lev 19:18),[48] but the interlocutor is not satisfied: Who is the neighbor that he must love (Luke 10:29)?

The passage in Leviticus was not ambiguous concerning the proper object of love. The immediate context of Leviticus 19:18 refers to fellow Israelites; but the broader context of the same passage also requires one to love Gentiles in the land as oneself (Lev 19:34). Given the penchant of Jesus's Jewish contemporaries for linking together texts on the basis of a common key term or phrase, this command to love Gentiles in the same context would have been difficult to miss. Then as today, however, people often exercised strong prejudices that affected interpretation and application. So Jesus temporarily circumvents the exegetical question with a story that provides the same answer.

Subsequent interpreters often missed the specifically ethnic focus of the interaction, ignoring the literary context of the parable and focusing on more traditional theological questions. Most famous is Augustine's allegorization of the parable's details in light of the story of creation, fall, and redemption.[49] Some recent interpreters, however, have revived part of his interpretation, namely, the God-as-Samaritan view, by suggesting a different meaning in the parable's pre-Lukan context.[50] Like many of Luke's parables, however, no "pre-Lukan context" for this story is available to us and, despite detractors,[51] the parable makes sense in its present context.[52]

---

46. B. Ber. 28b, bar.; Tamid 32a; cf. Luke 3:10; Acts 2:37; 16:30. Helmut Flender, *St Luke: Theologian of Redemptive History*, tr. R. H. and Ilse Fuller (London: SPCK, 1967), 10, rightly compares the exchange in Luke 18:18, which is pre-Lukan.

47. Some view this interaction as hostile (see e.g. John J. Pilch, "Lying and Deceit in the Letters to the Seven Churches," *Biblical Theology Bulletin* 22 [1992]: 129; Bruce J. Malina and Jerome H. Neyrey, "Honor and Shame in Luke–Acts: Pivotal Values of the Mediterranean World," in *The Social World of Luke–Acts: Models for Interpretation*, edited by Jerome H. Neyrey [Peabody, MA: Hendrickson, 1991], 51), though this remains open to debate.

48. The language of Jesus's commendation was standard for correct answers (e.g. 4 Ezra 4:20).

49. Augustine, *Quaestiones Evangeliorum* 2.19, reported in C. H. Dodd, *The Parables of the Kingdom* (London: Nisbet & Company, 1936), 11–12.

50. See Douglas E. Oakman, "Was Jesus a Peasant? Implications for Reading the Samaritan Story," *Biblical Theology Bulletin* 22 (1992): 123.

51. Rudolf Bultmann, *The History of the Synoptic Tradition*, 2nd ed., tr. John Marsh (Oxford: Basil Blackwell, 1968), 192.

52. See e.g. Kenneth E. Bailey, *Through Peasant Eyes: More Lucan Parables, Their Culture and Style* (Grand Rapids, MI: Eerdmans, 1980), 33. This is an "example story" as opposed to a similitude (Robert M. Johnston, "Parabolic Interpretations Attributed to Tannaim" [PhD diss., Hartford Seminary Foundation, 1977], 636).

Although Jülicher's insistence on interpreters finding only one point in a parable goes too far,[53] this parable invites only limited points of comparison between its story world and that of Luke's audience. Both the setting of the story and its opening situation are realistic yet distinct from the primary action, suggesting that they support the more dramatic storyline which follows. As is widely recognized today, the parable's "descent" to Jericho (10:30) is part of the geographical setting, not a theological commentary. The steep road from Jerusalem to Jericho descends over three thousand feet over a span of seventeen miles, and may not have been in the best condition (the Roman road dates from after 70).[54] Robbers provided a frequent threat to travelers,[55] and this man, by traveling alone and apparently on foot, might have provided an easier target than many others (10:30).[56] This particular road was known for robberies throughout history and into modern times.[57] The robbers wounded and stripped the man, leaving him "half dead" (10:30), a phrase which (like its converse, "half alive") normally depicted a person on the verge of death.[58] That they beat him may suggest that he resisted;[59] but perhaps they were especially desperate in wishing to strip him.[60]

At this juncture the points in the story begin to communicate more moral implications and surprises, at least for the legal teacher Jesus addresses in Luke's narrative world: those assumed to be the most obvious representatives of the wounded man's own group do not help him. Luke's own informed readers may be less surprised, given the aggression shown by some members of the

---

53. See Craig S. Keener, *A Commentary on the Gospel of Matthew* (Cambridge, MA: Eerdmans, 1999), 372–375, 381–384; Craig L. Blomberg, *Interpreting the Parables* (Downers Grove, IL: InterVarsity Press, 1990).

54. Edwin M. Yamauchi, *The Stones and the Scriptures: An Introduction to Biblical Archaeology* (Grand Rapids, MI: Baker, 1972), 104–105.

55. E.g. Phaedrus, *Fables* 4.23.16; 2 Cor 11:26; m. Ber. 1:3; b. A.Z. 25b; Ber. 11a; B.K. 116b; Pes. Rab Kah. 27:6; Gen. Rab. 75:3; Ex. Rab. 30:24. See also sources in Ludwig Friedländer, *Roman Life and Manners under the Early Empire*, 4 vols., tr. Leonard A. Magnus, J. H. Freese, and A. B. Gough (New York: Barnes & Noble, 1907, 1965; New York: E. P. Dutton & Company, 1908, 1913), 1:294–296.

56. Though the poor may have been less frequent targets (Dio Chrys. *7th, Euboean Disc.* 9–10).

57. Bailey, *Peasant Eyes*, 41–42; Joachim Jeremias, *The Parables of Jesus*, 2nd rev. ed. (New York: Scribner's, 1992), 203.

58. E.g. Eurip. *Alcestis* 141–143; Livy 23.15.8; 40.4.15; Corn. Nep. *Generals* 4 (Pausanias) 5.4. Rabbis also used this category, which for them would imply unconsciousness (Bailey, *Peasant Eyes*, 42).

59. Bailey, *Peasant Eyes*, 42.

60. Robbers sometimes murdered their victims (*Greek Anth.* 7.310, 516, 581, 737; Gen. Rab. 80:2; 92:6).

priesthood toward Jesus elsewhere in the gospel (Luke 9:22; 19:47; 20:1, 19; 22:2–4, 52, 66; 23:10; 24:20; though see also Luke 1:5; 5:14; 17:14; Acts 6:7).

A priest, seeing the wounded man, avoids drawing near him, instead passing on the other side of the road (10:31). Jewish law required priests, Levites, and other Israelites to help a dying person even if death was imminent.[61] Most people would have regarded rescuing a living person from robbers as morally appropriate, provided that this could be done with minimal risk to the rescuers.[62] But because a "half-dead" person was to all practical appearances dead, he might be dead for all they knew, and they may have judged the risk of ritual contamination too great.[63] Jewish law, to be sure, did not forbid involvement with a corpse, but one would contract biblical impurity for seven days (Num 19:11).[64] An early second-century Jewish teacher noted that all who pass by a corpse on the highway cover their noses and hurry off.[65]

The preoccupation of at least some priests with ritual purity may be illustrated by the later Jewish story of a priest who found a knife in the body of his dying son and paused to declare the knife ritually pure.[66] According to stricter Jewish traditions, if so much as one's shadow touched a corpse, one contracted corpse-impurity;[67] one could also contract it by contact with graves.[68] But in any case, the priest is also "descending" on that road, that is, heading for Jericho where many wealthy priests lived;[69] whatever ritual duties he had to do in the temple he had already fulfilled! This would not obviate the concern for ritual purity,[70] but it could diminish its priority.

---

61. Brad H. Young, *Jesus and His Jewish Parables: Rediscovering the Roots of Jesus' Teaching* (New York: Paulist, 1989), 240, 269 n. 15; cf. I. Abrahams, *Studies in Pharisaism and the Gospels*, 1st ser. (New York: KTAV, 1967; repr. of Cambridge: Cambridge University, 1917), 110.

62. Among Egyptians, see Diod. Sic. 1.77.3.

63. Cf. E. P. Sanders, *Jewish Law from Jesus to the Mishnah: Five Studies* (London: SCM; Philadelphia: Trinity Press International, 1990), 41–42; Marcus J. Borg, *Conflict, Holiness and Politics in the Teachings of Jesus*, Studies in the Bible and Early Christianity 5 (New York: Edwin Mellen, 1984), 104–105. For strictness in cases of doubt, see e.g. Sifra Taz. pq. 1.123.1.6; but positive duties should also normally take precedence over negative ones in Jewish tradition (p. B.M. 2:5, §1; for uncleanness, cf. p. Nazir 7:1, §7).

64. For necessary involvement with corpses, cf. Sanders, *Jewish Law*, 34.

65. ARN 11A.

66. Cf. Young, *Jesus and His Jewish Parables*, 239–241.

67. Sanders, *Jewish Law*, 232.

68. Cf. e.g. CD 12.15–17; Jos. *Ant.* 18.36–38; Sanders, *Jewish Law*, 34.

69. For Jericho's wealthy priestly community, see J. Schwartz, "On Priests and Jericho in the Second Temple Period," *Jewish Quarterly Review* 79, no. 1 (1988): 23–48.

70. He might prove unable to collect and eat from his tithes; see Bailey, *Peasant Eyes*, 44.

A Levite, also expected to be pious, likewise passes on the other side (10:32). Some commentators argue that whereas Sadducean regulations forbade priests to defile themselves with a corpse on the road, Levites were under no such obligation.[71] Yet another factor may play a role: one could distinguish Jews from Samaritans by their clothes but not by physical features, and this man was "stripped" (10:30). For all these religious professionals knew, he might not be a Jew anyway.[72] On the Jericho road, however, a Jew would be much more likely. It is possible that the priest and the Levite, like most analogies that modern preachers draw to them, simply refuse to risk danger (if robbers remain present) or serious inconvenience.

Many ancient Jewish parables make comparisons among priests, Levites, and Israelites, so some scholars suggest that Jesus's audience, including the legal scholar, may have expected the third and righteous character to be a common Israelite.[73] Normally these parables emphasize the greater purity requirements for the priest, but some other Jewish groups criticized the corruption of Jerusalem's priesthood,[74] suggesting possible expectation of such a contrast in favor of the Israelite at least in its original life-setting. But the proposal that most peasants would have disliked priests and Levites as urban characters[75] does not accord well with the respect accorded priests in our diverse extant sources.[76] To be sure, Jerusalem aristocrats generated disdain among their enemies, but Jesus does not identify the priest as a Sadducee (Josephus even reports Sadducees oppressing poorer priests, although most in Jericho would not have been poor).

Whatever Jesus's interlocutor's expectation of the third character, Luke's informed audience would expect him to be shocked to learn that the true hero of the story is a Samaritan (10:33). The idea of a "good Samaritan" was as much an oxymoron to them as the idea of a "friendly PLO member" might be to an Israeli Christian (or "Israeli police officer" to a Palestinian Christian), a

---

71. Jeremias, *Parables of Jesus*, 203. When both a priest and a Levite are available, the Levite should defile himself; when a Levite and an Israelite, the Israelite should defile himself (p. Nazir 7:1, §15).

72. Bailey, *Peasant Eyes*, 42–43. One was not supposed to help a sinner (Sir 12:13).

73. Jeremias, *Parables of Jesus*, 203. See e.g. p. Taan. 4:2, §4; sometimes only two members of the triad appear (e.g. p. B.B. 6:1, §3). Bernard Brandon Scott, *Hear Then the Parable: A Commentary on the Parables of Jesus* (Minneapolis: Augsburg Fortress, 1989), 200, suggests that the unexpected third character forces the hearer to identify with the victim instead of the hero.

74. See Sanders, *Jewish Law*, 42, 91, citing Psalms of Solomon and the Damascus Covenant.

75. Scott, *Hear Then the Parable*, 79, 197.

76. E.g. Jos. *Apion* 2.186; Philo *Hypothetica* 7.13; 1QS 2.19–20; Diod. Sic. 40.3.5.

"benevolent advocate of sharia" to Christians in some parts of northern Nigeria, and so forth.[77] This Samaritan serves the same function in Jesus's parable that the benevolent, God-fearing centurions do in Luke 7:3–5, 9 and Acts 10:2–4: confronting a "good" member of a group we have experienced or perceived as hostile challenges our prejudices.

Anointing wounds with oil was standard practice, and wine was probably used to disinfect the wound (10:34).[78] Strict Jewish piety preferred to avoid Gentile oil,[79] and probably some felt that Samaritan oil would become susceptible to the same impurity; the wounded man's need, however, takes clear precedence over such concerns. Then the Samaritan laid the man on his donkey and himself accepted a servile position by leading the donkey.[80] Donkeys normally could fit two people if necessary,[81] but traders often had donkeys loaded with merchandise.[82] Perhaps more to the point, the wounded man (presumably still unconscious) will not be sitting upright, and given his wounds the Samaritan may think it best to allow him more room. Yet the Samaritan risks not only comfort, but possibly also his own safety. By bringing the wounded man into a Jewish city, the Samaritan risks provoking hostile questions. "An American cultural equivalent would be a Plains Indian in 1875 walking into Dodge City with a scalped cowboy on his horse, checking into a room over the local saloon, and staying the night to take care of him."[83]

Jesus makes this Samaritan not merely one who goes out of his way more than any Samaritan or most Jews his audience knew, but one who sacrifices to aid this person he did not even know. Two denarii (10:35) might cover the man's stay in the inn for over twenty days; "I will repay" (10:35, author's translation)

---

77. Cf. e.g. J. Ramsey Michaels, *Servant and Son: Jesus in Parable and Gospel* (Atlanta: John Knox, 1981), 128. Some derive the notion of the "good Samaritan" from 2 Chr 28:5–15 (F. S. Spencer, "2 Chronicles 28:5–15 and the Parable of the Good Samaritan," *Westminster Theological Journal* 46, no. 2 [1984]: 317–349; Geza Vermes, *The Religion of Jesus the Jew* [Minneapolis: Augsburg Fortress, 1993], 110 n. 40), but though parallels exist, the case is less than clear.

78. Jeremias, *Parables of Jesus*, 203. On anointing wounds with oil, see e.g. Isa 1:6; m. Shab. 14:4.

79. Sanders, *Jewish Law*, 274.

80. For this as the servile position, see e.g. Esth 6:11 (cited by Bailey, *Peasant Eyes*); and the story in Gen. Rab. 32:10; 81:3; Deut. Rab. 3:6; Song Rab. 4:4, §5; for the low status of ass-drivers, Diog. Laert. 6.5.92.

81. Bailey, *Peasant Eyes*, 51. This may, however, assume that both persons are sitting upright, which would not be the position in which the injured man would be placed.

82. Naphtali Lewis, *Life in Egypt under Roman Rule* (Oxford: Clarendon, 1983), 140; cf. the story in Abrahams, *Studies* 1, 110.

83. Bailey, *Peasant Eyes*, 52.

was a legally binding formula in that period.[84] Because the wounded man no longer has any resources of his own, the Samaritan must provide for him or the man, on recovery, will risk the serious legal consequences that accrued to debtors in this period.[85] Jesus's point is that Jews and Samaritans who obey God's law must love one another as neighbors in God's land.[86] In the larger context of Luke–Acts, this helps pave the way for Philip's Samaritan mission (Acts 8:5–13) which in turn prepares the church for the Gentile mission.

Jew and Gentile in Romans

In the first half of the twentieth century in most of the American South, law prohibited black people and white people from eating together. Early Christians experienced some similar barriers based on custom: Jewish people were discouraged from eating with Gentiles, so for Jewish Christians to do so would scandalize their contemporaries (Acts 10:28; 11:3). (Conservative Palestinian Jews considered questionable even entering Gentile homes,[87] though this custom primarily grew from the hatred of idolatry.[88]) But then, how could Christians from the two groups participate in the Lord's Supper as one body? Whether the divisions were according to class (1 Cor 11:19–22) or culture (Gal 2:11–14), Paul opposed them uncompromisingly. Although private reproof was normally considered appropriate both in Jewish tradition and in Jesus's teaching,[89] Paul publicly reproved Peter, regarding his accommodation

---

84. Jeremias, *Parables of Jesus*, 204.

85. Bailey, *Peasant Eyes*, 53–54. Oakman, "Was Jesus a Peasant?," 122, cites m. Yeb. 16:7 to criticize leaving a sick man at an inn; but despite the severe reputation of inns, that very text indicates that Levites could leave a companion at such a place. In any case, the promise to pay for the man affords him protection (Oakman, 123).

86. Cf. Bailey, *Peasant Eyes*, 54–55. For the emphasis here on loving one's enemy (as in Matt 5:43–44), see Brad H. Young, *Jesus the Jewish Theologian* (Peabody, MA: Hendrickson, 1995), 168.

87. Cf. m. Pes. 8:8; Ohol. 18:7; Jos. *War* 2.150; Shemuel Safrai, "Religion in Everyday Life," in *The Jewish People in the First Century: Historical Geography, Political History, Social, Cultural and Religious Life and Institutions*, ed. Shemuel Safrai and M. Stern (Assen: Van Gorcum, 1987), 829; N. T. Wright, *The New Testament and the People of God* (Minneapolis: Fortress; London: SPCK, 1992), 239–240.

88. Cf. ARN 8A; b. Pes. 9a.

89. For the expectation of private reproof in Jewish tradition, see e.g. Jos. *Ant.* 3.67; 1QS 6.26–7.9; 7.15–16; m. Ab. 3:11; b. Sanh. 101a; Shab. 119b; Tam. 28a; Arak. 16b; Lawrence H. Schiffman, *Sectarian Law in the Dead Sea Scrolls: Courts, Testimony and the Penal Code*, Brown Judaic Studies 33 (Chico, CA: Scholars, 1983), 97–98; in Jesus's teaching, see Matt 18:15–17.

of ethnic separatism as compromising the integrity of the gospel itself (Gal 2:11–21).

We see this principle most clearly when Paul addresses the church in Rome. Here he uses the universal theological principle that Christ is the only way of salvation to address a particular concrete situation: Jewish and Gentile Christians were divided from one another.[90] Paul first met Aquila and Priscilla in Corinth, after they left Rome in response to the emperor's edict commanding at least many Jews to leave Rome (Acts 18:1–2).[91] By the time Paul writes to the Roman Christians, however, this couple has returned to Rome (Rom 16:3–4), indicating that Claudius's edict is no longer in effect (presumably because he is dead).[92] Thus it seems likely that Paul wrote after a number of Jewish Christians had returned or emigrated to Rome and encountered Gentile Christians who had functioned for several years with minimal Jewish guidance.

That Paul addresses matters of food customs and holy days (Rom 14:1–6) in such a setting is not surprising. Following the dominant views of their own Roman culture,[93] these Gentile Christians probably could not appreciate Jewish Christians' food laws and holy days. Many of the Jewish Christians, conversely, probably questioned the orthodoxy of Gentile Christians who did not observe biblical teachings about foods (Lev 11). Thus Paul begins his letter (Rom 1–11) by establishing that all people must approach Israel's God on the same terms, on the basis of Jesus Christ.

First, Paul establishes that everyone is equally lost (cf. 3:9–20). He begins with the uncontroversial lostness of the Gentiles, focusing on the examples of idolatry and homosexual behavior (1:18–27). Jewish texts regularly denounce idolatry, and treat it as largely (though not exclusively) a Gentile sin;[94] they

---

90. I have also addressed this material from Romans and Ephesians in my "The Gospel and Racial Reconciliation," in *The Gospel in Black and White: Theological Resources for Racial Reconciliation*, ed. Dennis Ockholm (Downers Grove, IL: InterVarsity Press, 1997), 118–123.

91. Also Suet. *Claudius* 25.4. Scholars currently debate the extent of Claudius's expulsion (cf. Dio Cassius 60.6); note the analogous expulsion under Tiberius in Suet. *Tiberius* 36, but also the relatively uninterrupted Jewish life in Rome (*Corpus inscriptionum judaicarum* 1:lxxiii).

92. For various reconstructions of the situation behind Romans, see Karl P. Donfried, ed., *The Romans Debate*, rev. ed. (Peabody, MA: Hendrickson, 1991); Mark D. Nanos, *The Mystery of Romans* (Minneapolis: Fortress, 1996).

93. Plut. *Table-Talk* 4.4.4, *Mor.* 669C; *Superst.* 8, *Mor.* 169C; Molly Whittaker, *Jews and Christians: Graeco-Roman Views* (Cambridge: Cambridge University Press, 1984), 73–80; J. N. Sevenster, *The Roots of Pagan Anti-Semitism in the Ancient World*, NovTSup 41 (Leiden: E. J. Brill, 1975), 136–139.

94. E.g. Bel and Dragon; Ep. Jer.; Ep. Arist. 134–138; Sib. Or. 3.8–35; 4.4–23; Test. Sol. 26; tos. Bek. 3:12; Peah 1:2; Sanh. 13:8; Sifra VDDeho. par. 1.34.1.3; Sifre Num. 112.2.2; Sifre Deut. 43.4.1; 54.3.2.

treat homosexual behavior as virtually exclusively a Gentile vice in this period.[95] Then, however, he adds a vice-list that includes sins such as envy, pride, and slander, which Jewish people also acknowledged as their own (1:28–32).[96] Like Amos (Amos 1:3 – 2:8) or Wisdom of Solomon, Paul denounces Gentile sins so that he may address Jewish sins.

Second, Paul shows that God has provided salvation for all people on the same terms. Jewish people commonly believed that they would be saved by virtue of their descent from Abraham, but Paul emphasizes that spiritual rather than merely physical descent from Abraham is what matters (Rom 4). God had, after all, chosen Abraham when he was still a Gentile (4:10–12), as Paul's contemporaries also acknowledged.[97] But regardless of who was descended from Abraham, all of us have descended from Adam, and share Adam's sin and death (5:12–21). This argument should have recalled postbiblical Jewish discussions of Adam for the Roman Jewish Christians.[98] Paul acknowledged that the law was a special gift to Israel (3:2), and that it was good (7:12, 14). But whereas the law enabled one to know what was good, it could not transform the human heart to be good; identifying one's evil impulse was not the same as conquering it.

Third, Paul addresses the relationship between ethnic Israel and the Gentiles more directly in chapters 9 through 11. Jewish people believed that God had chosen them in Abraham, but Paul establishes that not all ethnic descendants of Abraham in the Bible qualified for the promise (Rom 9:6–13). He argues that God can sovereignly choose people on any basis he pleases – in this context, not simply on the basis of one's ethnicity, but rather on the basis of one's response to his Christ (Rom 9:24–33).

But while Jewishness could not guarantee salvation, neither should Gentile Christians disregard their Jewish siblings or their heritage. Gentiles were saved by being grafted into the people of God (probably understood as spiritual proselytes, as in Rom 2:29). But if God could break off unbelieving Jewish

---

95. E.g. Ep. Arist. 152; Sib. Or. 3.185–186, 596–600, 764; 4.34; 5.166, 387, 430; tos. Hor. 2:5–6.

96. Envy (e.g. Wisd. 6:23; Ep. Arist. 224; Jos. *Ant.* 2.13; *War* 1.77); pride (e.g. 1QS 4.9; Sir. 3:28; 10:7, 12–13; 13:1, 20; 22:22; 25:1; Philo *Post.* 52; m. Ab. 1:13); and slander (e.g. 1QS 7.15–16; Philo *Spec. Laws* 4.59–60; Sifre Deut. 1.8.2–3; 275.1.1).

97. For Abraham as a model proselyte, see e.g. *Mekilta Nezikin* 18:36ff; b. Suk. 49b; Gen. Rab. 39:8.

98. Cf. e.g. Sir. 25:24; 1 En. 98:4; Life of Adam and Eve 44.3–4; Sifre Deut. 323.5.1; 339.1.2; and especially 4 Ezra 3:7, 20–22, 30; 7:118–26; 2 Bar. 17:2–3; 23:4; 48:42–45; 54:15, 19; 56:5–6.

branches who fit into that heritage more naturally, he could certainly break off the foreign Gentile branches (11:17–22).[99]

Finally, having established that God planned to justify both groups through Christ alone, Paul turns to moral exhortation based on this premise. Christians must serve one another like one body with many diverse members (12:3–16), recognize that the epitome of the law is love (13:8–10), respect one another's customs so long as they are used to glorify God (14:1 – 15:2), and embrace models of ethnic reconciliation like Christ (15:8–12) and Paul himself (15:25–27). Paul's closing exhortation is to beware of those who sow division (16:17). Paul grounds ethnic reconciliation in the gospel.

The New Temple in Ephesians 2

Ephesians, like Romans, seems to address churches divided in part along Jewish–Gentile lines. Scholars regularly debate the authorship of Ephesians; here I can only mention in passing that I accept Pauline authorship (with or without an amanuensis), believing that the general audience, the passage of time, and Paul's continued adaptation of his message for philosophically literate audiences is sufficient to explain the limited stylistic divergences from Paul's earlier letters. Certainly a setting of Paul's imprisonment makes good sense of the passage at hand.

Ephesians opens with a blessing which applies to the entire church many Old Testament designations for Israel (Eph 1:3–14: e.g. chosenness; inheritance; possession). Before turning to the new temple comprised of both Jew and Gentile in 2:20–22,[100] the letter declares both Jew and Gentile one in Christ (2:14). On the premise of Pauline authorship, this declaration is both situationally relevant and dramatic: not long after Paul dictated these words, riots broke out in Caesarea, the city of Paul's earlier imprisonment, with Jews and Syrians slaughtering one another.[101]

---

99. Given the use of "Israel" in the immediate context, I believe, *pace* many scholars, that Paul also expected an eventual turning of his people to faith in Christ; cf. Johannes Munck, *Christ and Israel: An Interpretation of Romans 9–11* (Philadelphia: Fortress, 1967), 136; George E. Ladd, "Israel and the Church," *Evangelical Quarterly* 36 (1964): 206–213.

100. Some Jewish documents apply the image specifically to Israel's elect (e.g. 1QS 8.5–9; Bertril Gärtner, *The Temple and the Community in Qumran and the NT* [Cambridge: Cambridge University Press, 1965], 16–46).

101. Jos. *War* 2.266–270, 457–458. For other massacres in reprisal, see *War* 2.458–468; *Life* 25.

Paul goes on in Ephesians 2:14 to announce that Christ has shattered the dividing wall of partition between Jew and Gentile. He writes as if his hearers will immediately understand the dividing wall to which he refers, and it does not take us long to imagine how Paul's hearers (either during his lifetime or shortly afterward) would have understood his point.

Paul's audience in the region around Ephesus must have known why Paul was writing to them from prison (3:1 – "for the sake of you Gentiles"; 4:1; 6:20); they were aware of the charge that he had transgressed a "dividing barrier" in the temple (Acts 21:28). Because of stricter interpretations of biblical purity regulations, the "outer court" that once welcomed Jews and Gentiles together (1 Kgs 8:41–43) now divided them. The Court of Israel allowed only Jewish men; the Court of Women, beyond which Jewish women could not pass, was on a lower level and further from the priestly sanctuary. Finally, still further from the sanctuary was the new outer court, beyond which Gentile seekers of Israel's God could not pass. Signs at entrances to the Court of Women warned Gentiles that proceeding further invited death.[102]

Paul entered the temple to affirm his Jewish identity for those who thought that he had accommodated the Gentiles too much (Acts 21:21–26).[103] Nevertheless, some Jews who knew of Paul's ministry among Gentiles in Ephesus recognized an Ephesian Gentile with Paul near Jerusalem's temple, and inferred that he had taken the Gentile into the temple. Once this rumor spread, a riot quickly ensued (Acts 21:27–30), leading to Paul's detainment.

But Paul quickly displays his cultural versatility. When his interrogator hears his good Greek and learns that he is a citizen of a prominent city (21:37, 39),[104] he allows him to address the crowd – which Paul proceeds to address in his Semitic language (21:40; possibly Hebrew, probably Aramaic). Emphasizing particular aspects of one's account for a particular audience was standard rhetorical practice.[105] Paul's fluency in Aramaic invites the crowd's attention (22:2), and he emphasizes every possible point of identification with

---

102. Jos. *Ant.* 15.417; *War* 5.193–200; 6.124–126. For the extant inscription, see Efrat Carmon, ed., *Inscriptions Reveal: Documents from the Time of the Bible, the Mishna and the Talmud*, tr. R. Grafman (Jerusalem: Israel Museum, 1973), 76, 167–168, §169; Josephus, *The Jewish War*, ed. Gaalya Cornfeld (Grand Rapids, MI: Zondervan, 1982), 354–356.

103. Paul's activity, if understood, would have appeared virtuous within Judaism; cf. Acts 18:18; 21:24 with Jos. *Ant.* 19.293–294; *War* 2.313–314.

104. On civic pride or honor, see e.g. Isocrates *Panegyricus*; *Panathenaicus*; Diog. Laert. *Lives* 7.1.12; Heraclitus *Ep.* 9; Quint. *Inst. Or.* 3.7.26; *Rhet. ad Herenn.* 3.3.4; Gen. Rab. 34:15.

105. E.g. Callirhoe in Char. *Chaer.* 2.5.10–11 omits Chaereas's kick.

his hearers, including having been raised in Jerusalem at the feet of Gamaliel and receiving ministry from a law-abiding Jewish Christian (22:3–5, 12).

But ultimately Paul alienated his audience, even though he was still expounding the *narratio*, the opening narration of his speech. Paul had earlier appealed to Stoic values with a different audience, finding common ground with his hearers through much of his speech (17:22–29). He had alienated many members of that audience, however, when he advanced an essential part of the gospel he could not accommodate to his hearers' worldview (17:30–32). Now Paul again alienates his audience with what he seems to accept as a nonnegotiable part of his gospel: God's concern for other peoples (22:21). Reflecting the tensions known to exist in the period shortly before the Jewish war, his audience resumed their riot (22:22–23).

Given the likely return to Asia of both Paul's Gentile companion and his accusers (Acts 24:18–19), congregations there surely knew the story that had led to his current imprisonment. For Paul and for the Jewish and Gentile Christians of western Asia Minor, no greater symbol of the barrier between Jew and Gentile could exist than the dividing barrier in the temple (Eph 2:14). Paul declares that in the new temple of God's Spirit, the cross of Christ has abolished that barrier.[106] Paul appears to have followed in Jesus's footsteps in proclaiming a new temple in which Jew, Samaritan, and Gentile would worship together (Eph 2:14–22; cf. John 4:20–24).

Conclusion

Jewish–Gentile conflict was pervasive in the earliest church, inviting comment from various early Christian writers. The theme of the gospel's challenge for surmounting ethnic prejudices (generally to the extent of commitment to the Gentile mission, hence incorporation into the church) appears in more New Testament passages than we could survey in one chapter. We have merely sampled a passage in John, a passage in Luke, a brief summary of Romans, and a passage in Ephesians (by way of Acts). John and Luke used Jesus's ministry to or comments about Samaritans in ways that likely summoned their audiences to consider and surmount ethnic prejudices in their own day. Paul demands ethnic unity in Christ as an integral part of the gospel he preaches (presumably as part of his mission to the Gentiles). Modern interpreters can explore ways

---

106. Mark 11:17 suggests (given the temple context of both Isa 56:7 and Jer 7:11) that at least some early Christians understood Jesus's act in the temple as directed partly against its segregation; see further my *Commentary on Matthew*, 499–501.

to apply such passages in countering ethnic divisions which continue to plague much of the church today.

Bibliography

Abrahams, I. *Studies in Pharisaism and the Gospels*, 1st ser. New York: KTAV, 1967. Reprint of Cambridge: Cambridge University Press, 1917.

Bailey, Kenneth E. *Through Peasant Eyes: More Lucan Parables, Their Culture and Style*. Grand Rapids, MI: Eerdmans, 1980.

Barrett, C. K. *The Gospel according to St John: An Introduction with Commentary and Notes on the Greek Text*. 2nd ed. Philadelphia: Westminster, 1978.

Blomberg, Craig L. *Interpreting the Parables*. Downers Grove, IL: InterVarsity Press, 1990.

Bonneau, Norman R. "The Woman at the Well: John 4 and Genesis 24." *The Bible Today* 67 (Oct. 1973): 1252–1259.

Borg, Marcus J. *Conflict, Holiness and Politics in the Teachings of Jesus*. Studies in the Bible and Early Christianity 5. New York: Edwin Mellen, 1984.

Bowman, John. *Samaritan Documents Relating to Their History, Religion and Life*. POTTS 2. Pittsburgh: Pickwick, 1977.

Brown, Raymond E. *The Gospel according to John*. 2 vols. Anchor Bible 29 and 29A. Garden City, NY: Doubleday, 1966–70.

Buchanan, George Wesley. "The Samaritan Origin of the Gospel of John." In *Religions in Antiquity: Essays in Memory of Erwin Ramsdell Goodenough*, edited by Jacob Neusner, 149–175. SHR, NumenSup 14. Leiden: Brill, 1968.

Bultmann, Rudolf. *The History of the Synoptic Tradition*. 2nd ed. Translated by John Marsh. Oxford: Basil Blackwell, 1968.

Carmon, Efrat, ed. *Inscriptions Reveal: Documents from the Time of the Bible, the Mishna and the Talmud*. Translated by R. Grafman. Jerusalem: Israel Museum, 1973.

Corpus inscriptionum judaicarum. Edited by Jean-Baptiste Frey. 2 vols. Sussidi allo studio delle Antichità cristiane 1 and 3. Rome: Pontificio Istituto di Archeologa Cristiana, 1936–52.

Corpus papyrorum judaicarum. Edited by Victor A. Tcherikover, Alexander Fuks, and Menahem Stern. 3 vols. Cambridge, MA: Harvard University Press for Magnes Press, 1957–64.

Dar, S. "Three *Menorot* from Western Samaria." *Israel Exploration Journal* 34, nos. 2–3 (1984): 177–179.

Delaney, Carol. "Seeds of Honor, Fields of Shame." In *Honor and Shame and the Unity of the Mediterranean*, edited by David D. Gilmore, 35–48. AAA 22. Washington, DC: American Anthropological Association, 1987.

Dexinger, Ferdinand. "Limits of Tolerance in Judaism: The Samaritan Example." In *Jewish and Christian Self-Definition*, edited by E. P. Sanders, 2:88–114. 3 vols. Philadelphia: Fortress, 1980–82.

Dodd, C. H. *The Parables of the Kingdom*. London: Nisbet & Company, 1936.

Donfried, Karl P., ed. *The Romans Debate*. Rev. ed. Peabody, MA: Hendrickson, 1991.

Eickelman, Dale F. *The Middle East: An Anthropological Approach*. 2nd edition. Englewood Cliffs, NJ: Prentice Hall, 1989.

Evans, C. A., and S. E. Porter, eds. *Dictionary of New Testament Background*. Downers Grove, IL: InterVarsity Press, 2000.

Flender, Helmut. *St Luke: Theologian of Redemptive History*. Translated by R. H. and Ilse Fuller. London: SPCK, 1967.

Freed, Edwin D. "Did John Write His Gospel Partly to Win Samaritan Converts?" *Novum Testamentum* 12 (3 Jul. 1970): 241–256.

———. "Samaritan Influence in the Gospel of John." *Catholic Biblical Quarterly* 30 (4 Oct. 1968): 580–587.

Friedländer, Ludwig. *Roman Life and Manners under the Early Empire*. 4 vols. Translated by Leonard A. Magnus, J. H. Freese, and A. B. Gough. New York: Barnes & Noble, 1907, 1965; New York: E. P. Dutton & Company, 1908, 1913.

Gärtner, Bertril. *The Temple and the Community in Qumran and the NT*. Cambridge: Cambridge University Press, 1965.

Gilmore, David D. *Honor and Shame and the Unity of the Mediterranean*. Washington: American Anthropological Association, 1987.

Glasson, T. Francis. *Moses in the Fourth Gospel*. SBT. Naperville, IL: Alec R. Allenson, 1963.

Horst, Pieter W. van der. "De Samaritaanse diaspora in de oudheid." *Nederlands Theologisch Tijdschrift* 42 (1988): 134–144.

Ilan, Tal. *Jewish Women in Greco-Roman Palestine*. Tübingen: J. C. B. Mohr; Peabody, MA: Hendrickson, 1996.

Jeremias, Joachim. *Jerusalem in the Time of Jesus*. Philadelphia: Fortress; London: SCM, 1969.

———. *The Parables of Jesus*. 2nd revised edition. New York: Scribner's, 1972.

Johnston, Robert M. "Parabolic Interpretations Attributed to Tannaim." PhD diss., Hartford Seminary Foundation, 1977.

Josephus. *The Jewish War*. Edited by Gaalya Cornfeld. Grand Rapids, MI: Zondervan, 1982.

Keener, Craig S. "Adultery, Divorce." In *Dictionary of New Testament Background*, edited by C. A. Evans and S. E. Porter, 6–16. Downers Grove, IL: InterVarsity Press, 2000.

———. *A Commentary on the Gospel of Matthew*. Cambridge, MA: Eerdmans, 1999.

———. "The Gospel and Racial Reconciliation." In *The Gospel in Black and White: Theological Resources for Racial Reconciliation*, edited by Dennis Ockholm, 117–130. Downers Grove, IL: InterVarsity Press, 1997.

———. *Paul, Women and Wives*. Peabody, MA: Hendrickson, 1992.

Kraabel, Alf Thomas. "New Evidence of the Samaritan Diaspora Has Been Found on Delos." *Biblical Archaeologist* 47 (1984): 44–46.

Ladd, George E. "Israel and the Church." *Evangelical Quarterly* 36 (1964): 206–213.

Levinskaya, Irina. *The Book of Acts in Its First Century Setting*. Vol. 5, *Diaspora Setting*. Grand Rapids, MI: Eerdmans; Carlisle: Paternoster, 1996.

Lewis, Naphtali. *Life in Egypt under Roman Rule*. Oxford: Clarendon, 1983.

Longenecker, Richard N. *Paul, Apostle of Liberty*. Grand Rapids, MI: Baker, 1976.

Maccini, Robert Gordon. *Her Testimony Is True: Women as Witnesses according to John*. JSNTS 125. Sheffield: Sheffield Academic Press, 1996.

Malherbe, Abraham J. *Moral Exhortation: A Greco-Roman Sourcebook*. LEC 4. Philadelphia: Westminster, 1986.

Malina, Bruce J., and Jerome H. Neyrey. "Honor and Shame in Luke–Acts: Pivotal Values of the Mediterranean World." In *The Social World of Luke–Acts: Models for Interpretation*, edited by Jerome H. Neyrey, 25–65. Peabody, MA: Hendrickson, 1991.

Marshall, I. Howard. "Historical Criticism." In *New Testament Interpretation: Essays on Principles and Methods*, edited by I. Howard Marshall, 126–138. Grand Rapids, MI: Eerdmans, 1977.

———, ed. *New Testament Interpretation: Essays on Principles and Methods*. Grand Rapids, MI: Eerdmans, 1977.

McNamara, Martin. *Targum and Testament*. Grand Rapids, MI: Eerdmans, 1972.

Michaels, J. Ramsey. *Servant and Son: Jesus in Parable and Gospel*. Atlanta: John Knox, 1981.

Munck, Johannes. *Christ and Israel: An Interpretation of Romans 9–11*. Philadelphia: Fortress, 1967.

Nanos, Mark D. *The Mystery of Romans*. Minneapolis: Fortress, 1996.

Oakman, Douglas E. "Was Jesus a Peasant? Implications for Reading the Samaritan Story." *Biblical Theology Bulletin* 22 (1992): 117–125.

Pamment, Margaret. "Is There Convincing Evidence of Samaritan Influence on the Fourth Gospel?" *Zeitschrift für die neutestamentliche Wissenschaft* 73 (1982): 221–230.

Pilch, John J. "Lying and Deceit in the Letters to the Seven Churches." *Biblical Theology Bulletin* 22 (1992): 126–135.

Purvis, James D. "The Fourth Gospel and the Samaritans." *Novum Testamentum* 17 (3 Jul. 1975): 161–198.

———. "The Samaritans and Judaism." In *Early Judaism and Its Modern Interpreters*, edited by Robert A. Kraft and George W. E. Nickelsburg, 81–98. SBLBMI 2. Atlanta: Scholars, 1986.

Robinson, John A. T. "The Destination and Purpose of St. John's Gospel." *New Testament Studies* 6 (2 Jan. 1960): 127–128.

Safrai, Shemuel. "Religion in Everyday Life." In *The Jewish People in the First Century: Historical Geography, Political History, Social, Cultural and Religious Life and Institutions*, edited by Shemuel Safrai and M. Stern, 793–833. Assen: Van Gorcum, 1987.

Safrai, Shemuel, and M. Stern. *The Jewish People in the First Century: Historical Geography, Political History, Social, Cultural and Religious Life and Institutions*. Assen: Van Gorcum, 1987.

Sanders, E. P. *Jewish Law from Jesus to the Mishnah: Five Studies*. London: SCM; Philadelphia: Trinity Press International, 1990.

Schiffman, Lawrence H. *Sectarian Law in the Dead Sea Scrolls: Courts, Testimony and the Penal Code*. Brown Judaic Studies 33. Chico, CA: Scholars, 1983.

Schwartz, J. "On Priests and Jericho in the Second Temple Period." *Jewish Quarterly Review* 79, no. 1 (1988): 23–48.

Scott, Bernard Brandon. *Hear Then the Parable: A Commentary on the Parables of Jesus*. Minneapolis: Augsburg Fortress, 1989.

Sevenster, J. N. *The Roots of Pagan Anti-Semitism in the Ancient World*. NovTSup 41. Leiden: E. J. Brill, 1975.

Smalley, Stephen S. *John: Evangelist and Interpreter*. Exeter: Paternoster, 1978.

Spencer, F. S. "2 Chronicles 28:5–15 and the Parable of the Good Samaritan." *Westminster Theological Journal* 46, no. 2 (1984): 317–349.

Vermes, Geza. *The Religion of Jesus the Jew*. Minneapolis: Augsburg Fortress, 1993.

Wegner, Judith Romney. *Chattel or Person? The Status of Women in the Mishnah*. New York: Oxford, 1988.

Whittaker, Molly. *Jews and Christians: Graeco-Roman Views*. Cambridge: Cambridge University Press, 1984.

Wright, N. T. *The New Testament and the People of God*. Minneapolis: Fortress; London: SPCK, 1992.

Yamauchi, Edwin M. *The Stones and the Scriptures: An Introduction to Biblical Archaeology*. Grand Rapids, MI: Baker, 1972.

Young, Brad H. *Jesus and His Jewish Parables: Rediscovering the Roots of Jesus' Teaching*. New York: Paulist, 1989.

———. *Jesus the Jewish Theologian*. Peabody, MI: Hendrickson, 1995.

11

Implications of Acts 15 for Forgiveness, Peace, and Reconciliation Today

Rowland D. Van Es, Jr.
Lecturer, St Paul's University, Limuru, Kenya

Abstract

This chapter presents a case study of the Jerusalem Council and the forgiveness, peace, and reconciliation between two different groups there, the Jewish Christians and the Gentile Christians. Using a new model of cross-cultural Christian interaction, I show how three key early church leaders (James, Peter, Paul) helped to bring about forgiveness, peace, and reconciliation between the two groups in Acts 15. This new model (and especially the role of Peter) serves as a template for working with various groups experiencing conflict and disagreement today, especially intra- or interreligious conflict caused by different cultural viewpoints, values, beliefs, and opinions about the essential practices or key requirements of one's faith.

Key words: Jerusalem Council, reconciliation, cross-cultural interaction, cultural hermeneutics, contextualization, inculturation.

Outline

Part 1 will introduce my new model of cross-cultural Christian interaction (from my unpublished ThM thesis). Part 2 will show how the gospel was received and contextualized differently in Jewish culture (by James et al.)

than in Gentile culture (by Paul et al.). Part 3 will then critically examine the Jerusalem Council in Acts 15 and the key roles of James, Paul, and Peter using my model as a lens for understanding what happened there. Part 4 will trace the modern implications of my model (by using it in both African and American culture today) as a way of promoting forgiveness, peace, and reconciliation among different religious groups and other communities with internal conflicts and disagreements, especially those caused by contrasting positions based on different viewpoints deriving from different cultural perspectives.

A New Model to Diagram Cross-Cultural Interaction with the Gospel

The church council at Jerusalem was held to resolve a conflict between those who believed everyone must be circumcised to be saved and those who did not believe so. According to Acts 15:2, Paul and Barnabas "had no small dissension and debate with them" (NRSV). It was essentially a matter of clean vs. unclean and whether to enforce the law of Moses upon Gentiles or make an exception for them. It could have ended badly and split the church. Instead, it ended with compromise and a model for us of the way to deal with cross-cultural differences from contextualizing the gospel.

One way to think about this biblical story is to conceptualize it as a diagram of the interaction of the gospel with two very different cultures, the Jewish culture and the Gentile culture. When any two cultures interact, there are areas of agreement but also areas of disagreement. As a Venn diagram it would look like the figure below, where area A is what is unique to the Jews (eating kosher, men being circumcised, etc.), B is the cultural overlap (common customs and practices), and C is what is unique to the Gentiles (not eating kosher, men not being circumcised, etc.).

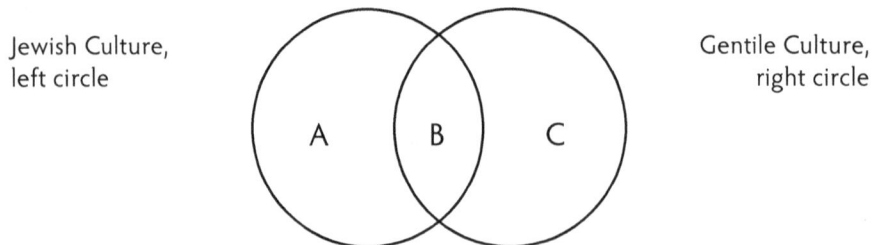

Jewish Culture, left circle   A   B   C   Gentile Culture, right circle

Now imagine what happens when the gospel is introduced to both Jewish and Gentile cultures. As a Venn diagram, it would be like adding a third circle to the diagram above. This time I will use numbers instead of letters to describe the seven zones found in this new model[1] of the gospel entering (or being inculturated into or incarnated into) two different cultures:

Gospel,
middle circle

Jewish Culture,
left circle

Gentile Culture,
right circle

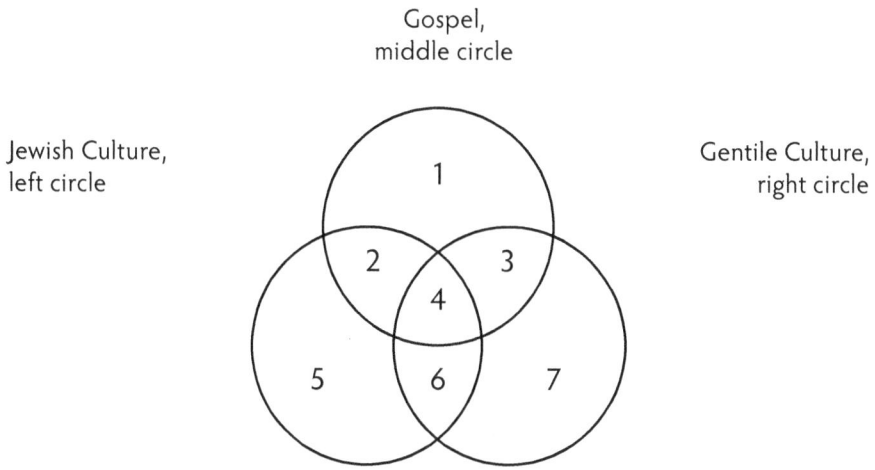

Zone 1 is the gospel that has not yet been revealed or incarnated in either culture. It is the "not yet" of the kingdom of God. In the first century that would have included women in office, the freedom of all slaves, and so on: what many of us take for granted today but was unheard of (even unimaginable) then, given the common cultural beliefs, practices, and assumptions of that time.

Zone 2 is the part of Jewish culture that did overlap with the gospel and was "in step" with (did fit well into) the gospel. This is what Jesus, James, and other early church fathers (and mothers) affirmed, accepted, even blessed in Jewish culture, but was *not* part of (no overlap with) Gentile culture. This is the gospel contextualized for Jewish background believers (but *not* for Gentiles). It also includes the *adiaphora*, things that are morally neutral (neither for nor against the gospel) found in Jewish culture (but *not* found in Gentile culture) that Jewish Christians continued to do.

---

1. Of course, my model is not entirely new. I acknowledge the influence of Robert J. Priest's model in "Missionary Elenctics: Conscience and Culture," *Missiology* 22, no. 3 (Jul. 1994): 298, 309, but his model deals only with conscience, whereas my model includes all aspects of culture: behavior, beliefs, and underlying worldview of a people.

Zone 3 is the part of Gentile culture that did overlap with the gospel and was "in step" with (did fit well into) the gospel. This is what Jesus, Paul, and other early church fathers (and mothers) affirmed, accepted, even blessed in Gentile culture, but was *not* part of (no overlap with) Jewish culture. This is the gospel contextualized for Gentile background believers (but *not* for all Jews). It also includes the *adiaphora*, things that are morally neutral (neither for nor against the gospel) found in Gentile culture (but *not* found in Jewish culture) that Gentile Christians continued to do.

Zone 4 is part of the overlap between Jewish and Gentile cultures that also overlapped with the gospel. This is the "best" of both cultures, what was affirmed, accepted, even blessed in both. It is because of this zone that the church could have common practices for both Jews *and* Gentiles. It also includes the *adiaphora*, things that are morally neutral (neither for nor against the gospel) in both cultures that believers in both cultures continued to do as Christians living in that era.

Zone 5 is the part of Jewish culture that did *not* overlap with the gospel and was "out of step" with (did not fit into) the gospel. This is what Jesus, Paul, and the early church fathers (and mothers) challenged, confronted ("repent!"), and cursed in Jewish culture as being against the gospel message. Examples are Jesus attacking the Pharisees, Sadducees, and money changers.

Zone 6 is the part of the overlap between Jewish and Gentile culture that did *not* overlap with the gospel. This is perhaps where Hellenistic Jews and Gentile proselytes lived. Some of their practices fit with the gospel (Zone 4) but much of them did *not*, and that was Zone 6. It was their mutual blind spot, what neither culture objected to but should have rejected in light of the gospel.

Zone 7 is the part of Gentile culture that did *not* overlap with the gospel and was "out of step" with (did not fit into) the gospel. This is what Jesus, Paul, and the early church fathers (and mothers) challenged, confronted ("repent!"), and even cursed in Gentile culture as being against the gospel message. Examples are temple prostitution, infanticide, idolatry, and Greek vices.

Faith and Religious Practice as Seen from the Perspective of Each Culture

The Perspective of James and Other Jewish Christians

Coming from their Jewish background, Jewish Christians saw Jesus as the long-awaited Messiah and therefore assumed they could continue living as messianic

Jews. Jewish behavior from Old Testament laws and traditions dictated the following customary practices and religious beliefs:

Jews practiced Kosher food laws (no pork or shellfish, etc.); circumcision for all men; but no sodomy; and no infanticide. Jews were monotheists, saw salvation as involvement, saw faith as faithfulness, and obeyed all 613 commandments of the Torah. Their worldview was based on a circular view of time, and of life as a dynamic unity, and they had an earthly spirituality. Jews saw the world (this life) as good, something to be embraced.[2]

As Christians, there were many of their former beliefs and practices that were compatible with the gospel and which they continued as Jewish Christians. So, even as Christians, they continued to circumcise their boys (as Jesus was on his eighth day), and they continued to keep kosher (refrained from pork and shellfish, etc.). They also continued to observe most of the 613 commandments and continued to go to synagogue. Much of what Jesus taught reinforced their former faith and life.

James, the brother of Jesus, the head of the church in Jerusalem, represents this "conservative" faction. According to Bruce Chilton, James was a Nazirite who was concerned with purity and the temple. Thus he initially sides with the Pharisees of the "circumcision party" who insisted on circumcising all Christian believers, including all the Gentiles.[3]

Eventually, these Jewish Christians were expelled from the synagogue for their belief in Jesus as the Messiah and the Son of God, and so on. It was probably only after this expulsion (ca. AD 90) that they adopted a more critical stance toward Judaism and re-examined some of their Jewish beliefs and practices in light of Jesus Christ and some of his more "radical" beliefs and teachings.

The Perspective of Paul and the Gentile Christians

Coming from their Gentile background, the Gentile Christians saw Jesus and the Christian faith quite differently from the Jewish Christians. Depending on their previous religion, they saw him as either a wise teacher, a philosopher with

---

2. Marvin R. Wilson, *Our Father Abraham: Jewish Roots of the Christian Faith* (Grand Rapids, MI: Eerdmans, 1989), 135–162.

3. Bruce D. Chilton, "James in Relation to Peter, Paul, and the Remembrance of Jesus," in *The Brother of Jesus: James the Just and His Mission*, ed. Bruce Chilton and Jacob Neusner (Louisville, KY: Westminster John Knox, 2001), 138–159.

the key to life, a man who revealed the secrets of a new mystery religion, and so on. Remember that the Greeks were "extremely religious" (Acts 17:22 NRSV).

As Gentiles they had the following cultural beliefs and practices (in stark contrast to the Jews): no kosher food laws (they ate pork and shellfish); they did not practice circumcision (they saw it as barbaric); they did practice infanticide and sodomy; they believed in many gods and goddesses; they collected lists of virtues and vices; they saw salvation as escape from this world; and they viewed faith as thinking/being more than as acting/doing. They had a linear view of time; saw life as dualistic; had a heavenly spirituality (body as "prison of the soul"); and saw this world (and this life) as bad, something to be escaped.[4]

For Paul and Barnabas, other Christian missionaries among the Gentiles, and the first Gentile converts, some of this was good and could continue to be practiced, while some of it was bad and had to be stopped. But much of this was *adiaphora*, a matter of indifference (morally neutral and not a matter of salvation). So, for example, Paul could quote a Greek poet (Acts 17:28) and could include Greek virtues and vices in his own lists in his letters to the early churches he started.

Paul also appealed to their way of thinking and their philosophical mindset because he knew that "Greeks desire wisdom" (1 Cor 1:22 NRSV). Thus Paul tolerated their eating pork, their being uncircumcised, and other cultural beliefs and practices that he considered nonessentials or *adiaphora* (morally neutral). As a Roman citizen educated in Greek, he was very familiar with Gentile culture. Paul understood them and so was able to build many bridges to their culture.

For Bruce Chilton, "the radical quality of Paul's position needs to be appreciated. He was isolated from every other Christian Jew."[5] Like Jesus, Paul was considered "unclean" for much of what he did by becoming "all things to all people" (1 Cor 9:22 NRSV) and for eating with them.

Revisiting the Jerusalem Council and Understanding It Using This New Model

All of the above is the context that led to the Jerusalem Council. Now we can better appreciate why there was "no small dissension and debate" between

---

4. Wilson, *Our Father Abraham*, 135–162, where Wilson contrasts Hebrew logic to Greek logic, and different views of time and history, etc.

5. Chilton, "James in Relation to Peter," 141.

them. The issue they discussed was circumcision, but that was just the tip of the iceberg of all their differences and disagreements.

For the Jewish Christians, circumcision was a matter of salvation, for without it "you cannot be saved" (Acts 15:1 NRSV). For the Gentile Christians, circumcision was just a "custom of Moses" and was *not* essential for salvation. In fact, for Greeks, it was barbaric, unnecessary, and a barrier to their becoming Christians. The Jews would have had a similar reaction if they had been required to eat pork to be saved – like Peter's first reaction to his vision of unclean food in Acts 10:14, "never!"

How to resolve this impasse? How to move forward to bring peace and reconciliation between these two very different groups with very different understandings of the faith? First, the Jewish Christians heard of Paul's work of conversion among the Gentiles, and that "brought great joy" to all (15:3 NRSV). But the Pharisee party nevertheless demanded that "it is necessary for them to be circumcised" to keep the law of Moses (15:5 NRSV). No salvation outside of the Jewish law of Moses.

Then Peter acts as a bridge-builder. After "much debate" (15:7) among the apostles and church elders, Peter stood up to speak. He related his role as an apostle to the Gentiles and told the story of how they had received the Holy Spirit just as the Jews did. This showed God had "cleans[ed] their hearts by faith" and had made "no distinction between them [Gentiles] and us [Jews]" (15:8–9 NRSV). Remember it is a matter of salvation and "clean" vs. "unclean" they are debating. God has now given the Holy Spirit to both the uncircumcised/unclean and the circumcised/clean.

The background to Peter's speech in Acts 15 is his own experience in Acts 10: his triple vision of clean and unclean (10:9–16), and his meeting with Cornelius, a Gentile described as "a centurion, an upright and God-fearing man, who is well spoken of by the whole Jewish nation" (10:22 NRSV). It is only after visiting Cornelius that Peter finally declares, "I truly understand that God shows no partiality, but in every nation anyone who fears him [God] and does what is right is acceptable to him" (10:34–35 NRSV). His testimony is based on his vision and personal encounter with a Gentile.

Peter then made a speech/sermon, and while he was still speaking the Holy Spirit fell on all who heard him (10:44). Note that the circumcised Jews were "astounded that the gift of the Holy Spirit had been poured out even on the Gentiles" (10:45 NRSV) and that they were "speaking in tongues and extolling God" (10:46 NRSV). Then Peter baptized them with water since they had obviously received the Holy Spirit (10:47). All this precipitated the Jerusalem

Council because those in Judea heard about it and criticized him for entering Gentile homes and eating Gentile food (11:1–3).

Back in Jerusalem, Peter (15:10 NRSV) asks them a question: "Why are you putting God to the test by placing on the neck of the [Gentile] disciples a yoke that neither our ancestors nor we have been able to bear?" This is an astonishing question and admission by a Jew. Then Peter continues, "On the contrary, we believe that we [Jews] will be saved through the grace of the Lord Jesus, just as they [Gentiles] will" (15:11 NRSV). So salvation is by grace, *not* by works of the law (as for Paul).

No wonder James Dunn called Peter "the bridge-man who did more than any other to hold together the diversity of first-century Christianity."[6] Peter is thus the mediator between the "conservative" James and the "radical" Paul in the Jerusalem Council. Without Peter, no compromise would have been made. He speaks both for the apostles and for the church.

Fitting the Key Events of Acts 15 into This New Model

The circumcision party, led by the Judeans, James, and the Pharisees, held that "unless you are circumcised according to the custom of Moses, you cannot be saved" (15:1 NRSV) and wanted the Gentiles "ordered to keep the law of Moses" (15:5 NRSV). In my model, this group saw only *Zone 2* as the gospel, not just for themselves but for all other believers as well (even the Gentiles).

Paul and Barnabas, on the other hand, "had no small dissension and debate with them" (15:2 NRSV) because they saw no need to require circumcision for the Gentiles, especially since they had obviously received the Holy Spirit *without circumcision*. They were saved by grace, *not* by works of the law (circumcision). In my model, this group saw *Zone 3* as the gospel for the Gentiles, who did not need to be part of Zone 2 (gospel for the Jewish-background believers).

Peter can then be placed in *Zone 4*: he could see that Zone 2 was good for the Jewish Christians and also that Zone 3 was good for the Gentile Christians. Peter is the "bridge-man" between the two groups. James finally agreed with Peter on circumcision but added the provision from Genesis 9:4 that they must also "abstain only from things polluted by idols and from fornication [and from whatever has been strangled] and from blood" (as quoted in Acts 15:20).

---

6. James D. G. Dunn, *Unity and Diversity in the New Testament: An Inquiry into the Character of Earliest Christianity* (Philadelphia: Westminster, 1977), 385.

This puts James on the boundary between Zones 2 and 4. He still wanted Gentiles to keep Noah's covenant (which applied to all people, not just Jews). As Craig Keener summarized Acts 15, "Jewish Christians were free to maintain culturally Jewish customs and Gentile Christians to maintain culturally Gentile customs, so long as both faithfully obeyed God's teachings."[7]

Use of Both Scripture and Tradition in Acts 15

David and Cynthia Strong also see the Jerusalem Council as a model for globalizing theology. They looked at how Scripture was used at the council. Among other passages, James quoted Amos 9:12, where Gentiles bear God's name and stand in a covenant relationship with God *without* first becoming Jewish proselytes. So "James supports Peter's, Barnabas's, and Paul's reports that God had accepted the Gentiles without their first becoming proselytes and being circumcised."[8] Then the other church leaders finally accepted *un*circumcised Gentiles too.

Implications for Forgiveness, Peace, and Reconciliation Today

There are still many areas of disagreement in Christian communities today. In the 1800s Protestants in the US fought over slavery and in the 1900s they fought over the ordination of women. Catholics and Protestants disagree about celibacy for clergy and about Communion. Christians are divided over drinking, national and international politics, and so on. We will probably always have some areas of disagreement, even while having much larger areas of agreement.

In the past, these disagreements have led to church schisms and civil wars (Thirty Years' War, Hundred Years' War, American Civil War). Today many denominations are splitting or are on the verge of splitting over human sexuality and the place of homosexuals in the church despite many key beliefs held in common.

The way forward is modeled by Peter, the "bridge-man," who saw things from both sides and was able to negotiate a compromise between James,

---

7. Craig Keener and Medine Moussounga Keener, *Reconciliation for Africa: Resources for Ethnic Reconciliation from the Bible and History* (Nairobi: Life Challenge Africa, 2010), 28.

8. David K. Strong and Cynthia A. Strong, "The Globalizing Hermeneutic of the Jerusalem Council," in *Globalizing Theology: Belief and Practice in an Era of World Christianity*, ed. Craig Ott and Harold A. Netland (Grand Rapids, MI: Baker Academic, 2006), 130.

who was concerned with purity, and with Paul, who considered his previous insistence on purity as "rubbish" (Phil 3:8) to be abandoned for the sake of his missionary work among Gentiles. Peter was concerned with finding peace, getting both groups to forgive each other and be reconciled as brothers and sisters, God's children, in Christ.

Is it possible to have both unity *and* diversity? The New Testament indicates that it *is* possible. There were a variety of gifts, but the same spirit. There was (and is) a wide variety of different church structures, organizations, and offices, but still only "one, holy, catholic, and apostolic church." As Augustine reportedly said, "In essentials, unity; in non-essentials, liberty; in all things charity." On Acts 15 Richard Longenecker has said, "The decision reached by the council must be considered one of the boldest and most magnanimous in the annals of church history."[9]

Another Example from Early Church History

In early church history, according to Kondothra George, in relation to Jewish culture "there was both continuity in tradition and break with the Torah." Concerning Gentile culture, while some church fathers "unequivocally denounced some expressions of popular paganism," they were also "unanimous in showing respect for the wisdom and the virtues shown by some 'philosophers' [like Socrates and Plato] in the pagan Hellenistic world."[10]

In terms of my model, "continuity in tradition" is Zone 2; "break with Torah" is Zone 5. What was "denounced" in popular paganism is Zone 7, while "showing respect for the wisdom and virtues" of the "philosophers" in the "pagan Hellenistic world" is Zone 3. Continuity and break; some things fit and some did not. It took time and spiritual discernment to sort out which traditions of both cultures were OK, and which traditions of both cultures were not OK.

Two Examples from More Recent Church History

In the history of Christian missions to India, several Protestant churches decided to form one new church to offer a united witness to the Hindu

---

9. Richard Longenecker, *New Testament Social Ethics for Today*, 39, quoted in Wilson, *Our Father Abraham*, 49.

10. Kondothra M. George, "Cross-Cultural Interpretation: Some Paradigms from the Early Church," *International Review of Mission* 85, no. 337 (Apr. 1996): 217–226.

culture instead of confusing them with many different versions of Christianity. Churches of Anglican, Methodist, Congregational, Presbyterian, and Reformed traditions joined together into the Church of South India in 1947.

The Presbyterian and Reformed churches, who hold the office of elder (*presbyter*) as the key one, compromised with the Methodists and Anglicans, who hold the office of bishop (*episkopos*) as the key one, and accepted that the new Church of South India would have bishops, even though it was not part of their own ecclesiology. This was no small matter for Presbyterians named after the office of elder. No wonder that the negotiations took almost thirty years, from 1919 to 1947.[11]

A similar effort at unity and compromise is seen in the World Council of Churches document "Baptism, Eucharist, and Ministry" (Faith and Order Paper no. 111, 1982). In discussing each of these divisive issues, the members of the Faith and Order Commission urge member churches to understand the background of our various differences regarding each key issue but to still affirm the practice and belief of the other churches within the WCC. The aim is mutual recognition, *not* uniformity of practice, by every different Christian denomination in the world.

Those who baptize infants are urged to accept those who practice believers' baptism, and vice versa. Those who use only wine and wafers for the Eucharist are urged to accept those who use only grape juice and bread for Communion, and vice versa. Those who don't accept women into ordained ministry are urged to accept those who do, and vice versa. Those who are ordained only by bishops are urged to accept those who are ordained by laying on of hands of church elders, and vice versa. No one practice is singled out as exclusively valid over the others.

These are not just small differences of opinion or casual variations in church practice and polity. They go to the heart and core of denominational identity. What is a Baptist without believers' baptism by immersion? What is a Presbyterian without the rule of elders? What is an Anglican or Episcopalian without the rule of bishops? Yet we can disagree on all of this and still agree that we are all Christians and part of the "one, holy, catholic, and apostolic church" and in the WCC. This is a good example of "In essentials, unity; in non-essentials, liberty; in all things charity."

---

11. For this history see "History," Church of South India, https://www.csisynod.com/aboutus.php.

Implications of This Model for Forgiveness, Peace, and Reconciliation Today

When it comes to cross-cultural conflict in areas of sexuality or politics, or other religious beliefs and practices, can we also see instances where the gospel may look different depending on the context where it is being contextualized? There will be similarities but also some major differences.

Kevin Vanhoozer, writing about theological method in our era of world Christianity, speaks of the need for both canonicity *and* catholicity. Canonicity is accepting Scripture as the supreme rule, and particularly the story of Jesus as the church's authoritative script.[12] Catholicity is accepting the need for contextualization and particularly for "vernacular performance," or what he calls "regional theater," when we present or perform the story of Jesus locally.[13]

In my model, canonicity is found especially in Zone 4 that we all agree on. Catholicity would be seen in Zone 2 for one culture and in Zone 3 for another culture. Thus there can be both unity (canonicity) and diversity (catholicity): there is no need to demand uniformity in everything. After all, the gospel has always played out differently in each culture. This is what Vanhoozer refers to as the necessary "improvisational wisdom" of the gospel,[14] which is actually a form of "disciplined spontaneity,"[15] and similar to Paul Hiebert's own term "critical contextualization."[16]

Vanhoozer also says that "Doctrine develops as the church encounters new challenges and seeks to do what is theodramatically fitting" in each culture.[17] After all, even within the Bible "the truth of Scripture is plural and polyphonic." So he concludes, "In sum, the task of systematic theology is to train actors with good improvisatory judgment, actors who know what to say and do to perform and advance the gospel of Jesus Christ *in terms of their own cultural context*."[18]

Believers from different cultures have different backgrounds, beliefs, views, and practices. And they need to express their faith in ways that fit in their

---

12. Kevin J. Vanhoozer, "One Rule to Rule Them All? Theological Method in an Era of World Christianity," in *Globalizing Theology: Belief and Practice in an Era of World Christianity*, ed. Craig Ott and Harold A. Netland (Grand Rapids, MI: Baker Academic, 2006), 112.

13. Vanhoozer, "One Rule," 116–117.

14. Vanhoozer, 113.

15. Vanhoozer, 114.

16. Paul G. Hiebert, "Critical Contextualization," *International Bulletin of Missionary Research* 11, no. 3 (1987): 104–112.

17. Vanhoozer, "One Rule," 120.

18. Vanhoozer, 121.

own cultural context. There is no need to fight about all of these practices. Many of them are *adiaphora*, matters of indifference, neutral, nonessential. Others may appear essential to one group (as circumcision was and still is for some) but as nonessential or even barbaric to another group (as FGM is seen by some). We are all products of our own culture in these matters; we see the same things very differently.

As Schreiter put it, "expressions of the Christian message show a continuing indeterminacy . . . While indeterminacy may initially offend dogmatic sensibilities, it should not be so shocking when we recall that the center of the Christian message is not a proposition but a narrative . . . Narrative thrives on a certain amount of indeterminacy which allows the story to be retold. Thus we will continue to encounter new modes of expression of the Christian message."[19] This is like Vanhoozer's regional theater or vernacular performance by actors using good improvisation.

How do we ensure that these various local expressions of the faith are still faithful to the gospel? Schreiter has proposed five criteria that must all be met by the local Christian performance: First, it has a cohesiveness that manifests a consistency. Second, the worshipping context shows that the law of believing follows the law of prayer (*lex credenti, lex orandi*). Third, the praxis of the local community shows that what they do is central to who they are. Fourth, the local church is willing to stand under the judgment or correction of other churches. Fifth, it is also willing to move outward in mission and even to challenge other churches.[20]

In my view, these five criteria of Schreiter are all found in the two of Vanhoozer: catholicity and canonicity. Being canonical will give the local Christian community a cohesiveness that will be seen in their beliefs and prayers. Catholicity comes from their local and global praxis. Criteria 4 and 5 are two sides of the same coin: they will be affected by and will affect other churches.

---

19. Robert J. Schreiter, *The New Catholicity: Theology between the Global and the Local* (Maryknoll, NY: Orbis, 1997), 130–131.

20. Robert J. Schreiter, *Constructing Local Theologies* (Maryknoll, NY: Orbis, 1985), 118–120.

Applying This New Model in Africa and America Today

Consider what happens when we apply the model above, not to the Jewish and Gentile cultures of the past, but to African and American cultures today (with Africa on the left, and America on the right):

African Culture, left circle

Gospel, middle circle

American Culture, right circle

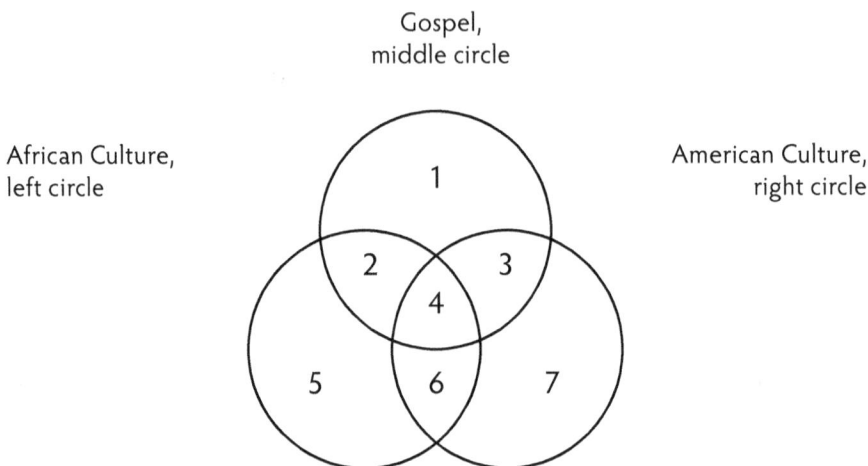

Zone 1 is still the gospel that has not yet been revealed or incarnated into either culture. It is the "not yet" of the kingdom of God. It includes things we may find unimaginable even now given the cultural beliefs, practices, and assumptions of our era (before human-cyborg hybrids, etc.). Some of it we may be able to see by studying the gospel in Asia or Latin America; other parts remain a mystery that will only be revealed to us in the future by the Holy Spirit in the church.

Zone 2 is the part of African culture that does overlap with the gospel and is "in step" with (fits well into) the gospel. This is Christ *in* Africa, Christ *of* Africa, what can be affirmed, accepted, and blessed in African culture, but is *not* part of (has no overlap with) American culture. This is the gospel contextualized just for African-background believers (but *not* for Americans). It also includes the *adiaphora*, things that are morally neutral (neither for nor against the gospel) found in African culture (but *not* found in American culture) that African Christians continue to do. Examples include African Christology (Jesus as Ancestor) and African Narrative Theology.

Zone 3 is the part of American culture that does overlap with the gospel and is "in step" with (fits well into) the gospel. This is Christ *in* America, Christ *of* America, what can be affirmed, accepted, even blessed in American culture, but is *not* part of (no overlap with) African culture. This is the gospel contextualized for American-background believers (but *not* for Africans). It also includes the *adiaphora*, things that are morally neutral (neither for nor against the gospel) found in American culture (but *not* found in African culture) that Americans can continue to do. Examples may include egalitarianism, individualism, and American contextual theologies.

Zone 4 is part of the overlap between African and American cultures that also overlaps with the gospel. This is the "best" of both cultures, what is affirmed, accepted, even blessed in both. It is because of this zone that many churches can have common practices in Africa and America. It also includes the *adiaphora*, things that are morally neutral (neither for nor against the gospel) in both cultures that believers in both cultures can continue to do as Christians living in our era. Examples may include African-American music and spirituality, and a new respect for creation.

Zone 5 is the part of African culture that does *not* overlap with the gospel and so is "out of step" with (does not fit into) the gospel. This is what missionaries to Africa and African evangelists still challenge, confront ("repent!"), and condemn in African culture as being against the true gospel. Examples may include witchcraft, the subjugation of women, and other negative cultural practices.[21]

Zone 6 is the part of the overlap between African and American culture that does *not* overlap with the gospel. This is where many modern Africans and Americans live lives "of the world." It is our mutual blind spot, what neither culture objects to but should reject in light of the gospel. Examples may include how money, sex, and power are still being misused in both these cultures.

Zone 7 is the part of American culture that does *not* overlap with the gospel and is "out of step" with (doesn't fit into) the gospel. This is what missionaries there and American evangelists must still challenge, confront ("repent!"), and condemn in American culture as being against the gospel message. Examples may include American materialism, hedonism, nationalism, and materialism.[22]

Using This New Model for Resolving Denominational Disagreements Today

Is it possible to agree to disagree about some of our key practices, beliefs, views, and customs? What is essential for salvation is what the church has

---

21. Justin S. Ukpong, "Inculturation: A Major Challenge to the Church in Africa Today," *African Ecclesial Review* 38, no. 5 (1996): 258–267.

22. Wilbert R. Shenk, *Changing Frontiers of Mission* (Maryknoll, NY: Orbis, 1999), 184.

always believed and confessed, that "Jesus is Lord." If we can recite the Apostles' Creed and the Nicene Creed together and then celebrate Communion, must we also insist on uniformity in all the other areas that we disagree about (and probably always will), like the Jews who thought that *only* those who had been circumcised would be saved?

We must remember the diversity of the New Testament and the great diversity throughout church history. This is not always a bad thing. What one culture considers "unclean" is seen by another culture as clean, and vice versa. Who are we to judge? There is room for more: there is room for tolerance to maintain peace and unity *without* uniformity. Some things are *not* really essential; some things are *not* matters of salvation. "For with the judgment you make, you will be judged" (Matt 7:2 NRSV).

Remember the lessons of the new model or diagram of Acts 15: we are all affected by the biases of our own culture. Culture gives us insight but can also blind us to our own faults and to all our biases. We need to see ourselves and each other as God sees us. There is much more of the gospel yet to be revealed by the Holy Spirit in the church and in others. Zone 1 is still coming as the earth is being redeemed and God's will is being done here "on earth as it is in heaven." The Holy Spirit, "the Spirit of truth," will teach us all things, and lead us forward (John 15:15, 26).

The other lesson is to see that there can exist a contextualized version of the gospel that fits in the other person's culture but does not necessarily fit in yours. African churches can live in Zone 2 but it is for Africa, *not* for America. American churches can live in Zone 3 but it is for them, *not* for Africa. We can still both enjoy Zone 4, the gospel for both cultures, while looking out for Zone 6, our mutual blind spot. Africans should judge between Zones 2 and 5, and Americans should judge between Zones 3 and 7, even as we both remember that many things are *adiaphora*, morally neutral, matters of indifference to our salvation. Issues on the very cutting edge will be disputable and some groups within the culture may accept them while other groups still will not. Remember how sure we once were about slavery being OK but women clergy not being OK?

Using Scripture and Tradition in Settling Denominational Disagreements Today

Just as James appealed to an Old Testament precedent, so we can also appeal to precedents in the Old and New Testaments as well as to subsequent events and decisions in our church history that agree with the Holy Spirit and with the principles found in Scripture, even if they may disagree with the letter of the law or some of the commandments given in one context that may no longer fit our own context. As Paul says, "for the letter kills, but the Spirit gives life" (2 Cor 3:6 NRSV).

Webb, in *Slaves, Women, and Homosexuals*, shows how Christians (using Scripture) used to justify slavery but the Spirit eventually led the church to condemn it (even though it is legal and *never* explicitly condemned in Scripture). Christians (again using Scripture) also used to justify patriarchy and keeping women away from the pulpit but the Spirit has now led most churches to welcome the ordination of women (even though *nowhere* in Scripture were women ordained).

For Webb, we must never read the Bible with a static hermeneutic; rather we must always read it dynamically.[23] We must move *beyond* the literal words of the text (which are addressing ancient cultures) and move forward in the direction of the Spirit of the text, heading toward the ultimate ethic, what he calls Z and what I have called Zone 1: what is yet to be revealed to us through the Holy Spirit. Just as we reject both slavery and patriarchy today, we may reject other practices tomorrow. It would be against the gospel to reintroduce slavery or reinforce patriarchy now.[24]

Conclusion

There have always been and will always be strong disagreements within Christianity (and within other religions). Many disagreements, even over matters of salvation (such as those in Acts 15), are the result of cross-cultural differences. The way the Jerusalem Council settled the matter was to look at Scripture for a precedent, listen to the testimony of various actors and church leaders, trust the Holy Spirit, and respect the faith of the other party. This led them to a compromise: the Jews could continue to practice circumcision, but the Gentiles could continue *not* to do so.

The Gentiles did agree to certain other rules, however, to maintain table fellowship with Jews. As Paul advised Christians in Romans, sometimes the "stronger" party has to sacrifice some of its freedoms for the sake of the "weaker" party. The goal is not to offend and not to lead the other party into

---

23. William J. Webb, *Slaves, Women and Homosexuals: Exploring the Hermeneutics of Cultural Analysis* (Downers Grove, IL: IVP Academic, 2001), 31–34, where his model is introduced and redemptive spirit explained.

24. Webb, *Slaves, Women and Homosexuals*: see 3 for slavery and 38 for patriarchy.

sin. Once again, love fulfills the law. It's not just about freedom but about our witness. To be effective, our witness must be contextual, but being contextual, it may stretch orthodoxy.

When we have religious and/or denominational conflict, let's be humble in our own convictions. Let us trust that God may be doing a new thing again and accept that only God judges the heart. Jews did not associate with Samaritans, but Jesus spoke to a Samaritan woman by a well. Jews thought eating pork was unclean and being uncircumcised made one unsaved, but Paul ate pork and other "polluted" meat from the market and ate with uncircumcised men to evangelize them. Peter spent his whole life eating only kosher food and associating with Jews, but God gave him a vision and a voice that said, "Do not call anything impure that God has made clean" (Acts 10:15) and then sent him to the home of the Gentile Cornelius to learn that he should also "not call anyone impure or unclean" (10:28). Why are we so quick to call other people unclean?

The gospel can look different in different cultures. Jewish and African Christians can live in their Zone 2, allowing Gentile and American Christians to live in their Zone 3. Much that we disagree about is *adiaphora*. We can all agree on Zone 4 while using the spirit of discernment to help us see what is wrong with Zones 5, 6, and 7. We must all be willing to repent of our sins, even those we are culturally blind to, living in the world and being part of our culture, even the part that does not fit with the gospel. On this side of heaven we live in "fear and trembling" about some matters.

Paul Hiebert reminds us that "Unity in the body of Christ does not rest on uniformity, but on our common 'blood,' which is the blood of Christ. We are now members of one family, and that identity cannot be taken from us, no matter how much we disagree or quarrel. Unity in the Church is a sign of the Kingdom of God now invading the earth."[25] We are united, not uniform.

We do not all have to eat the same food or drink the same wine (or drink wine at all). Like Paul, we must be willing to "become all things to all people," so that we might "by all means save some" (1 Cor 9:22 NRSV). We must be humble, admitting that there is much that we still don't know for sure and that God can always surprise us with grace, mercy, and new truth yet to be revealed.

---

25. Paul G. Hiebert, *The Gospel in Human Contexts: Anthropological Explorations for Contemporary Mission* (Grand Rapids, MI: Baker Academic, 2009), 193.

As Lewis Smedes said, "After all is said and done, being right is not the most important thing in the world, being forgiven is."[26] For the sake of reconciliation, let us forgive one another, and live at peace, despite all our differences today, celebrating our common humanity and all the areas where we do agree, and having Christian charity for those areas where we still disagree for now, especially for those who are fellow Christians, members of the one Christian family.

Bibliography

"Baptism, Eucharist and Ministry." Faith and Order Paper No. 111. Geneva: World Council of Churches, 1982.

Chilton, Bruce D. "James in Relation to Peter, Paul, and the Remembrance of Jesus." In *The Brother of Jesus: James the Just and His Mission*, edited by Bruce Chilton and Jacob Neusner, 138–159. Louisville, KY: Westminster John Knox, 2001.

Dunn, James D. G. *Unity and Diversity in the New Testament: An Inquiry into the Character of Earliest Christianity*. Philadelphia: Westminster, 1977.

George, Kondothra M. "Cross-Cultural Interpretation: Some Paradigms from the Early Church." *International Review of Mission* 85, no. 337 (Apr. 1996): 217–226.

Hiebert, Paul G. "Critical Contextualization." *International Bulletin of Missionary Research* 11, no. 3 (1987): 104–112.

———. *The Gospel in Human Contexts: Anthropological Explorations for Contemporary Mission*. Grand Rapids, MI: Baker Academic, 2009.

Keener, Craig, and Medine Moussounga Keener. *Reconciliation for Africa: Resources for Ethnic Reconciliation from the Bible and History*. Nairobi: Life Challenge Africa, 2010.

Priest, Robert J. "Missionary Elenctics: Conscience and Culture." *Missiology* 22, no. 3 (Jul. 1994): 291–315.

Schreiter, Robert J. *Constructing Local Theologies*. Maryknoll, NY: Orbis, 1985.

———. *The New Catholicity: Theology between the Global and the Local*. Maryknoll, NY: Orbis, 1997.

Shenk, Wilbert R. *Changing Frontiers of Mission*. Maryknoll, NY: Orbis, 1999.

Smedes, Lewis B. *Choices: Making Right Decisions in a Complex World*. San Francisco: Harper & Row, 1988.

Strong, David K., and Cynthia A Strong. "The Globalizing Hermeneutic of the Jerusalem Council." In *Globalizing Theology: Belief and Practice in an Era of World Christianity*, edited by Craig Ott and Harold A. Netland, 127–139. Grand Rapids, MI: Baker Academic, 2006.

---

26. Lewis B. Smedes, *Choices: Making Right Decisions in a Complex World* (San Francisco: Harper & Row, 1988), 121.

Ukpong, Justin S. "Inculturation: A Major Challenge to the Church in Africa Today." *African Ecclesial Review* 38, no. 5 (1996): 258–267.

Vanhoozer, Kevin J. "One Rule to Rule Them All? Theological Method in an Era of World Christianity." In *Globalizing Theology: Belief and Practice in an Era of World Christianity*, edited by Craig Ott and Harold A. Netland, 85–126. Grand Rapids, MI: Baker Academic, 2006.

Webb, William J. *Slaves, Women and Homosexuals: Exploring the Hermeneutics of Cultural Analysis.* Downers Grove, IL: IVP Academic, 2001.

Wilson, Marvin R. *Our Father Abraham: Jewish Roots of the Christian Faith.* Grand Rapids, MI: Eerdmans, 1989.

12

Reconciliation as Separation

Socio-Location and Validity of Othering in 1 John

Julius Kithinji

Head of Department of Theology, St. Paul's University-Limuru, Kenya

Abstract

Postcolonial theorists have on many occasions presented binarism and othering as organizing principles of the empire. The covert presence of such categories in the Bible has been used to present the Bible as a text of the empire, much to its detriment. The Epistle of 1 John presents a protracted argument/response between the Johannine community (insiders) and the secessionists (others). The secessionists are assailed in this epistle and presented in the worst light. In fact, they are seen as the antichrist. This categorization would seem to render the epistle as applying imperial tactics to silence and criminalize its others. It would seem to negate the doctrine of reconciliation and love for the enemy that is the central ethic of the Christian gospel. Owing to this, the task of this research is mainly to distance the epistle from imperial literature that propagates othering, binarism, and marginalization of different identities. The importance of such an exercise is to diversify the understanding of peace and reconciliation by reinforcing the supremacy of the entire Bible over and against generalized human unity and reconciliations.

Key words: postcolonial, 1 John, Johannine, reconciliation, peace, secede/ schism, marginalization, conflict, othering.

Introduction

The Epistle of 1 John addresses a context where one group has seceded (2:19) and the "other" has remained. The nature of the seceding group and the occasion for its secession are described by the group that has remained and therefore we may never know the factors that necessitated this schism from the perspective of the seceding group. The secession is described in high order words and strong vocabulary such that it is escalated to a status typical of the end of the world (ἐσχάτη ὥρα ἐστίν, 2:18) and equated with the *eschaton*. The perspective becomes more complicated because these things are written by a member of the Johannine community whose identity remains the subject of protracted scholarly debate. If the author had given some clue as to his identity, we could have greater grounds to build confidence in his description of this event. However, no introduction whatsoever, by name or otherwise, has been given by this author. We have only a few textual indicators that make us agree with the traditional view that John the apostle, who was also the son of Zebedee and "one of the Twelve," was the author. Chief among these textual indicators is the level of authority that he expresses toward his recipients to the point of infantilizing them as "children"(Παιδία),[1] and his particular confession that he (together with others – possibly other apostles) had seen, heard, and touched (θεάομαι) the Christ.[2] More than that, the opening verses inescapably remind one of the contents of the writings by John in the fourth gospel (John). Such details help us conclude that the account of this schism, this division, is narrated or constructed by one who had witnessed it. We can, therefore, have confidence in his accusations against the seceding group.

Without going into other questions that relate to dating and the original readership of this epistle, which Rasiah S. Sugirtharajah terms "questions of conjecture,"[3] in this chapter I engage with textual or epistolary evidence regarding questions on the situation and nature of the conflict and disunity that faced the recipients of this epistle, and argue for a more advanced way in which such intricate and delicate disunity can be addressed without recourse to denigration of the other. As I delve into the argument of this chapter, it is

---

1. Tat-Siong Benny Liew, "Tyranny, Boundary and Might: Colonial Mimicry in Mark's Gospel," *Journal for the Study of the New Testament* 73, no. 1 (1999): 7–31. In Liew's view, infantilization is an insulting form of patronization at best and an extreme form of victimization at worst.

2. The deponent Greek verb *theomai* includes in its meaning a sense of physical examination.

3. Rasiah S. Sugirtharajah, "The First, Second and Third Letters of John," in *A Postcolonial Commentary on the New Testament Writings*, ed. Fernando F. Segovia and R. S. Sugirtharajah (Edinburgh/London: T&T Clark, 2009), 413.

important to note that, as indicated above, I maintain the assumptions of many scholars who assign this epistle a place in the so-called Johannine literature.[4] I hold that the whole of the Johannine literature is the product of the same author and recasts properly the thinking not only of the Johannine community but also largely of John the apostle. Therefore, in my view, the epistle was written by the person who was most probably John the son of Zebedee and the beloved disciple of Jesus (John 21:20–25). This epistle may have been written for the so-called Johannine community to address a great dissension[5] or schism[6] that was occasioned by the view of Christ (christological controversy) taken by the fourth gospel. Further, I hold that the nature of the problem is a local dispute with generalizable traits. This is for instance evidenced in the references to "many antichrists" (2:18) and "many false prophets" (4:1). Although Gregory Goswell argues that "lack of specifics facilitates its general application,"[7] in my view this is purely a local problem with limited dimensions for universal application.

For the purposes of this chapter, allow me to sympathetically read this division from a postcolonial perspective.[8] In doing this, I note with Higuera Smith that postcolonial approaches to the Bible can indeed yield fruitful insights that will contribute to the health of the interpretive enterprise within evangelicalism while, at the same time, not destroying the way the evangelical church has embraced the authority of Scripture.[9] Since postcolonial biblical criticism overtly deals with interpretations that purportedly free the Bible from imperial entanglements, the question that presents itself in this chapter is not only of the usefulness of this mode of reading for 1 John but also of imperial inputs that render the epistle liable to undue criticism and hinder the efficacious offer of salvation to all.

---

4. See for example Gregory Goswell, "The Johannine Corpus and the Unity of the New Testament Canon," *Journal of the Evangelical Theological Society (JETS)* 61, no. 4 (2018): 717–734.

5. Carl R. Holladay, *Introduction to the New Testament: Reference Edition* (Waco: Baylor University Press, 2017).

6. Donald Guthrie, *New Testament Theology* (Downers Grove, IL: InterVarsity Press, 1981), 979.

7. Goswell, "Johannine Corpus," 726.

8. For a fuller discussion on how the postcolonial criticism can broaden parameters within which postcolonial studies can fruitfully be related to New Testament studies, see chapter 2 of Jeremy Punt's *Postcolonial Biblical Interpretation* (Boston: Brill, 2015).

9. Kay Higuera Smith, Jayachitra Lalitha, and L. David Hawk, eds. *Evangelical Postcolonial Conversations: Global Awakenings in Theology and Praxis* (Downers Grove, IL: InterVarsity Press, 2014), 21.

1 John at a Glance

For centuries, the Johannine literature has nourished generations of Christians and the church in general as the epistle that promotes brotherhood and sisterhood in love. It has been perused for the doctrine of assurance of salvation and the certainty of forgiveness. The Epistle of 1 John is one of the favorite texts of many, for its spiritual tone can adequately be rated as the wisdom of the wise. This epistle abounds in the language of love in the midst of conflict. Even for those who do not believe in a Johannine community, if there is any text that could support the existence of the Johannine community, 1 John does. The community seems to be a closed society. The group may be in the norming stage,[10] the intricate nature of which is evidenced by the patronizing and infantilizing language employed in the epistle.

The teachings of this epistle have been questioned by some, mainly due to what some would say is its seemingly inconsistent logic. For example, in 1:8 and 2:1 the epistle describes the inescapable sinfulness of humanity. Elsewhere, such as in 3:9–10, the epistle declares that πᾶς ὁ γεγεημένος ἐκ τοῦ θεοῦ ἁμαρτίαν οὐ ποιεῖ (all begotten of God cannot do sin) and describes sinners as children of the devil. However, the main controversy the epistle raises is that of separation from the world, in which the world stands for the outside community. The epistle retains a subtle binarism as it drafts an insider and outsider community and reserves the latter for its worst criticism.

Anatomy of the Conflict

Inasmuch as 1 John is a salvific narrative, unfortunately it presents a sad story. It is the story of a dividing and divided church. Any edifying or efficacious message can be gleaned only within the confines of a bitter conflict. Reading the conflict from the perspective of an inferred postcolonial author assumes that the real author presents a one-sided reading of the conflict (i.e. only from the point of view of the insiders or the in-group).[11] Such a reading views the conflict as involving a hegemonic and privileged group, one with the power of the pen, versus a marginal group. It accuses mainstream commentaries for tending to follow the argument of the hegemonic/privileged group, to the detriment of the silenced group and hence agonizes that, much of the information we will ever

---

10. Bruce J. Malina, *The New Testament World: Insights from Cultural Anthropology*, 3rd ed. (Louisville, KY: Westminster John Knox Press, 2001).

11. See also Hisayasu Ito, "Johannine Irony Demonstrated in John 9: Part 1," *Neotestamentica, Journal of the New Testament Society of Southern Africa* 34, no. 2 (2000): 368.

have concerning the seceding group is a preserve of its perceived "enemies," which unfortunately is the group to which the author belongs.

The dismay and agony of the author are that a number of people seem to have been warming to the opposite camp, a point which is echoed by Goswell.[12] These others seem not only to have been gaining momentum but also convincing many and commanding power, and their influence could not be ignored. If chapter 4 is to be read in a literal sense, it can be argued that they had taken on a global sphere of influence. In particular, "they are from the world . . . and the world listens to them" (4:5).

Another dimension to the conflict can be presented from George G. Findlay's perspective.[13] On this view, the occasion for the composition of 1 John was a full-blown conflict with a name-calling schism between those who stood for a Jewish version of the Christian faith and those who preferred a progression in the faith that incorporated dimensions of the existence of an intermediary Son. The latter group was fully convinced by the logic of the Gospel according to John that the Son was the only avenue to the Father, such that to be without the Son was also to be without the Father (see John 14:6). On this view, the two groups claimed to be authentic proponents of their positions in understanding Christ, but the group holding to the Jewish traditional view left (ἐξ ἡμῶν ἐξῆλθαν) since they could not accept the new doctrine.[14]

In these circumstances, the remaining community had become an independent Christian body. The report we have in 1 John is that a group had broken from the ranks of the community. And although both groups were aware of the assertions of Christianity, their understanding was different. Moreover, each of the disputing parties claimed that its appropriation of the gospel was the correct one. Those who had seceded from the Johannine community so stressed the divine principle in Jesus that they almost overlooked his earthly career. Therefore, they ostensibly believed that the humanity of Jesus, while real, was not needful for one's salvation. Their supreme view was that eternal life had been made available to humanity by Christ who had lived the life we live. Therefore, the author who advances the view of the remaining group faults the seceding group on three grounds. First, their view was steeped in a

---

12. Goswell, "Johannine Corpus," 727.

13. George G. Findlay, *Fellowship in the Life Eternal: An Exposition of the Epistles of St John* (London: Hodder & Stoughton, 1909), accessed 21 March 2019, http://faculty.gordon.edu/hu/bi/ted_hildebrandt/New_Testament_Greek/Text/Findlay-1John/Findlay-1John.pdf. See also John Paul Heil, *1–3 John: Worship by Loving God and One Another to Live Eternally* (Eugene, OR: Cascade, 2015), 161–172.

14. Findlay, *Fellowship in the Life Eternal*, 229.

romanticizing of God that equated perfection with sinlessness (2:9–11). Second, it underemphasized keeping the commandments (3:21–23). Third, according to Findlay, they sustained a distorted view on the subject of neighborly love and what it meant to be born of God (2:28–29).[15] Consequently, a moral and theological dispute had divided these children of God. They were parting company and the author, "in a strategic arousal of emotions"[16] and though full of love, had to take a decisive position to cut off the hand so as to retain the body (see Matt 5:30).

Colonial Discourse in 1 John

To measure the dispute in 1 John using a postcolonial analysis, we must first appreciate that in postcolonial biblical criticism it is not texts that contain meaning waiting to be discovered but meaning is properly construed in a text-reader interaction.[17] For this reason, many postcolonial theorists have railed against texts that tend to imbibe colonial tendencies that offer a "worlded" existence.[18] The Epistle of 1 John is vulnerable in the face of a postcolonial hermeneutics because many postcolonial readers argue that it is a record of a dispute which contains several characteristics of colonial discourse. As Sugirtharajah has noted, colonial discourses and disputes eschew diversity and, as such, do not tolerate dissent or debate.[19] Colonial discourses are welded in exclusive non-truths and they staunchly stick to the dimension of conservative "reality." In colonial discourse, it is the empire that talks, and subaltern speech is an unexpected and even unimaginable component. For such readers, elements of colonial discourse are exhibited in this epistle through intolerance because the "other's" theological viewpoint is shunned and detested.

On such an account, Sugirtharajah and Segovia have argued that the author's hermeneutical device for dealing with theological dissidence is to come up with his own definition of Christianity based on his understanding

---

15. Findlay, 231.

16. David A. deSilva, "The Strategic Arousal of Emotion in John's Visions of Roman Imperialism: A Rhetorical Critical Investigation of Revelation 4–22," *Neotestamentica: Journal of the New Testament Society of South Africa* 42, no. 1 (2008): 11.

17. Jeremy Punt, *Postcolonial Biblical Interpretation: Reframing Paul* (Leiden/Boston: Brill, 2015).

18. "Worlding" is a reference to a "world System theory" as an organizing principle. See Heidi Hadsell and Christoph Stuckelberger, *Overcoming Fundamentalism: Ethical Responses from Five Continents* (Nairobi: Acton, 2009), 185.

19. Sugirtharajah and Segovia, *Postcolonial Commentary*, 414.

of the person of Christ. This is done by way of excluding those with divergent views or who hold a different interpretation from his.[20] This claim, according to Sugirtharajah, is pegged on the "beginning" which has become some sort of hermeneutical key for the author. The beginning is the point in which the author seeks sanctuary and validation in the face of competing theological ideas. It is for this reason that Sugirtharajah encourages readers not only to be wary of the author but also to denounce the author's exhibition of colonial fears of unscripted inventions and improvisations.[21]

1 John also becomes vulnerable in the face of postcolonial analysts because of the perception that the author has become some sort of umpire or referee of disputed theological standpoints. His argumentation and refutation of his opponents is seen as extreme, and compared to Jesus, it can be noted that Jesus always left some room for his opponents to buy his viewpoint and reform.[22] In a postcolonial hermeneutic, therefore, it is inevitable to see 1 John as engaged in colonial discourse and hence seen to encourage othering. Since postcolonial studies have permeated interpretive spaces in the African academy and tend to present such stand points, (1) they cannot be ignored and (2) theorists have to imagine how to respond to their perspectives.

Textual Complexities in 1 John's Plot

The Epistle of 1 John rails at the "others" because they have lacked love and are liars: "Whoever claims to love God yet hates a brother or sister is a liar" (4:20a). It seemingly complicates the matter by offering the example of Jesus. According to John, the perfect example of Jesus and the adequate proof of love is that "Jesus Christ laid down his life for us. And we ought to lay down our lives for our brothers and sisters" (3:16). In the gospel, John writes, "Greater love has no one than this: to lay down one's life for one's friends" (John 15:13). In the epistle, John institutionalizes this injunction to the level of a commandment, indicating his recommendation and group's position. Therefore, we read: "And he has given us this command: Anyone who loves God must also love his brother and sister" (1 John 4:21). A complication that can arise here is where a reading tries to understand why the two sides of this dispute could not see how this exhortation was related to them. Further, how the wider value of texts

---

20. Sugirtharajah and Segovia, 414.

21. Sugirtharajah and Segovia, *Postcolonial Commentary*, 414.

22. See Luke 13:3 as an example, where Jesus told his opponents that "unless you repent, you too will all perish."

like Ephesians 2:11–14, that Christ "has destroyed the barrier, the dividing wall of hostility," and Colossians 3:13, "forgive one another," could have been preferred and seen as applicable to this conflict.

In as much as such complication could arise and grant postcolonial readings grounds to offer an apology for the seceding group, there is need to notice that according to John, this group had serious defects. In several verses, John propagates hermeneutics of refutation for those who possessed a contrary confession (1:3; 3:23; 4:13; 5:1; etc.) that denied the lordship of Christ. There is no doubt that in his view, these were people who had failed the trial of suffering for their belief. He presents them as having abandoned the group, proving that they had never been genuine members of the believing community (2:19), because true believers never give in to worldliness. Where Paul's position (2 Thess 2:3) and Revelation (13:1–18) was that the antichrist would pave the way for the last days which would commence with a time of tribulation, 1 John actually states that many antichrists are present in the world. In the words of Craig S. Keener, "anyone who will not spill his blood for Christ's sake is a tool of those by whom that blood is spilt."[23] Further, as Keener observes, the group that has left is accused because they would not believe in a Savior whom the remaining group had touched (ἐψηλάφησαν) and handled (1 John 1:1), and they would not believe that the man who had been called Jesus could be hailed as the Son of God.[24] They would seem to have believed in a human Jesus, but one who was only a man; to judge by the opening verses, they must also have held to some doctrine of a Savior, perhaps reasoning, like Cerinthus, that the spiritual Christ adopted Jesus during his baptism and abandoned him during his passion.[25]

---

23. See Craig S. Keener, *The IVP Bible Background Commentary: New Testament*, 2nd ed. (Downers Grove, IL: IVP Academic, 2014), 711.

24. See Keener, *IVP Bible Background Commentary*, 707. See also Daniel R. Streett, *They Went Out from Us: The Identity of the Opponents in First John* (Berlin: De Gruyter), 2011.

25. Information concerning Cerinthus chiefly comes from the writings of Irenaeus and Eusebius. Cerinthus may have been an early Christian heretic (CE 100) who taught a half-baked Christology, that Jesus was a mere man but at baptism the divine "Christ" (an eternal and divine power) came upon him. The "Christ" left Jesus the man at some point prior to the crucifixion since the divine Christ, being spirit and thus good, cannot suffer. Thus, Cerinthus divided the earthly Jesus (who is human/flesh) from the heavenly Christ (who is spirit). See also Ladd, *Theology of the New Testament*, 34.

A Hermeneutics of Self-Inclusion

The phrase "hermeneutic of self-inclusion" is quickly gaining currency in biblical circles. I first heard of this phrase from Jewel Hyun[26] who said that she caught it from Philomena Mwaura.[27] Since I have not read anything on hermeneutics from Mwaura, I started to muse over what it could mean for the present topic. In my view, a hermeneutic of self-inclusion is an interpretation of self so as to belong. A hermeneutic of self-inclusion involves a personal acceptance that one regards oneself as belonging to God's family without depending on imperial and hegemonic arithmetic and interpretations of who belongs and who does not, who is in and who is out.

The point of postcolonial critiques is that in 1 John, the interpreting community is presented as having the privileged position of creating the test of criteria of who is in a right standing, and further the privilege of applying those criteria upon its opponents and having the mandate to disqualify the other from the prize. They argue that the Johannine community has been denied other biblical principles and laws of biblical justice, especially those spelled out in the Sermon on the Mount, that mere human beings cannot be adequate judges and therefore should not judge "one another" (Matt 7:1–2). This is what compels them to give up on others and accounts for division and irreconcilable differences. Although, this is not the exact position in 1 John, it can be noted many shallow interpretations of 1 John can be used to fuel an undue schism. If it comes to that, it is acceptable that people who find themselves willfully defined negatively by the community with the hegemonic and epistemological privilege of defining, especially in matters related to God and peace, ought at such times to react by concocting a hermeneutics of self-inclusion. To others' dismay, they must see themselves as part of the greater group and interpret their perceived state within the confines of belonging to the kingdom of God.

The Bible advocates this hermeneutics of self-inclusion and warns against the extreme exclusion of the other by those who count themselves included. Paul says to let no one disqualify you for the prize (Col 2:18) and not to judge others (Rom 14:1–4).[28] Jesus on several occasions gave parables that revealed

---

26. Jewel is the president of Matthew 28 Ministries and a known author; e.g. Keumju Jewel Hyun and Diphus C. Chemorion, eds., *The Quest for Gender Equity in Leadership: Biblical Teachings on Gender Equity and Illustrations of Transformation in Africa* (Eugene, OR: Wipf & Stock, 2016).

27. Philomena Mwaura is a professor of religious studies at Kenyatta University, Kenya.

28. Rom 14:4: "Who are you to judge someone else's servant? To their own master, servants stand or fall. And they will stand, for the Lord is able to make them stand."

and cautioned that the privileged side may be in the "error of privilege."[29] The error of privilege is what blinds the other from seeing the possibility of other interpretations. In the Old Testament, the main task of the privileged community Israel is not to boast of their privileged position as a community already included by Yahweh but to figure out the inclusion of the other. When Israel fails to see this broad mandate, its role is replaced by the Jesus community, the new Israel. It is heretical for any Christian community to conclude hastily on the other that they are beyond redemption, that the efficacy of the blood of Jesus is limited by some state.

Apart from postcolonial interpreters, other interpreters who equate the voice of 1 John as that of God advocating for unnecessary schism are at fault in the way they render the text by their interpretation as a dangerous document for any peace attempts. If only read within their hermeneutic, 1 John, while retaining its good warning against secession and schism, becomes a redundant monolithic ethic for a closed and inward-looking society. Further, their hermenuetics misses the bigger picture of redemption, that is, the dealing of God with humanity. Easily noticeable in such readings is the case of insider bias; insiders who are biased because they shallowly accept Johannine perspectives rather than the deep Johannine logic that is rooted in the gospel teachings.

Although the Epistle of 1 John may seem to apply a temporary state or situation to issue an eternal injunction and an exclusive state on the other, compared to Paul (when faced with a similar situation at Galatia), the epistle is actually in the overall saying "Brothers and sisters, if someone is caught in a sin, you who live by the Spirit should restore that person gently. But watch yourselves, or you also may be tempted" (Gal 6:1).[30] This view exonerates 1 John from being an ethics manual for a closed community. For this reason, my point is that broader applications of Christian morality should foresee broader applications of the same. If such is negated by any community, then it calls for a hermeneutic of self-inclusion.

---

29. For example, in Matt 20 where Jesus gives the parable of the workers in the vineyard to imply that the standards of the kingdom of God defy the othering and difference that is part of this sinful life.

30. Philip B. Payne, *Man and Woman, One in Christ: An Exegetical and Theological Study of Paul's Letters* (Grand Rapids, MI: Zondervan, 2009), 273.

Subordinating the Subordinationist Teaching

Clearly expressed in the ongoing argument is that it is not easy to read 1 John as a member of the "other" group or as one who stands neutral from cultural, religious, and ideological differences that stand between the groups envisaged in 1 John. On topics on which the biblical interpretation evidences considerable diversity, we must critically evaluate Scripture by Scripture if we are to perceive Christ's mind for a united body, the church. Those who have rightly discerned the mind of the Lord should exercise such interpretative boldness where faithfulness to Jesus Christ requires it. For example, it is not hard to discern that 1 John has excellent insights for Christian unity. However, as one reads deeper, they are confronted with the presumption that the "outsider" group cannot be won back to Christ. Here, those who secede are branded as antichrists (2:22, ὁ ἀντίχριστος), children of the devil (3:10, τὰ τέκνα τοῦ διαβόλου), and liars (2:22, ὁ ψεύστης) (and though they may have been so, these may not be beyond evangelism). Though the epistle recognizes the danger of continuous association with "backslidden believers," there is need to imagine ways that they can be restored.

Christian unity is more complex than one group dismissing another because of its developing orthodoxy. For too long, subordinating teachings have cared too little about God's love for dissenting and lost groups. The love found in this epistle should, therefore, be understood within the entire New Testament understanding of the same. It is extremely necessary to use aspects of the Bible to evaluate other parts. Just as we use Pauline texts to illuminate other Pauline texts, so in the same manner we can use Johannine texts to illuminate Johannine texts, and so forth.

Reading 1 John for Unity and Reconciliation

The way to honor the Bible is to seek to understand what it says, not to force its evidence into agreement with prior ideas about biblical authority. Reading the Bible openly reveals material that may seem to conflict with the God we have come to know in Jesus Christ. Christ himself found such instances in Scripture especially in the "but I say to you" sections. A hermeneutical danger is always posed when we fail to read particular scriptures within the entire ethic of Jesus Christ. As such, particular scriptural traditions can be and have been used to justify sub-Christian morality, such as patriarchy, polygamy, racism, and slavery.

Similarly, some aspects of the ethic of dis/unity in 1 John cannot be read in isolation. If this is done, it can lead to othering, which is a characteristic of colonial literature. Such reading can make the text a celebration of hegemonic groups which easily may mistake secession as the only option for unity. As has been noted above, some aspects of the latter part of the epistle can be interpreted to promote disunity if not understood within the greater context of the unity of love that the entire epistle proposes.[31] In such instance, one who honestly seeks biblical unity for conflicting communities should not just stop at 1 John but should consider the plenary voice of the Bible.

Reading 1 John for reconciliation and unity, while recognizing the place of its initial audience, therefore, requires reading it within the entire canon of the New Testament. Since it is the twenty-seven books that are canonized, Christians must admit that it is the entire canon of the New Testament that is the New Testament: not just part of the books or phrases that are the New Testament, but all the books held in totality. The rule of the hermeneutical circle is that we must balance the whole with the parts and the parts with the whole. Further, scriptural tradition must be buttressed by Christian reasoning, Christian tradition, Christian experience, and God's continuous revelation: the totality of godly experience. The usefulness of 1 John is in exposing how the gospel can wittily be opposed and how the believing group can be protected. Although 1 John does not go beyond this and as such cannot stand on its own, we must recognize that, none of the canonical texts can stand on their own, and so must be supplemented by the logic of the entire New Testament. If this is not recognized, then the standalone perspective of 1 John can become permissible and easily pass for doctrine.

Conclusion

In the words of Higuera Smith, "postcolonial approaches to the Bible can indeed yield fruitful insights that will contribute to the health of the interpretive enterprise within evangelicalism while, at the same time, not destroying the way the evangelical church has embraced the authority of Scripture."[32] By use of 1 John, this chapter has demonstrated that some aspects of a postcolonial reading of the Bible can be useful while others can be detrimental to the authority of the Bible. More importantly, this reading reveals that for communities living within the dictates of modern ethics that celebrate difference and modern trends of churches that romanticize schism on flimsy grounds, misreading of 1 John

---

31. Ronald R. Ray, *Systematics Critical and Constructive 1: Biblical-Interpretive-Theological-Interdisciplinary* (Eugene, OR: Pickwick, 2018), 204.

32. Higuera Smith et. al., "Evangelical Postcolonial Conversations," 21.

mainly from a postcolonial perspective can form fertile grounds for conflict, separation, and resignations to the other. However, read within the primacy of unity and reconciliation of creation that God so desires, 1 John and the Bible as a whole become valuable resources for critiquing the misappropriation of unity and for constructing models of Christian unity. Inasmuch as Christian reconciliation does not necessarily mean uniformity, nevertheless Christ must remain the sole ingredient for such unity. The potentials of a postcolonial interpretation of the Bible lie in how evangelicals can utilize the space offered by the framework to return the gaze of the Bible to its interpretative methods and not vice versa.

Bibliography

deSilva, David A. "The Strategic Arousal of Emotion in John's Visions of Roman Imperialism: A Rhetorical Critical Investigation of Revelation 4–22." *Neotestamentica: Journal of the New Testament Society of South Africa*, 42, no. 1 (2008): 1–34.

Edwards, M. J. "Martyrdom and the 'First Epistle' of John." *Novum Testamentum* 31, no. 2 (1989): 164–171.

Findlay, George G. *Fellowship in the Life Eternal: An Exposition of the Epistles of St. John*. London: Hodder & Stoughton, 1909. Accessed 21 March 2019. Digitized by Ted Hildebrandt, Gordon College, 2006. http://faculty.gordon.edu/hu/bi/ ted_hildebrandt/New_Testament_Greek/Text/Findlay-1John/Findlay-1John.pdf.

Goswell, Gregory. "The Johannine Corpus and the Unity of the New Testament Canon." *Journal of the Evangelical Theological Society* (*JETS*) 61, no. 4 (2018): 717–734.

Guthrie, Donald. *New Testament Theology*. Downers Grove, IL: InterVarsity Press, 1981.

Hadsell, Heidi, and Christoph Stuckelberger. *Overcoming Fundamentalism: Ethical Responses from Five Continents*. Nairobi: Acton, 2009.

Heil, John Paul. *1–3 John: Worship by Loving God and One Another to Live Eternally*. Eugene, OR: Cascade, 2015.

Higuera Smith, Kay, Jayachitra Lalitha, and L. Daniel Hawk, eds. *Evangelical Postcolonial Conversations: Global Awakening in Theology and Praxis*. Downers Grove, IL: InterVarsity Press, 2014.

Holladay, Carl R. *Introduction to the New Testament: Reference Edition*. Waco: Baylor University Press, 2017.

Hyun, Keumju Jewel, and Diphus C. Chemorion, eds. *The Quest for Gender Equity in Leadership: Biblical Teachings on Gender Equity and Illustrations of Transformation in Africa*. Eugene, OR: Wipf & Stock, 2016.

Ito, Hisayasu. "Johannine Irony Demonstrated in John 9: Part 1." *Neotestamentica, Journal of the New Testament Society of Southern Africa* 34, no. 2 (2000): 361–371.

Keener, Craig S. *The IVP Bible Background Commentary: New Testament*. 2nd ed. Downers Grove, IL: IVP Academic, 2014.

Ladd, George Eldon. *A Theology of the New Testament*. Grand Rapids, MI: Eerdmans, 1993.

Liew, Tat-Siong Benny. "Tyranny, Boundary and Might: Colonial Mimicry in Mark's Gospel." *Journal for the Study of the New Testament* 73, no. 1 (1999): 7–31.

Malina, Bruce J. *The New Testament World: Insights from Cultural Anthropology*. 3rd ed. Louisville, KY: Westminster John Knox Press, 2001.

Payne, Philip B. *Man and Woman, One in Christ: An Exegetical and Theological Study of Paul's Letters*. Grand Rapids, MI: Zondervan, 2009.

Punt, Jeremy. *Postcolonial Biblical Interpretation: Reframing Paul*. Leiden/Boston: Brill, 2015.

Ray, Ronald R. *Systematics Critical and Constructive 1: Biblical-Interpretive-Theological-Interdisciplinary*. Eugene, OR: Pickwick, 2018.

Streett, Daniel R. *They Went Out from Us: The Identity of the Opponents in First John*. Berlin: De Gruyter, 2011.

Sugirtharajah, R. S., and Fernando F. Segovia, eds. *A Postcolonial Commentary on the New Testament Writings*. Edinburgh/London: T&T Clark, 2009.

13

The Gospel of Honor for Shame-Based Cultures

Rethinking Mission Theology in Violent Societies in Africa

Martin Munyao

Global Research Institute Scholar and Part-Time Lecturer

Daystar University

Abstract

Significant studies have been done on cross-cultural missions. Many of these studies have concerned themselves with polemics and apologetics to defend the Christian faith. Some have also focused on understanding other faiths' theology to equip missionaries with theological tools to navigate other religious spaces for evangelistic engagement. However, little is being done to gain an understanding of the theological and cultural dynamics created by honor–shame cultures. African culture is largely based on honor–shame. In shame-based cultures, shame fuels violence. Even though violence may be religiously or politically instigated, shame plays a significant role.

This chapter will first explore the dynamics of shame-based cultures in African societies. The goal is to inspire an appreciation of honor–shame values prevalent in Africa and how they affect human relationships. African society is not a homogeneous unit; it is a multicultural context and can be very complex. Nevertheless, the underlying values of honor and shame are ubiquitous in the African setting. Even though rarely talked about, these values are behind interethnic and interreligious conflict, thus promoting unhealthy competition and conflict among diverse communities. The pathology of shame is very deep, affecting not only the emotional and psychological elements of humanity but also the spiritual.

Second, the chapter will demonstrate from the Bible how Mediterranean and Middle Eastern cultures are steeped in honor and shame. Thus, the biblical narrative is full of interethnic violence and bloodshed. Arguably, Scripture is replete with honor and shame language. Consequently, the Bible is already contextualized for honor and shame cultures. This provides a hermeneutical framework within which to engage violent communities in Africa with the gospel. Unfortunately, the West's biased legal gospel which is dominant in Africa does not speak to shame-based cultures. Its truncated theology of humanity, sin, and salvation does not scratch the itch in most African societies, that is, shame and loss of face (God's face).

Lastly, this chapter will attempt to mainstream an honor–shame missiology for African societies to mitigate interethnic violence. The underlying dynamics of violence in Africa such as honor killings and interethnic clashes are shame-based and can find their linkage in the shame-based ancient Mediterranean cultures.

Key words: honor–shame, Africa, shame-based cultures, mission theology, cross-cultural relationships, honor killings, the gospel of Shame–Honor.

Introduction

Large-scale violence in Africa is religiously, ethnically (tribal), or politically instigated.[1] Its impact on African societies is, without doubt, devastating as it inhibits not only cohesion along religious, ethnic, and political divides but also development on the continent. Major scholarship and studies (Deng,[2] Karbo,[3] and Muloongo et al.[4]) have been undertaken to foster peace mediation and conflict resolution among waring African communities. While this brings

---

1. Gerrie ter Haar, *Religion: Source of Conflict or Resource for Peace?* (London: Brill, 2004), 6.

2. Francis M. Deng, "Ethnicity: An African Predicament," *The Brookings Review* 15, no. 3 (1997): 30–31.

3. David J. Francis, ed., "Peace-Building in Africa," in *Peace and Conflict in Africa* (London/New York: Zed Books, 2008), 116.

4. Keith Muloongo, Roger Kibasomba, and Jemima N. Kariri, eds., *The Many Faces of Human Security: Case Studies of Seven Countries in Southern Africa* (Pretoria: Institute for Security Studies, 2005), 1–2.

benefits by stopping the bloodshed and restoring warring communities, tensions are still felt, threatening sustainable peace. Thus shalom (God's peace) may not be realized in its entirety.

Underneath the tension, threats of war, and war itself is an underlying dynamic: the cultural value of honor and shame. The humiliation that comes from losing land or livestock to another community, losing water holes for cattle, stolen elections, and so on, can trigger deep shame. Shame and honor are rooted in the social–communal fabric of African societies. Honor is a scarce and coveted value, while shame is shunned. These values are inherent in the community-based African societies. They sit at the core of the African worldview and thus inform decisions, intentions, and actions that protect the group's interests first, even if it means using violence. Africa's New Testament scholar Mbuvi states:

> Honor and shame are group values underlying strong kinship ties and giving high value to ancestry . . . And since honor is a scarce commodity, it is obtained at a cost and can either be ascribed or achieved. The honor-and-shame culture is characterized by an ongoing "challenge-riposte," usually in the public domain . . . In such a culture, honor is also controlled and dispensed by the individuals called the "significant other."[5]

Thus, shame in the African setting is associated with weakness and humiliation, while honor is strength and is desired whether achieved or ascribed. Shame has both positive and negative connotations. As used in this research, shame is "the basic awareness of the opinion of others and the fear of censure."[6] In this sense, shame is considered to be a virtue (value) in the African setting. Honor, on the other hand, is "the value of a person in his or her own eyes, hence a claim to worth along with the social acknowledgment of worth."[7] Viewed this way, honor and shame therefore function as a social sanction that comes with a certain level of performance in accordance with the expectations of the group. Hence shame and honor serve as an element of social control in collectivistic societies such as those in Africa.

---

5. Andrew Mbuvi, "African Theology from the Perspective of Honor and Shame," in *The Urban Face of Mission: Ministering the Gospel in a Diverse and Changing World*, ed. Harvie M. Conn, Manuel Ortiz, and Susan S. Baker (Phillipsburg, NJ: P&R, 2002), 287.

6. Jerome H. Neyrey, *Honor and Shame in the Gospel of Matthew* (Louisville, KY: Westminster John Knox, 1998), 30.

7. Bruce J. Malina, *The New Testament World: Insights from Cultural Anthropology* (Louisville, KY: Westminster John Knox, 1993), 31.

Honor and Shame in African Societies

One of the crucial questions we might ask is this: Is Africa shame-based? Western cultural anthropologists in collaboration with the evangelical missionary enterprise of the nineteenth century classified African society within the categories of fear–power, also labeled under an animistic worldview.[8] However, recent scholarship has argued that this "fear classification for Sub-Saharan Africa cultures can hinder us from seeing the significant presence and interrelationship of honor/shame dynamics."[9] To be sure, there is a fundamental overlap between fear and shame in African societies. For example, dishonoring of our ancestors is feared, and could bring shame.

Kinship and Blood

It is of prime importance that honor in the African setting be understood as a group value. This is because African societies are collective and not individualistic by nature. What this means is that "Their cultural outlook prioritizes the groups' survival and distinction over individual preferences."[10] Therefore, "honor and shame are largely group values where different individuals that make up the group share the same values of honor and shame."[11] The result of this is a strong kinship bond where blood relationship is the community binding factor. In this sense, individuals coming from the same ethnic group pride themselves not only on sharing the same language but, more deeply, on the honor of the same roots, ancestry, and blood.

Thus, if honor is found in familial and community sharing of ancestry and blood, then the same honor ought to be replicated within the unity of blood. Mbuvi argues that "honor is also replicated in blood; therefore, the good name of a family signifies that honor. To know the family name is to know the honor rating of that family."[12] No wonder honor killings are rampant and rarely understood as unacceptable in North African societies, as they are deeply

---

8. Samuel E. Chiang and Grant Lovejoy, eds., *Beyond Literate Western Contexts: Honor and Shame and Assessment of Orality Preference* (Hong Kong: International Orality Network, 2015), 78.

9. Sandra Freeman, "Honor/Shame Dynamics in Sub-Saharan Africa," *Mission Frontiers* 37, no. 1 (Feb. 2015): 32.

10. Jayson Georges and Mark D. Baker, *Ministering in Honor–Shame Cultures: Biblical Foundations and Practical Essentials* (Downers Grove, IL: IVP Academic, 2016), 45.

11. Andrew Mbuvi, "The Ancient Mediterranean Values of 'Honour and Shame' as a Hermeneutical Lens of Reading the Book of Job," *Old Testament Essays* 23, no. 3 (2010): 754.

12. Mbuvi, "Ancient Mediterranean Values," 754.

seated in the social–cultural fabric of the communities. This also explains the public stoning of women in Sudan who are caught in adultery, or the chopping off of thieves' limbs. Any individual shortcoming that might bring dishonor on the community will be eliminated in public even if by way of violence.

The Issue of Limited Good

Leading anthropologist and New Testament scholar Neyrey defines "limited good" as related to shame-based societies as "how certain people perceived all the world's goods (that is, wealth, land, education, happiness, honor, etc) as absolutely limited in supply."[13] In Africa, communities view the world as though all desirable objects occur in a finite quantity. At the functional level of everyday life experience, if one gains, the others lose; it's a zero-sum game. In most African societies, honor is always in limited supply. By implication, there is only so much honor to go around. If an individual from a certain community gains something of value – for example, an election victory or land – then the social position of the competitor's communities is diminished.

This common feature of honor–shame cultures leads to fierce competition. Success is generally countered by aggression or envy, a notable cause behind most interethnic clashes and tribal-based wars. This is because "honor is a scarce commodity and thus has to be obtained at a cost which would normally result in envy between friends and, even more so, among equals."[14] This leads to another dynamic of honor and shame among African societies, known as challenge and riposte.

Challenge and Riposte

As seen earlier, honor is in short supply, so oral public contests are common in the sphere of African social life. This is publicly displayed in a technique known as "riposte." This term is borrowed from a sporting technique in fencing, which, interestingly, is a very rare sport in Africa. It means "a quick return thrust following a parry. Socially, it means a quick clever reply to an insult or criticism."[15] This technique marks conversations in the public space, and they can quickly incite violence through the push and shove of words.

---

13. Neyrey, *Honor and Shame*, 18.

14. Mbuvi, "Ancient Mediterranean Values," 755.

15. Werner Mischke, *The Global Gospel: Achieving Missional Impact in Our Multicultural World* (Scottsdale, AZ: Mission ONE, 2015), 104.

According to Mischke, there are four steps to this social code of challenge and riposte:

> Claim to worth or value
> Challenge to that claim or refusal to acknowledge the claim
> Riposte or defense of the claim
> Public verdict or success awarded to either claimant or challenger.[16]

In Africa, this phenomenon is common in political rallies before, during, and after election contests. They are designed to pitch honor for a certain community or family, and a subsequent challenge of the same claim of honor by another community representative. The intention is to disparage one's claim of worth, fame, or status which has been acquired through community processes. While the subtleness of the technique is evident, it can raise interethnic tensions that can quickly escalate into armed violence. The community that is bound to lose in the contest does not go down without a fight. Members of the community will do what it takes, even shedding blood and killing to protect the honor of their leader, who is also considered to be a patron.

Patronage and Reciprocity

In a bid to fight for the honor of a patron, another dynamic of shame-based societies in Africa is brought out, called reciprocity and patronage. Patronage and reciprocity is the reciprocal socio-economic relationship between a patron and a client. The patron bestows favors on the clients in exchange for social capital in the form of honor. As Georges and Baker put it, "The superior patron provides material goods to a client, and the client repays with nonmaterial goods such as loyalty, obedience or gratitude."[17]

From an outsider's perspective, this might appear like corruption or dependency syndrome in African cultures. However, that is not necessarily the case. From an esoteric viewpoint, "In developing countries where people acquire goods through relationships, patronage is the de facto economic system. Honor, not money, serves as the primary currency facilitating the transaction of goods and services."[18] In return, patrons who are mostly politicians or people of higher social status receive respect and allegiance from the beneficiaries. With an understanding of patronage and reciprocity, one begins to appreciate

---

16. Mischke, *Global Gospel*, 104.
17. Georges and Baker, *Ministering in Honor–Shame Cultures*, 51.
18. Georges and Baker, 52.

the group mentality behind individuals of honor in the society where social capital is given in return. An entire community can opt for violence to protect the honor and respect of their patron or kingpin, knowing that, in return, they will receive benefaction.

Honor and Shame in the Bible

The Scriptures are full of violence, a reality that many readers will either naively read past or simply dismiss as archaic behavior that marked the ancient Mediterranean societies. However, for one to fail to see or to dismiss the violence in most biblical narratives, one has to read past honor and shame dynamics that color the Scriptures. I contend in this section that from the book of Genesis to Revelation, the Bible is replete with honor and shame. "Since the pivotal cultural value of honor and shame is characteristic of the Middle East, and since the Bible grew out of Middle Eastern Culture, then it can be assumed that the pivotal cultural value of the Bible is also: *honor and shame*."[19] For example, in the Old Testament: "When Yahweh defended his honor by annihilating the Assyrian forces, the Assyrian king 'withdrew to his own land in disgrace' and was murdered by his own sons in the temple of his god (2 Chron 32:21). The whole account is couched in the language of honor and shame. Assyria sought to shame Yahweh, but God's power and greatness were vindicated; therefore, his public honor and reputation were upheld, and Assyria was publicly shamed."[20]

In the New Testament writings too, the language of honor and shame was used as a technique for censuring and shaming followers of the tiny and newly formed revolutionary "Christlike" movement that was mistaken as a cult and was turning the world upside down. DeSilva writes:

> The authors of the New Testament devote much of their attention, therefore, to insulate their congregation from the effects of these shaming techniques, calling the hearers to pursue lasting honor before the court of God whose verdict is eternal. These authors continue to use the language of honor and shame to articulate the value system of the Christian group, and to build up the church into a court of reputation that will reinforce commitment to those

---

19. Mischke, *Global Gospel*, 42.

20. Timothy C. Tennent, *Theology in the Context of World Christianity: How the Global Church Is Influencing the Way We Think about and Discuss Theology* (Grand Rapids, MI: Zondervan, 2007), 85.

values through honoring those who distinguish themselves in acts of love, service and faithful witness and through censuring those who fail to embody those values.[21]

Similar examples in the Bible have faced biblical criticism which casts doubt on the character of a God who takes up land from its ancestral owners and gives it to Israelites through violent and bloody means. The violence in the Bible can, however, be interpreted through the hermeneutical lens of honor and shame in order to minister to violent societies in Africa. This calls for a brief interrogation of honor and shame dynamics in the Bible that correspond to those of African cultures.

Kinship and Blood in the Bible

In the Bible, "Honor was frequently attached to one's birth, and family name."[22] That is why genealogies were important in both Old and New Testaments. Abraham's honor, for example, was extended through his blood descendants of Isaac, Jacob, and David in whose line Jesus was born. Therefore, the significance of blood relationships in the Bible is woven in the fabric of the ancient Mediterranean culture. Kinship and blood often caused honor competition among Israelites.

An example can be seen in the story of Rechab and Baanah, who avenged the blood spilt by their enemies by killing their enemies' offspring (2 Sam 4:7–11). Their "default culture recognized that family blood was a justifiable catalyst for honor-based violence; family-versus-family revenge was indeed culturally acceptable."[23]

Just as in many honor and shame societies of Africa today, blood feuds in Bible days were common as blood replicated the honor of the family. In such societies, loyalty to your kin and blood honor trump the law. In fact, the law becomes irrelevant when family honor through blood is in jeopardy, hence violent encounters.

The crux of violence in the Bible is evidenced in the execution of lawbreakers and those who disturbed the Greco-Roman authoritative status quo. Revolutionaries were subjected to excruciating pain and death through the cross. Jesus Christ suffered this form of violence, as a result of which

---

21. David deSilva, *Honor, Patronage, Kinship and Purity: Unlocking New Testament Culture* (Downers Grove, IL: InterVarsity Press, 2000), 43.

22. Tennent, *Theology in World Christianity*, 86.

23. Mischke, *Global Gospel*, 156.

"the blood of Christ" is talked about that brings salvation. Was the blood of Christ avenged? Why would God choose such a violent means of securing the salvation of the world? This needs to be understood through the lens of the shameful death of Christ and his honorable victory to life.

But the blood of Christ is different. Consider the apostle Paul's view of the honor in Jesus's blood in Ephesians 2:13–16. It has an entirely different catalyst. While honor in blood is the catalyst for family and ethnic feuds in the Bible, the blood of Jesus is different: it brings healing, reconciliation, and acceptance among warring ethnicities to form the new community of God. "Divine forgiveness releases people from the social bondage of shame and carries profound social overtones."[24] Tension and possible violence are lessened where there is forgiveness.

The Issue of Limited Good in the Bible

There was only so much honor to go around in Bible cultures, hence it was a limited good. Since honor, being a social capital, was limited, it quite often led to violence. A classic example in the Old Testament is in the story of Saul and David and the war against the Philistines (1 Sam 18:6–9). After David slew Goliath, the words of the women who sang in celebration at the return of David and the army, who carried with them great honor, threatened Saul's acquisition of the same: "'Saul has struck down his thousands, and David his ten thousands.' And Saul was very angry, and this saying displeased him. He said, 'They have ascribed to David ten thousands, and to me they have ascribed thousands, and what more can he have but the kingdom?' And Saul eyed David from that day on" (1 Sam 18:7–9 ESV).

Honor competition is at the heart of Saul's jealousy that makes him entertain thoughts about assassinating David. "In an honor/shame culture, honor is a 'limited good' (a zero-sum game), hence the power of this value to influence behavior – particularly to generate conflict – is raised to another order of magnitude."[25] Since Saul's ascribed honor was being threatened by David's achieved honor, it was only conceivable for him to plot evil.

---

24. Georges and Baker, *Ministering in Honor–Shame Cultures*, 101.
25. Mischke, *Global Gospel*, 99.

Challenge and Riposte in the Bible

Public conversations in the Bible were characterized by the social–cultural value that is pervasive in the ancient Mediterranean world known as challenge and riposte. "The most common way to acquire honor was 'in the face-to-face game of challenge and riposte,' which was an integral part of daily life."[26] If family or community honor was lost in the court of public opinion, it could lead to being avenged by blood.

Most of Jesus's public discourses were marked by this intelligent push-and-shove game of words. An example is Jesus's story of Matthew 12:8–16, 23. The contest follows a fourfold path:

1. Claim of worth or value: Jesus claimed to be the Son of Man. "For the Son of Man is lord of the Sabbath" (Matt 12:8 ESV).

2. Challenge to that claim or refusal to acknowledge the claim: the crowd challenged Jesus's claim. "Is it lawful to heal on the Sabbath?" (Matt 12:10 ESV).

3. Riposte or defense of the claim: Jesus gave the sheep–man comparative analogy to quickly return the challenge and healed a man with a withered hand on a Sabbath day (Matt 12:11–14).

4. Public verdict of success awarded to either the claimant or the challenger: in amazement, people ascribed Jesus messianic status. "Can this be the Son of David?" (Matt 12:23 ESV).

A combination of the values of limited good and the challenge and riposte can result in a greater propensity for violence. When one is disgraced publicly in Middle Eastern societies it can easily result in attacking others in order to avenge community honor.

This understanding can be used to explain terror-related violence. A humiliated individual or group, due to the shame of their collective identity, is behind the religious extremism that leads to attacking others. For example, it can be argued that the actions of Muslim extremist groups can be traced back to the shaming and humiliation of the Muslim community by others.[27]

---

26. Tennent, *Theology in World Christianity*, 86.

27. Mischke, *Global Gospel*, 119–122.

Patronage and Reciprocity in the Bible

Patronage is a very common practice in the Bible. Biblical patriarchs were considered to be patrons – for example, Abraham, Isaac, Jacob, David – and association with them bestowed blessings among the beneficiaries. Officials were also patrons in relation to their subjects who were the clients. There was a "dance of grace" that existed between them, for as the patron gave gifts, the clients reciprocated with honor in the public space.[28]

Consider the story of the centurion and his servants (Luke 7:2–5). This high-status person in the government had done favors for his subjects. "He is worthy to have you [Jesus] do this for him, for he loves our nation, and he is the one who built us our synagogue" (7:4b–5 ESV). However, the chief of patrons in the Bible is Jesus. People, especially women, experienced a form of violence that was unique to social outcasts – for example, the hemorrhaging woman, the woman caught in adultery, and Mary Magdalene. Jesus bestowed honor on them by association, removing their shame, and ascribing them honor in public. The emphasis is not so much on the forgiven sin as the restoration back into the community of these individuals. "Jesus's public relationships honored those with 'achieved shame'"[29] who were experiencing violence because of it.

Therefore, as a patron, Jesus bestowed healing, forgiveness, restoration of status, belonging, and humanity back onto individuals. To reciprocate, the individuals gave their allegiance to Jesus in honor of his mercy and grace. As Bates has posited, "*Pistis*, which has traditionally been translated as 'faith' in Paul's Letters, is better understood as allegiance when speaking of how the gospel of Jesus unleashes God's power for salvation."[30] Therefore, reciprocation of God's grace is by allegiance as understood among the cultures in the Bible. This has a lot of similarity with the African concept of receiving grace and returning favor. It's an avenue for reconciliation in the African mindset.

Linking Biblical and African Cultures for the Gospel in Africa's Violent Societies

African societies are collectivistic in their set-up of communities and interrelationships. "Most people in collectivistic societies structure their life

---

28. D. A. deSilva, "The Noble Contest: Honor, Shame, and the Rhetorical Strategy of 4 Maccabees," *Journal for the Study of the Pseudepigrapha* 7, no. 13 (1 Apr. 1995): 44, https://doi.org/10.1177/095182079500001303.

29. Georges and Baker, *Ministering in Honor-Shame Cultures*, 102.

30. Matthew W. Bates, *Salvation by Allegiance Alone: Rethinking Faith, Works, and the Gospel of Jesus the King* (Grand Rapids, MI: Baker Academic, 2017), 77.

to avoid shame and maintain honor."[31] Without doubt this affects how people perceive and relate to each other ethnically. A missional harmony is required of the Christian witness carried out in Africa. This is because collectivism also impacts Africans' reception of Jesus's message and their subsequent reading of the Scripture. African biblical scholar Mbuvi has argued that "The primary core values that underlie both the African culture and the biblical cultures are those of honor and shame."[32] If the Bible is steeped in honor–shame language and African cultures are honor and shame cultures, then the Bible is already contextualized for African culture. "Due to the various points of resemblance between the African and the first-century cultures, it is indeed possible to approach the Bible optimistically."[33] The implication of this is that the Bible may not require further contextualization for violent societies in Africa. There is too much honor-based violence in the Bible and that can be used to reverse cultural values that trigger interethnic violence in order to bring about peace and prepare adversary groups to reimagine honor. As collectivistic societies, African communities will be prepared for the reception of the Good News. If various African ethnicities long for honor and God's plan is for all people from all walks of life and ethnic diversities to seek and find their honor in him, then Christian witness can be that of creating a linkage between biblical and African cultures for the gospel in Africa's violent societies as a missional harmony. Missionaries and Christian workers, in serving among African violent societies, need to read honor-based violence and killings in harmony with Africa's shame-based context to reveal to the readers a new lens for understanding God's honor. God intends humanity to become his family, bearing his honor.[34] With this understanding, the chances to reduce honor killings and other violent practices that are supported in the respective cultural framework among African communities can highly be mitigated. "The African view of honor and shame could be an interpretive tool for reading the biblical text."[35] Thus, given that violence in various cultures is shame-based, that African culture is based on honor and shame, and that honor and shame

---

31. Jayson Georges, "Why Has Nobody Told Me This Before?: The Gospel the World Is Waiting For," *Mission Frontiers* 37, no. 1 (February 2015): 7.

32. Mbuvi, "Ancient Mediterranean Values," 755.

33. E. Mahlangu, "The Ancient Mediterranean Values of Honour and Shame as a Hermeneutical Procedure: A Social-Scientific Criticism in an African Perspective," *Verbum et Ecclesia* 22, no. 1 (2001): 87.

34. Georges, "Why Has Nobody Told Me This Before?," 10.

35. Mahlangu, "Ancient Mediterranean Values," 88.

are pervasive in the Bible, the Scripture can speak to various levels of violence in Africa.

How can this be done?

Removing Western Cultural and Theological Blinders

Evangelical Christianity as perceived and practiced in Africa today is heavily intertwined with its Western counterpart. Obviously, the West's evangelical missionary enterprise carried with it vestiges of Western culture, and these were sometimes mistaken for biblical culture. Such vestiges are individualism and an understanding of salvation as a personal decision. Thus, violent acts in the Western context are an individual's decision that will bring about consequences for the individual. However, like ancient Mediterranean cultures, African cultures are collectivistic and community-oriented. The biblical culture and worldview are far removed from Western culture, but closely resemble the African worldview. Unfortunately, the Western evangelical missionary enterprise has not only set the norm for biblical interpretation but also truncated the gospel, through Western eyes, for the African audience. This has presented a huge cultural and theological blind spot to honor and shame. For instance, war and violence in both Testaments are understood to be caused by the human sin nature. Shame, loss of honor, and desire for the restoration of honor are lost in the biblical interpretation. But African societies are community-based. "This strong community orientation elevates the role of honor and shame to a significant level. It is an element of social control affecting gender roles and political organization and provides a framework for all aspects of life in African societies . . . In this framework, the public sphere, as the domain of the male, becomes a zone of challenge and conflict."[36]

This aspect significantly resembles the biblical worldview. It is therefore crucial for African readers to remove their acquired Western guilt–innocence lenses and wear their own cultural and theological lenses of honor and shame in order to see violence in the Bible the way God sees it. Linking between biblical themes of honour and shame, and Africa's cultural leaning towards the same, involves looking for instances of violence in the Bible and closely reading the honor games, dances of grace, and reciprocation involved.

---

36. Mbuvi, "African Theology," 289.

Wearing African Cultural Lenses

So far we have seen that African cultures, as diverse as they may be, are steeped in honor and shame. Therefore, it goes without saying that putting on honor and shame lenses to first interpret the biblical cultures and then study the violence in our own cultures is the intuitive approach. From an African perspective, violence is a result of groups, families, or communities protecting their honor, or the honor of their patron.

War and violence in the Bible were quite often employed to either defend God's honor or to offend and shame God's enemies. As a matter of natural instinct, Africans, including believers (Christians), will naturally defend their own community when under attack by others. Does this match Israel's behavior in their defense of God's honor?

Jesus brings a different way of giving honor without necessarily using the pathway of violence.

Noting Jesus's Subversion of "Honor" in All Cultures

In the coming of Jesus Christ, all cultural inclinations that are against God's commands have radically been subverted in the gospel. For instance, Jesus shows an alternative to revenge: "You have heard that it was said, 'An eye for an eye and a tooth for a tooth.' But I say to you, Do not resist the one who is evil. But if anyone slaps you on the right cheek, turn to him the other also" (Matt 5:38–39 ESV). In this statement, Jesus completely subverts cultural norms on revenge when an offense has been committed. How can this be possible in a culture where dishonoring a wrongdoer is the honorable thing to do?

Jesus taught a more honorable way of giving honor to one's enemies, namely, no revenge. Nonviolent retaliation becomes the new way of giving honor. Of course, this does not sit very well with most African Christians. Saying no to revenge is almost impossible for most African communities. That is why Christians have historically been implicated in violent acts during times of chaos.

However, the New Testament does suggest shaming as an antidote to the toxic desire for bad honor. On certain occasions, Paul explicitly shamed believers. For example, he wrote, "I say this to your shame" (1 Cor 6:5; 15:34 ESV); "Take note of those who do not obey what we say in this letter; have nothing to do with them, so that they may be ashamed" (2 Thess 3:14–15 NRSV). Therefore, there is a biblical precedent for public shaming of Christians who either incite or engage in violent acts, to cause them to refrain from their behavior. Can African Christians adopt this strategy as a cultural warning against involvement in violence? Georges and Baker offer some insight into this: "The threat of potential shame acts as a cultural stop sign, helping to preserve dignity and avoid offensive actions. Even though the experience of shame will be painful, we can affirm a group's shaming when (1) the action in question is something God would consider shameful, and (2) the intent of the shaming is restoring the person to right living and right relationship with God and others. This 'reintegrative' shaming is restorative and temporary."[37]

For violent retaliation to stop in Africa, a discipleship is needed that is holistic and does not assume the gospel. Such discipleship must involve an element of biblical shaming that seeks to reintegrate offenders back into the community. While shaming in non-African cultures might seem to be oppressive and hateful, it might be a helpful ministry resource in the African context. This approach might carry weight especially when opinion leaders in the community champion the idea of public shaming and value change for peace.

The community must make refusal to retaliate as something of a higher value and greater honor. Unfortunately, this subversion of cultural dynamics has not been touched by Western guilt–innocence categories and gospel presentations. This does not mean that the Western perspective is wrong – no! Rather, it means that the evangelical missionary enterprise's presentation scratches where there is no itch. This calls for a rethinking of mission theology for violent societies in Africa.

Rethinking Mission Theology in Africa

To achieve an objective rethinking of mission theology for African societies, a reading of African and biblical cultures in retrospect and prospect is needed. This chapter proposes that a retrospective look at Western culture's guilt–innocence value categories be done in light of Western missionary work in Africa, as well as a prospective look at the honor–shame values of the African people which are shared with the ancient Mediterranean cultures. Therefore, the following needs to be done in order to imagine a mission theology that addresses honor and shame in Africa to reduce or stop violence.

---

37. Georges and Baker, *Ministering in Honor–Shame Cultures*, 44.

From Legal to Regal Language

Kinship and blood, patron and client relationships, kings and subjects are some of the honor–shame dynamics inherent among the African people. African cultures pay detailed attention to royalty and power dynamics. The biblical narrative is also very keen on regal (royal) language.

A gospel presentation as traditionally passed on to the African church is packed with legal language. God is viewed as a judge: Christ will sit on the judgment seat and judge the living and the dead. Even though clearly understood, that description may not necessarily resonate with the African mind.

Reconciling warring tribes in Africa using legal language may not bear much fruit. According to the traditional missionary church, reconciliation is conceptualized and explained in legal form. "Because Jesus reconciles us to God, our efforts towards moral perfection are in vain . . . When Jesus returns to the earth, God will judge all people justly and punish sin."[38] Seeking to view a patron as a judge is imposing impossible categories on an African person.

However, the vision of the Lord as a King who sits on his throne, full of beauty, splendor, and glory, with the apparel of a king, who joins his army for war, is revered in African thinking. A description of his army coming to war against God's enemies, when told in African stories and narratives, is bound to spark a sense of fear mixed with honor and glory.

Talk of a King who has a kingdom that is from everlasting to everlasting will influence an African mind to rethink his or her state of allegiance. By this, there is a need to acknowledge the place of our blood in kinship and relationships, but show the superiority of Jesus's blood in uniting communities. When talking of the "everlasting," the African mind is pervaded with the issue of "the afterlife." Hence Jesus's royalty securing the everlasting kingdom needs to be incorporated into African mission theology.

From Guilt/Innocence to Shame/Honor

A gospel presentation, as traditionally told, goes like this: Humans violated God's law and are guilty; God's justice requires that all guilty violations must be punished; however, God offered his Son, Jesus Christ, to die in our place for us to access forgiveness and reconciliation. This gospel presentation is fitting for

---

38. Jayson Georges, *The 3D Gospel: Ministry in Guilt, Shame, and Fear Cultures* (n.p.: Timē Press, 2014), 36.

the Western mind which is normally based on guilt–innocence.[39] The problem is that guilt is not necessarily present in the African ontology.

Freeman, a missionary in Botswana, once exclaimed, "Why does there seem to be no sense of guilt here, except when there is also shame in getting caught?"[40] Freeman went on to explain that when given a chance between not sinning against God and disobeying a respectable person, an African person would most likely choose to sin in order to obey and not dishonor the patron. This presents a serious challenge to discipleship in Africa's violent societies. When an African Christian must choose between lying (to protect an elder's reputation and honor) or speaking the truth (which will shame and dishonor the elder) that person will often think, "God will forgive me and my elder will not, so I will lie."[41]

Honor must therefore be demonstrated through restoring an offender into the community/group. Since God's desire for salvation is to build a new community (Eph 2), biblical shaming should seek to restore violent offenders into the church. Therefore, gospel presentation and discipleship should be reintegrative.

Unfortunately, shaming as understood in popular gospel presentations isolates and alienates. This explains why interethnic violence is justifiable even in some of the communities most reached by Christianity in Kenya. An understanding of how honor–shame dynamics in a community can be decoded by the gospel will bring a breakthrough in solving longstanding conflict and tension zones in the continent. African mission theology must be revised through honor–shame language to incorporate and exercise biblical shaming because it is theologically fitting as well as restorative in African communities.

How does this look, both theologically and culturally? Theologically, violence and violent acts are shameful in God's eyes. Christians must be able to see how their ethnic fragmentation that fuels interethnic violence is dishonoring to God, thus shaming them. The sin of violence is brought into light through biblical shaming. Piper, in his book *Future Grace*, puts it this way: "Well-placed shame (the kind you ought to have) is the shame we feel when there is good reason to feel it. Biblically that means we feel ashamed of something because our involvement in it was dishonoring to God. We ought

---

39. Tennent, *Theology in World Christianity*, 79.

40. Freeman, "Honor/Shame Dynamics," 32.

41. Freeman, 33.

to feel shame when we have a hand in bringing dishonor upon God by our attitudes or actions."[42]

The intensity of violence that was meted out on Jesus on the cross is to be reflected upon in order to transform communities' ideas about the shame-to-honor status reversal. Jesus absorbed the climax of violence, a reality that informs honor and shame communities to decode their perception of violence. "A key element in understanding the atonement is to recognize the centrality of shame to crucifixion itself."[43] Jesus bore the fullest extent of shame on the cross to honor us with a superior honor. Because of his honor, we can honor one another, regardless of our differences.

Reimagining Interfaith Dialogue

With an understanding of challenge and riposte as a fuel to violence, there is a need for the church to reimagine interfaith dialogue through the eyes of honor; to realize that at the heart of religious fundamentalism are the honor and shame dynamics of push and shove. The shame of losing ground/territory is behind Al-Shabaab's and ISIS's agendas. Therefore, interfaith discourse ought to be cognizant of the shame and humiliation suffered by religious extremist organizations.

The evangelical church should re-strategize its approach to engaging with other religions. While evangelism and proselytization are at the background of its mission, it needs to realize that giving honor to other religious groups can win people for the kingdom of God more efficiently and with dignity. Interfaith dialogue must not end with a win–lose situation.

Finally, there is a need to avoid the win–lose approach to evangelism and instead emphasize the win–win situation in Jesus's new community of faith. Clever play on words and use of African stories and dirges, proverbs, and symbolism should also be used in interfaith encounters. Honor is communicated through symbolism and figures of speech.

Hospitality Ministry to Refugees

To reverse the sin of isolation and alienation, the ministry of hospitality is a tool that can be used to unite communities. In most instances, wars end up with

---

42. John Piper, "Faith in Future Grace vs. Misplaced Shame," in *Future Grace: The Purifying Power of the Promises of God* (Colorado Springs, CO: Multnomah, 2012), 129.

43. Georges and Baker, *Ministering in Honor-Shame Cultures*, 108.

the forceful displacement of people from their homes, fleeing to seek refuge in neighboring countries. Kenya has been a host to refugees from neighboring countries for the last four decades. Credit ought to go to organizations that work hard to take care of refugees in Kenya. However, quite often, human dignity is lost in the manner in which this help is given. Shame is at the root of the dehumanization that refugees have to endure. Dehumanization ranges from poor and inhumane housing conditions, to lack of decent amenities and lack of access to nutritious food for women and children.

Violence and inhumanity are increased by the manner in which help is given. It is in offering hospitality to those in distress that one might encounter trends of challenge and riposte. November offers some practical tips for ministering in a society that uses honor challenges:

1. "When someone responds unusually harshly, consider what may be behind his or her words or actions."[44] Remember that, quite often, the message is in what is not being said.

2. "Remember, claiming honor can look like boasting or bravado."[45]

3. "Honor challenges can be used to build relationships."[46] Be careful to use a wise response which gains honor and acceptance. Seek to restore honor in the way you engage in a conversation.

The church in Africa ought to be encouraged to seize this opportunity to offer the ministry of hospitality to refugees. However, while offering help to refugees from war-torn countries, it is paramount to do so with dignity in order to restore their honor in humanity as part of gospel proclamation.

Conclusion

Shame fuels violence. The cultural values of honor and shame are pervasive in African societies yet are under-studied in current missiological engagement. The explicit cultural values of honor–shame are often hidden in bare sight. Appreciating honor–shame cultural values and their impact on Christian theology will boost an understanding of violent societies in Africa. A

---

44. J. November, *Honor/Shame Cultures: A Beginner's Guide to Cross-Cultural Missions*, ed. R. Hewett (independently published, 2017), 60, https://books.google.co.ke/books?id=gND7swEACAAJ.

45. November, *Honor/Shame Cultures*, 61.

46. November, 61.

reimagination of mission theology through honor–shame lenses is required for the church to develop tools for ministering in Africa's violent societies.

In the event of conflict, reconciliation ought to be approached as honor restoration, since honor is a limited good in African societies. This is an opportunity for community leaders of warring tribes in Africa to give honor to their enemies with the assistance of Christian leaders. Such Christian leaders must be conversant with the underlying honor–shame dynamics in play, which lead either to humiliation or to mutual respect. Just as biblical honor is both ascribed and achieved, so are honor categories in African cultures. Honor in the Bible and the desire to avoid shame can be used to disciple African communities in a different way to deter violence or reconcile communities.

A reminder to give honor and use biblical shaming can be leveraged to both deter Africans from participating in violent acts and restore violent offenders back into the community. While ministering in an African context, the church needs to be sensitized to the pervasiveness of the honor–shame dynamics present. For African Christians, discipleship must warn people of the temptation to defend one's honor as it could spark violence. Finally, just because someone does not defend his or her honor does not mean that person does not have it. Good honor is ascribed by God through the familial relationship that Christians share with God. Hence Christians are honorable children of God carrying all the honor there is on earth because of their kinship relationship with Jesus Christ.

Bibliography

Bates, Matthew W. *Salvation by Allegiance Alone: Rethinking Faith, Works, and the Gospel of Jesus the King*. Grand Rapids, MI: Baker Academic, 2017.

Chiang, Samuel E., and Grant Lovejoy, eds. *Beyond Literate Western Contexts: Honor and Shame and Assessment of Orality Preference*. Hong Kong: International Orality Network, 2015.

Deng, Francis M. "Ethnicity: An African Predicament." *The Brookings Review* 15, no. 3 (1997): 28–31.

deSilva, D. A. *Honor, Patronage, Kinship and Purity: Unlocking New Testament Culture*. Downers Grove, IL: InterVarsity Press, 2000.

———. "The Noble Contest: Honor, Shame, and the Rhetorical Strategy of 4 Maccabees." *Journal for the Study of the Pseudepigrapha* 7, no. 13 (1 Apr. 1995): 31–57. https://doi.org/10.1177/095182079500001303.

Francis, David J. "Peace-Building in Africa." In *Peace and Conflict in Africa*, 113–130. London/New York: Zed Books, 2008.

Freeman, Sandra. "Honor/Shame Dynamics in Sub-Saharan Africa." *Mission Frontiers* 37, no. 1 (Feb. 2015): 32–33.

Georges, Jayson. *The 3D Gospel: Ministry in Guilt, Shame, and Fear Cultures*. N.p.: Timē Press, 2014.

———. "Why Has Nobody Told Me This Before?: The Gospel the World Is Waiting For." *Mission Frontiers* 37, no. 1 (Feb. 2015): 6–10.

Georges, Jayson, and Mark D. Baker. *Ministering in Honor–Shame Cultures: Biblical Foundations and Practical Essentials*. Downers Grove, IL: IVP Academic, 2016.

Haar, Gerrie ter. *Religion: Source of Conflict or Resource for Peace?* London: Brill, 2004.

Mahlangu, E. "The Ancient Mediterranean Values of Honour and Shame as a Hermeneutical Procedure: A Social-Scientific Criticism in an African Perspective." *Verbum et Ecclesia* 22, no. 1 (2001): 85–101.

Malina, Bruce J. *The New Testament World: Insights from Cultural Anthropology*. Louisville, KY: Westminster John Knox, 1993.

Mbuvi, Andrew. "African Theology from the Perspective of Honor and Shame." In *The Urban Face of Mission: Ministering the Gospel in a Diverse and Changing World*, edited by Harvie M. Conn, Manuel Ortiz, and Susan S. Baker, 279–295. Phillipsburg: P&R, 2002.

———. "The Ancient Mediterranean Values of 'Honour and Shame' as a Hermeneutical Lens of Reading the Book of Job." *Old Testament Essays* 23, no. 3 (2010): 752–768.

Mischke, Werner. *The Global Gospel: Achieving Missional Impact in Our Multicultural World*. Scottsdale, AZ: Mission ONE, 2015.

Muloongo, Keith, Roger Kibasomba, and Jemima N. Kariri, eds. *The Many Faces of Human Security: Case Studies of Seven Countries in Southern Africa*. Pretoria: Institute for Security Studies, 2005.

Neyrey, Jerome H. *Honor and Shame in the Gospel of Matthew*. Louisville, KY: Westminster John Knox, 1998.

November, J. *Honor/Shame Cultures: A Beginner's Guide to Cross-Cultural Missions*. Edited by R. Hewett. Independently published, 2017. https://books.google.co.ke/books?id=gND7swEACAAJ.

Piper, John. "Faith in Future Grace vs. Misplaced Shame." In *Future Grace: The Purifying Power of the Promises of God*. Colorado Springs, CO: Multnomah, 2012.

Tennent, Timothy C. *Theology in the Context of World Christianity: How the Global Church Is Influencing the Way We Think about and Discuss Theology*. Grand Rapids, MI: Zondervan, 2007.

14

Interreligious Dialogue as Means for Public Theology

Promises and Challenges for Social Justice and Democracy in Kenya

Elias K. Ng'etich
Lecturer, the Department of Religious Studies
Moi University, Eldoret, Kenya

Abstract

Interreligious dialogue is arguably an outstanding feature of the contemporary globalized world. The belief that no single culture, religion, or ideology has ultimate claim to be the voice of truth is a key challenge that necessitates the need for interreligious dialogue. The church in Kenya needs a paradigm shift in its understanding of what it means to be the church in a pluralistic society with diverse competing religious groups. This calls for an accommodative space for constructive theological engagement with the world, not just in spreading the gospel but also in contexts of democracy and social justice. It is the argument of this research that interreligious dialogue as an instrument of public theology ought to be a commitment of the church in Africa as it can propel a personal, social, and cultural revolution in a milieu of religious and political diversity. Though there is no adequate theology of interreligious dialogue, there is nevertheless a need to engage in public theology with a view to promoting and enhancing social justice and democracy in contexts. In this respect, the research argues various theological strands for dialogue with respect to public theology, broadening its implications to the challenges and promises of interreligious dialogue explorations in the Kenyan context, particularly regarding social justice and democracy.

Key words: interreligious dialogue, public theology, social justice, Vatican II, democracy.

The Concept of Interreligious Dialogue

In its etymology, the term "dialogue" has roots in the Greek word *dia* which means "through" and *logos* meaning "word." Taken literally, therefore, dialogue can mean "through word." Dialogue thus has the implication of talking or conversing with a view to understanding one another. In a religious context, interreligious dialogue is predominantly a conversation occurring in the context of diverse religious backgrounds and beliefs. Interreligious dialogue must happen not only between people of different faiths but in an environment of acceptance and mutual trust. The atmosphere must be conducive. Interreligious dialogue is about more than just becoming informed or enlightened about other religions; it is also a chance to fundamentally re-experience one's own faith. At its best, the dialogue helps to remove historical prejudices, ultimately leading to new possibilities for working together for the common good.[1] Interreligious dialogue means "all positive and constructive interreligious relations with individuals and communities of other faiths which are directed at mutual understanding and enrichment."[2] As such, it covers in its breadth an examination of different religious persuasions grounded in respect and love.[3] As Father Francis Arinze notes, interreligious dialogue in the African context ought to be aimed at peace matters and not just be mere conversations.[4] He observes that interreligious dialogue is a necessary skill and a worldview worth embracing with openness of mind. It is indeed true that, being a significant aspect of human life, interreligious dialogue can be utilized creatively as an indispensable instrument of evangelization. Jacques Dupuis's definition of

---

1. S. Wesley Ariarajah, "Interfaith Dialogue," in *Dictionary of the Ecumenical Movement,* ed. Nicholas Lossky et al., 2nd ed. (Geneva: WCC, 2002), 314.

2. Pontifical Council for Inter-Religious Dialogue, "Dialogue and Proclamation," accessed 9 August 2019, http://www.vatican.va/roman_curia/pontifical_councils/interelg/documents/rc_pc_interelg_doc_19051991_dialogue-and-proclamatio_en.html.

3. Pontifical Council for Inter-Religious Dialogue, "Dialogue and Proclamation."

4. Cardinal Francis Arinze, *Meeting Other Believers* (Nairobi: Paulines Publications Africa, 1997), 9–10.

interreligious dialogue best expresses the thoughts of this research in relation to interreligious dialogue and democracy: "As a specific, integral element of evangelization, dialogue means all positive and constructive interreligious relations with individuals and communities of other faiths, which are directed at mutual understanding and enrichment, in obedience to truth and respect for freedom. It includes both witness and the exploration of respective religious convictions."[5]

The Case of Vatican II and the Interreligious Dialogue in the Catholic Church

Taking place between 1962 and 1965, the Vatican II Council emerged historically both as a formidable force in the Catholic Church and as the most momentous religious event of the twentieth century. By its establishment, the Council wrought numerous changes that reformed the Church to influence not only all the Christian churches but also other religions and their political convictions. In essence, the Council aimed to deepen the spirituality and zeal of the Catholic Church to constructively face the innumerable challenges facing it on a global scale. In responding to contemporary challenges and at the same time clearly and intelligently teaching the gospel, the Catholic Church was, in essence, practicing public theology. The permeation of the gospel through all levels of society demanded a change of approach with regard to evangelization because of the reality of religious pluralism. Out of Vatican II sixteen documents emerged, most of which had a bearing on interreligious dialogue and evangelization.

Of relevance to this discussion are the "Pastoral Constitution on the Church in the Modern World (*Gaudium et Spes*)," 7 December 1965; the "Decree on the Church's Missionary Activity (*Ad Gentes*)," 7 December 1965; and the "Declaration on the Relationship of the Church to Non-Christian Religions (*Nostra Aetate*)," 28 October 1965. These documents continue to be a source of spiritual wealth given to the Church even in the context of diverse political ideologies. They illustrate the grace to effectively evangelize, by way of dialogue, the society in which we find people of different faiths. Since Vatican II, the Church has constantly sought to implement this mandate. This should be a wakeup call to other denominations to actively respond to

---

5. Jacques Dupuis, *Toward a Christian Theology of Religious Pluralism* (New York: Orbis, 2002), 358–359.

the political challenges of our times through public theology in the form of interreligious dialogue.

The commitment of the Catholic Church to dialogue since Vatican II is an undeniable historical fact. The official teaching of the Church and its establishment of interreligious commissions with various levels of engagement bears witness to this commitment. The institution of the Second Vatican Council by Pope John XXIII had great success and bearings on the mission of the Catholic Church. A key aspect was its pronouncement that all humanity was within reach of God's grace. As a significant theological development, this declaration recognized interreligious dialogue, among other things, as a crucial feature of the Church's call to evangelism. Theologically, within the Vatican II documents, *Gaudium et Spes* teaches that at Christ's incarnation, God united himself in some sense with every human being and that this applies not only to Christians but to all persons of goodwill, in whose hearts grace is active invisibly.[6] *Nostra Aetate*, the Vatican II declaration on non-Christian religions, suggests that there is a ray of that truth which enlightens all other traditions.[7] The Vatican II declaration "On the Missionary Activity of the Church," *Ad Gentes*, recognizes the Scriptures as the seed which God uses to reach out to all nations of the earth.[8] *Lumen Gentium*, the "Constitution on the Church," refers to the good which is established in the rites, cultures, and customs of people.[9] Vatican II was a call for Catholics to dialogue and collaborate graciously with people from different faiths. Interreligious dialogue thus became a vital part of the life and mission of the Catholic Church worldwide. To ignore the importance of interreligious dialogue is therefore out of line with the Church's official teaching. To fail to be involved in dialogue is, to some extent, to hold back the effectiveness of the Church's evangelization.

---

6. "Pastoral Constitution on the Church in the Modern World: *Gaudium et Spes*, Promulgated by His Holiness, Pope Paul VI, on December 7, 1965," accessed 9 August 2019, http://www.vatican.va/archive/hist_councils/ii_vatican_council/documents/vat-ii_const_19651207_gaudium-et-spes_en.html.

7. "Declaration on the Relation of the Church to Non-Christian Religions: *Nostra Aetate*, Proclaimed by His Holiness Pope Paul VI on October 28, 1965," accessed 9 August 2019, http://www.vatican.va/archive/hist_councils/ii_vatican_council/documents/vat-ii_decl_19651028_nostra-aetate_en.html.

8. "Decree *Ad Gentes* on the Mission Activity of the Church," accessed 9 August 2019, http://www.vatican.va/archive/hist_councils/ii_vatican_council/documents/vat-ii_decree_19651207_ad-gentes_en.html.

9. "Dogmatic Constitution on the Church: *Lumen Gentium*, Solemnly Promulgated by His Holiness Pope Paul VI on November 21, 1964, accessed 9 August 2019, https://www.vatican.va/archive/hist_councils/ii_vatican_council/documents/vat-ii_const_19641121_lumen-gentium_en.html.

Vatican II furthered a richer and more accurate self-understanding of the Church to expand its missional mandate to include dialogue with other faiths. This self-understanding also influenced the Church's ecclesiology in relation to worldwide missions and what it means to be church. The Church would not have reached this point were it not for the challenges of the time. As noted by Bonaventure Kloppenburg, "The Church is a pilgrim, set down in the midst of history and therefore inevitably and deeply marked and conditioned by events,"[10] and so it was with Vatican II. The Council distinguished itself more by a new approach to unity and evangelization than by explanations of Christian doctrine. Specifically, the Vatican II Council's missionary attitude in the face of the contemporary challenges provided an opportunity to enter into dialogue and cooperation with non-Catholics and non-believers. This has largely equipped the Church as the worldwide agent of salvation. This was a critical shift theologically. Such a shift ought not to be limited to a denomination or section of the Christian church but rather should be expanded as a means of God's voice on contemporary issues relating to social justice and democracy as well as the evangelization process.

Interreligious Dialogue and Public Theology

The presence of competing religious perspectives confronts our contemporary world in a new and forceful way, especially as regards the public sphere on issues of politics, democracy, and social influence. The key question is, with a recognition of genuine religious diversity, what approach should we take in using our Christian faith for the common good in contexts of competing religious perspectives? My suggestion is public theology. This is because, in essence, public theology is a means by which the Christian faith enters the public space as an influential conversational tool in extending God's kingdom through social and political transformation. The concept is clearly set out by the Berlin Institute of Public Theology when it states in its Mission Statement that "Public Theology, understood as theologically informed interdisciplinary discourse on public issues and the scholarly reflection thereof, is of paramount importance in modern societies which tend to be pluralistic in regard to religions and comprehensive worldviews. It involves the plural perspectives of faith into public debates and allows for a critical reflection of those perspectives.

---

10. Bonaventure Kloppenburg O.F.M., *Ecclesiology of Vatican II* (Chicago: Franciscan Herald Press, 1974), 2.

Thus, it enables public scrutiny of those perspectives while enriching public discourse by the contribution of religious perspectives."[11]

This sounds good as an approach or a means by which theological perspectives and ideas can penetrate and transform the public discourse for the common good; however, it is controversial. This is because there is no single established methodology that is universally acceptable to scholars, nor has there been a recognized theology in reference to public theology. I would suggest that the way of interreligious dialogue is perhaps plausible. In the contemporary pluralistic context, Christian public theology has to effectively bring on board other religions in order to bring about the common good in spite of varied theological perspectives. This also is not comprehensive because no theology has yet been developed on interreligious dialogue. As a contemporary concern, public theology by means of interreligious dialogue has to wrestle with two major concerns: first, the growing dialogue between different religions in varied contexts; and second, the role of these religions in the democratic nation state in a period of international geopolitical change and realignment. Interreligious dialogue, though only a recently emerging concept, is already transforming the way in which religion is being approached, studied, and embraced in the global environment. Dialogue takes numerous forms but, most importantly, not only affects the identity of a particular religion but also makes an impression on the place of religion in society as a whole.

The need for public theology especially in the African context is inevitable. Public theology by means of interreligious dialogue ought to strengthen Christianity's relations with other religions and with a positive consequential impact on social practices, networks, and institutions that promote functions ascribed to civil society. As such, interreligious dialogue should be a means of trust that nurtures participatory citizenship for the holistic development of society. Meaningful and creative interreligious dialogue makes Christian faith into a significant force in the public sphere. The need and call for public theology come at a time when the role of religion in society is suspect and when even its demise is anticipated, certainly in the Western world. Religions in Africa continue to impact the public sphere in different ways.

Interreligious dialogue is necessary because it has a connection with political and international relations. Alan Race and Ingrid Shafer note that "As a persistent marker of cultural and national identity, religion as such continues

---

11. Berlin Institute for Public Theology (Theologische Fakultät der Humboldt-Universität zu Berlin), "Mission Statement," accessed 17 January 2019, https://www.theologie.hu-berlin.de/de/bipt.

to exert influence as a player in negotiations to chart a way through the maze of political fragmentation which paradoxically accompanies the unifying momentum of globalization."[12] The practice of public theology by any given religion faces difficulties. The tensions of religion bringing society together or causing division and disintegration, between religious revival and decline, and of the competing and conflicting interests of religious groups and civil society greatly hinder the practice of interreligious dialogue.

Public Theology and Civil Society as Contested Space

> Civil society is that part of social life that lies beyond the immediate reach of the state and which . . . must exist for a democratic state to flower. It is the society of households, family networks, civic and religious organizations, and communities that are bound to each other primarily by shared histories, collective memories and cultural norms of reciprocity.[13]

The above quotation has the usefulness of specifying the kinds of social institutions associated with civil society. It is however inadequate in addressing how civil society is supposed to produce its democratizing effects. Historically, religion has been a critical resource for the moral foundations without which the state in all its endeavors to establish social justice and democratic leadership crumbles. George Washington noted this in his "Farewell Address" in 1776: "Of all the disposition and habits which lead to political prosperity, religion and morality are indispensable supports . . . Let it simply be asked where the security for property, for reputation, for life, is if the sense of religious obligation deserts the oaths, which are the instrument of the investigation in courts of justice."[14] Interreligious dialogue and democracy reinforce one another.

Democracy is necessary in order to create the space for mutual respect in which dialogue can flourish, and dialogue is necessary in order to keep democracy alert to the different needs and gifts that spring from diverse cultural histories. In this sense, interreligious dialogue and democracy offer each other both challenges and opportunities. The challenges are clearly seen

---

12. Alan Race and Ingrid Shafer, *Religions in Dialogue: From Theocracy to Democracy* (Aldershot: Ashgate, 2002), 4.

13. Mike Douglass and John Friedmann, eds., *Cities for Citizens: Planning and the Rise of Civil Society in a Global Age* (London: John Wiley, 1998), 2.

14. W. B. Allen, ed., *George Washington: A Collection* (Indianapolis: Liberty Classics, 1988), 521–522.

in the African, and specifically the Kenyan, context when theologians, say, of Christian and Muslim religions, develop their own reasoning in relation to a democratic vision. This challenge arises because each religion speaks from its roots and histories, yet with a willingness to listen and learn. Another challenge is that, just as interreligious dialogue takes a number of forms, so inevitably does the embodiment of democracy in the world's diverse cultural, national, and religious settings. In a democratic context where the principles of freedom, toleration, and human rights are highly prized, the different religions are challenged to re-examine their attitudes and effectiveness regarding the basic vision of democracy itself. Democracy, therefore, makes its own demands on the religions to move beyond stereotyping and suspicion by developing models of cooperation and pluralistic understanding. This can only be accomplished from a deep sense of religious trust, dialogical commitment, and intellectual integrity.

Dialogue

Dialogue is more than mere conversation; it is a worldview of meanings and reflections. In the context of religion, dialogue is a way of thinking and seeing beyond your belief systems with a view to understanding and not judging. To be involved in dialogue is, therefore, to risk and become vulnerable, to go beyond the absolutes in order to learn from "the other." It is to have a tête-à-tête with someone with different views, with the aim of learning from the other. Dialogue is a discipline that calls for the suspension of prejudice and seeing the viewpoint of the other. Our learning and growing in the process of dialogue does not mean we impose our views or change the views of others; it is not, therefore, a debate but a constructive conversation. It is indeed right, as noted by Race and Shafer, that "true and genuine dialogue removes obstructions that tend to cloud our vision as it releases passionate moral energy, intensifies social responsibility and deepens spirituality. Such intensive encounters energize participants to translate dialogical potency and passion into socially responsible action."[15]

The church and its public theology manifesto and the political community of varied contexts are independent and autonomous from each other. The church's public theology must rise to the occasion in any given context to address and respond to both the personal and the social challenges of the respective communities. Through interreligious dialogue, public theology can

---

15. Race and Shafer, *Religions in Dialogue*, 9.

help foster healthier cooperation between the two, bringing about positive and transformative services and ministries for the common good. Interreligious dialogue as a means of public theology should address issues of social living. Without common concern for the political context, interreligious harmony will promote a false and unjust harmony.[16] Christian public theology by means of interreligious dialogue can work politically and democratically for the liberation of poor and marginalized people.

Social Justice

Since, according to Christian theology, all human dignity is grounded in the image of God, the best service that the church and Christians in general can offer is to empower people to control their lives. This reality extends the struggle for justice to cover gender and ecology. In the midst of the ambivalence of cultural, political, and economic realities, public theology should prepare the way for social and political transformation based on social justice. Indeed, within Christian communities there are movements of justice and compassion. All these are true marks of public theology that need to be embraced right from the local church context; they are clear indicators of the presence of God through human agency in the world.

The biggest challenge to this in the Kenyan context, as echoed from Western history, is the separation of religion and state. Christianity seems to be quite distant from the state, but, on the other hand, Islam and other religions greatly seek to influence the apparatus of the state to reflect their religion. Religion will still remain a basic source of ethics in any given state. The foundation of most societal ethics for the state remains the various religions. Historically that has been true for Western civilization, especially in relation to Judeo-Christian religious traditions. Public theology has in its agenda the responsibility to clarify democracy. This is because the relationship between Christianity and democracy is an uncertain one: challenges arising in democracy emanate from various multicultural and multifaith contexts, and public theology has to deal with this dilemma. Theologically, democracy is to be valued, measured, and judged in relation to the framework of the understanding of the kingdom of God. There has to be a balance between the inner life of the soul and the outer life of society. The former informs the latter. We must not be so eschatological that we neglect the needs of the world today.

---

16. Race and Shafer, 61.

Implications, Challenges, and the Promise of Interreligious Dialogue as a Means for Public Theology in African Context

Today God calls the church in Africa, particularly Kenya, to dialogue through the challenges we are facing. Refugees and migration continually bring people of other religions closer to us. Terrorism and the tension often witnessed between Christians and Muslims offer an opportunity to fully understand Islam and dialogue with them. Unfortunately, fear and suspicion have reigned. With dialogue, misunderstandings and hostilities are rebuffed. Dialogue is indispensable to uphold peace. By way of dialogue, the church can make the good news known; this is evangelization. Evangelization involves proclamation with a view to inviting others to believe in that which is being proclaimed. Dialogue involves bearing witness to Christian beliefs as espoused by the church, while also being open to sincerely listen to others. These are the two arms of evangelization that perfectly supplement each other. They do, however, have challenges.

Hindrances to Interreligious Dialogue as an Instrument of Public Theology

Polemics

The attempt to always link Christianity to colonialism, imperialism, and aggressive missionary strategies undermines the whole process of public theology. Historically, Christianity has had other forms that have not embraced these behaviors and have even succeeded in opposing them. We cannot advance dialogue by telling any faith community's story in the darkest of terms and with reference to the basest motives and most eccentric popular belief.

Lack of Self-Critical Identity

Dialogue may sometimes involve debates that strongly address troubling issues. It should be understood, however, that in debating, we are not in an exercise of deconstructing the faith of others. Difficult conversations within religious contexts can positively lead to great learning and listening.

The Promise of Public Theology in the Kenyan Context

Dialogue should be sought in the context of institutions and structures supported by authority. For public theology to have positive success it has to be collaborative and project-oriented, aiming at such projects as peacemaking, conflict resolution, and humanitarian and pastoral needs. Public theology has the promise of taking advantage of scholarship in support of activism that ensures critical oversight and a close relationship to real communities of real people. The promise of public theology in Africa and Kenya, in particular, is related to the goals of education and to a broad-based understanding of what each faith is, believes, and does. Its promise lies also in the acknowledgment of social and scientific progress that can foster viable cultural exchange as part of the dialogue process.

Conclusion

In light of the above, I propose that interreligious dialogue as a means of public theology can enhance not only a wide interface of contacts, including theology, spirituality, and ethics, but also education, scientific exchange, culture, and political transformation. Interreligious dialogue should be aimed not at creating a single religion but at diminishing intolerant impulses by means of mutual understanding, respect, and cooperation in the context of public theology. In particular, interreligious dialogue as a means of public theology can work on conflict resolution, humanitarian assistance, education, social justice, peacemaking, and sober democratic principles. It is the work of public theology, therefore, to create the climate within which social justice and democratic principles can proceed in a fruitful manner.

Christian dialogue is profoundly entrenched in the Trinity and is best expressed in love for all humanity irrespective of their religious background. The church is empowered and strengthened to dialogue by the power of the Holy Spirit who provides effectual grace to thus reach out to other religions on amicable and conducive platforms. As 1 Peter 3:15 states, for the church to practice public theology effectively through interreligious dialogue they are required to be grounded and well informed in their faith. Interreligious dialogue, it must be noted, is not about conceding faith but about gently regarding the beliefs of others with a view to extending God's kingdom.

It is through the call of public theology that the church makes sincere efforts to make the gospel known by other religions as well as to understand other faiths. Through willingness to dialogue, the church shows solidarity with the whole human family regardless of religion, race, or culture. This ought to be our mission in the Kenyan context. To take advantage of technological advances, religious tensions, and migrations to strengthen bonds of friendship with non-Christians should be our goal as the church.

Interreligious dialogue brings out the best in all religions in a uniting and redeeming manner, thus minimizing the disruptive and manipulative tendencies of religions that have been witnessed in the past. In contrast to such divisive and manipulative roles, interreligious dialogue seeks to develop the unifying and liberating potential of all religions. Justice, peace, and human well-being thus become the relevance of religion. Interreligious dialogue not only becomes a means of evangelization, but also fosters peaceful and meaningful neighborliness with members of other religions, thus enhancing social justice and strengthening democratic principles.

Bibliography

Allen, W. B., ed. *George Washington: A Collection*. Indianapolis: Liberty Classics, 1988.

Ariarajah, S. Wesley. "Interfaith Dialogue." In *Dictionary of the Ecumenical Movement*, edited by Nicholas Lossky et al. 2nd ed. Geneva: WCC, 2002.

Arinze, Cardinal Francis. *Meeting Other Believers*. Nairobi: Pauline's Publications Africa, 1997.

Baum, Gregory, O.S.A. *The Teachings of the Second Vatican Council; Complete Texts of the Constitutions, and Declarations*. Westminster, MD: Newman Press, 1966.

Berlin Institute for Public Theology (Theologische Fakultät der Humboldt-Universität zu Berlin). "Mission Statement." Accessed 17 January 2019. https://www.theologie. hu-berlin.de/de/bipt.

"Declaration on the Relation of the Church to Non-Christian Religions: *Nostra Aetate*, Proclaimed by His Holiness Pope Paul VI on October 28, 1965." Accessed 9 August 2019. http://www.vatican.va/archive/hist_councils/ii_vatican_council/ documents/vat-ii_decl_19651028_nostra-aetate_en.html.

"Decree *Ad Gentes* on the Mission Activity of the Church." Accessed 9 August 2019. http://www.vatican.va/archive/hist_councils/ii_vatican_council/documents/ vat-ii_decree_19651207_ad-gentes_en.html.

"Dogmatic Constitution on the Church: *Lumen Gentium*, Solemnly Promulgated by His Holiness Pope Paul VI on November 21, 1964. Accessed 9 August 2019. https:// www.vatican.va/archive/hist_councils/ii_vatican_council/documents/vat-ii_ const_19641121_lumen-gentium_en.html.

Douglass, Mike, and John Friedmann, eds. *Cities for Citizens: Planning and the Rise of Civil Society in a Global Age*. London: John Wiley, 1998.

Dupuis, Jacques. *Toward a Christian Theology of Religious Pluralism*. New York: Orbis, 2002.

Flannery, Austin, O.P., ed. *Vatican Council II: Constitutions, Decrees, Declarations – A Completely Revised Translation in Inclusive Language*. Northport, NY: Costello, 1996. Accessed 9 August 2019. www.urbandharma.org/pdf/NostraAetate.pdf.

Fletcher, Jeannine Hill. "As Long As We Wonder: Possibilities in the Impossibility of Interreligious Dialogue." *Theological Studies* 68 (2007): 531–554.

Kloppenburg, Bonaventure, O.F.M. *Ecclesiology of Vatican II*. Chicago: Franciscan Herald Press, 1974.

Knitter, F. Paul. "Catholics and Other Religions Bridging the Gap between Dialogue and Theology." *Louvain Studies* 24 (1999): 319–354.

"Pastoral Constitution on the Church in the Modern World: *Gaudium et Spes*, Promulgated by His Holiness, Pope Paul VI, on December 7, 1965." Accessed 9 August 2019. http://www.vatican.va/archive/hist_councils/ii_vatican_council/documents/vat-ii_const_19651207_gaudium-et-spes_en.html.

Pontifical Council for Inter-Religious Dialogue. "Dialogue and Proclamation." Accessed 9 August 2019. www.vatican.va/roman_curia/pontifical_councils/interelg/documents/rc_pc_interelg_doc_19051991_dialogue-and-proclamatio_en.html.

Race, Alan, and Ingrid Shafer. *Religions in Dialogue: From Theocracy to Democracy.* Aldershot: Ashgate, 2002.

Willis, Michelle. *Vatican II: Summary and Reflection of Vatican II Documents.* Ocean East Publishing, 2008. http://docplayer.net/21012148-Vatican-ii-summary-and-reflection-of-vatican-ii-documents-michelle-willis-2008-ocean-east-publishing.html.

15

Integrative Systems of Pastoral Care and Counseling for Victims of Violence in Kenya

A Biblical, Classical, Clinical, Prophetic, Contextual, and Reframing Approach for African Christianity

Ndung'u J. B. Ikenye

Professor and Clinical Psychologist

St Paul's University, Limuru, Kenya

Abstract

There are multiple forms of violence in Kenya today: marital and family violence, sexual violence, political and economic violence, and religious and interethnic violence. This chapter answers the following questions: (1) What are the Christian responses as interventions (in terms of individual, familial, and communal systems) to the victims of these multiple kinds of violence? (2) What kind of pastoral care and counseling (competent and effective Christian theory and practice of care) is needed for the victims of violence in Kenya? This chapter uses a case study of Kenya in the qualitative method of research to answer these two questions. It proposes a biblical, classical, clinical, prophetic, contextual, and reframing model and method of pastoral care and counseling as an integrative systems approach to healing Kenyan victims of the multiple forms of violence. This integrative systems approach begins with the use of the classical functions of pastoral care and counseling: healing, guiding, reconciling, and sustaining. In order to expand the paradigm of pastoral functions in Kenyan contexts, the chapter proposes that decolonization, faithing, disciplining, discipling, and empowerment be added to the classical functions. Christians who are victims of the multiple forms of violence are informed by their faith in Christ and walk in the Holy Spirit; thus, as proposed in this chapter, they have an option to engage the multiple forms of violence for the purposes of forgiveness, peaceful coexistence, healing and reconciliation, and development. The integrative systems theory, model, and practice of pastoral care and counseling recommended here is the message of Christ to all peoples and nations of the world (acknowledgment of sin and sinfulness, confession, forgiveness, absolution, and acceptance) and to Kenyan Christians specifically.

Key words: multiple forms of violence; biblical, classical, clinical, prophetic, contextual, and reframing pastoral care and counseling.

Introduction

Contemporary Kenyan ways of life (personal, communal, and national) are governed by a mixture of multidimensional and complex systems, local and international in the global village, all affecting systems of violence in Kenya. There is a contradiction (lack of consistency and continuity of ethos and values in life) and paradoxical (blessings and curses of life are not explicit but implicit in life) existence in postcolonial Kenya as multiple systems seek to coexist: jumping from one era and ethos of existence (from traditional to modern and postmodern systems), dependency, reactionism, and circumstances of the moment (including existential poverty and mental poverty). These contradictory and paradoxical systems of existence lead to anger expressed outwardly and toward others, leading to multiple forms of violence, or to depression as anger expressed inwardly or as violence toward self. As this study will show, multiple aspects of contemporary life are affecting systems of violence in Kenya. This chapter has four sections: part 1 covers the background to pastoral care and counseling; part 2 covers the dynamics of violence in Kenya; part 3 covers the multiple forms of violence in Kenya; and part 4 discusses the theory, method, and practice of pastoral care and counseling for the victims of violence.

This chapter argues that these three eras, each with its own ethos (traditional, modern, and postmodern), as well as personal, communal, and national circumstances, stand as the backbone to contemporary Kenyan life and to systems of violence and their transmission. For the purposes of this study, we use[1] six theoretical resources to form a wide lens to address the multiple levels and dimensions to the systems of violence and also to address the systems of intervention: Graham who uses the psychosystemic approach (psyches of persons and forces of the world around persons) in pastoral care and counseling in linking symptoms, crises, and change to strategic love and redemptive justice; McNeill who uses care and cure of the human soul (essence of human personality) interchangeably as tasks of pastoral care and counseling with special focus on guidance of souls in the New Testament; and Clebesch and Jaekle who focus on defining pastoral care and four pastoral functions, and also on the aspects of the "representative function of clergy, troubled persons, meaningful troubles and helping acts." Hiltner and Colston are helpful in bringing up the issues of setting, expectation, relationship, and aims and limitations of pastoral care and counseling and the role and office; Clinebell and Wise are helpful in their focus on the biblical basis of pastoral care and counseling as communicating the inner meaning of the gospel and the role of insight (truth), faith, forgiveness, rites and rituals, mature and immature religious attitudes, prayer and use of Scripture versus magical formulae; and our theory and practice introduces African Christian experience that includes testimony of holistic salvation, liberation from colonial Christianity, and empowerment and nurture of a mature and meaningful African faith in the context of ethnicity and culture. These six authors inform the integrative theory and practice of pastoral care and counseling for victims of violence. We also use Miller and Ikenye to determine the dates and dynamics of the

---

1. Larry Kent Graham, *Care of Persons, Care of World: A Psychosystems Approach to Pastoral Care and Counseling* (Nashville: Abingdon, 1992), 13–69; John T. McNeill, *A History of the Cure of Souls* (New York: Harper & Row, 1951), vii–xii, 67–87; William A. Clebesch and Charles R. Jaekle, *Pastoral Care in a Historical Perspective* (New York: Jason Aronson, 1975), 4–10, 33–66; A. Hiltner and Lowell G. Colston, *The Context of Pastoral Counseling* (Nashville: Abingdon, 1961), 24–42; F. Lake, *Clinical Theology: A Theological and Psychological Basis to Clinical Pastoral Care* (London: Darton, Longman & Todd, 1986), 29–37; Howard Clinebell, *Basic Types of Pastoral Care and Counseling* (Nashville: Abingdon, 1994), 25–46; Carroll A. Wise, *The Meaning of Pastoral Care* (New York: Harper & Row, 1966; reprint ed. 1989), 1–34; Carrol A. Wise, *Pastoral Counseling: Its Theory and Practice* (New York: Harper & Brothers, 1951), 1–167; Ndung'u Ikenye, *African Christian Counseling: Method, Theory and Practice* (Nairobi: Envoy Graphics and Print Systems, 2002), 49–93; Ndung'u Ikenye, *African Pastoral Counseling: An Integrative Theory, Research, Method and Model of Practice in African Christianity* (Thika, Kenya: Joroi Counseling Consultants and Researchers, 2014), 23–96; and Caroline Knowles, "Theorising Race and Ethnicity: Contemporary Paradigms and Perspectives," in *The Sage Handbook of Race and Ethnic Studies*, ed. Patricia H. Collins and John Solomos (Los Angeles: Sage, 2010), 1–42.

three eras and their ethoses, namely, traditional, modern, and postmodern.[2] In these three eras, there is a trend of transmission of violence in the context of politics, religion, economy, philosophy, relationships, functioning in families and extended kinship, and emotions. These three eras and ethoses form the backbone of individual, marital, ethnic, and cultural systems of violence. Violence in this context is understood as person-oriented and id-, ego-, and superego-oriented, beginning from early childhood conflicts; as marital-oriented, beginning with marital problems; as family-oriented, beginning with problems of relationships in family systems; and in collective violence, as communal systems of violence as perpetrated by traditionalism, tribalism, monoculturalism, colonialism, and neocolonialism – meaning that violence, as discussed in this chapter, is perpetrated and perpetuated in the personal and communal self and national–international systems of violating the lives of others. Multiple levels of intervention using the integrative approach in pastoral care and counseling are proposed to bring healing into the lives of victims who experience violence.

Definition of Pastoral Care and Counseling in the African Christian Context (Ikenye)[3]

The second part of this chapter is focused on transforming the lives of the victims of personal, marital, familial, and collective violence. A systems approach[4] is used to develop the integrative Christian approach to healing and transforming lives of victims of violence: biblical, classical, clinical, prophetic, contextual, and reframing methods and models of pastoral care and counseling. This means that African Christian pastoral care and counseling for the victims of violence is defined[5] as the "art and science of in-depth caring ministry of communicating the inner meaning of the gospel through a relationship with one another and God" and the pastor or a designated and set-apart person; meeting persons at their multiple points of need within the biblical, classical, clinical, contextual, prophetic, reframing paradigms, and within the church traditions of care and

---

2. D. Rhoades, "Social Justice Issues in Pastoral Care," in *Dictionary of Pastoral Care and Counseling*, ed. Rodney J. Hunter (Nashville: Abingdon, 1990), 1189–1190; James B. Miller, "The Emerging Postmodern World," in *Postmodern Theology: Christian Faith in a Pluralist World*, ed. F. Burnham (San Francisco: Harper & Row, 1989), 1–13; and Ndung'u Ikenye, *Decolonization of the Kenyan Soul* (Nairobi: Envoy Graphics and Print Systems, 2002), 14–21.

3. Ikenye, *African Pastoral Counseling*, 52.

4. C. W. Stewart, "Systems Theory," in Hunter, *Dictionary*, 1250–1251.

5. Ikenye, *African Pastoral Counseling*, 14–21.

counseling ministry in the "ethical, psychological, ethnic and cultural contexts of optimal living; through mature pastoral relationships and within the core call of the Great Commission; and toward holistic and wholistic salvation in the communal contexts of ethnicity and culture of embeddedness."

The classical and clinical approach uses the four functions of pastoral care and counseling: healing, guiding, reconciliation, and sustaining.[6] For the purposes of expanding the paradigm of functions for the African contexts, this research proposes that decolonization, faithing, and empowerment be added to the classical functions of pastoral care and counseling.[7] The prophetic approach focuses on biblical aspects of truth-telling in season and out of season, of God's will for all people. The pastor's role is a priestly function, emphasizing that the truth sets people free, brings healing and reconciliation, and sustains and guides Christians.[8] The contextual approach focuses on the people of God sharing their contextual stories of the violence, pain, and suffering that affects the whole self;[9] thus the sharing of personal and communal stories will provide an opportunity for healing and reconciliation, and they will be sustained in their crisis moments and through the periods after the trauma. The reframing approach[10] focuses on envisioning, retelling, and rewriting of personal and communal stories as people weave their stories, pain, and suffering with the Christ-based and Christ-centered story, a story of a new self which is born in Christ. The six-systems model of theory and practice of care and counseling forms an integrative and multidimensional understanding and intervention systems perspective in the theory and practice of African Christian pastoral care and counseling. In this model and method, the counselor begins with Scripture and the Christian faith experience at the core of the model, theory, and practice. As a part of the theory and practice, we are reminded by Patton[11] that personal and communal systems and contexts of care and counseling will require remembering and re-remembering as parts of "being and doing"[12] and

---

6. Clebesch and Jaekle, *Pastoral Care*, 32–66.

7. Ndung'u Ikenye, *Modeling Servant-Leaders for Africa* (Eldoret, Kenya: Zapf Chancery, 2010), 32–36.

8. Charles V. Gerkin, *Prophetic Pastoral Care* (Nashville: Abingdon, 1991), 15–22, 32–67. John Patton, *Pastoral Care in Context: An Introduction to Pastoral Care* (Louisville, KY: Westminster John Knox, 1993), 159–184.

9. Patton, *Pastoral Care*, 159–184.

10. Donald Capps, *Reframing: A New Method in Pastoral Care* (Minneapolis: Fortress, 1990), 9–54.

11. Patton, *Pastoral Care*, 15–60.

12. Patton, 5–6.

bringing us into relationship with ourselves, our communities, and God. A systems approach in the integrative method in theory and practice of pastoral care and counseling will allow all these elements to interact as lenses in the lives of victims, and work together for holistic healing and transformation.

Systems of Violence in Kenya
Dynamics of Victimization in Violence

Victims are subjected to oppression, deprivation, suffering, and manipulation. Miller[13] argues that victimization and victims have to be understood within "sociological processes of change," especially in relation to change of values. Miller[14] further argues, and for our purposes, about the victims of institutional and cultural patterns (victims of cultural and ethnic violence) and in relationship to historicity. Miller's victimology can be interpreted for victims of cultural and ethnic violence. Victims of ethnic and cultural violence are characterized by experiences of powerlessness, stripping off power to be and to make choices, stereotyping, narrow definition of roles, inappropriate defining of roles and functions, constriction of interactions, constrictions on operating in their environments, and changes in status. On the other hand, the oppressed through violence also become oppressors; therefore victims of violence become perpetuators of cycles of violence.

Miller[15] argues that victims also struggle with a range of emotions, including anger, grief, guilt, shame, and anxiety. Kenyans from the three eras and ethoses (traditional, modern, and postmodern) have been victims of violence and also perpetuators of violence, and their most expressed feeling is anger; turned inward, they are victims of depression; and turned outward, they are victims of violence directed at other persons. Njogu and Wekesa[16] show that political violence in the 2013 elections had two concerns: a democratic process which "is both inclusive and representative; and resolution of deep-seated ethnic claims and grievances." But political violence in Kenya works hand in hand with ethnic and cultural wars, "a strong ethnic dimension, with polarization and divisions along ethnic, economic, regional and other cleavages being a common feature."[17]

---

13. D. E. Miller, "Victimization," in Hunter, *Dictionary*, 1301–1303.

14. Miller, "Victimization," 1301–1303.

15. Miller, 1301–1303.

16. Kimani Njogu and P. Wafula Wekesa, *Kenya's 2013 General Election* (Nairobi: Twaweza Communications, 2015), 17.

17. Njogu and Wekesa, *Kenya's 2013 General Election*, 17.

This means that violence in Kenya is used to achieve particular goals (long-term and short-term); violence is perpetuated by collective frustration and aggressive tendencies; and violence is fueled by internal conflicts; by long-term feelings of "stuckness" and lack of change; and by contradictions in community operations where the common good and the individual good are mixed with disparities between the rich and poor, impunity, and corruption.

Kenyan victims of violence can be divided into four types: victims who have inflicted violence on themselves (abusers of alcohol, drugs, and other substances; and suicides); victims of institutional violence (ethnic violence, cultural violence, family violence, kinship violence, gender-based violence); victims of group and intergroup violence (political violence, economic violence, philosophical violence, and gang violence); and victims of personal assault (rape, physical violence, murder by husband and vice versa, female and male genital mutilation, sexual abuse, verbal abuse, wife and husband battering, and child abuse). Violence and victims of violence in Kenya are becoming more complex day by day (politically based, religious-based, social-based, gender-based, family-based, class-based, economic-based, terrorist-based, and sexual-based).

Traditional (Premodern) Era and Violence: Before Colonization of Kenya (Before Berlin Conference, 1885)

Kenyan life used to be informed by a traditional ethos, customs, proverbs, and values, both ethnic and cultural. These traditional systems of guidance to functioning were orally transmitted rules of living. Traditions were seen as the source of authoritative knowledge about functioning, and that dictated what was violence and not violence, what was healthy and optimal, and what was pathological, unhealthy, and harmful to human life of individuals and their communities of embeddedness. This traditional system of life is viewed by Kenyans as comprehensive, unified, and connected; and as the "good old days," the "old African order," and a period of peace.[18] This traditional system was also viewed as humane, spiritual, meaningful, fulfilling, purposeful, cohesive, orderly, and relational. Njuguna[19] also mentions that there were "skirmishes, alliances and raids." Culture and ethnicity were the sources of an integrated identity for persons and their communities of embeddedness.

---

18. Francis Mwangi Njuguna, *Kenya: Down Memory Lane* (Nairobi: FM Njuguna, 2015), 14–43.

19. Njuguna, *Kenya*, 16.

We argue that ethnicity and culture as traditional systems of life were also based on patriarchal systems, the birthplace of violence. The "We-Ethos" of this era in Kenya can be criticized for silencing the "I-Ethos" that came with modernity, especially for women and children. Violence at all levels in this era was intertwined with the structures and systems of the family, ethnic community, and cultural functioning. The structural systems of "silencing" and systems of violence against the "I" of women and children built an inner anger, shame, and guilt as well as intolerance, emotional fusion, hate, self-disregard, shame, and guilt in response to the abuses, mainly by men in the family and in the name of family kinship, ethnicity, and culture. It seems that the perpetrators of violence were not only sadistic and masochistic individuals, but also that the community devalued its own women and children in the name of keeping the status quo of ethnicity and culture.

Modern Era and Violence: After 1900–1950, Colonization, Modernization, and Christianization

The second level of Kenyan life was that of modernity. This era and ethos was both a "blessing" and a "curse." On one side, modernization, Christianization, and democratization were a blessing as Kenya was exposed to other worlds. Modernity around the world began with the triumph of "critical rationality, [and] social struggle over authority (political and religious, horizontal dualism)."[20] The modern ways of life that came to Kenya involved Westernized expansionism of empires and their systems of operation, including colonization and its systems of oppression, exploitation, and abuse; and new economic systems that produced classism and neighborhoods, rural and urban communities. As much as modernity affirmed new systems, order, unity, coherence, progression, situationist solutions, and a new form of spirituality, this ethos resulted in the second level of violence. Modernity also came to Kenya with the glorification of individualism; "I," materialism, and the quest for power all became the birthplace of communal and individual forms of violence.

This modern era in Kenya saw abuse, exploitation, divide and rule, negative stereotyping, tribalism, and a class system in which the power of the "powerful" continues to be a thorn in the flesh of Kenyans. The insider–outsider mentalities of this era in Kenya demonstrated the strength to carry out violence on a legal basis. These legalized systems of violence (*de jure* systems of violence) were added to the preexisting traditional systems of violence,

---

20. Miller, "Emerging Postmodern World," 3–8.

especially against women and children. Violence through governance and dislocation of persons by the British governor in Kenya was also evidence of the legalization of violence.[21]

The other issue related to individual and communal violence is "Bible on one hand and the gun on the other," or the *Gutiri muthungu na Mubea* mentality, meaning there is no difference between the priest and the colonialist.[22] The first anti-violence issue led by some missionaries was "women circumcision," namely, female genital mutilation (FGM).[23] The second set of anti-violence issues led by some missionaries was forced labor, Mau Mau oaths, polygamy and dowry, and witchcraft and consulting with traditional healers.[24] The third anti-violence issue was all-out war (*de facto* system of violence) by the Mau Mau and other groups of men and women who decided to fight against white oppression and occupation of Kenya as a colony.

What can be observed from the modern era is that there was violence between individuals as well as legal systems of imperial violence perpetrated by the British government system within the local Kenyan community. This violence was physical, social, religious, functional, economic, linguistic, mental, and philosophical. We can also observe that violence meted out on women and violence meted out on men, or on both men and women, increased in intensity.[25] We also observe that modernization, democratization, and Christianization did not break down the systems of ethnic and cultural violence perpetrated in the traditional era. Additionally, fighting for individual and community rights escalated into other forms of violence: ideological, economic, political, and religious violence.[26] As the new colonial Kenya evolved and developed, colonial systems of violence were born and hidden in legal systems of the state (disruption of life, disunity among Kenyans, and isolation, causing further friction, exploitation, and indignity).[27] A new consciousness, "I-ism," was also born and nurtured as individual voices grew; individual rights and

---

21. Caroline Elkins, *Imperial Reckoning: The Untold Story of Britain's Gulag in Kenya* (New York: Henry Holt, 2005), 1–31; and David Anderson, *Histories of the Hanged: Britain's Dirty War in Kenya and the End of the Empire* (London: Phoenix, 2006), 1–53.

22. Njuguna, *Kenya*, 71–89.

23. Njuguna, 54–57.

24. Njuguna, 54–57.

25. Elkins, *Imperial Reckoning*, 31–368.

26. Englelbert Mveng, "Christianity and the Religious Culture of Africa," in *African Challenge*, ed. Kenneth Y. Best (Nairobi: All Africa Conference of Churches, 1975), 1–24.

27. Anderson, *Histories of the Hanged*, 41–53, 289–327; and Jomo Kenyatta, *Suffering without Bitterness* (Nairobi: East African Publishing, 1968), Foreword, v–xvii.

communal rights came with the new consciousness.[28] This new consciousness also involved questions of land ownership and governance at the national level, both of which were now understood as critical issues.[29]

By the end of World War II (1945), this new consciousness started to burn like fire and a new communal neurosis erupted among Kenyans as they fought colonial dictatorship, indifference, the reign of terror, use of detentions and extermination, and administrations that repressed, abused, and used social racism to propagate. As the abused become the abusers, now Kenyans started to fight the colonizers. Ikenye and Malomba[30] argue that control by the colonizers had become a system of dehumanization and Kenyans had to reclaim respect, dignity, values, and all-round emancipation (political, economic, social, and spiritual). These freedoms were ushered into Kenyan life at independence on 12 December 1964. We argue, however, that political independence did not break down the systems and cycles of violence perpetrated in the traditional and modern eras; instead, more forms of violence have been experienced in Kenya.

Postmodernity (1990 to the Present Day) and Ethnocultural Violence: Paradoxical Experience of Freedom and Bondage

Third, postmodern ways of life in Kenya have rejected both "traditionalism and modernism" as orders for living, yet traditional ways of life still govern the hearts of many Kenyans, especially in times of personal and communal crisis and pain. Kenyan life is now postcolonial with new systems of government in accordance with the Kenya 2010 constitution: the executive, legislative, justice, and public service. Yet there is an underlying system of life, namely, neocolonial life, in which one feels that the colonialists have a great deal of power over the Kenyan government. Postmodernity as a postcolonial reality in Kenya came with "subjective knowing" which is relational, conversational, and functional. Postmodernity became the third birthplace of the current systems of violence in all parts of life: social, functional, economic, familial, relational, political, religious, ideological, and philosophical. With these new forms of knowing and commitments, postmodernity in Kenya came with blurred systems that produced a crisis of personal, communal, and legal functioning

---

28. Elkins, *Imperial Reckoning*, xi–xvi.

29. Kenyatta, *Suffering without Bitterness*, 332–339.

30. Ikenye, *Decolonization of the Kenyan Soul*, 14–21; and Wunyabari O. Malomba, "Decolonization: A Theoretical Perspective," in *Decolonization and Independence in Kenya 1940–93*, ed. B. A. Ogot and W. R. Ochieng (Nairobi: East African Educational, 1995), 7–24.

and boundaries, a crisis of identity, and lack of differentiation (breakdown of id, ego, and superego boundaries); and the painful unconscious systems continued to flow from underneath, with violence now being acted out at all levels in individual, familial, communal, and national life.

The history and ethoses of these three Kenyan systems (traditional, modern, and postmodern) show that violence is a complex and multidimensional reality in personal, communal, and national life. The magnitude of life changes in Kenya shows that systems of violence – and more specifically, communal, individual, marital, and familial forms of violence – are born and yet have a history, continuation, and propagation. As postmodernity took root in Kenyan life, it was characterized by new possibilities for women and men; new responsibilities emerged; and shifts in the operational paradigm brought challenges that were far-reaching for individual, familial, communal, and national functioning.[31] The internalized systems of violence (traditional, modern, and legal) were primitive systems of acting-out in violence. Violence of doubt and skepticism became more hidden (what was said and done differed from the hidden systems of violence). Political correctness of the political class and the powerfully privileged remained with violent systems at home, in the workplace, and at the national level. This means that postcolonial and postmodern reconstructionism of national, cultural, and ethnic levels is at the manifest level (on-top operations), yet systems of violence remain in the underlying systems (latent level). As is commonly said, the devil is in the detail. People in Kenya today are more violent than before.[32] This research has discovered that violence and reactionism continued to increase in 2018 and 2019 and that ethnic and cultural labels, such as self–other, insider–outsider, we–they systems, increase animosity and continue to heighten multiple forms of violence. Kenyans wear the mask "we are all equal and inclusive," but in reality violence is evident; divide and rule is evident; rich and poor and class systems divide; and rulers and ruled exist. All of this propagates systems of violence at individual, familial, marital, communal, and national level.

31. William R. Ochieng, "Structural and Political Changes," and Robert M. Maxon, "Social and Cultural Changes," in Ogot and Ochieng, *Decolonization and Independence*, 83–147.

32. Ikenye, *Decolonization of the Kenyan Soul*, 14–21; D. C. Chemorion, Esther Mombo, and C. B. Peter, *Contested Space: Ethnicity and Religion in Kenya* (Limuru, Kenya: Zapf Chancery Publishers Africa, 2013), 99–200; and Njogu and Wekesa, *Kenya's 2013 General Election*, 16–31, 48–63, 112–123.

Culture of Violence and Multiple Forms of Violence in Kenya Today

Under the constitution, the national government of Kenya has four arms:[33] the president is the head of the executive branch; speakers lead the Senate and Parliament as the legislature; the chief justice heads the judiciary; and devolved governments are headed by governors. Scholars and politicians argue that these four arms of governing Kenya since independence have not been an "impartial arbiter"[34] for the last fifty-four years as Kenya, as an independent nation from British colonization, has grown and promoted multiple systems of growth, development, and efficiency and yet has continued the colonial legacy of multiple forms of violence. Kenyans in public and private discourse continue to send contradictory messages on culture and ethnicity that perpetuate the glorification of violence.

One of the basic assumptions in this research is that colonization and decolonization, as well as ethnicity and culture, affect all departments of life (personal and communal). Our holistic approach to African life was proposed by Mbiti, Nichols, and Schwartz[35] and it involves all departments of life. Bowen Family Systems theory[36] is discussed and interpreted and in the context of this chapter is applied to multiple systems of violence. We have concluded that violence in Kenya involves individual and communal systems of feelings, thoughts, attitudes, attachments in relationships, and functioning as a whole. We have also concluded that life in postcolonial times as a whole is systemic and multidimensional and therefore functioning is connected to systemic capabilities and regulations in changing times. Life in Kenya also has to do with systems of nature, nurture, development, transmission, and interactions to inform functioning systems. This means that multiple forms of violence, as shown in this research, affect and are affected by psychosocial and biological perspectives (heredity, nurture, and development) and by human perspectives (love of one another, natural erotic instincts, natural loss of love that leads to anger and violence, aggression, and death instincts – "thanatos") – all affecting

---

33. *Kenya Constitution*, 2010, 17–19.

34. P. Godfrey Okoth and Bethwell A. Ogot, *Conflict in Contemporary Africa* (Nairobi: Jomo Kenyatta Foundation, 2002), 2–3.

35. John S. Mbiti, *African Religions and Philosophy* (Nairobi: Heinemann, 1979), 2–5; Michael P. Nichols and Richard C. Schwartz, *Family Therapy: Concepts and Methods* (Boston: Allyn & Bacon, 2002), 366–405; William C. Nichols, *Marital Therapy: An Integrative Approach* (Boston: Allyn & Bacon 1988), 43–48.

36. Murray Bowen, *Family Therapy in Clinical Practice* (Northvale, NJ: Jason Aronson, 1985), 103–240, 285–450; and D. V. Papero, "Bowen Family Systems and Marriage," in *Clinical Handbook of Couple Therapy*, ed. Neil S. Jacobson and Alan S. Gurman (New York: Guilford Press, 1995), 11–23.

strategies and structures of being and functioning as well as experiences, cognition, behavior, problem-solving, and spiritual functioning. This also means that multiple facets of violence have to do with transmission, from traditional culture and ethnicity (traditional Kenyan culture had systems of violence) to modernity (the colonial experience was an experience of ethnic and cultural violence at a personal and a collective level). Kenyan experience of postcolonial life has continued to propagate colonial and traditional systems of violence. These experiences of violence are connected to individual, communal, and national anxiety. Manifestations of this anxiety (physical and psychological) include "wariness, suspicion, physical tensions, fatigue and irritability."[37]

Bowen Family Systems theory[38] and its nine concepts ("differentiation of self, triangles, nuclear family emotional system, family projection process, emotional cutoff, multigenerational transmission process, sibling position, societal regression," and systems of anxiety) demonstrate that a systems approach to violence in Kenya is complex, with multiple causes and effects.[39] This means that violence affects the functioning of individuals and communities in terms of their lack of capacity to separate emotional and intellectual systems in order to have ideal functional systems and relationships. Anxiety not only affects differentiation in functioning but also creates triangles to manage the anxiety.[40] This means that an anxious person (husband, children, and wife), anxious nation, anxious individuals, and anxious communities create unhealthy alliances, reactiveness, and problems of communication (perception, sensitivity, interpretation, behavior, and personalization of issues), all of which cause and perpetuate violence.

The Kenyan history of violence begets violence as a projection process, meaning that there is a history of violence in Kenyan life; societal regression is an emotional and social illness attached to violence; and transmission of violence and processes of violence from one generation to another speaks to violence from traditional and modern times, and into our postmodern and postcolonial times. Papero argues that anxiety in the system increases as relationships worsen and further distance, silence, avoidance, conflicts, and dysfunctions increase, leading to more violence.[41] Hence, without "coaching

---

37. Nichols and Schwartz, *Family Therapy*, 366–372; Nichols, *Marital Therapy*, 43–48; Bowen, *Family Therapy*, 203–240, 285–450; and Papero, "Bowen Family Systems," 11–23.

38. Bowen, *Family Therapy*, 103–240.

39. Bowen, 103–240, 285–450; and Papero, "Bowen Family Systems," 11–23.

40. Bowen, *Family Therapy*, 283–450.

41. Papero, "Bowen Family Systems," 11–23.

to create a climate where all are involved and are close in relationships,"[42] dysfunctions, including violence, will increase in the system. Worsened function is characterized by more distance, conflicts, loss of functioning capacities, loss of togetherness and love, reactionism, and increase of irrationality (as a part of societal regression). This means that violence will increase and more violence systems will be born.

The fourth part of this chapter develops a systems integrative theory, method, and model of individual and communal care, counseling, and transformation of the whole (spiritual, mental, relational, attitudinal, and functional adjustment) and also for the purposes of decolonization, restoring and transforming the Kenyan soul (personal and communal rebirth of the soul), and healing of violence. If individual and communal care, counseling, and transformation are not used, the systems of deprivation in the following systems of violence propagated in Kenyan life mean that collective violence and its systems of embeddedness are bound to escalate violence. There is plenty of evidence of escalation of violence being a product of not only personal and communal discontent, frustration, and complex stressors, but also lived notions of poverty, injustice, and unachievable goals and expectations. Our observation of African psychological anthropology shows that the systems of violence discussed below demonstrate problems of balance in the id, ego, and superego, meaning that aggression will continue to grow and violence will continue to increase if systems of prevention and intervention are not put in place.

Multiple Forms of Violence in Kenya: Evidence, Exploration, and Interpretation

Mwaniki, Omare, and Kamaara, speaking about the pre-election violence of 2006, reflected that during that period violence included hate speech which was an exchange of abuse words;[43] and that violence was propagated by patriarchy in living systems where men saw themselves as bosses while relegating women to servitude. This means that ethnic and cultural violence in Kenya is connected to

---

42. Papero, 11–23.

43. Lydia Mwaniki, "Ethnicity and December 2007 Post-Election Violence in Kenya: A Post-Colonial Examination and a Theological Response," in *Our Burning Issues: A Pan African Response*, ed. Edison M. Kalengyo, James Amaze, and Deji Ayegboyin (Nairobi: All African Conference of Churches, 2013), 185–201; and Simon Omare and Eunice Kamaara, "Ethnicity and Political Violence in Kenya and the Role of the Church," in Kalengyo, Amaze, and Ayegboyin, *Our Burning Issues*, 203–220.

ethnic and cultural dominance, threats and control, and feelings of insecurity. Omare and Kamaara further argue that ethnic and cultural violence is triggered by the perpetuation of ethnic and cultural suspicions, tensions, open animosity, and pitting communities against each other.[44] Ikenye argues that our models of pastoral care and counseling must use an interdependent African model and liberation of individuals and their communities of embeddedness, and hence develop a comprehensive incarnational approach.[45] Nyong'o argues that politics, ideologies, personality-oriented and ethnically based parties, and a battered economy, including bad land policies, all featured during the electioneering period of 2012–13, have left Kenyans bitter due to increased inequalities, disruption to life, destruction of property, increase of distrust, and the propagation of violence.[46] Mwaniki argues that negative ethnicity caused by fear, feelings of insecurity on minority and majority ethnic groups, and broken relationships perpetuate cycles of violence, including sexual violence.[47] Mutullah argues for and against a negotiated democracy, which does not solve the problems of individuals, "*Wanjiku*," women, children, and men, who are the real victims of violence; and this view is also supported by Omare and Kamaara.[48] Thus, violence is multifaceted and multidimensional, and our responses must also meet those multiple dimensions.

Class-Oriented Violence in Kenya

Another form of violence according to our observation is class-oriented violence, noted more in Nairobi, Mombasa, Kisumu, and Nakuru, all urban communities, where the poor attack, maim, or destroy the lives and properties of the poor, or the poor attack or seek to destroy the lives of the rich, or vice versa. The economic sabotage is a neocolonial system where one stands at the door, does not go in, and does not let others go in either. The other side of this dynamic is that while the rich get richer, the poor get poorer. Furthermore, violence allows poverty to grow to unmanageable levels; and

---

44. Omare and Kamaara, "Ethnicity and Political Violence," 203–220.

45. Ndung'u Ikenye, "Pastoral Care and Counseling in the African Ethnic Context," in Kalengyo, Amaze, and Ayegboyin, *Our Burning Issues*, 233–239.

46. P. Anyang' Nyong'o, "Drivers of Victory and Loss," in Njogu and Wekesa, *Kenya's 2013 General Election*, 80–95.

47. Mwaniki, "Ethnicity and December 2007," 185–201.

48. Winnie V. Mutullah, "Negotiated Democracy: A Double-Barrelled Sword," in Njogu and Wekesa, *Kenya's 2013 General Election*, 344–360; and Omare and Kamaara, "Ethnicity and Political Violence," 203–220.

systems of imperialism, capitalism, and dependency are continued in public and personal life. This means that oppression at personal, communal, and national levels is left unattended and bitterness further increases; as a result, more violence almost becomes the order of the day. Our deductions are based on evaluations from Philips.[49]

Neocolonial Violence in Kenya

Ethnic and cultural violence in Kenya as a neocolonial and postcolonial experience takes the form of political violence, ideological violence, and economic violence. Regarding political violence, our observation is that the notion of the state, the constitution, and the structures and institutions as developed and articulated by the constitution are not respected and therefore are held according to neocolonial attitudes that are self-defeating, and they only increase struggle in the name of self-liberation and self-awareness, as well as antagonism and abusive critiques. In Kenya's political economy, the labor democrats with their capitalistic definitions and actions do not differ from the social democrats with their community thoughts joined with socialism. Instead of creating philosophically based parties, ethnic power and the tyranny of many are used, and they become birthplaces of further violence and the demonization of one another.

Religious Violence in Kenya as a Paradox, and Divide and Rule

Religion is a cultural way of life,[50] and yet religion has theoretical, practical, sociological, cultural, ethnic, artistic, ethical, and personal meanings. In connection with this chapter, Western European Christianity has cultural underpinnings and yet goes beyond cultural meanings, especially as it relates to Scripture. Niebuhr proposes that encountering Christ be considered as "Christ against Culture, Christ of Culture, Christ above Culture, Christ and Culture in Paradox and Christ the Transformer of Culture."[51] The African religious paradox of religious violence is expressed in missionary Christianity and postcolonial Christianity as "against," "of," "above," "in Paradox," and "the Transformer" where the religion of ethnicity and culture breeds religious

---

49. Kevin Philips, *The Politics of Rich and Poor* (New York: Random House, 1990), 3–52.

50. R. S. Ellwood, "Religion," in Hunter, *Dictionary*, 1054.

51. H. Richard Niebuhr, *Christ and Culture* (New York: Harper & Row, 1951), 45–229; and Mbiti, *African Religions*, 1–28.

violence at personal and communal levels. The way Christ was presented during the missionary era and the way in which Christ is being presented in the postcolonial era "was and still is" paradoxically a breath of violence.[52] Galgalo calls Christianity the "stranger within," without evidence of transformation of lives and communities.[53] The "Bible on one hand and gun on the other hand"[54] have produced the paradox as missionaries supported injustices, exploitations, inequalities, oppression, and discrimination. This violence is still experienced in Kenya today, the postcolonial period; hence Galgalo's sentiments are still real.

Religious Violence in Kenya: Dividing and Ruling from the Heart

Religion for Kenyans (African Traditional Religion and Christianity) is ethnic and cultural in nature. Religion speaks to the heart and the heart is personal, ethnic, cultural, and therefore communal as well. The hearts of Kenyans were, after all, not "untutored, heathen, primitive, polytheistic, animist, illogical and worshipping idols and ancestors."[55] Thus the personal and communal identity of being a Christian is transformative, and yet if conversion is not based on authentic and genuine faithfulness and changes in actions, behavior, relating, and functioning, the cycles of religious violence will continue in this postcolonial era, and divide and rule mentalities that propagate violence will rule the hearts of Kenyans. Scholars in African Traditional Religion(s) and African Christianity argue that African traditional beliefs and customs are held seriously as the religion of life.[56] This means that African Traditional Religion is the religion of the African soul (heart, mind, oral history, rites, rituals, beliefs, activities), as the religion handed down from generation to generation and the religion that permeates all departments of African life; and missionary activity, as good as it is, has a component of religious violence; and that African Traditional Religion remains strong in the midst of progressive changes in emancipation, human rights, tolerance, democracy, justice, freedom, and

---

52. Njuguna, *Kenya*, 46.

53. Joseph Galgalo, *African Christianity: The Stranger Within* (Limuru, Kenya: Zapf Chancery Publishers Africa, 2012), 4–30.

54. Njuguna, *Kenya*, 46–76.

55. E. G. Parrinder, *African Traditional Religion* (London: SPCK, 1962), 9–20.

56. E. Bolaji Idowu, *African Traditional Religion: A Definition* (London: SCM, 1973), 1–21, 203–210.

redemptive development in governance, development, and politics. Yet "We are being consumed by hatred, ethnic conflict, and brutal violence."[57]

Philosophical (Worldview) Violence in Kenya

The European worldview as a modern and postmodern way of life came with colonization, modernization, and Christianization.[58] The European worldview, like all other worldviews, includes causality, cosmology, anthropology, teleology, ontology, epistemology, axiology, and futurology. For the people of Kenya, there was no greater violence that the British colonizers and missionaries could have done than impose this worldview. Kenyans' ethnocultural identity, relational and communal reality, explanations of optimal and pathological behavior, and gender-based forms of organization were shifted, and this shift was violence.

Family Violence in Kenya

Violence begins with the unwritten norms of family, extended family, and kinship systems under the traditional, modern, and postmodern ethos. A definition of violence is "anything that results in injury to the other member of the family . . . physical, emotional, mental and behavioral."[59] Thus the use of force or any form of abuse, coercion, destruction, domination, disturbance, threat, or violation qualifies as violence; all these end in hurting another person in the family, and take away freedom. Mbiti[60] argues that family and kinship are central to the African life (being and doing), philosophy, and worldview: "I am, therefore we are, and since we are, therefore I am." This means that the balance of "I–We" is life, and colonial imbalances (forced or taught) to this philosophy are violence to family and within family, and to the extended family, clan, and kinship system. The narratives of common origin, shared identity and sense of belonging, oneness, and togetherness which were broken down by the colonialists and missionaries did violence to the family as a whole. The

---

57. Jose B. Chipenda, "Foreword," in *Peacemaking and Democratisation in Africa: Theoretical Perspectives and Church Initiatives*, ed. Hizkias Assefa and George Wachira (Nairobi: East African Educational, 1996), ix–xiv.

58. D. C. Chemorion, *Introduction to Christian Worldview* (Nairobi: Nairobi Academic Press, 2014), 27–29.

59. Harvey Wallace, *Family Violence: Legal, Medical and Social Perspectives*, 4th ed. (Boston: Pearson Education, 2005), 1–29.

60. Mbiti, *African Religions*, 100–109.

shifts and prescriptions were valuations of violence and ethical violence to the Kenyan family.

Our argument is that family violence, that between family members (husband–wife, husband–wife–children, and extended family and kinship against women and children) is all homemade. These multiple forms of violence in the family are perpetrated by intimate member(s) who are well known to the victim(s). Factors that contribute to family violence include psychosocial problems; problems of costs, reward, and punishment; frustration and aggression; interacting environmental issues; and learning from the culture of violence in the family or ethnic community. Our interpretation of media reports in Kenya shows that isolation and control, power differentials, are especially used by those with more resources who are therefore powerful, and those without or with fewer resources experience powerlessness. Violence and powerlessness produce people with substance and drug abuse, and with pathological self-perception issues, including low self-image, low-self-esteem, and lack of self-actualization – all of which result in shame and guilt that are acted out in violence. Other issues include relational problems such as pathological disconnects and conflicts, problems in balanced functioning, reactivity, unrealistic reactivity, and anxiety.

Youth Violence in Kenya

Youth violence has permeated the present generation more than any previous generation. Today's young generation of Kenyans is growing up with depictions of aggression and violence. We would argue that violence is being normalized in forms of media entertainment. Most parts of Kenya have organized gangs or militias. The youth are initiated through rituals into violence-oriented groups. The nurturing contexts of Kenyan youths have been infiltrated by all forms of violence, thus affecting the youth. Issues of poverty, mean-spirited approaches to life demonstrated by parents and guardians, and inadequate teaching and training in life skills all lead to youths becoming perpetrators of violence or victims of violence. Reiss and Roth[61] define youth violence in terms of behavior that inflicts physical and emotional harm on other persons, meaning that violence includes threats and attempts to harm others, murder, aggravated

---

61. A. J. Reiss and J. A. Roth, eds., *Understanding and Preventing Violence* (Washington, DC: National Academy, 1993), 22.

assault, rape, and robbery. Howard and Jenson[62] argue that youth violence is caused by individual factors (population, biological, psychological, familial, school, and peer), situational factors (victim–victimizer relationship, behavior of victims, substance abuse, presence/availability of a weapon), and macro contextual factors (poverty, population density and mobility, community disorganization, and media influences). While these scholars are speaking to the American scene, we can learn from them and mirror those causes to the Kenyan scene. On Kenyan television and in other forms of media we see youths who are impulsive, hyperactive, and aggressive in behavior, deviant attitudes, negative emotions, and family conflicts, all roots of youth violence in urban and rural areas.

Relational Problems and Violence in Kenya

Neocolonial patterns of violence in Kenya are a relational problem. Nichols[63] argues that relational problems are concerned with four core issues (commitment, caring, communication, and conflict/compromise): commitment to the value of the relationship which leads to its maintenance and continuation; caring love that leads to emotional attachment; communication as an ability to communicate verbally and symbolically to share meaning; and conflict/compromise patterns in dealing with conflict to maintain intimacy. Thus dealing with violence requires attending to and breaking down the cycles discussed by Chemorion, Mombo, and Peter,[64] including crisis of identity, crisis of boundaries, crisis of interethnic stories and memories, and crisis of love. Relational problems expressed in violence have expanded into ideological problems and mentalities of divide and rule, control and manipulation, and threatening systems; political problems where social democrats and labor democrats have not defined their philosophies on a national basis; power struggles which have been relegated to ethnic power bases, the power of numbers, and power of alliances; those ruling and the ruled; and economic wars which make class systems and financial distribution a painful experience.

---

62. Matthew O. Howard and Jeffrey M. Jenson, "Causes of Youth Violence," in *Youth Violence: Current Research and Recent Practice Innovations*, ed. Matthew O. Howard and Jeffrey M. Jenson (Washington, DC: NASW Press, 1999), 19–42.

63. Nichols, *Marital Therapy*, 13–43.

64. Chemorion, Mombo, and Peter, *Contested Space*, 9–96, 100–250.

Interpretation and Propagation of Violence

Our observation and argument is that violence is far from coming to an end as we look at systemic multiple causes and effects. The first issue for consideration is the trauma of the ongoing changes in individuals, communities, and Kenya at large. The constant factor in Kenyan life is change itself. What we are observing in Kenya today is stressed people, with multiple stressors. These stressors are the hotbeds of violence as Kenyans react to and act out their frustrations. One of our basic assumptions about violence is that egocentrism, negative identity, monoculturalism, ethnocentrism, neocolonialism, and crises of values and virtues all perpetuate systems of violence.

In egocentrism, the perpetrator focuses on communal violence and uses a self-centered interpretation of personal and communal life: "the interpreter's consciousness is his or herself." Hinkle and Hinkle[65] argue that surrendering the self is a necessity in pastoral care and counseling and it stands at the limits of culture and psychotherapy. This self-centeredness of the perpetrator is sadistic, masochistic, and narcissistic, and it is born in a person through nature (heredity) and nurture (parenting). When ethnicity and culture are the perpetrators of violence, the systems of ethnic and cultural violence become self-centered, sadistic, and masochistic. These systems of violence also demonstrate the breakdown of communal reality, ideals, values, customs, beliefs, and conscience.

In ethnocentrism, the center of violence is tribalism, negative ethnicity, negative ethnocultural identity. Hinkle and Hinkle[66] argue that in ethnocentrism, the individual or community is "unwilling or unable to address experience outside of a particular ethnic heritage," meaning that the person or community is ethnically encapsulated and lacks differentiation. Thus the person or community carries unrealistic and irrational narratives (personal and communal) of perceptions, stereotypes, and assumptions. Individuals or communities in Kenya have created these perceptions, stereotypes, and assumptions (social debts and obligations) that are unrealistic and based on fantasies. These operational systems in the individual and ethnic mind keep ethnic communities apart, divided and abusing one another, and violence increases and grows on these systems.

---

65. John E. Hinkle and Gregory A. Hinkle, "Surrendering the Self: Pastoral Counseling at the Limits of Culture and Psychotherapy," in *Therapeutic Practice in a Cross-Cultural World*, ed. Carole R. Bohn (Decatur, GA: Journal of Pastoral Care, 1995), 77–98.

66. Hinkle and Hinkle, "Surrendering the Self," 80.

The third level of interpretation of violence is monoculturalism. The statement that "one who knows one culture knows no culture" carries a lot of weight for our living together in our world.[67] The world we live in does not encourage people to live "alone and exclusive." Rather, in Kenya and in our world, we must cross over and join others in their world. Our observation is that each Kenyan ethnic and cultural community has priced, valued, protected, and cherished that which they call "Us, Our Own" and closed the door to others, therefore making it exclusively theirs. In fact, "local tourism" is still exclusive. Monoculturalism is a closet mentality, and it closes the cultural community in upon themselves in perspective, values, and the meaning of life. As a system of violence, the individual and communal perpetrating system impose themselves, their core values, and their value system. In Kenya, this happened under colonization but the same is true of neocolonization. The violence in monoculturalism is the imposition by any means necessary, including dehumanization, abuse, self-idealization, and devaluation.

The contemporary call of the African Christian church is to provide competent and effective pastoral care and counseling that speaks to the African Christian soul in context and, in particular, meets persons and communities at their multiple points of need.

A Paradigm of African Pastoral Care and Counseling for Victims of Violence

Table 15.1 demonstrates the new paradigm of African pastoral care and counseling to the victims of violence in Kenya. The table shows the theory, model, and method of practice as applied to Kenyan contexts and to victims in pastoral care and counseling.

Pastoral Care and Counseling for Victims of Multiple Systems of Violence in Kenya: Integrative Systems Approach in Theory and Practice

The biblical approach of pastoral care and counseling is foundational to all forms of Christian approaches to countering violence in the lives of victims. The text 2 Corinthians 5:19 (NASB), "God was in Christ reconciling the world to Himself," is basic to dealing with violence, meaning that reconciliation as

---

67. David W. Augsburger, *Pastoral Counseling across Cultures* (Philadelphia: Westminster Press, 1986), 18.

Table 15.1: African Christian paradigm of pastoral care and counseling

Theory, Model, and Method	African Pastoral Care	African Pastoral Counseling
Overall Goal of the Integrative Systems Pastoral Care and Counseling: Holistic transformation	*Goal:* Meeting persons and communities at their multiple points of need	*Goal:* In-depth and multidimensional meeting persons and communities at their points of need
Other Goals: Competent and effective practice	*Pastor:* Pastoral and personal identity As a calling from God	*Counselor:* Stance of acceptance and positive regard of Christian parishioner
Integrative Systems Methods, Models, and Techniques: Biblical, classical, clinical, contextual, prophetic, and reframing	*Practice:* Contact, listening, inquiry, entry, diagnosis, intervention, and maintenance of Spirit-filled life	*Practice:* Contact, listening, inquiry, entry systems, diagnosis, intervention, maintenance of optimal living, and growth-oriented
Christian-Centered: Transformation in Christian living: Personal, communal, and national coherent and peaceful life	*Christian-Centered:* Holistic and wholistic self, conversion at justification, righteousness and processes of sanctification, and Christian discipline	*Christian-Centered:* Holistic and wholistic self, faithing as a process of incarnating Christ in all spheres of the Christian life as an active faith
Goals for African Pastoral Functions to Victims of Violence: Healing, restoring, guiding, reconciliation, faithing, empowerment, liberation, discipling, disciplining, decolonization, and prophesying	*Function:* Healing, restoring, guiding, reconciliation, faithing, empowerment, liberation, discipling, disciplining, decolonization, and prophesying	*Function:* Healing, restoring, guiding, reconciliation, faithing, empowerment, liberation, discipling, disciplining, decolonization, and prophesying

a transformation process for the victims of violence is understood and lived with the revelation of Christ, and that his invitation to truth, the way, and life is experienced as a relational process. This divine and vertical intention of God (salvation as faith in Christ) is central to reconciliation, as a focus of faith in

Christ is transformative reconciliation. The second aspect of reconciliation and transformation is ontological and horizontal, as a relational process among Christians. In both cases, forgiveness is also central: forgiveness in Christ and forgiveness between the brothers and sisters (victims of violence). This means that without forgiveness there is no reconciliation. Establishment of communion is done by the cross (meditational atonement). Third, reconciliation must also be understood as the work of the Holy Spirit. The gifts of the Holy Spirit (Gal 5:22–25) are lived in the power and efficacy of God's work of love, a work of reconciliation. This means that the work of the cross is brought to the present reality of pain and suffering of the victims of violence (Gal 3:26–28; 6:14–15). Four, the gospel is a reconciling gospel. This implies Christians live the gospel of reconciliation and transformation as reconciled persons, to Christ, and through Christ; and are called to live that life with one another. Thus the law of the new self and new creation is not only about living and walking with Christ but also bringing others into that reconciliation: reconciliation is missional. Hence the church's mission is to affirm the imperative of the ministry of reconciliation (1 Cor 12:13; Col 3:11, "oneness"). The biblical theory, model, and method of pastoral care and counseling therefore calls the Christian community to restore the victims of violence to a life of fullness and productivity, as an inclusive and loving community.

The classical pastoral care and counseling paradigm provides a theoretical model and practical resource for healing, sustaining, guiding, and reconciling, thus working through the pain of personal and communal violence.[68] For the purposes of this research, we have extended this paradigm to reframing as proposed by Capps.[69] We continue to hold an earlier proposal that African pastoral care and counseling must include the functions of faithing, empowering, liberating, and decolonizing.[70] We also include a feminist approach as proposed by Moessner,[71] where weaving the web of relationships is women-friendly and women's sensitivities inform the delivery of pastoral care and counseling. We also include cross-ethnic and cross-cultural sensitivities (ethnocultural narratives and paradigms) as proposed by Ikenye.[72] Table 15.2

---

68. Clebesch and Jaekle, *Pastoral Care*, 32–66.

69. Capps, *Reframing*, 9–54.

70. Ikenye, *African Pastoral Counseling*, 54, 59–86.

71. Jeanne Stevenson Moessner, *Through the Eyes of Women: Insights for Pastoral Care* (Minneapolis: Fortress, 1996), 1–49.

72. As a transformational resource for healing individual and collective systems of violence see Ndung'u J. B. Ikenye, "Contextualization of Pastoral Theology in African Christianity Care and Counseling," in *African Contextual Realities*, ed. Rodney L. Reed (Carlisle: Langham Global

demonstrates our integrative approach to pastoral care and counseling in theory and practice as applied in Kenyan Christianity for victims of violence.

Christians Encountering Systems of Violence Perpetrated on Individuals and Communities

Healing and growth are systems of pastoral care and counseling that can heal a personal and communal soul after the crisis of collective, individual, and communal violence. This process requires conversation: between God, and between parts of the self and parts of the community, thus working toward a healthy personal and communal soul in the context of Christian life and mission. This means that African Christian faith, ethnicity, and culture, by means of community dialogue and conversation (genuine sharing), can be moved from the negative image of self and the negative image of community (powerless as intrusion and constriction) to the new creation image and new self in Christ. Healing and growth are possible through conversation, sharing stories, and strategic remembering (social, personal-psychological, ecological, and spiritual) as proposed by Assefa and Wachira, and Ikenye.[73] We argue that healing and growth have to do with levels of awareness that help to structure the personal and communal soul after experiences of personal and communal violence. Pastoral care and counseling, as a system of working toward health and growth and as a method of reframing, involves conversation as equals, especially as Christians, at the table, revisioning, remembering, and reinventing the personal and communal soul, and thus will use African traditional systems of spirituality and African Christian awareness.

Conclusion

In the treatment of all forms of violence, the goal is transformation (of self, community, and nation) which will include the rebirth of personal and communal systems of meaningful relationships where attachment, differentiation, individuation, and object constancy are encouraged through genuine dialogue and living out faithfulness and righteousness. In cross-ethnic and cross-cultural contexts of Kenya, pastoral care and counseling will work in individual and communal mature systems of caring, tolerance, and living

---

Library, 2018), 31–55.

   73. Assefa and Wachira, *Peacemaking and Democratisation*, 34–71; Ikenye, *Decolonization of the Kenyan Soul*, 22–36.

Table 15.2

Eras of Violence	Systems of Violence in Kenya	Systemic Contradictions and Violence
Traditional Life and Systems of Violence	Violence in family and kinship systems: relational problems acted inwardly or outwardly	Egocentrism, individual-based violence: Id-oriented problems Attachment-oriented problems
Modern Life and Systems of Violence	Violence in imposition of Westernized core value and value systems in colonization and modernization	Ethnocentrism: tribalism equals negative ethnicity
Blurred Life and Systems of Violence	Colonial: violence in marginalization; demonization of ethnic and cultural values; religious violence	Monoculturalism: seeing and imposing one lens core value and value system
Crisis Life and Systems of Violence	Postcolonial: projections of colonial violence (legal and illegal violence) Internalization of violence	Neocolonialism: Kenyans hurting one another as they were hurt by colonialists Forgetting the pain and suffering Anxiety and depression turned inward, and outward anxiety and depression (hurting self and hurting others)
Postmodern, Postcolonial, and Neocolonial Life of the Christian in Kenya	Neocolonial Africa to African Oppressions and violence as if colonialists never left Colonialists using international systems of oppression abuse and as if they never left Relational violence between Christians in marriage, family, and church communities and domestic abuse = trauma to the personal and communal soul	Crisis of virtues, values, and broken relationships = systems of acting out, denial, and shame leading to disconnection of the soul (personal and communal), physical abuse, sexual abuse, husband–wife abuse = violence begets violence, terror (intrusions, constriction), disconnection, and captivity

Biblical Christian Pastoral Care and Counseling Healing, Guiding, Sustaining, Reconciliation	Approaches: Classical, Clinical, Contextual, Reframing, Prophetic, in Personal and Communal Soul	Personal, Communal Revisioning, Reinventing, and Restructuring of Self and Communal Soul
Biblical, classical: faith, confession, and forgiveness Clinical: resistance and use of defenses	Liberation of individual, personal, and changing systems on being, doing, behaving, feeling	Revisioning
Listening with empathy, Bernard of Clairvaux	Women-friendly change in care and counseling	Remembering
Interpathy: crossing over for healing St Francis of Assisi: prayer of unity and diversity	Cross-cultural and cross-ethnic care and counseling Stages of personal and communal growth and development	Reinventing living together
Remembering: cognitive of shared stories as spiritual exercise, of healing, sustaining, reconciling and guiding Ignatius Loyola Confession: individual and communal John Knox, from sin-sick soul to varieties of religious experience William James	Cross-ethnic and cross-cultural perspective Nurturing positive ethnicity and culture Building positive personal and social environment Building systems of dialogues within ethnic and cultural identities Developing harmonious and integrated systems of mutual living	Prophetic, liberative Confronting and condemning all systems of violence Changing systems of collective violence in ethnicity and culture Personal and communal systems of health and growth after violence = salvation and revival; John Wesley and East African Revival
Differentiation, unity, and diversity = maturity of persons and communities in the context of Christian faith	Holistic empowerment: Holistic self Physical self Mental self Spiritual self Relational self Ethnocultural self Environmental self Christian self	Restructuring of power = empowerment after the experience of violence = self-communal-contextual empowerment = remembering, mourning, and reconnections

with one another, as opposed to the competition experience that increases all forms of violence. We use the classical and clinical together to meet the victims of violence at their multiple points of need. This requires the art and science of pastoral care and counseling.

This chapter has answered the following questions: (1) What are the Christian responses as interventions (in terms of individual, familial, and communal systems) to the victims of these multiple kinds of violence? And (2) what kind of pastoral care and counseling (competent and effective Christian theory and practice of care) is needed as care and counsel to the victims of violence in Kenya? The research has recommended the use of the integrative method and model in transforming the pain and wounds of violence in Kenyan contexts. This approach uses a biblical, classical, clinical, prophetic, contextual, and reframing model and method of pastoral care and counseling as an integrative systems approach. This integrative systems approach begins with the use of classical functions of pastoral care and counseling: healing, guiding, reconciling, and sustaining. For the purposes of expanding the paradigm of pastoral functions in Kenyan contexts, this research has proposed that decolonization, faithing, disciplining, discipling, and empowerment be added to the classical functions of pastoral care and counseling. Kenyan Christians who are victims of multiple forms of violence are encouraged to use their spiritual heritage of faith in Christ and walking in the Holy Spirit. Pastors and pastoral counselors are encouraged to use their unique heritage in Christ and influence victims of violence to engage the multiple forms of violence for the purposes of forgiveness, peaceful co-existence, healing and reconciliation, and development.

Bibliography

Adams, Carol J., and Marie M. Fortune, eds. *Violence against Women and Children: A Christian Theological Sourcebook*. New York: Continuum, 1995.

Anderson, David. *Histories of the Hanged: Britain's Dirty War in Kenya and the End of the Empire*. London: Phoenix, 2006.

Assefa, Hizkias, and George Wachira. *Peacemaking and Democratization in Africa: Theoretical Perspectives and Church Initiatives*. Nairobi: East African Educational, 1996.

Augsburger, David W. *Pastoral Counseling across Cultures*. Philadelphia: Westminster Press, 1986.

Baldwin, John R., et al., eds. *Redefining Culture: Perspectives across the Disciplines*. Mahwah, NJ: Lawrence Erlbaum Associates, 2006.

Baum, Gregory, and Harold Wells, eds. *Reconciliation of Peoples: Challenge to Churches*. Geneva: World Council of Churches; Maryknoll, NY: Orbis, 1997.

Bohn, Carole R., ed. *Therapeutic Practice in a Cross-Cultural World*. Decatur, GA: Journal of Pastoral Care, 1995.

Bowen, Murray. *Family Therapy in Clinical Practice*. Northvale, NJ: Jason Aronson, 1985.

Capps, Donald. *Reframing: A New Method in Pastoral Care*. Minneapolis: Fortress, 1990.

Chemorion, Diphos C. *Introduction to Christian Worldview: Meaning, Origins and Perspectives*. Nairobi: Nairobi Academic Press, 2014.

Chemorion, Diphos C., Esther Mombo, and C. B. Peter. *Contested Space: Ethnicity and Religion in Kenya*. Limuru, Kenya: Zapf Chancery Publishers Africa, 2013.

Clebesch, William A., and Charles R. Jaekle. *Pastoral Care in a Historical Perspective*. New York: Jason Aronson, 1975.

Clinebell, Howard. *Basic Types of Pastoral Care and Counseling*. Nashville: Abingdon, 1994.

Crabb, Lawrence J., Jr. *Effective Biblical Counseling*. Grand Rapids, MI: Zondervan, 1977.

Elkins, Caroline. *Imperial Reckoning: The Untold Story of Britain's Gulag in Kenya*. New York: Henry Holt, 2005.

Enns, Fernando, Scott Holland, and Ann Riggs, eds. *Seeking Cultures of Peace: A Peace Church Conversation*. Scottdale, PA: Cascadia; Geneva: World Council of Churches, 2004.

Fortune, Marie M. *Sexual Violence: The Unmentionable Sin*. Cleveland, OH: Pilgrim Press, 1983.

Freilich, Morris, ed. *The Meaning of Culture*. Lexington, MA: Xerox College, 1972.

Galgalo, Joseph. *African Christianity: The Stranger Within*. Limuru, Kenya: Zapf Chancery Publishers Africa, 2012.

Gerkin, Charles V. *Prophetic Pastoral Care*. Nashville: Abingdon, 1991.

Glazer, Nathan, and Daniel P. Moynihan. *Beyond the Melting Pot*. 2nd ed. Cambridge, MA: MIT Press, 1963, 1970.

Graham, Larry Kent. *Care of Persons, Care of World: A Psychosystems Approach to Pastoral Care and Counseling*. Nashville: Abingdon, 1992.

Griswold, Wendy. *Cultures and Societies in a Changing World*. Los Angeles: Pine Forge, 2008.

Hiltner, A., and Lowell G. Colston. *The Context of Pastoral Counseling*. Nashville: Abingdon, 1961.

Holsopple, Mary Yoder, et al. *Building Peace: Overcoming Violence in Communities*. Geneva: WCC, 2004.

Howard, Matthew O., and Jeffrey M. Jenson. *Youth Violence: Current Research and Recent Practice Innovations*. Washington, DC: NASW Press, 1999.

Hunter, Rodney J., ed. *Dictionary of Pastoral Care and Counseling*. Nashville: Abingdon, 1990.

Idowu, E. Bolaji. *African Traditional Religion: A Definition*. London: SCM, 1973.

Ikenye, Ndung'u. *African Christian Counseling: Method, Theory and Practice*. Nairobi: Envoy Graphics and Print Systems, 2002.

————. *African Pastoral Counseling: An Integrative Theory, Research, Method and Model of Practice in African Christianity*. Thika, Kenya: Joroi Counseling Consultants and Researchers, 2014.

————. "Contextualization of Pastoral Theology in African Christianity Care and Counseling." In *African Contextual Realities*, edited by Rodney L. Reed, 31–55. Carlisle: Langham Global Library, 2018.

————. *Decolonization of the Kenyan Soul: Theory and Practice of Minding the Collective and Individual Soul*. Nairobi: Envoy Graphics and Print Systems, 2002.

————. *Modeling Servant-Leaders for Africa*. Eldoret, Kenya: Zapf Chancery, 2010.

————. "Pastoral Care and Counseling in the African Ethnic Context." In *Our Burning Issues: A Pan African Response*, edited by Edison M. Kalengyo, James Amaze, and Deji Ayegboyin, 233–239. Nairobi: All African Conference of Churches, 2013.

Jacobson, Neil S., and Alan S. Gurman. *Clinical Handbook of Couple Therapy*. New York: Guilford Press, 1995.

Kenyatta, Jomo. *Suffering without Bitterness*. Nairobi: East African Publishing, 1968.

Knowles, Caroline. "Theorising Race and Ethnicity: Contemporary Paradigms and Perspectives." In *The Sage Handbook of Race and Ethnic Studies*, edited by Patricia H. Collins and John Solomos, 1–42. Los Angeles: Sage, 2010.

Lake, F. *Clinical Theology: A Theological and Psychological Basis to Clinical Pastoral Care*. London: Darton, Longman & Todd, 1986.

LeVine, Robert A. *Culture, Behavior and Personality*. New York: Aldine, 1982.

Levi-Strauss, Claude. *The Savage Mind*. Chicago: University of Chicago Press, 1996.

Leys, C. *Under-Development in Kenya: The Political Economy of Neo-Colonialism*. London: Heinemann, 1975.

Magesa, Laurenti. *Anatomy of Inculturation: Transforming the Church in Africa*. Nairobi: Paulines Publications Africa, 2004.

Mathema, C. *Wealth and Power: An Introduction to Political Economy*. Harare: Zimbabwe Publishing, 1988.

Mbiti, John S. *African Religions and Philosophy*. Nairobi: Heinemann, 1979.

McNeill, John T. *A History of the Cure of Souls*. New York: Harper & Row, 1951.

Miller, James B. "The Emerging Postmodern World." In *Postmodern Theology: Christian Faith in a Pluralist World*, edited by F. Burnham, 1–13. San Francisco: Harper & Row, 1989.

Moessner, Jeanne Stevenson, *Through the Eyes of Women: Insights for Pastoral Care*. Minneapolis: Fortress, 1996.

Moore-Gilbert, Bart. *Postcolonial Theory: Contexts, Practices, Politics*. London: Verso, 1997.

Mveng, Englelbert. "Christianity and the Religious Culture of Africa." In *African Challenge*, edited by Kenneth Y. Best, 1–24. Nairobi: All Africa Conference of Churches, 1975.

Mwaniki, Lydia. "Ethnicity and December 2007 Post-Election Violence in Kenya: A Post-Colonial Examination and a Theological Response." In *Our Burning Issues:*

A Pan African Response, edited by Edison M. Kalengyo, James Amaze, and Deji Ayegboyin, 185–201. Nairobi: All African Conference of Churches, 2013.

Nichols, Michael P., and Richard C. Schwartz. *Family Therapy: Concepts and Methods.* Boston: Allyn & Bacon, 2002.

Nichols, William C. *Marital Therapy: An Integrative Approach.* Boston: Allyn & Bacon, 1988.

Niebuhr, H. Richard. *Christ and Culture.* New York: Harper & Row, 1951.

Njogu, Kimani, and P. Wafula Wekesa, eds. *Kenya's 2013 General Election: Stakes, Practices and Outcomes.* Nairobi: Twaweza Communications, 2015.

Njoya, Timothy Murere. *Human Dignity and National Identity: Essential for Social Ethics.* Nairobi: Jemisik Cultural, 1987.

Njuguna, F. Mwangi. *Kenya: Down Memory Lane.* Nairobi: Francis Mwangi Njuguna, 2015.

Nsamenang, A. Bame. *Human Development in Cultural Context: A Third World Perspective.* Newbury Park, CA: Sage, 1992.

Ogot, B. A., and W. R. Ochieng. *Decolonization and Independence in Kenya 1940–93.* Nairobi: East African Educational, 1995.

Okoth, P. Godfrey, and Bethwell A. Ogot. *Conflict in Contemporary Africa.* Nairobi: Jomo Kenyatta Foundation, 2002.

Omare, Simon, and Eunice Kamaara. "Ethnicity and Political Violence in Kenya and the Role of the Church." In *Our Burning Issues: A Pan African Response*, edited by Edison M. Kalengyo, James Amaze, and Deji Ayegboyin, 203–220. Nairobi: All African Conference of Churches, 2013.

Parrinder, E. G. *African Traditional Religion.* London: SPCK, 1962.

Patton, John. *Pastoral Care in Context: An Introduction to Pastoral Care.* Louisville, KY: Westminster John Knox, 1993.

Philips, Kevin. *The Politics of Rich and Poor.* New York: Random House, 1990.

Reiss, A. J., and J. A. Roth, eds. *Understanding and Preventing Violence.* Washington, DC: National Academy, 1993.

Rokeach, Milton. *Understanding Human Values: Individual and Societal.* New York: Free Press, 1979.

Wallace, Harvey. *Family Violence: Legal, Medical and Social Perspectives.* 4th ed. Boston: Pearson Education, 2005.

Wa-Mungai, Mbugua, and George Gona. *(Re)Membering Kenya: Identity, Culture and Freedom.* Nairobi: Twaweza Communications, 2010.

Were, Gideon S., and Derek A. Wilson. *East Africa through a Thousand Years: A History of the Years A.D. 1000 to the Present Day.* New York: African Publishing, 1968.

White, Heath. *Postmodernism 101.* Grand Rapids, MI: Brazos, 2006.

Wise, Carroll A. *The Meaning of Pastoral Care.* New York: Harper & Row, 1966. Reprinted 1989.

———. *Pastoral Counseling: Its Theory and Practice.* New York: Harper & Brothers, 1951.

List of Contributors

J. Gregory Crofford currently is a Resident Chaplain at Ascension-Seton Hospitals (Austin, Texas, USA). He served for twenty-three years as a missionary, with posts in Côte d'Ivoire, Benin, Haiti, South Africa, and Kenya. His responsibilities included pastoral education, educational administration, and church development. He holds a PhD in Theology from the University of Manchester (UK) and is an ordained minister in the Church of the Nazarene.

Ndung'u J. B. Ikenye is the Program Leader in Counseling Psychology and Pastoral Theology at St Paul's University. He is also a Clinical Psychologist in Private Practice for Individual, Marriage, Family, and Organizations. Professor Ikenye is an ordained priest and Archdeacon in the Anglican Church, Diocese of Thika, Kenya, and Diocese of Chicago, USA. Prof. Ikenye holds a PhD in Counseling, Personality, and Culture from Northwestern University, USA, a DMin in Counseling and Psychotherapy, and an MTS in Pastoral Psychology from Garrett-Evangelical Theological Seminary, USA. He is a member or fellow of several professional bodies in the fields of counseling and psychology.

Craig S. Keener (PhD, Duke University) is F. M. and Ada Thompson Professor of Biblical Studies at Asbury Theological Seminary. He is author of twenty-eight books, six of which have won awards in *Christianity Today*; more than a million copies of his books are in circulation. In 2020 Craig is president of the Evangelical Theological Society. Craig is married to Dr Médine Moussounga Keener, who was a refugee in her home country of Congo for eighteen months. His blog is at http://www.craigkeener.com/.

Julius Kithinji currently heads the Department of Philosophy, Theology, and Biblical Studies in the Faculty of Theology at St Paul's University, Limuru, Kenya. He has been at St Paul's since 2016, teaching courses in New Testament, Greek exegesis, and biblical interpretation. Kithinji is also an ordained Methodist church minister and serves on several church steering committees.

Emily M. Kyalo has been a lecturer in Machakos University, Kenya, since 2012. She served as the Chair of the Department of Social Sciences in 2014–2015. Currently, she is pursuing a PhD in Clinical Psychology at Daystar University in Nairobi, Kenya. She holds a Master of Arts in Counselling Psychology from Daystar University, Nairobi, Kenya.

Peter Mageto is an ordained Methodist minister and educator who has been serving in the Circuit (attached clergy at Lavington United Church) and higher institutions of learning. Currently, he is the Deputy Vice Chancellor of Africa University in Mutare, Zimbabwe. Prior to that, he served as acting Vice Chancellor for the University of Kigali, Rwanda, and as Deputy Vice Chancellor for Academic and Student Affairs, Kenya Methodist University. He received his Bachelor of Divinity from St Paul's United Theological College, Limuru, and his Master in Theological Studies and Doctor of Philosophy in Ethics from Garrett-Evangelical Theological Seminary, Chicago, USA.

Marco Methuselah is a lecturer at St Paul College, Mwanza, Tanzania. He also works as an associate pastor at PAG Mwanza and as a college registrar. He graduated with a diploma in Bible and Theology at PAG Bible College, Mwanza, Tanzania, in 1991. He pursued his Master of Arts in Theological Studies at Africa International University (AIU) in 2015. Currently, he is doing his PhD in Theology and Culture at Africa International University (AIU).

Micah Moenga is currently an adjunct lecturer at Pan Africa Christian University (PACU). He is also an ordained Calvary Assemblies of God minister and serves as a lead pastor of Grace and Power of God International Ministry, a ministry of Calvary Assemblies of God. Micah holds a bachelor's degree in Bible and Theology from PACU, and a master's in Biblical Studies and a postgraduate diploma in Education, both from Africa International University (AIU). He is currently pursuing his PhD in Biblical Studies at AIU.

Timothy J. Monger is a missionary in Tanzania who since 2010 has been serving with Emmanuel International, which equips churches in holistic mission among the poor. He has been the Country Director since 2018. He is also a part-time lecturer at St Paul College, Mwanza. He received his BA from the University of Oxford and his Master of Christian Studies from Regent College, Vancouver.

Zebedi Muga is a senior lecturer at St Paul's University and has served at SPU since 1998. He teaches in the Department of Biblical Studies, Theology, and Philosophy. He has supervised master's and PhD students for a number of years. Muga teaches Old Testament, Biblical Hebrew, Church History, and Mission Studies, and has vast research interests in biblical and social issues. Dr Muga is an ordained minister of the Anglican Church (ACK) and is a member of several church and community committees and organizations.

Martin Munyao is a Global Research Institute (GRI) scholar and an adjunct lecturer at Daystar University, Nairobi. He holds a PhD degree in Missiology from Concordia Theological Seminary in Fort Wayne, IN. Currently he is working on his postdoctoral work at the Center for Missiological Research (CMR) at Fuller Theological Seminary in Pasadena, CA, USA.

David K. Ngaruiya is an Associate Professor at International Leadership University, where he is currently the Director of PhD in Theological Studies. He holds a PhD in Intercultural Studies from Trinity Evangelical Divinity School. He served as Chair of the Africa Society of Evangelical Theology in 2015–2016. He also served as one of the directors of the *Africa Leadership Study* published by Orbis in New York.

Elias K. Ng'etich is a lecturer in the Department of Religious Studies in Moi University, Kenya. He is also an ordained minister of Africa Inland Church, Kenya. Elias is currently completing his PhD studies in Sociology of Religion with a focus on Pentecostalism and social development in Kenya at the University of Cape Town, South Africa.

Benson Phiri serves as Academic Dean at Nazarene Theological College of Central Africa. He also serves as Senior Pastor at Falls Church of the Nazarene in Lilongwe, Malawi. He holds a Bachelor of Theology and Master of Arts in Religion from Africa Nazarene University. Currently, he is pursuing a PhD in Religion at Africa Nazarene University.

Rodney L. Reed is a missionary educator who has been serving at Africa Nazarene University in Nairobi, Kenya, since 2001. Currently he is the Deputy Vice Chancellor of Academic Affairs, a position he has held since 2010. Prior to that he served as the Chair of the Department of Religion for nine years. He holds a PhD in Theological Ethics from Drew University and is an ordained minister in the Church of the Nazarene.

Benjamin Straub is the Dean of the School of Bible at Central Africa Baptist University in Kitwe, Zambia, where he has taught theology, apologetics, and Koine Greek since 2012. He holds a MDiv and a ThM in Systematic Theology, and is currently pursuing a MEd in Educational Leadership.

David K. Tarus is Executive Director, Association for Christian Theological Education in Africa (ACTEA), a continent-wide organization that serves theological institutions through the facilitation of academic recognition and capacity-building programs. He is a graduate of McMaster Divinity College, Canada (PhD Christian Theology), Wheaton College Graduate School, USA (MA Historical & Systematic Theology), and Scott Christian University, Kenya (Bachelor of Theology). He is an ordained minister in the Africa Inland Church, Kenya.

Kamande Thuo is both a Bible translation consultant and a part-time lecturer in the Languages, Linguistics, and Translation Department at Africa International University (AIU). He received both his master's and doctoral degrees (PhD) in translation studies from AIU, and his research interest is mainly in the interpretation and translation of non-literal language.

Rowland Van Es is a mission partner of Reformed Church Global Mission who has been serving at St Paul's University in Limuru, Kenya, since 2004. Currently, he is the Interim Head of Department for History, Missions, Religion, and Practical Theology. Prior to 2004 he and his wife Jane also served in the Gambia, Malawi, and Sierra Leone. He has an MDiv and a ThM from Western Theological Seminary and an MA from Michigan State. He is an ordained minister in the Reformed Church of America.

Judy Wang'ombe is a lecturer at Africa International University, Kenya. She received her Master of Divinity (Biblical Studies) from Africa International University and Master of Theology in missions. She later did her PhD in interreligious studies at AIU as well. She has served as a missionary in various parts of Kenya.

Harun Wang'ombe is a missions pastor at Karen Community Church, Nairobi. He is a PhD candidate in interreligious studies at Africa International University (AIU). Prior to that he served as a missionary in Northern Kenya among different communities.

Subject and Names Index

Scripture Index

www.ingramcontent.com/pod-product-compliance
Lightning Source LLC
Chambersburg PA
CBHW070548270326
41926CB00013B/2240